LIBERATING OUR IMAGINATIONS

SEMEIA STUDIES

Jacqueline M. Hidalgo, General Editor

Editorial Board:
Rhiannon Graybill
Suzanna Millar
Raj Nadella
Emmanuel Nathan
Kenneth Ngwa
Shively T. J. Smith
Wei Hsien Wan

Number 106

LIBERATING OUR IMAGINATIONS

The Bible and Minoritized Literature

David Janzen

 PRESS

Atlanta

Copyright © 2025 by David Janzen

All rights reserved. No part of this work may be reproduced or transmitted in any form or by any means, electronic or mechanical, including photocopying and recording, or by means of any information storage or retrieval system, except as may be expressly permitted by the 1976 Copyright Act or in writing from the publisher. Requests for permission should be addressed in writing to the Rights and Permissions Office, SBL Press, 825 Houston Mill Road, Atlanta, GA 30329 USA.

Library of Congress Control Number: 2025938641

To my parents, who introduced me to literature,

and to Patricia, who greatly deepened my appreciation of it

CONTENTS

Abbreviations ix

1. Contextual Hermeneutics and the Emancipatory
   Literary Imagination 1

2. A Revolutionary in Search of a Revolution: Empire and the
   Powerless in *The Sympathizer* and Daniel 41

3. The Hard Law of Love: Community Identity and
   Inclusion in *Angels in America* and Ezra-Nehemiah 85

4. The Grace They Could Imagine: Suffering and the
   Subaltern Community in *Beloved* and Lamentations 129

5. As Liminal as Possible: Human Identity and
   Relationship with the Divine and Nonhuman in
   Freshwater and Genesis 1–11 175

6. Conclusion: The Hermeneutical Process of Reading after
   Minoritized Literature 123

Bibliography 233
Ancient Sources Index 271
Modern Authors Index 280

ABBREVIATIONS

AB	Anchor Bible
ABC	*Assyrian and Babylonian Chronicles*
ABR	*Australian Biblical Review*
ACS	African Christianity Series
AcT	*Acta Theologica*
AIL	Ancient Israel and Its Literature
ANEM	Ancient Near East Monographs/Monografias sobre el Antiguo Cercano Oriente
AS	*Aramaic Studies*
AsJT	*Asia Journal of Theology*
AUS	American University Studies
b.	Babylonian Talmud
BBR	*Bulletin for Biblical Research*
BETL	Bibliotheca Ephemeridum Theologicarum Lovaniensium
BI	Biblical Intersections
Bib	*Biblica*
BibInt	*Biblical Interpretation*
BibLib	Bible and Liberation
BibWor	Bible in Its World
BIS	Biblical Interpretation Series
BJS	Brown Judaic Studies
BLS	Bible and Literature Series
BMW	Bible in the Modern World
BN	*Biblische Notizen*
BR	Biblical Research
BRPBI	Brill Research Perspectives in Biblical Interpretation
BSNA	Biblical Scholarship in North America
BT	*The Bible Translator*
BTB	*Biblical Theology Bulletin*

BW	The Bible and Women
BWANT	Beitrage zur Wissenschaft vom Neuen Testament
BZ	*Biblische Zeitschrift*
BZABR	Beihefte zur Zeitschrift für altorientalische und biblische Rechtsgeschichte
BZAW	Beihefte zur Zeitschrift für die alttestamentliche Wissenschaft
CBQ	*Catholic Biblical Quarterly*
CCTS	Controversies in Contextual Theology
CSP	Contemporary Sociological Perspectives
CTM	*Concordia Theological Monthly*
DSD	*Dead Sea Discoveries*
EANEC	Explorations in Ancient Near Eastern Civilizations
ECL	Early Christianity and Its Literature
EJL	Early Judaism and Its Literature
EstBib	*Estudios bíblicos*
ET	English Translation
FAT	Forschungen zum Alten Testament
FCB	Feminist Companion to the Bible
Gen. Rab.	Genesis Rabbah
GPBS	Global Perspectives on Biblical Scholarship
GTR	Gender, Theory, and Religion
HBM	Hebrew Bible Monographs
HBS	History of Biblical Studies
HDR	Harvard Dissertations in Religion
HeBAI	*Hebrew Bible and Ancient Israel*
HThKAT	Herders Theologischer Kommentar zum Alten Testament
HTS	*HTS Theological Studies*
ICC	International Critical Commentary
IECOT	International Exegetical Commentary on the Old Testament
Int	*Interpretation*
ISBL	Indiana Studies in Biblical Literature
ITS	Intersectionality and Theology Series
IVBS	International Voices in Biblical Studies
JAJ	*Journal of Ancient Judaism*
JAJSup	Journal of Ancient Judaism Supplements
JANES	*Journal of the Ancient Near Easter Society*

JANER	*Journal of Ancient Near Eastern Religions*
JBL	*Journal of Biblical Literature*
JETS	*Journal of the Evangelical Theological Society*
JFSR	*Journal of Feminist Studies in Religion*
JHNES	The Johns Hopkins Near Eastern Studies
JHS	*Journal of Hellenic Studies*
JJS	*Journal of Jewish Studies*
JSJ	*Journal for the Study of Judaism in the Persian, Hellenistic, and Roman Periods*
JSJSup	Journal for the Study of Judaism in the Persian, Hellenistic, and Roman Periods Supplement Series
JSNT	*Journal for the Study of the New Testament*
JSOT	*Journal for the Study of the Old Testament*
JSOTSup	Journal for the Study of the Old Testament Supplement Series
JSP	*Journal for the Study of the Pseudepigrapha*
JSQ	*Jewish Studies Quarterly*
JTS	*Journal of Theological Studies*
JTSA	*Journal of Theology for Southern Africa*
Ketub.	Ketubot
LHBOTS	The Library of Hebrew Bible/Old Testament Studies
LSTS	The Library of Second Temple Studies
MELUS	*Multi-Ethnic Literature of the United States*
MSJ	*The Master's Seminary Journal*
MT	Masoretic Text
NEA	*Near Eastern Archaeology*
Neot	*Neotestamentica*
OBT	Overtures to Biblical Theology
OG	Old Greek
OIS	Oriental Institute Seminars
OSHT	Oxford Studies in Historical Theology
OTE	*Old Testament Essays*
OTL	Old Testament Library
OTR	Old Testament Readings
OTRM	Oxford Theology and Religion Monographs
PCI	Post-Contemporary Interventions
PHSC	Perspectives on Hebrew Scriptures and Its Contexts
PMLA	*Proceedings of the Modern Language Association*
Proof	*Prooftexts: A Journal of Jewish Literary History*

PRSt	*Perspectives in Religious Studies*
RB	*Revue biblique*
RBS	Resources for Biblical Studies
RCC	Religion, Culture, Critique
RevExp	*Review and Expositor*
RIBLA	*Revista de Interpretación Bíblica Latinoamericana*
RINAP	Royal Inscriptions of the Neo-Assyrian Period
RIPBC	Routledge Interdisciplinary Perspectives on Biblical Criticism
RNCTRTBS	Routledge New Critical Thinking in Religion, Theology and Biblical Studies
SAA	State Archives of Assyria
SBS	Stuttgarter Bibelstudien
SBLDS	Society of Biblical Literature Dissertation Series
SBLSymS	Society of Biblical Literature Symposium Series
SemeiaSt	Semeia Studies
Sif. Deut.	Sifre Deuteronomy
SJOT	*Scandinavian Journal of the Old Testament*
SLC	Studies in Latino/a Catholicism
SP	Samaritan Pentateuch
SRA	Studies of Religion in Africa
SSPC	SUNY Series in Psychoanalysis and Culture
STDJ	Studies on the Texts of the Desert of Judah
SVTP	Studia in Veteris Testamenti Pseudepigraphica
T. Asher	Testament of Asher
TBC	*The Bible and Critical Theory*
TCS	Texts from Cuneiform Sources
TJT	*Toronto Journal of Theology*
TTC	Transdisciplinary Theological Colloquia
TTCSGOT	T&T Clark Study Guides to the Old Testament
TynB	*Tyndale Bulletin*
VT	*Vetus Testamentum*
VTSup	Supplements to Vetus Testamentum
WMANT	Wissenschaftliche Monographien zum Alten und Neuen Testament
WUNT	Wissenschaftliche Untersuchungen zum Neuen Testament
ZAW	*Zeitschrift für die alttestamentliche Wissenschaft*

1
CONTEXTUAL HERMENEUTICS AND THE EMANCIPATORY LITERARY IMAGINATION

Introduction

The character of Daniel, the focus of the second chapter of this monograph, is someone torn between competing imperial interests. After Nebuchadnezzar's defeat of Jerusalem, Daniel, along with others from the city's royal household and nobility, is deported to the court in Babylon and educated to serve the victorious empire (Dan 1:3–4). He eventually grows quite close to his new king, as chapter 2 discusses, but during the reign of Belshazzar—Nebuchadnezzar's son according to the chronology of the book of Daniel—he receives two visions (7:1; 8:1) that warn him of the monstrous nature and violence of human kingdoms (7:2–8, 19, 21; 8:4, 6–11, 24) and that tell him they will be replaced by an eternal one authorized by heaven (7:27). Yet Daniel does not leave the imperial service after receiving these revelations, and by the time Darius the Mede replaces Belshazzar in the book's story, Daniel's fealty to his new ruler is such that he is promoted to an office in which he exerts more power than anyone else in the empire except the king (6:4 [ET 3]) and in which he refuses to damage imperial interests (6:23 [22]).[1] Despite the visions that he has already received about the transitory nature of human empires, something that stands in stark contrast to the kingdom that will last forever (מלכות עלם), which Daniel has been told will replace them, Daniel addresses Darius with the standard Aramaic greeting that loyal servants use before monarchs in

---

1. As the introduction of chapter 2 briefly explains, I will be following the book's story as reflected in the MT. In the OG of 6:23 [ET 22], Daniel tells Darius that no ἁμαρτία "error, guilt" was found in him in regard to the king, which is not precisely the same thing as his claim in the MT that he did no חבולה "damage" to the king.

the book: מלכא לעלמין חיי "O king, live forever" (6:22 [21]).[2] Daniel, it seems, has not yet absorbed the import of his visions to the degree that the heavenly powers might have wished and remains a faithful servant to a violent political entity that he still does not seem to realize ultimately has no future. In fact, one can see the revelations of the latter chapters of the writing as heaven's attempt to force Daniel to choose a side and decide to which kingdom his loyalty should truly belong.

However, the book of Daniel is so focused on imperial power, earthly and otherwise, and on elite characters such as Daniel and the kings he serves that it does not consider the plight of the powerless whom empires treat as if they were nothing or address the question as to whether they would be better off in the eternal kingdom of Daniel's first vision than they are under the rule of kings such as Nebuchadnezzar and Darius. As a result, readers with ethical commitments to support disadvantaged communities in their resistance to forces of socioeconomic subjugation might hope that Daniel will eventually notice the subalterns to whom neither the book's earthly empires nor heavenly revelations pay any attention. There is actually a glimmer of hope in his story, as we will see, that he is on the cusp of being able to recognize the existence of the powerless and that he might even be willing to prioritize their needs and liberative struggles over the demands of loyalty by kingdoms who exhibit no concern for the subaltern at all.

There is perhaps a parallel to be drawn between the character of Daniel and the modern field of biblical studies, which has also had difficulty noticing and prioritizing the interests, concerns, and goals of the minoritized, groups that are disadvantaged because of a "relation of domination and subordination, superiority and inferiority, at work in all axes of human identity, whereby one formation erects itself as dominant while casting others as minorities" (Liew and Segovia 2022, xiii). Biblical studies was constructed as a discipline to privilege historical questions[3] and largely continues to do so, even though there are hundreds of millions of people subjugated by oppressive political and socioeconomic structures who regard the Bible as an important resource in their resistance against those forces. The hermeneutical basis of this book, however, is rooted in the idea

---

2. All translations of biblical passages in this monograph are my own.

3. For studies of factors that shaped the modern field of biblical studies, and that in particular led to the dominance of historical study within it, see Sheehan 2005; Howard 2006; Legaspi 2010.

that the field of biblical studies should privilege interpretive approaches that subjugated groups could conceivably find to be of liberative use, an idea that is itself based in the ethical belief that we should support movements of resistance to structural oppression whenever that is reasonably possible. Just as those of us with that belief would hope that Daniel could become a character who could learn to recognize the existence of those subjugated by the empire and even grow to prioritize their emancipatory struggles, we would also hope that the field of biblical studies could evolve in such a way that the focus of its mainstream becomes driven by the ethical concerns of the minoritized rather than by the historical issues that currently dominate it. The more broadly emancipatory hermeneutical priorities are embraced by the discipline, the more it can become like other fields in which ethical concerns shape the research of many of their practitioners. There are, after all, political scientists who use their academic expertise to weigh in on questions surrounding unequal access to voting, sociologists who direct their research to the ways in which the police can be used as agents of social control within different kinds of communities, and economists who study the dangers posed by a vastly unequal distribution of wealth. It is not beyond the reach of human imagination to envision biblical studies as evolving into a field dominated by an ethical commitment to support movements of resistance against structural oppression.

When biblical studies first emerged as a modern discipline, it focused on historical issues, and it is not surprising when students, taught to prioritize such matters, pursue them when they become scholars and, in turn, push their students to do the same. Historical research comes to be second nature to the field's practitioners, a basic professional habit we often do not bother to question, and doing the same sort of work for a long period of time can eventually seem fundamental to one's self-understanding.[4] Habit, then, forms part of the explanation as to why historical rather than political and liberative concerns dominate biblical studies, and why, in the most recent survey of Society of Biblical Literature members available at the

---

4. So, for example, when Richard Rorty (1998, 343–44) wrote of the possibility of a shift in perspective in the field of philosophy toward antirepresentationalism, he acknowledged that it would not be possible for all philosophers to begin to see the world in that way, since the work of some of them was so deeply grounded in very different understandings of their discipline and the kinds of work they should do within it. Looking at the field differently, he wrote, is not possible for some because it would demand abandoning a key sense of their identity.

time of writing, more respondents chose the category of historical criticism as a basic description of their interpretive approach than any other option the survey offered (Society of Biblical Literature 2019, 7). Habit alone, however, is not a good enough reason for the field to continue to be dominated by historical rather than emancipatory questions and concerns, especially as many scholars, in particular ones from contexts that expose them on a daily basis to the depredations of structural oppression, have described at length the ethical failures of this habit. There is as much a moral necessity for the field of biblical studies to change as there is for the character of Daniel to do so, and the change required is similar in both cases, involving a refocusing of attention on the minoritized and a commitment to support their movements of resistance to structural injustice.

The greater the number of interpretive strategies we can devise to break the discipline of its habit of prioritizing historical work, then, the greater will be its potential to produce research that could be of emancipatory use, a process that will make biblical studies a more ethical discipline, a more useful and better one, at least from the standpoint of those who are ethically committed to supporting liberative struggles whenever that is possible. I adopt and model one very accessible strategy in this book that can serve such an emancipatory goal: reading biblical texts through the lens of contemporary literature by authors in social locations that give them personal experiences of the humiliations and terrors of structural subjugation. Exposure to a broad range of such experiences can deepen the emancipatory imaginations of biblical scholars, and new ways of thinking about oppression and resistance can spur us to see and interpret biblical texts in better and more ethical ways.

The following section of the chapter discusses critiques of biblical studies' hermeneutical mainstream by minoritized scholars, so that the need for alternative reading strategies such as this one, described in more detail in the chapter's third section, is clear. Each of the following chapters models this approach and addresses a different kind of ethical problem within academic biblical interpretation that prevents scholars from actualizing our commitment to support movements of resistance to subjugation. But since many scholars habituated to function in the field's mainstream assume that historical criticism is not only a necessary part of scholarly work in biblical studies but must also have priority over and be used to judge the validity of other kinds of interpretation, the fourth section of this chapter will argue that such a prohistorical hermeneutical stance is not a necessary way to conceive of academic biblical interpretation and that it is perfectly possible to produce valid textual meaning through interpretation that does no historical research at all and instead prioritizes emancipatory concerns of minoritized communities. In the final section of the chapter, I discuss the epistemic humility necessary when doing biblical interpretation that privileges the experiences of those in minoritized socioeconomic contexts different from one's own. In the approach I adopt and model here, we read after, or through the lenses of, authors in different social locations, looking to the experiences of subjugation and resistance they describe from their contexts. The epistemic humility necessary to a virtuous application of this hermeneutical process of *reading after* means that, as interpreters, we are not speaking for biblical readers in contexts different from our own nor prescribing how they should interpret a particular text. We are learning from them, with the hope that our interpretations might spark emancipatory imaginations in a variety of contexts and so be of some liberative use, even if we cannot prescribe to those in contexts outside of our own if and how they should use such readings.

The White Context of Mainstream Biblical Studies

To begin by providing context for the interpretive strategy I adopt in this book, one important reason why approaches like this one are so necessary for the field of biblical studies lies precisely in the fact that those in dominant socioeconomic locations have shaped the research of its mainstream. The Society of Biblical Literature surveys reveal an academic discipline that is overwhelmingly male and white[5] and thus defined demographically by a membership largely located in privileged social contexts. Because context shapes interpretation, a matter addressed in more detail later in the chapter, describing the field as white is more than an observation about demographics but an ethical and political critique of its general failure to challenge structural oppression. When biblical scholars, who tend to have their greatest public influence through their professional positions and social standing granted to them through academic institutional affiliation, decide that they have nothing to say about issues of subjugation in their professional work, their silence indicates a tacit acceptance of struc-

---

5. In the 2019 Society of Biblical Literature survey, over 75 percent of respondents identified as male (Society of Biblical Literature 2019, 8). Only those who indicated that they were born in the United States were asked about their ethnicity; of those, more than 85 percent identified as white (10).

tural oppression. As Tikva Frymer-Kensky (2006, 162) put it, if one can do something about a problem but chooses to do nothing at all, "one becomes part of the problem," and when biblical scholars have nothing to say about political and socioeconomic injustice in the academic roles in which they generally exercise the most influence, they communicate that this injustice is not important enough for them or their field to worry about.

No piece of academic work is ever apolitical, in short, and the field as a whole could even be understood to speak in favor of oppressive socioeconomic forces when it awards degrees, book contracts, promotions, and tenure to scholars who produce work that never challenges structural norms that benefit those in the demographic categories to which the great majority of the discipline belongs, even as those forces impoverish, humiliate, and terrorize those in other social locations. Because biblical studies largely functions by privileging historical criticism, writes Vincent Wimbush (2017, 13), his own training as a historical critic brought him to the realization that he was being educated "to be a good ideological 'civil servant,' tradent, interpreter of, apologist for, the Western regime." This rigid prioritization of historical questions, as if the Bible held no liberative relevance for millions of people subjugated by oppressive structures, serves a status quo that tends to benefit white males. Wimbush's experience reflects that of other members of the discipline from minoritized contexts, who often feel compelled to produce the historical work of white scholarship in order to enter and remain part of the field and are often chastised when their research fails to live up to that white norm.[6]

This critique of the field was leveled by its members from minoritized contexts almost as soon as they began to react against the dominance of historical study in the discipline in the late twentieth century. For example, not long after second-wave feminism began to impact biblical studies, Mary Ann Tolbert (1983, 117) pointed out that feminist readings of biblical texts were often disparaged by her colleagues as subjective and so of less importance and validity than the mainstream historical work done by those who did not privilege the emancipatory concerns of women. Scholars who made such a distinction between feminist scholarship and work they understood to be objective were ones who believed that valid and important research in biblical studies is not influenced by the concerns

---

6. For some examples of such experiences, see Nzimande 2008; Schneider 2019, 129–30; Anderson 2022; Weems 2022; Nadella 2023, 188–89.

of interpreters and so not influenced by interpreters' contexts, whether in regard to gender identity or any other aspect of their social location. Through such an assumption, the field creates a special and normative status for historical-critical work; it alone, as the fourth section of this chapter discusses, is often understood to truly lead out meaning inherent to the biblical texts rather than impose meaning on them as approaches driven by the concerns of minoritized interpreters are often seen to do.

The normative status the field confers on historical research results in widespread suspicion of work that prioritizes the concerns and needs that arise in the contexts of those subjugated to oppressive forces, as well as in a tendency to mark out and ghettoize such scholarship. From the discipline's mainstream perspective, such nonnormative approaches fail to be objective and thus fail to grasp the meaning of the text, since interpreters omitting the necessary first steps of historical work will inevitably arrive at subjective and therefore inaccurate conclusions in regard to textual meaning. This is why the field still largely communicates to its members that they cannot privilege liberative concerns and that current political realities cannot be the place where one begins when trying to determine what a biblical text means. From this mainstream point of view, research with that kind of political focus can be done only as a second step, guided by the primary historical study that determines the meaning of a text that its ancient author intended to communicate, what is often understood in the field as the original text. The result, as we will see below, is that research with liberative aims is seen by the discipline's mainstream to be valid only insofar as it conforms to the historical work that necessarily precedes it. That historical study is understood to be objective and what must be done first; any other kind of research is secondary, optional, and judged by its conformity to historical findings.

The result of such a belief, says Wongi Park (2021), is a white field, an area of academic discourse that privileges a status quo that benefits people defined as white. The social structures of this status quo determine what race individuals are seen to have and convey immense socioeconomic privilege to those understood to be white. But by claiming that these forces have nothing to do with the way in which biblical scholarship is conducted, since historical work is described as objective and so as uninfluenced by social and political contexts, the discipline simultaneously hides the whiteness at its core. As a consequence, actors in the field are habituated to do work that does not prioritize struggles against oppressive structures that benefit those in dominant social locations. This marginalization of questions of social justice is what has led Wimbush and others, such as Jacqueline Hidalgo (2023, 54), to the realization that the mainstream of the discipline trains its members to become apologists for structures of subjugation.

Biblical studies is hardly the only academic discipline constructed in this way for, as Sara Ahmed (2007) notes, modern colonialism created a world in which social structures privilege those understood to be white, while peoples minoritized as nonwhite were understood to be less intelligent and moral, in need of European colonial leadership and control. Whiteness becomes what is normal, something rooted in the types of attitudes and contexts that are not noticed because they have become habitual and that structure the work academics do.[7] Suzie Park (2019, 249), for example, writes of frequently being asked to *do* Asian American readings of biblical texts, requests that make her uncomfortable since they assume that her background and biases and interests influence her interpretations in ways that would not be true of those doing white biblical scholarship, the kind of historical-critical work that the field normally understands as needing no ethnic qualification because it is seen as contextless. Gale Yee (2021, 60–64), who is also often asked to provide Asian and Asian American perspectives on various issues in biblical studies, gets at the same issue when she points out that no one ever asks for a white male or German interpretation, a fact that communicates the assumption that the historical work that scholars from those social locations generally produce is perspectiveless and objective. As a white discipline, writes Abraham Smith (2022, 122–23), biblical studies provides tacit support for white privilege, with the result, says Musa Dube (2018, 10–11), that the field trains scholars from minoritized groups to "lose the ability to speak in their own tongue, to ask their own questions" when their intellectual formation takes place in a discipline that consistently communicates to them that the questions that matter for the field have nothing to do with liberation from structural subjugation. In that kind of educational context, says Janette Ok (2023), students from disadvantaged groups can question their own sanity because their perceptions of reality and as to what is of importance are continually dismissed by teachers and peers.

---

7. For studies of the relationship that coloniality created and maintains between race and the production of knowledge, see, e.g., Wynter 2003; Quijano 2024, 73–84.

All of these scholars point to the problem of attempts on the part of the discipline to merely tolerate on its margins hermeneutical approaches that its mainstream marks out as subjective, since this process of ghettoizing functions only to further solidify that mainstream's view of its own centrality, objectivity, and contextlessness as it produces work that does not need to be identified with a subjective term like feminist or womanist or queer or postcolonial (Nadar 2023, 183). Scholars from dominant social locations—those who, like me, are straight, white middle-class males—often simply do not notice the field's whiteness, not only because we have been trained and habituated by it to practice our work in particular ways that we learn to accept as normative, but also because the contexts in which we live and produce our scholarship do not force us to constantly negotiate social structures that mark us as outsiders who should be regarded with suspicion. Being recognized as white is, as the legal scholar Cheryl Harris (1993) argues, to have at one's disposal a whole series of social and economic benefits enshrined in and protected by law, such that whiteness can be regarded as valuable property. In the United States, she writes, all white people have a stake in racism because their racial identity conveys so many economic, legal, and political benefits.

I do not mean to imply that white biblical scholars who insist on the necessity and priority of historical study are consciously racist or sexist or homophobic or classist, merely that those of us in privileged social locations benefit from socioeconomic structures that have shaped the academy and obscured the white context from which our work proceeds. As Kwok Pui-lan (1995, 86) pointed out some decades ago, historical biblical study "is perhaps the most suitable praxis for white, male, middle-class academics, because they alone can afford to be 'impartial,' which literally means 'non-committed.' Oppressed women and men of all colors find that the historical-critical method alone cannot help them to deal with the burning questions they face." All acts of knowing, argues Eduardo Mendieta (2012), are political acts, the result of decisions as to where one should turn one's attention, and he points out that a kind of "epistemic privilege" is available to those of us in dominant social locations, because we can avoid knowing about the results of structural oppression or noticing that our supposedly objective and contextless academic work is as deeply rooted in context as any other hermeneutic. So when historical criticism is the dominant interpretive approach of biblical studies, it not only advances the interests of those of us in privileged social locations, but allows us to exercise what Abraham Smith (2023, 132–33) refers to as "epistemic violence" that claims priority and superiority over hermeneutical concerns rooted in contexts of resistance that the more privileged among us often do not notice. Even when we do notice these concerns and contexts, we tend to see them as entirely unrelated to the so-called objective scholarship we believe to be so important.

If biblical scholars truly wish to honor our ethical commitments to support emancipatory struggles and transform the field into one with relevance for movements that resist structural oppression, then our research will have to be driven by issues of concern for liberative struggles rather than by historical questions. This is work in which the discipline must look for leadership from scholars located in groups whose contexts continually expose them to the negative effects of that oppression, since those communities' long experiences of it make their members experts when it comes to the kinds of emancipatory movements that are most likely to meet with success in their specific social locations. The biblical scholars located in such contexts, then, will be best equipped to know what sorts of research and teaching in our field might best serve such movements. For obvious reasons, then, this sort of scholarly work begins with the experiences and struggles of disadvantaged communities, and this is why, for example, African American biblical scholarship begins with the experiences of African Americans (e.g., Smith 2017, 24–25), womanist and Black feminist biblical scholarship begins with the experiences of African American women (e.g., Crowder 2016, 33–36), African feminist scholarship begins with the experiences of African women (e.g., Mbuwayesango 2014, 75–76), and so on.

However, to adopt the position that only Asian Americans could produce academic analysis of biblical texts that might have some relevance for Asian American liberative struggles or that only Latina scholars could do the same for Latinas' emancipatory needs would be to greatly diminish the field's potential. It would reinforce the existing status quo of white male dominance in biblical studies by supporting the ghettoizing of scholarship from vulnerable social locations, as the research of Pasifika scholars, for example, becomes something of interest only to them. It would absolve those from dominant social locations—the majority of the field—of any obligation to try to produce work that could be of use in emancipatory struggles, since demographically privileged academics have not experienced the negative effects of structural oppression to any degree like their minoritized colleagues. It would also ignore the important insight arising from intersectional analysis that the struggles of different resistance movements are often related, even if different groups experience structural intersections of power differently;[8] this is why, writes Vivian May (2015, 34), a key facet of intersectionality is "a radical *coalitional political orientation* grounded in solidarity, rather than sameness, as a basis for working collectively to eradicate inequalities" (emphasis original).

A field aiming to be of emancipatory value is one that works collaboratively in this regard and with the understanding that it is possible for anyone to produce research that could be of liberative use. However, only those whose social locations have resulted in a lifetime's worth of experience with the negative effects of social injustice, and with strategies of resistance to it, have the expertise to decide whether any given piece of academic work could be useful for a resistance movement in their specific context. We could describe this approach as pluriversal rather than universal, since it looks to the experiences, insights, and hermeneutical approaches of many different groups as potentially useful in emancipatory struggles and abandons the notion of the universal necessity and priority of historical criticism in interpretation, which becomes just one of many acceptable ways to read biblical texts.[9] Many scholars in the discipline doing research driven by liberative needs have reflected on how they have looked to colleagues from other minoritized social locations for inspiration, demonstrating the benefits of this sort of collaborative approach. Randall Bailey (2010, 20), for example, writes that so little Black biblical scholarship was available when he was a graduate student that he read feminist biblical interpretation to develop emancipatory approaches to the texts that would fit his context as an African American scholar and that he "became convinced of the interrelationships of liberation movements." Jimmy Hoke (2021, 13) says that a study of feminism helped them to see the personal as political and that they use queer theory in biblical interpretation where it intersects with a feminist agenda. Grant Macaskill (2021, 45) looks to the ways in which queer theory destabilizes binaries and revalorizes words and concepts used in oppressive ways as aspects of a hermeneutic useful for disability studies in biblical interpretation.

---

8. As Patricia Hill Collins (2019, 25–26) notes in this regard, women of color are marginalized both in antiracist and feminist activism, and understanding that they experience racism differently than men of color and sexism differently than white women involves, in part, the need to see the struggles of racism and sexism as intertwined within their specific social location.

9. For discussion of pluriversality in the sense I mean here, see, e.g., Grosfoguel 2012; Mignolo and Walsh 2018.

We could consider as well Angeline Song's (2022) specific experience of interpreting the story of 1 Kgs 21, in which Ahab and Jezebel kill Naboth in order to appropriate his land. From the standpoint of her cultural rootedness in Singapore among the Peranakans, those of multiethnic Malay and Chinese descent, who had been forced to sell their land to the government, Naboth's initial rejection of Ahab's offer to purchase his ancestral land seemed to her like an attempt to insult the king. But after she moved to Aotearoa New Zealand and read the story with the Māori, she encountered a way of thinking of ancestral land that is "as uncorrupted by the ideological clutter of colonialism, nationalism, and/or neocolonialism as it could possibly be" (213), with the result that she reevaluated her own position on land and on resisting assimilation into dominant Western culture and so reevaluated as well her earlier interpretation of Naboth's story. It makes sense, then, to think that those of us who believe biblical studies should be a field driven by ethical concerns and emancipatory hermeneutics would aim to find inspiration for our research by broadening our exposure to the work of colleagues in a variety of social locations whose work is directed by liberative goals.

This is not the only step we can take, however, to produce better and more ethical scholarship ourselves. Song's shift in her interpretation of 1 Kgs 21, for example, was the result not of reading the work of fellow scholars but of personal contact with people whose somewhat different context persuaded her to read the story differently. The kind of physical and cultural relocation that led to Song's reevaluation of a biblical narrative is generally not feasible for most of us, of course, and not all of us will be able to move to Aotearoa to learn about Māori history and culture and interpret the Bible with them, or to Guatemala and learn K'iche' to become better acquainted with the transformative struggles of that particular Maya people. We need to look for other more accessible means to broaden our range of discursive partners in ways that will help us meet liberative hermeneutical goals, ways that can complement our interaction with the emancipatory work our colleagues from various disadvantaged contexts are already doing.

Liberative Hermeneutics and the Literary Imagination

One such approach, the one this book adopts and models, is the strategy of reading biblical texts after and in the light of contemporary literature by authors from minoritized communities deeply affected by long histories of social injustice. A key aspect of emancipatory biblical hermeneutics is its rootedness in the experiences of different communities intimately aware of the depredations of structural oppression, and so it follows that the broader our exposure to the experiences of different minoritized groups is, the more we will be able to exercise our imaginations to better meet our liberative goals. With Juliana Claassens (2018, 157–59) and others, I can see a hermeneutical benefit in using contemporary fiction to develop what Martha Nussbaum (1995, xvi) calls a "literary imagination," something that is "an essential ingredient of an ethical stance that asks us to concern ourselves with the good of other people whose lives are distant from our own." Literature can immerse us in social worlds very different from those we know and draw us to empathize with protagonists rooted in such contexts (9), and this means, Nussbaum writes, that we should approach literature with a "political agenda" (1997, 89). As we encounter and empathize with characters of different genders, races, and classes, readers can begin to see how forces such as sexism, racism, and classism have shaped the world in ways they themselves have not experienced (94–95). Literary novels can sometimes fail to see certain subjugated groups, Nussbaum acknowledges (97), but they can also make comprehensible to readers the experiences of people who are located in contexts very different from their own (111).

I am not the first biblical scholar to find a liberative potential in a call to read contemporary literature politically in order to develop and expand a literary imagination that can help us read biblical texts in better, more ethical ways, and it has been scholars from minoritized contexts in particular who have adopted this interpretive strategy. For example, Chin Ming Stephen Lim (2020) reads Ruth with *Esperanza*, a play by Souk Yee Wong and Hong Seng Tay, in which the eponymous character is a Filipina domestic worker for a Chinese family in Hong Kong who abuse her. The character of Esperanza, writes Lim, allows us to see Ruth as disenfranchised and to read the biblical book as a cautionary story about her subjugation to those unaware of their privilege. Or, to take another example, Rhiannon Graybill (2021, 30–57) reads biblical rape stories like those of Dinah in Gen 34 and Tamar in 2 Sam 13 with the work of the Black feminist science fiction author Octavia Butler in order to get at the "fuzziness" of our understandings of rape. Butler's writings help Graybill see the biblical stories as narratives that challenge a concept of rape as a sexual act defined only by a withholding of consent, something that can push readers to see how coercion, race, and distinction of status between those involved should affect our conception of rape outside of a consent/nonconsent binary.

As another example, Claassens (2020, 127–52) reads Lam 1 in dialogue with J. M. Coetzee's novel *Disgrace*, as both are pieces of literature with female rape victims. In both texts, she concludes, the victims' trauma becomes something that serves male interests and exculpates male elites from their wrongdoings, which leads her to create space in which she can imagine how the victims in both texts could tell their stories if given the chance to narrate. And to take just one more example, Mosese Ma'ilo (2018) reads the story of the prodigal son from Luke 15 through the lens of a novel by the Samoan-born author Albert Wendt that reflects the experiences of Pasifika islanders. In the novel, an island family leaves Samoa for Aotearoa New Zealand in the hope of making a better life for themselves, but they find it to be no utopia, and yet when the family's son returns to Samoa, he eventually leaves once more, disillusioned with life in his ancestors' homeland. The novel complicates the binary picture we see in the Lukan story of a distant land one should avoid and a homeland one should desire, Ma'ilo concludes, and does so in a way that, when read with the prodigal son story, makes the biblical narrative better reflect the experience of islanders in a postcolonial context.

Since the particular hermeneutical goal I have in mind is to broaden biblical scholars' exposure to the life experiences of those in disadvantaged contexts different from their own, then to meet this goal it matters that we choose works by minoritized authors featuring minoritized characters. If this is a reading strategy from which all of us can benefit as we attempt to broaden our literary and liberative imaginations, it is arguably those from the most privileged social locations who stand in most need of it. The case is not only that we are the ones with the least exposure to the negative effects of structural injustice, but also that we live in cultures in which narratives crafted by those who experience those negative effects on a daily basis are rarely heard, since Western media overwhelmingly features stories with straight white male protagonists. To illustrate that last point, we could consider, for example, the study by Walt Hickey (2014) of all 1,615 movies made in the United States between 1990 and 2013 about which he could find both financial information and analysis on the basis of the Bechdel Test, an evaluation of movies based on three criteria: if they have more than one female character; if female characters ever speak to each other; and if they ever speak to each other about a topic other than a man. A movie passes the test if it meets all three of the criteria, but even by this low bar of gender inclusiveness, Hickey's study found that only 53 percent of the movies passed, even though passing the Bechdel Test had no effect on return of investment or, when controlling for the movie's budget, on gross profits. Other tests that measure the inclusion of women and minoritized characters in and staff who work on films demonstrate a bias in Western cinema toward stories about males and white characters, something that may reflect the fact that more men than women control the creation and production of movies. When the fifty top-grossing films in 2016 in North America were graded according to the Feldman Score, which awards points based on women's creative input (in roles such as writer, director, and department head) as well as on the prominence and victimization of female characters, three-quarters of them failed (Hickey et al. 2017).

Within Western media, film is not the only art form dominated by white male artists who create white male protagonists with whose interests and concerns audiences are implicitly urged to identify and see as normative; similar problems exist in other media, such as literary fiction. For example, VIDA, a feminist literary organization, finds that almost all the major literary journals and reviews (included in what VIDA calls its Main Count) publish more works by men than by women, some by a wide margin (Maher 2019). The publishing industry in the United States is also overwhelming white, and the Lee & Low Diversity Baseline Survey of 2023, a diversity survey of American publishing houses and review journals, found that about 72 percent of their employees identified as white. While this is an improvement over the 2015 survey, where that number was 79 percent (Lee & Low Books 2024), it helps to explain why 95 percent of the fiction books produced by the major American publishing houses between 1950 and 2018 were written by white authors (So and Wezerek 2020).

Because all of us exposed to Western media are inundated with stories told and controlled by those in dominant social locations, stories that reflect their experiences and that generally feature protagonists who share their creators' social context, we can see the urgent need to develop the literary imagination Nussbaum discusses in order to read politically to achieve liberative hermeneutical goals. This is true especially for those of us who are from such privileged locations ourselves. The specific interpretive project that I pursue here, then, reads biblical texts after, or through the lens of, pieces of contemporary literature by authors in disadvantaged contexts, ones that have made them very familiar with the forces of structural oppression and with movements of resistance against them.

Each of the readings in the following chapters emphasizes a different hermeneutical problem that all scholars can encounter when trying to do work that could be of liberative value. If these are failures that result from biblical studies' traditional orientation to historical issues, they also reflect the white social location of the majority of members that shaped the field in the first place and continue to shape it, and so are problems of interpretation that those of us in such privileged contexts will face more frequently. In chapter 2, I read the story of Daniel after *The Sympathizer*, a novel by the Vietnamese American Viet Thanh Nguyen, in order to address the common problem of interpreters failing to even notice when a biblical text contains no disadvantaged characters at all. When we read Daniel after *The Sympathizer*, however, that absence in the biblical book is glaring. *The Sympathizer*, whose protagonist is a Vietnamese immigrant to the United States who says he "ranked among the meanest," is focused on the debilitating effects of empire and power, even anti-imperial power, on those who have no power at all. Like the unnamed narrator of the novel, the main character of Daniel is also forced to migrate to an imperial center, but he hardly ranks among the meanest, and while the story of the biblical book, like that of the novel, is very interested in the problems posed by imperial power, the fate of the powerless is not a matter its narrative concerns itself with. Encountering it after *The Sympathizer*, however, makes that absence of concern glaring, and it can push the reader to ask what ethical concerns this raises in regard to Daniel's portrayals of both earthly and heavenly kingdoms.

An important issue raised in *The Sympathizer* is that the powerless are often not permitted to represent themselves but are represented by the powerful, who depict them and their desires in whatever ways best serve the interests of the dominant. Exposed as we all are to a plethora of stories that feature protagonists with a great deal of socioeconomic privilege, it is possible that readers, especially ones from dominant social contexts, will overlook the silencing of subaltern characters in some biblical narratives and simply accept the ways they are represented by the more powerful and central figures in the stories. To highlight this interpretive challenge and the way the hermeneutical strategy I am modeling can help readers confront it, chapter 3 opens with a discussion of *Angels in America*, a work by the gay Jewish playwright Tony Kushner that features characters in the late twentieth-century gay community in New York ravaged by the AIDS crisis. The work is full of speech by figures forced to the margins of their society, and when we read Ezra-Nehemiah in light of it, it is difficult to miss the fact that, while the biblical writing privileges the perspectives of relatively powerful community members, the foreign women whom those characters demonize in the story and eventually expel from the community are never permitted to speak or represent themselves. *Angels in America* helps draw our attention to the silencing of those powerless figures in Ezra-Nehemiah, but the speech of the minoritized characters in the play fighting for inclusion in American society can also help us imagine how those women in Ezra-Nehemiah might speak if given the chance and how they might imagine community in a much more inclusive way than the more privileged individuals in the book do.

Even when subaltern characters do speak in biblical literature, readers—again, privileged ones in particular—might not even notice that they are speaking or might simply accept without question their speech that sometimes reflects a more dominant ideology that justifies their suffering. Chapter 4, however, marks this out as a problem in Lamentations by reading the book after *Beloved*, a novel by the African American Nobel laureate Toni Morrison. *Beloved*'s narrative focuses its attention on Black characters in the post–Civil War United States, many of whom survived the trauma of slavery. When read after the novel, it seems apparent that the voices speaking in Lamentations, a book written in the wake of Babylon's destruction of Jerusalem, come from a group who, like the Black community in *Beloved*, has survived events of massive trauma and whose members have been treated as if their lives are of no value at all. This particular interpretive act allows us to see that Lamentations presents us with speech of vulnerable characters whose suffering has much in common with that of the characters of the novel and who are struggling to transcend depictions of their lives as having less than human value in order to see themselves as worthy of a future that is more than just survival. Part of this struggle involves the problem of how to envision God, who is sometimes portrayed here, as in many other biblical books, as being willing to treat humans as if their lives do not matter. *Beloved* can, however, also help us see Lamentations as an unfinished conversation among different voices who have not yet settled on firm conclusions in regard to the worth of its speakers' lives, and can help us imagine how their speech might continue and perhaps even affirm the fact that their lives are valuable and that God's actions always reflect that fact.

Just as readers can ignore the ways in which biblical texts can be read as justifying the suffering of the oppressed, we can also sometimes miss the ways in which they can be interpreted in order to challenge aspects of an oppressive status quo, especially when they have often been read to do the opposite. This can certainly be a problem for readers from very privileged contexts who feel as if they do not stand in any need of socioeconomic liberation, for whom the burning hermeneutical necessity to read for emancipation will often be absent. The opening chapters of Genesis, for example, are, in some interpretive contexts, seen as an affirmation of a cisheteronormative binary of gender and sexuality, portraying a created order that, from this point of view, validates the condemnation of those who do not experience heterosexual desire or definitively identify as either male or female.

Chapter 5, however, begins with a reading of *Freshwater*, a novel by the transgender Nigerian-born writer Akwaeke Emezi; in it the human protagonist struggles to shape her identity in relationship with the gods who live within her. In light of this story, Gen 1–11 can be read as one of humanity and God negotiating a developing sense of human identity as both humans and the divine grow and evolve in relationship with each other. The matter of who humans are and what they are like is not settled in the first few chapters of Genesis, and we can see a portrayal of a God in these stories who is willing to adapt to the humans as they realize they are not entirely the beings God intended them to be at their creation, a reflection of the way the main human character and the gods of *Freshwater* adapt and change in relationship with each other. In the novel, this adaptation on the part of the human protagonist involves a release from the binary categories of human and divine, as well as from the traditional binary categories of gender and sexual orientation to which she had once conformed. In Gen 1–11, an initial binary distinction between human and divine collapses, just as understandings of gender and sexuality change as the story progresses. God largely accepts the human choice to blur initial boundaries of identity established at creation, and so the character of God as constructed in these chapters is one who is open to human choices for liminal existence when it comes to gender and sexuality as well. If, after reading *Freshwater*, we can see the humans in Gen 1–11 as queer or trans beings, their identity transcending the distinct categories of their creation, that is also true of the depictions of animals in these chapters. Genesis 1–11 has often been used to justify a disregard toward the natural world that has contributed to disastrous ecological crises, but the novel helps us see a portrayal of nonhuman animals in these chapters as beings whose identity cannot be clearly distinguished from that of humans and who cannot be treated as objects with no value that humans can use for whatever purposes they choose.

Finding as many ways as we can to abandon unethical hermeneutical beliefs and habits can only be beneficial for the discipline of biblical studies, and easily accessible interpretive approaches are also of pedagogical use; in the case of the one I adopt in this book, for example, students without much academic background in biblical studies will find it much easier to read biblical literature in the wake of works of fiction rather than technical scholarly writing. As the final section of the chapter discusses, however, it is important to exercise epistemic humility any time we interact with a different cultural context than one's own. We cannot assume that the hermeneutical process of reading biblical texts after the literature of authors from social locations of which one has no direct experience makes one an expert interpreter of that context with the ability to solve its problems. That section of the chapter reflects on the hermeneutical limitations as well as potential of this interpretive strategy. The readings I pursue in the following chapters are rooted in a hermeneutical process that looks to literature from contexts other than one's own so that we can deepen our liberative imaginations, but it does not provide us with the cultural proficiency to prescribe liberative biblical interpretations for any context outside of the one the interpreter inhabits. The strategy of reading after can help us create interpretations with emancipatory potential, but whether they are useful for any given context of resistance to structural subjugation is something that only members of a given community can decide. Before turning to that issue, however, I address a question that many of us educated in the mainstream of biblical studies might feel a need to grapple with before following the kind of interpretive strategy I am adopting here: Can we produce valid meaning in critical biblical interpretation if we begin our work with the experiences, interests, and concerns of those in minoritized social locations—precisely the hermeneutical endeavor the following chapters undertake—and do not prioritize historical questions or even avoid historical work entirely?

Context, Objectivity, and Textual Meaning

Biblical scholars are not only educated and habituated to act in a field that prioritizes historical questions, but for many mainstream scholars historical work is also a necessary and nonnegotiable aspect of any sort of academic reading of biblical texts. James Barr (2000, 40–45), for example, writes that what we can consider to be "genuine biblical criticism" must involve historical research. Such work alone is often understood to guarantee what John Barton (2007, 48–49) calls "reasonable objectivity," and from this point of view readers who abandon this sort of "genuine biblical criticism" abandon objectivity, meaning they let their own presuppositions speak for the text, producing only subjective and unscholarly readings.[10] I want to show in this part of the chapter, however, that these kinds of widely accepted claims, which end up subordinating all interpretive work to the so-called objective demands of historical study, have failed to understand the link that exists between texts, interpreters, and meaning. They have, as a result, failed to see that it is the context of an interpretive community that will always provide the norms and guidelines for proper interpretation, and this means that biblical studies could become a field dedicated to fighting structural oppression if its members decided to make it a community aimed at that goal.

Arguments that draw an equation between historical work and objectivity in biblical studies generally aim to make the case not only that biblical scholars must do historical work, but that it must be done first before scholars answer any nonhistorical questions they might have when reading texts, because we will be unable to discover any valid or authentic meaning from biblical writings without the historical research that brings it to light. Often a key assumption in this regard is that the biblical texts themselves somehow demand such an approach. Roy Harrisville (2014, 154), for example, refers to an "extra-linguistic reality" of biblical texts, something that, he writes, means that the text itself must act as an interpreter (162) because it has "a certain autonomy" (165), with the result that "the interpreter"—the human interpreter, in this case—"is not in control" (167). Biblical texts are "a reality independent of the critic," says F. W. Dobbs-Allsopp (1999, 265), and for him, this textual reality demands historical work to arrive at "a just estimation of the past on its own terms" (268). To "do justice to the reality of the text," writes David Law (2012, 235–36), "we should treat the text on its own terms and not impose upon it meanings which are not true to the phenomena of the text," and only historical research will "allow the voice of the text to be heard." Arguments based on these sorts of claims as to the nature of the biblical text generally do not conclude that biblical scholars should not go on to do liberative readings in their roles as scholars, but they do emphasize that the historical work must be done prior to any consequent interpretive move—such

---

10. For similar positions, see, e.g., Harvey 1996, 5; Perdue 2005, 341–42.

as using a biblical text to resist subjugation, for example—and that any such secondary step must not disagree with the historical conclusions as to what ancient authors meant to communicate.

Some mainstream defenses of the necessity of historical work more obviously foreground the notion that the point of biblical texts is to communicate the messages of their authors and redactors, something that demands historical research since these individuals wrote thousands of years ago in languages that are no longer spoken and lived in cultures that no longer exist. This idea is commonly taught to students in the early stages of their education in academic biblical exegesis,[11] and so it becomes a common assumption of the field's members. One of the best known articulations of this position by a biblical scholar is that of Krister Stendahl (1984, 22), who argued in the middle of the twentieth century that the primary task of the field is historical research that aims at discovering what biblical texts "meant when uttered or written by the prophet, the priest, the evangelist, or the apostle,"[12] scholarly work that "yields the original in its own terms, limiting the interpretation to what it meant in its own setting" (29). For Stendahl, this should not stop interpreters from going on to discuss what texts currently mean to contemporary audiences, but such meanings depend on "a strong exposure to the 'original' beyond the presuppositions and the inherited frame of thought of our immediate predecessors in the theological task" (41).

It is not uncommon to encounter claims by biblical scholars that scholarly research that presupposes interpreters' religious beliefs should have no place in the discipline (e.g., Davies 1995, 17–55; Berlinerblau 2002, 275–81; Fox 2010, 15), and Stendahl's meant/means distinction aims at finding a hermeneutical place for confessionally driven interpretation—something that, we can say now, would for him apply equally to recognizing the validity of readings animated by the emancipatory goals of subjugated popula-

---

11. For examples of its appearance in introductory guides to biblical exegesis, see, e.g., Fee 2002, 1; Hayes and Holladay 2007, 139; Blomberg and Markley 2010, xii. Susanne Scholz's (2017, 11–17) survey of biblical studies curricula in liberal arts colleges in the United States found that most students are taught historical criticism and often no other interpretive approaches; Dale Martin's (2008, 1–28) survey of the biblical studies pedagogy at ten seminaries and divinity schools in the United States came to the same conclusion. Scholz's (2017, 18–21) survey of the textbooks used for undergraduate courses in biblical studies found that they privilege historical issues.

12. This essay is a reprint of the original version of an entry published in 1962 in *The Interpreter's Dictionary of the Bible*.

tions—so long as such readings acknowledge and conform to historical conclusions about what the biblical authors meant to communicate. Stendahl (1984, 22), too, assumes that texts are active players in interpretation and that scholars must aim to produce interpretations that end up with a "description in terms indicated by the texts themselves"; we can check the validity of our interpretations, Stendahl writes, by comparing it with "the material itself." In this view of the discipline articulated by Stendahl and the other scholars mentioned above, historical work is always primary, and any other sort of reading must be secondary and dependent on those first steps of historical research, the conclusions of which are used to judge the validity of any other interpretation. These historical conclusions can alone be considered objective, since they involve treating "the text on its own terms," allowing "the voice of the text itself to be heard," and do not rely only on interpreters' subjective presuppositions in regard to textual meaning.

The notion that objective interpretation is safeguarded only through historical study is so common in the field that even those who support or aim to privilege emancipatory goals in their work, both those who fit within the field's demographic mainstream and those who do not, often repeat this claim. So, for example, while Paul Joyce (1994, 23–26) sees an important benefit to the field in expanding beyond historical-critical approaches, he also writes that "texts make some claim upon the reader" and that scholars should ensure that interpretations not aimed at establishing the authorial intention in a passage do not cut "quite against the grain of the original," which we can come to know only through historical work. While Daniel Patte (1995, 35–36, 48–51) sees historical criticism as dangerous insofar as it foregrounds the interests of white male interpreters, he still argues that these historical questions should have a "special status" within the discipline, and that without it we lose a sense of "legitimate and valid" academic readings. While Hans de Wit (2008, 24–25) writes that he is supportive of liberative interpretation, he refers to "the ethics of accountability for the historical past of the text" and says that, without the historical research that this demands, "one is quickly doomed to hear just the echo of one's own voice."

Johanna Stiebert's (2013, 8–17) work generally aims at emancipatory readings of texts, but she also says that historical criticism is a necessary part of any academic interpretive approach and writes that it is "problematic" when "contemporary feminist advocacy is superimposed on the biblical texts," and in a work on feminist biblical interpretation, Phyllis Bird (2015, 31–33) writes that scholars must first undertake historical work to establish the views of the biblical writers and only then go on to liberative analysis. In somewhat similar ways, Justin Ukpong (1999) writes that true liberative scholarship within an African context cannot be done without historical criticism, and Brian Blount (1995, 7) says that if biblical scholars do not interact with conclusions produced by historical-critical work, they might simply make the text say anything they want it to say. Sometimes scholars from minoritized social locations will advance variations on the mainstream claim in regard to the necessity of the priority of historical work. For example, some argue, rather as Wolfgang Iser (1978) did, that since no text can supply an infinite amount of information, readers are always in the position of having to fill in gaps left by texts, with the result that readers' own contexts and beliefs, which shape the ways they perform such gap-filling, will always contribute to their conclusions about textual meaning, but that, nonetheless, there is still an ancient text of which scholars must ask historical questions.[13]

This widespread belief in the discipline in regard to the necessity of historical work, something that is understood to make interpretation as objective as it can be, is one that is rooted in somewhat unclear and unhelpful understandings of concepts such as *text* and *meaning*, as I aim to demonstrate here. I have argued elsewhere that it makes little sense to believe that an inanimate object such as a text, which is a series of dots and lines on a page (or pixels on a screen, or symbols carved into stone, or the like) can have terms or speak or indicate or do anything else (Janzen 2021b, 29–56), and I will not repeat those arguments here. It is perhaps enough in that regard to make the fairly straightforward point that inanimate objects do not literally speak to us, so texts, as a series of physical marks, can make no demands on us as to what to prioritize in the work of interpretation, with the result that meaning is not inherent to a text but is something that its interpreters decide on. Here, however, I want to point out that arguments by biblical scholars in regard to general hermeneutical theories about how to arrive at textual meaning tend not to say much about what meaning actually is, although they often seem to assume that it is something inherent to a text; that, at least, seems to be the question-begging sense of what some scholars are arguing when they refer to the text as having autonomy and a voice readers must listen to, terms onto which

---

13. For arguments like this from minoritized biblical scholars, see, e.g., González 1996, 11–18; Ukpong 2001, 156–57; Cuéllar 2008, 16–17; Blount 2019, 11–12.

we should not impose our own meanings—which is why Stendahl can say that readers can check their conclusions about meaning against what the text apparently communicates apart from our interpretive efforts. I want to demonstrate here, however, why I am in agreement with Jeffrey Stout (1982, 3) when he writes that it is not clear what a general hermeneutical theory of meaning would actually refer to.

We arrive at conclusions about textual meaning all the time, of course, but useful discussions about meaning, as I will show here, only take place among those within the same interpretive context; *meaning* is not a term that is specific enough to be very helpful when we are trying to devise broad hermeneutical theories as to how all readers, no matter in what context they find themselves, should go about the work of interpretation. Meaning can never be something that is not dependent on the context of readers and the communities they belong to—although I believe this for a different reason than Iser did—and those communities will inform readers how to produce meaning in their interpretive work. And if textual meaning is dependent on interpretive context, then it is the concerns of interpreters and their communities, shaped by the contexts in which they find themselves, that determine what to prioritize, where to begin the work of interpretation, and what to aim for in that process. If those concerns are unrelated to answering questions about authorial intention or any other topic associated with the ancient contexts of biblical texts, then historical work is unnecessary for such readers.

To illustrate this idea, we can imagine different teachers asking different groups of students what a particular passage means. We could, for example, picture a secondary school teacher reading *Henry IV, Part 1* with their students and coming across the passage where Gadshill says, "I am joined with no foot landrakers, no long-staff sixpenny strikers, none of these mad mustachio purple-hued maltworms" (2.1.80–83). Since the speech contains words and phrases with which the students would likely be unfamiliar, the instructor's question as to what these lines mean would likely be focused on having the students provide definitions of particular vocabulary. On the other hand, if the same class were reading *Hamlet*, and the teacher asked what Hamlet means when he says, "The play's the thing / Wherein I'll catch the conscience of the king" (2.2.633–634), the question about meaning would have more to do with Hamlet's intentions insofar as they advance the plot.

We could imagine instead a different pedagogical context in which an undergraduate instructor in Latin American literature reading Gabriel

García Márquez's novel *Cien Años de Soledad* with students who are nonnative Spanish speakers arrives at the following passage:

—¿Qué esperabas? —suspiró Úrsula—. El tiempo pasa.
—Así es —admitió Aureliano—, pero no tanto. (2018, 226)[14]

In this context, a question about meaning might have something to do with vocabulary, perhaps in regard to the phrase *pero no tanto*, which some students, depending on their experience in reading Spanish-language literature, might find it difficult to make sense of here, but it may well have to do with the way this short piece of dialogue reflects the cyclical structure of the novel, in which the passing of time only seems to result in the same sorts of events repeating over and over in the lives of the members of the family at the book's center, which is why *el tiempo pasa* "time passes" in the novel, *pero no tanto* "but not so much."

In a different context, we could imagine a university or seminary instructor asking a class about the meaning of a biblical text, having indicated to students that they should use their academic background in the critical study of the Bible to explain why an author or redactor wrote a particular sentence or passage precisely as they did and why they placed it at a particular point in a narrative. The instructor might, in this context, ask their students for historical rather than literary solutions to the question of the meaning of the text, having them explain how an ancient author's economic or religious or geopolitical context was a causative factor in the decision to compose a given text in a specific way. In a different pedagogical context, the instructor might ask about the meaning of a newly discovered ancient inscription for the field of biblical studies, a question aimed at having students reflect on the ramifications of that text for the discipline. Of course, a teacher within a religious setting might ask what a particular biblical passage means for their students in regard to their own lives, perhaps in the sense of what light it might cast on some ethical dilemma they face or how it might function as guidance in their relationships with friends or coworkers. We could imagine instructors in different types of classrooms, teachers deeply influenced by Philo's or Origen's allegorical hermeneutics, for example, and they would direct their students to articulate very different kinds of meanings.

---

14. The first edition of the novel was published in 1967.

Because we can use the word *meaning* in such different ways—and the brief discussion above hardly exhausts the various senses it can have—deciding what it might refer to on any particular occasion will always be dependent on the context in which someone is asking about it. One could connect many of the meanings to which I have just referred to authorial intention, although different interpreters would come to different conclusions in deciding which ones have something to do with such intention; not everyone, for example, would agree that ancient authors intended to communicate allegorical meanings of the kind Philo saw. It is perfectly possible to talk about meaning in regard to a text without ever referring to the concept of authorial intention, and in a classroom discussion on the meaning of the Tel Dan inscription for the study of the history of ancient Israel, for example, the term *meaning* refers to the way the discipline has reacted or should react to that text, a matter distinct from the author's intention in composing it. In each of the classrooms mentioned above, the teachers' questions are nuanced by context, and if any useful conversation is to take place in these discussions, the students must be clear as to whether the teacher is asking about structure or allegorical sense or plot or their own personal relationships or the direction of an academic field when they use the word *meaning*. As a result, the only general sense that word has that would apply to all of these cases is that it is the end result of interpretation, and a teacher's decision as to whether the students had arrived at correct answers to their questions about textual meaning would depend on the pedagogical context.

Since it is context that determines the particular sense of questions about meaning, different contexts, beliefs, backgrounds, experiences, and interests will lead different groups of readers to look for and prioritize different things when it comes to interpretation and the meaning it produces, and so the word *meaning* will refer to different things in different contexts. This is why, Stout (1982, 7–8) concludes, what a particular group sees as good interpretation is whatever serves its interpretive interests, so we will only be able to distinguish a good interpretation from a bad one when we know what purpose it is supposed to serve, which is a question about the context of the interpreters (Stout 1986, 103–4). To return to our classrooms above, the search for meaning is a matter of what larger purpose is intended in the context of each classroom for the interpretive work the students are supposed to carry out. The interpretation or meaning—since meaning is whatever the act of interpretation produces—at which the students or any other group of readers arrive is determined by readers' intentions as they take account of the evidence of the text's dots and lines, writes Stanley Fish (1980, 161), and those intentions will be determined by context. The students in the class studying Shakespeare's plays should know what kind of meaning the teacher is expecting from them based on the instructions and questions they are given, just as the different contexts of the other classrooms have already provided specific interpretive frameworks that signal to students what counts as good and bad interpretation, which is to say what kinds of meanings (or end results of interpretation) are acceptable and what kinds are not.

This is why there is nothing wrong with referring to the meaning of a text once the context of interpretation is shared by all involved, since in those contexts everyone should be clear as to what specific questions they are trying to answer, while the word ends up being unhelpful when one is trying to define with specificity broad hermeneutical theories as to precisely what all interpreters are searching for, since different communities of interpreters can search for radically different things. The classrooms I imagined have teachers who are clear as to acceptable and desirable interpretive limits, with the result that their questions about meaning should be unproblematic for their students. It is because context creates those limits, Fish (1980, 291–92) notes, that interpreters are never in the position of believing that a text could mean anything at all; students are normally (or at least ideally) quite aware of the kinds of interpretations that will result in good grades and the kinds that will not, the result of being aware of the criteria of interpretation (and of grading criteria in their case) in specific contexts. Their teachers have (also ideally) provided them with so much direction and guidance and examples as to what counts as good interpretation that it becomes easier and easier for the students to see specific ways of reading as natural, and such enculturation immerses them within specific interpretive communities, as Fish (1980, 303–21; 1989, 320–24) and others call them, their interpretations producing what they come to see as the plain or literal or obvious or important or real meanings of texts. Once one becomes enculturated in this sense—as, for example, biblical scholars are when they train in the mainstream of their field—the interpretive habits one has developed make it difficult to see that context has shaped the meaning or interpretation one produces, because the modes of reading in which one engages have come to seem natural and are reflected in the work of one's teachers and peers, seeming to be the sort of thing that everybody does, or should do.

Of course, when contexts and belief systems differ radically from community to community, these different groups can begin with very different assumptions as to what sorts of questions they are trying to answer and what kind of meaning they should be producing. It is possible for one interpretive community to disagree so radically with another as to what to privilege when it comes to interpreting texts that they will often not accept the conclusions of the other group as valid; if one has become enculturated to think of the real meaning of a biblical text as linked to its author's intentions for it, for example, then one will not be able to see interpretive work that pays no attention to historical questions as valid or useful, or at least will see such work as valid only insofar as it acknowledges the priority of historical investigations that might help establish authorial intention.

In the end, the beliefs modeled in examples of interpretation and sometimes articulated theoretically in hermeneutical guidelines are what undergird the ways in which searches for meaning are to proceed within a given community, and when important aspects of these beliefs disagree markedly with those of another group, the two interpretive communities might not have much to talk about—beyond their disagreements, at least—when it comes to reading texts. The belief system that gives rise to the hermeneutical norms of each group has convinced its members that they have found the literal or plain or obvious meaning of the text, and only by convincing its members to change some of those beliefs could one convince them to interpret in different ways, since our belief systems place particular limits on how we will deal with the evidence with which the dots and lines on the page present us. As Fish (1980, 274–77) notes, texts seem to have obvious meanings because interpretive communities teach their members to deal with the evidence on the page in specific ways. There is no point in trying to convince the members of a very different interpretive community than one's own that their interpretation is wrong by appealing to that evidence, because it is one's hermeneutical belief system that leads one to construe those dots and lines on the page as a particular kind of evidence for a particular kind of reading. We need hermeneutical beliefs that make sense to us—which is to say, that fit well within the worldviews we already have—in order to interpret the evidence of those marks on the page, and so what one sees as evidence is dependent on the whole worldview or belief system in which one's hermeneutical commitments are rooted.[15]

---

15. Fish 1989, 52–56. For a longer discussion of the idea that evidence and facts are created by individuals and groups as they use their worldviews or belief systems

So when Barton (2007, 49) writes that biblical scholars must proceed with "reasonable objectivity," which is to say with "a refusal to simply read one's own ideas into the text or to have no sense of detachment from it," he articulates the point that all of the teachers discussed above would have emphasized or at least modeled to their classes: Students need to learn the interpretive community's hermeneutical norms if they want to read properly in that context, and this involves exercising self-discipline so as not to engage any of their personal beliefs that might conflict with those norms as they go about the process of interpretation. The students will need to learn what kinds of questions the interpretive community expects them to ask when reading a text, how to go about answering them, and what kinds of answers are acceptable if they want to do objective interpretation as that group would understand it. Any good interpretation is objective interpretation, because it will have been produced by sticking to the hermeneutical norms of the particular community that validates it—judges it to be acceptable and good, in other words—and so the act of being objective just amounts to making the kinds of interpretive moves a community finds acceptable, moves that do not conflict with the belief system on which the group's hermeneutic depends.

Words like *meaning* and *objectivity*, then, can point to very specific ideas within the context of a given interpretive community, but they will not tell us very much when we are trying to create broader trans-communal theories as to how interpretation works. So if the context of a particular interpretive community leads its members to read biblical texts without prioritizing historical questions such as those that surround authorial intention, they are still able to talk about the meaning of the text, because all interpretation produces meaning. What matters for an interpretive community, as Stout (1982, 3–4) points out, is what kind of purpose interpretations are supposed to serve, something rooted in important aspects of the worldviews of the members of that community. Other interpretive communities may not agree with their approach, of course, because they interpret from the contexts of different belief systems and want interpretations to serve different kinds of purposes, which means that they will aim to answer different sorts of questions.

---

to deal with sensory phenomena, see Wilfrid Sellars's discussion of the myth of the given (1997, 68–79).

One can see why, then, students and scholars in the field of biblical studies who have roots in communities forced to struggle for social justice might want to privilege their experiences of resistance when it comes to interpreting texts and might hope that their work would have some sort of liberative value for their communities, and one can see as well why those from the demographic mainstream of the field who want to honor their ethical commitments to be allies in these fights would want to join them with their professional work in some fashion. Biblical scholars from minoritized social locations have, in fact, broadened the field beyond its traditional orientation that prizes historical questions, even if that orientation still dominates the discipline's mainstream. In the contemporary period, ever since second-wave feminism began to impact the discipline in the 1970s, when less than 4 percent of the Society of Biblical Literature's membership was female,[16] minoritized scholars have fought to include research that begins with experiences of resistance to oppression and aims at producing readings that provide liberative resources for those emancipatory movements. Women, scholars of color, scholars from the Two-Thirds World, LGBTQ+ scholars, Indigenous scholars, and scholars with disabilities appear to have recognized long before most of their mainstream colleagues that meaning is always shaped by interpreters' contexts, experiences, communities, and worldviews.[17]

The hermeneutical approach of prioritizing minoritized experiences, questions, and goals does not rule out the use of historical work; as I mentioned above, many minoritized readers who prioritize liberative goals agree with the contention of the field's mainstream and say that some sort of historical research must be done when producing academic biblical interpretation, and for some, historical questions are key to the emancipatory work they aim to produce,[18] but this is an approach in which the contexts of the minoritized and their emancipatory concerns set the agenda.

---

16. To be specific, in 1970, 3.5 percent of Society of Biblical Literature's membership identified as female; see Taylor 2019, 19.

17. See, e.g., Schüssler Fiorenza 1999, 26–27; Clarke and Ringe 2009, 69; Dube 2010, 91; Darden 2015a, 16–17; Crowder 2016, 33–36; Scholz 2017, xx.

18. One can think, for example, of Elisabeth Schüssler Fiorenza's (e.g., 2000, 166–74) work on the historical Jesus, where she argues that the original Jesus movement was more egalitarian than the communities envisioned by the authors of the gospels, or Carol Meyers's (e.g., 2014) argument, rooted in archaeological studies, that ancient Israel was less patriarchal than biblical texts make it out to be, or Gale Yee's (2003, 59–79) historico-economic study of Gen 2–3, aimed at demonstrating the dangers

One can tell if this sort of interpretation is good interpretation if it does a good job of providing readings that could potentially be used in liberative struggles, because that is its purpose. If it happens to be work that involves some sort of historical investigation, then that aspect of it must be judged on the basis of how well that historical work has been done, but in such a case that would be a secondary rather than the primary way of judging the quality of the research. One could argue that no sense can be made of ancient biblical texts without at least the work of translation,[19] something that involves research into historical linguistics and textual criticism, for even someone using a translation produced by others is still relying on the historical work that the textual critics and translators did. Such dependence, however, is distinct from the matter of privileging historical questions in one's own research and deciding that they must be answered first; it would, after all, be perfectly possible to use an existing translation to ask questions of emancipatory importance to a minoritized group, an approach that expresses no interest in issues of authorial intention and that involves no actual historical research on the part of the interpreter producing that emancipatory work.

Those of us wishing to honor our ethical commitment to contribute to emancipatory struggles when that is reasonably possible, with the result that we want our work in the field of biblical studies to be guided by a liberative hermeneutic, need not be dissuaded by arguments from the mainstream that the biblical texts themselves demand prioritizing historical study that must be used as a yardstick to judge the validity of any other sort of interpretation, because texts are inanimate objects that cannot make demands; the decision to prioritize historical questions when reading ancient texts is precisely that, a decision, not a universal hermeneutical rule. The beliefs of those of us who want to contribute to emancipatory interpretation have simply committed us to being part of an interpretive community that, while it has much in common with biblical studies' mainstream, also sees a different purpose for interpretation, and anyone who thought that we should prioritize something besides emancipatory interests in our professional work would have the obligation of convincing us that it is wrong to believe that we should support liberative struggles against structural subjugation whenever

---

to women posed by a text composed to benefit a sector of the dominant class in an ancient society.

19. For a thoughtful discussion of this idea, see Roberts 1995.

that is reasonably possible. Interpretations that begin with and privilege emancipatory questions and interests rather than historical ones can produce meaning, because all interpretations produce meaning, and they can produce legitimate meaning, because legitimacy of interpretation is determined by the interpretive community, and minoritized scholars are already members of communities that prioritize support for emancipatory projects and have established such readings in the field of biblical studies, even if some members of the discipline's mainstream regard such hermeneutical approaches with suspicion.

Epistemic Humility and Reading after the Minoritized

Since there is no good reason why academic biblical interpretation must prioritize historical study or why it cannot privilege emancipatory goals at all stages of its work, we can see the importance of providing different strategies to pursue those liberative goals, such as the one I model in this book. If we want the field of biblical studies to become a more relevant discipline, in which even its mainstream becomes an interpretive community that produces work guided by its members' ethical commitment to support movements of resistance against forces of subjugation, then promoting a range of interpretive options that can help scholars develop their liberative imaginations by broadening their exposure to different contexts of subjugation and resistance seems like a straightforward goal. In this final section of the chapter, however, I reflect on the limitations as well as the promise of the particular interpretive strategy I pursue in the following chapters. Reading literature by minoritized authors from contexts other than one's own can generate liberative creativity and empathy for others who live in different social locations, as earlier sections of the chapter discuss, but we also need to be aware of what it cannot do.

We might think in this regard of the way that John Dewey (1998, 66) described the pragmatist movement in philosophy as one that aims "to develop ideas relevant to the actual crises of life."[20] It is important, he wrote, to distinguish *pragmatic* from *practical*, since the aim of pragmatism is "to free experience from routine and from caprice" rather than to create practical solutions to specific issues. "A pragmatic intelligence is a creative intelligence," he wrote, and while pragmatist philosophers orient

---

20. The essay was originally published in 1917.

their energies toward problems people face, "philosophy will not solve these problems; philosophy is vision, imagination, reflection" (67). Reading after minoritized authors from different contexts can be pragmatic in this sense insofar as it helps us escape the routines and habits of biblical studies' mainstream and generate vision, imagination, and reflection in liberative interpretation, but it cannot be prescriptive in regard to the practical use of its interpretive work for emancipatory struggles in contexts different from one's own. Only those who inhabit a particular social location know it well enough to tell if and how any scholarly work is of practical value for their specific site of resistance. The process of reading after is different from that of reading with, as I discuss below, and will only be done successfully within a context of deep epistemic humility, a recognition that one lacks the requisite knowledge and experience to tell those in social locations other than one's own what emancipatory interpretation should look like in their context. This is an important point for scholars in dominant demographic locations to keep in mind, because we are used to setting the agenda for biblical studies and, as the second section of the chapter explains, the effects of that have not always been positive.

In the end, only those within a particular community can decide if a given work of interpretation is of emancipatory use in their context, because they alone know enough about their situation of resistance to be aware of the strategies that would be effective there; for this reason, wrote Ukpong (2002, 21–22), the minoritized alone have epistemological privilege in liberative biblical interpretation. This is why there is no lack of minoritized scholars who reflect on the way in which the experiences of those in similar social locations and their resistance movements direct their work: Wil Gafney (2022, 139–56), for example, writes that her teaching is informed by the Black Lives Matter movement and thus begins textual study with Black experiences of violence and injustice in order to prepare students to confront it; Dora Mbuwayesango (2014, 71–76) says that African feminist biblical scholarship begins its interpretation with the experiences of African women with the aim of allowing them to realize their agency in liberation; Monica Melanchthon (2013–2015, 63) says that South Asian feminist readings always begin with the socioeconomic contexts of Asian women in order to empower them in liberative struggle; Nāsili Vaka'uta (2011, 3–5, 38–45) says he reads from the perspective of the Tongan lower class, beginning with their experiences of oppression and focused on their liberation; and Althea Spencer Miller (2015, 90–92) refers to her creolizing hermeneutic as one that begins with the lived reality of colonized peoples and aims at transforming their lives.

All these scholars—and many more could be added to the list—are providing examples of the central hermeneutic principle of emancipatory biblical interpretation. It begins with the experiences and ways of knowing of individual subjugated communities so that it can be useful for their liberation. And the epistemological privilege of the minoritized in liberative interpretation is based not only in the fact that they have far more knowledge of what oppression and liberation in their contexts look like than those from outside it could ever have, but also in the idea that they alone can take the lead in enacting their liberation. Ada María Isasi-Díaz (1996, 1), for example, makes that latter point when she writes that "liberation is not something one person can give another but … is a process in which the oppressed are protagonists, participants in creating a different reality from the present oppressive one." When those outside of a disadvantaged community assume that they can solve the community's problems for it and free its members from oppression, subalterns end up in the same situation in which they have always been, with people from outside of the group who understand little about their lives claiming that they know what is best for them, maintaining that the powerless should remain dependent on these outsiders in regard to how to think and act. This sort of approach would imply that members of vulnerable communities lack the intelligence and ability to discover emancipatory solutions and that they should not be the primary liberative actors who can make their own decisions as to what is best for them, but should be instead passive recipients of the largesse of those from dominant social locations, which is precisely the position taken by those who police their oppression.

Given this most basic principle of emancipatory hermeneutics, then, it is not surprising to find that not all minoritized scholars are open to participation in this endeavor, or at least in specific aspects of it, by those in other social locations. Esther Fuchs (2003, 96–98), for example, writes that she is suspicious of male scholarship that valorizes feminist studies of the Bible; male feminists cannot speak for female ones, she says, or else we are in a situation where men ignore female subjectivity and agency, the very thing feminist biblical scholarship means to oppose. Not all African American scholars believe non-Africana readers can do African American biblical interpretation, writes Mitzi Smith (2017, 51–52); not all Latine biblical scholars believe that readers from outside of the community can engage in Latine interpretation, writes Francisco Lozada (2017, 28–29); to be involved in womanist biblical criticism requires self-identification as an African American woman, writes Nyasha Junior (2015, 115–16). The case is not that minoritized biblical scholars in general do not want their colleagues in other social locations, including privileged ones, to conduct research that could be of use in emancipatory struggles—Shively Smith (2022, 41–42), to take just one example, writes that it is the responsibility of the entire field to include the work of minoritized scholars and to look to underrecognized hermeneutical models as new places to begin interpretation—but such participation involves careful consideration of how to do so in a useful way given the basic hermeneutical principle of liberative interpretation.

This is an issue of particular importance for biblical scholars from dominant social locations, those of us most used to setting the agenda for the field and with the least exposure to minoritized experiences and narratives, and so when scholars from disadvantaged contexts do extend an invitation to those with greater socioeconomic privilege to engage in liberative dialogue, it is with the caveat that this discussion respect all participants as equals (so, e.g., Guardiola-Sáenz 1997, 69; Sugirtharajah 2003, 138; Miller 2005, 219–20; Dube 2010, 97–99). As Love Sechrest (2022, 74) puts it, participation of those from the demographic mainstream in emancipatory struggles must be "characterized by epistemic humility," a stance that acknowledges the superior knowledge and epistemological privilege of the minoritized in regard to their own contexts and that would obviously reject the assumption that those uninterested in prioritizing historical questions in scholarly biblical interpretation are illegitimate discussion partners. Mitzi Smith (2017, 56–60) uses the term *hermeneutical humility* when referring to this latter issue; this sort of approach to interpretation, she writes, is characterized by a rejection of a hegemonic epistemology that insists that knowledge can derive only from dominant sources, and it asks interpreters to reflect on their own privilege and social locations as they begin the reading process.

If those of us from privileged social locations hope to do work that could conceivably be of use to movements of resistance to structural subjugation, then we must change our views as to how scholarship is to be done and learn how to prioritize a different epistemology than the field normally does, something that will demand manifesting our epistemic humility by developing strategies that can allow us to begin our work at different points and to learn to read after our minoritized colleagues by prioritizing their contexts, interests, and goals. And since, as this chapter has already pointed out, each social location is different, and different minoritized groups suffer from subjugation in different ways and have developed different strategies of resistance, epistemic humility is the appropriate epistemological stance any time a scholar from any social location interacts with a minoritized culture to which they do not belong. In adopting that stance, we can broaden our liberative imaginations in virtuous ways and so have a better foundation for emancipatory research.

Sechrest is not the only biblical scholar who refers to the importance of epistemic humility; Hidalgo, for example, uses the same term (e.g., 2018, 74), although she roots this concept in the notion that all interpretive approaches are limited by their readers' contexts, a hermeneutical reality that leads her to prefer the term *epistemic realism* (see, e.g., 2021, 40). If, as in Sechrest's use of the phrase, there is a warning here to scholars in majoritarian contexts that they not assume the universal priority and applicability of their experiences, epistemologies, and related hermeneutics, Hidalgo extends the sense of epistemic humility or realism to point to the need for a pluriversal understanding of biblical studies that conceives of historical criticism as just one reading strategy among many, no one of which has priority in the discipline as a whole over the others. We might compare this aspect of epistemic humility to Lewis Gordon and Jane Anna Gordon's (2006, ix) appropriation of Audre Lorde's metaphor of using—or being unable to use—the master's tools to dismantle the master's house: It is possible to use the master's tools, they write, but also to adopt other ones with the goal of building new houses, until the master's house loses its hegemonic status because it is simply one among many from which people may pick and choose for shelter. This extended sense of epistemic humility envisions a pluriversal (rather than universal) and collaborative hermeneutical field for the discipline, one in which critical work driven by emancipatory goals by scholars in many different contexts provides many interpretive options that are potentially of use for those in liberative struggles.

That being said, however, the concept of epistemic humility cautions those outside of a given community that they will not know it well enough to decide which of those options are useful for that context, a warning of particular importance for those of us from dominant social locations with little exposure to the realities and experiences of minoritized groups. As some biblical scholars emphasize, we must refrain from speaking in place of or for the powerless and should read with them instead, where *reading with* suggests a dialogue of equals. One well known example of this sort of approach is the work of the white South African scholar Gerald West who, during and after the apartheid era, has used his resources as a trained biblical scholar to read biblical texts with impoverished South African communities of color. To do so, West (1995, 214–15) begins with the issues and concerns raised by those communities,[21] writing that "those of us who are white middle-class males are not and cannot be organic intellectuals, but we can choose to be accountable to and to be in solidarity with the poor and oppressed. We can learn from them and we can serve them."

Not all scholars from vulnerable social locations, however, are convinced that this kind of interpretive process is well suited to exercising epistemic humility. When Eric Anum (2001, 111–15), for example, studied the sort of format in which a scholar from a dominant context engages minoritized readers in interpretation, he found that the latter see the scholars as imposing their agendas and are often in the position of feeling as if they have to tell the academic experts what they want to hear. Sarojini Nadar argues that scholars who are not members of the disadvantaged community whom they engage in interpretation—are not "organic intellectuals," as West puts it—will not really know the context well enough to speak with community members, and will inevitably speak to them.[22] Reading with the subjugated can sometimes allow privileged academics to analyze their own social locations and question their assumptions about the universal applicability of the historical questions they normally ask, notes Lim, but the process often ends in Western modes of analysis dominating the discussion (2019, 65–69). So, writes Walter Mignolo (2009, 173), regardless of one's academic discipline, nonorganic scholars have "*no right to guide the 'locals'*" in deciding what is appropriate interpretation and action in their contexts, since local communities alone will understand those contexts well enough to make such decisions (emphasis original).

The approach I model in this book, however, is an interpretive strategy rooted in a hermeneutic that involves reading after rather than with the minoritized from a different context than one's own. Whatever particular process of reading after that one chooses, it begins with silent listening to or reading the narration of those in social locations other than one's own and foregrounds those experiences in order to generate liberative vision, imagination, and reflection in interpretation. The particular speakers and

---

21. For a detailed description as to how West conducts these contextual Bible studies, see West 2001.
22. See her broader critique of this model in Nadar 2012.

authors to whom one listens may not, in the end, see a specific act of interpretation that someone produces after listening to them as useful in their specific site of resistance. But when we think of the extended sense of epistemic humility or realism as an attempt to create a collaborative and pluriversal discipline directed by emancipatory ethical commitments, each such interpretive act of reading after should, if competently done, have the potential to generate liberative imagination in some context.

If scholars, and particularly ones at privileged intersections of social identity, can take the concept of epistemic humility seriously, then there will be room for all of us who hope to contribute to emancipatory biblical interpretation to become better acquainted with life experiences of those at different intersections of identity and power than our own, and reading literature by contemporary minoritized authors is one way we can expose ourselves to such experiences and learn different kinds of stories about different kinds of protagonists than the ones we tend to be constantly exposed to. It is an accessible interpretive strategy, both insofar as it can open our hermeneutical investigations to different experiences of subjugation and resistance without, for example, demanding that one uproot one's life and move to another country, and insofar as it can be taught to students and those with little or no exposure to the academic study of biblical texts. With such a strategy even readers whose identity is rooted at dominant intersections of power can try to do something like the sort of thing Sechrest (2022, 24–26) says she does in her womanist hermeneutic, as she takes the situation of contemporary disadvantaged readers seriously, highlights the dangers of texts that often receive illiberative interpretations, and searches for what she calls rhyme, or similarities in the problems faced by characters in biblical stories and those that contemporary minoritized readers must confront. We interpreters with a great deal of socioeconomic privilege must not fool ourselves into thinking that reading a novel by a Black woman will provide us with the same sort of sensitivity and insight that an African American scholar like Sechrest has when looking for rhyme between biblical stories and African American experiences, but it will make it possible for us to search for connections between characters created by a contemporary Black woman author and ones in biblical stories, and so to ask questions a bit more like some of those our colleagues in different social locations bring to their interpretive work, as we will see in the following chapters.

In each case in which I model this particular way of reading after the minoritized in those chapters, I begin with minoritized experience, at least as reflected by one minoritized author in one work of literature that they have produced, and this provides me with a set of concerns that shape the questions I foreground when interpreting a biblical text, one that I have chosen because I have been struck by similarities between the two writings, something like the rhyme that Sechrest discusses. These concerns end up being different ones than those that drive historically oriented biblical interpretation, because they are all ones formulated with ethical and liberative concerns in mind, ones driven by my encounter with the minoritized literature after which I am reading, and so each chapter confronts a different ethical failure with which mainstream biblical interpretation struggles. In chapter 2, I ask why no one in Daniel, a book concerned with the problem of empire, ever demonstrates concern for those most vulnerable to the abuse of imperial power, something that raises an ethical problem with the heavenly kingdom that features so prominently in the second half of the work. In chapter 3 I am struck by the ethical problem of the silencing of Ezra-Nehemiah's powerless characters who are demonized by the powerful ones who are permitted to speak. In chapter 4, I ask about the ethical problems that arise when the victims of siege, rape, and starvation in Lamentations are blamed for their suffering that some of the book's speakers depict as just divine punishment. My investigation in chapter 5 is driven by the ethical problem of interpretations of the opening chapters of Genesis that have been used in the subjugation of queer communities, leading me to ask if they can be read in liberative and inclusive ways.

None of these sound like the sorts of questions traditionally prioritized by the mainstream of biblical studies, because reading after authors from minoritized intersections of power leads me to focus on very different concerns than those raised in historical-critical investigations of biblical texts. That does not mean that historical issues never arise in the following chapters, and because of my training and experience as a biblical scholar I find it difficult not to notice redactional critical issues when I read Genesis or text critical ones when I read Daniel or to avoid asking about the ancient Near Eastern context of some of Lamentations' explanations for the destruction of Jerusalem or about the compositional history of Ezra-Nehemiah. My positions on all of these issues have some effect on the way I read those texts, but they are secondary if not tertiary issues rather than my primary concerns; I address them because they happen to arise incidentally in discussions that are directed by and focus on very different ideas.

Reading after minoritized literature helps me to begin my interpretations of biblical texts with different questions and concerns than the mainstream of biblical studies has prioritized and to aim at producing interpretations that could be considered to include vision and imagination of use to liberative struggles. The degree to which any of these readings have practical use at any specific site of resistance will depend on those who inhabit that site, but each attempt to prioritize emancipatory interpretation ideally has the effect of making the discipline of biblical studies as a whole an ethically better field, one in which more of its scholars are able to acknowledge that all academic writing supports some sort of political stance, whether a scholar intends their work to do so or not, and a field in which more of its members aim to prioritize their ethical commitment to oppose injustice in their research and teaching.

2
A REVOLUTIONARY IN SEARCH OF A REVOLUTION: EMPIRE AND THE POWERLESS IN *THE SYMPATHIZER* AND DANIEL

Introduction

One ethical problem that any reader of the Bible might encounter in the interpretive process is a failure to notice the absence of subaltern characters in a biblical writing, although it is likely readers in dominant social locations who benefit from withholding their gaze from the subjugated that are most prone to manifest this particular hermeneutical act of omission. Stories that feature protagonists from privileged intersections of identity dominate Western culture, as chapter 1 discusses, with the result that many interpreters will often fail to notice a problem exists when reading narratives that feature only socially central characters and no minoritized ones at all. Yet since emancipatory interpretation begins with the experiences of the oppressed and aims to be useful in their liberative struggles, one of the most basic things that readers training themselves to listen to such experiences should be able to notice and recognize as problematic is the exclusion of powerless characters and any sort of concern about them in biblical narratives, the central issue in this chapter's reading of Daniel.

Some of that book's best known stories—such as Daniel in the lions' den (Dan 6) or the condemnation of his three fellow exiles to a furnace of fire (Dan 3)—reflect, as the other parts of the book do, what commentators often identify as Daniel's most obvious theme: God's sovereignty and absolute control of history (e.g., Collins 1993, 51–52; Boccaccini 2002, 171–72; Niskanen 2004, 85; Seow 2004, 219; DiTomasso 2005, 215). The gentile kings who cast faithful Jews into a lions' den or fiery furnace for not compromising their religious fidelity are thwarted in their murderous intentions by the God of Israel, who saves the religiously loyal in these two stories, and as other parts of Daniel make abundantly clear, plans to do away with kingdoms controlled by humans altogether, replacing them with one authorized by heaven that will last forever. This emphasis on the divine control of history is as clear in the stories of Daniel and his friends (Dan 1–6) as it is in Daniel's visions of the destruction of human empires and their replacement by one sanctioned by God (Dan 7–12) and reflect the period in which the book was put together. The consensus of modern critical scholarship is that the visions of the latter half of the book, or at least those that appear in Dan 8–12, were composed between 167 and 164 BCE as a response to a persecution of Palestinian Judaism by the governing Seleucid Empire.[1] Antiochus IV, the Seleucid king, imposed a religious and cultural suppression of Judaism in the region beginning in 167 in reaction to a revolt that began in Judea, and this led to yet a broader armed response from the Jewish population that took control of Jerusalem and resumed Jewish worship in the temple in 164.[2] While versions of the stories of Daniel and his friends were already in circulation before this time,[3] Antiochus's persecution was formative in the development of the anti-imperial message of the different ancient editions of the biblical book of Daniel.

My concern here, however, is not with the historical context in which the book was assembled but with its focus on divine sovereignty as something that manages to entirely ignore the suffering of the powerless. This becomes the focus of my interpretation because I read Daniel after *The*

---

1. It is not only modern scholars who arrive at this conclusion. Porphyry, a third-century CE philosopher, also argued that Daniel was written during the reign of Antiochus IV (see the prologue to Jerome's *Commentary on Daniel*). For a standard summary of the reasons why scholars find it untenable to date the book to the period centuries earlier in which it places Daniel and his friends, see Redditt 1998, 463–64. Some see an earlier edition of Dan 7 as attached to a developing corpus of Danielic traditions before the addition of Dan 8–12; see, e.g., Meadowcroft 1995, 272–75; McLay 2005, 218–19; Newsom 2012, 563–66.

2. Helpful and succinct scholarly discussions of the conflict between Antiochus IV and Judaism include Boccaccini 2002, 151–63 and Grabbe 2016, 21–26.

3. Stories of Daniel and Nebuchadnezzar may have been told as early as the Persian period (see, e.g., Kratz 1991, 124–48 and Newsom 2012, 560–61), although the origins of the stories in Dan 1–4 are more frequently dated to the Hellenistic period (see, e.g., Collins 1993, 24–38 and Henze 1999, 10–11).

Sympathizer,[4] a novel by the Vietnamese American Viet Thanh Nguyen. If, as I pointed out in chapter 1, the hermeneutical process of reading after the minoritized can result in something like what Sechrest describes as rhyme, in the case of interpreters reading a biblical text after a work of literature by a minoritized author from a social location different from their own, this would amount to seeing points of similarity between the characters and their situations and contexts in the two texts. We do see rhyme in this sense when reading Daniel after *The Sympathizer*, but this hermeneutical process also leads us to notice the complete absence of powerless characters in that biblical narrative. So intent is Daniel on making the case that God, not human power, controls history, and that a divine rather than an earthly empire will ultimately triumph, that the book devotes no space at all to the consideration of the fate of the powerless who have no say as to which empire will rule over them. Their absence makes their concerns invisible to the book's narrative.

The unnamed narrator and protagonist of *The Sympathizer* is a Viet Cong spy embedded in the command structure of a South Vietnamese general fleeing to the United States just ahead of the fall of Saigon to the North Vietnamese army in 1975. The narrator travels with the general, the general's family, and some of his officers to California in order to report on their activities to the new communist government of Vietnam. The white America these refugees encounter refuses to accept them, and while the general's officers long to return to Vietnam, even if only to die there fighting communists, the narrator's relationship with his home culture is rather more fraught, as his father was a French priest and even his own Vietnamese family despises him because of his multiracial heritage. This protagonist who is accepted by no culture, who as a spy is constantly forced to hide his true identity, and who can find what little social acceptance is possible only to the degree that he can sympathize with the different and warring groups among whom he lives, encounters problems rather like those faced by the Jewish characters in Daniel, who are also forced to move to the center of empire and whose lives are subject to the whims of powerful foreigners.

The rhyme we can perceive results in part from this similarity in the characters' lives in these two writings and in part from the fact that both

---

4. Nguyen 2015. References to page numbers from the novel will appear in the text of the chapter. Italicization in quotations are original to the novel.

works are concerned with the problems and dangers of assimilation and acceptance faced by outsiders forced to live in proximity to a dominant imperial culture. We cannot see these similarities, however, without also noticing that the situations of *The Sympathizer*'s unnamed narrator and that of the Jewish characters in Daniel are quite different, since the former is accepted by no culture while the latter were among the elite in Jerusalem and live in the imperial court in Babylon. While one could read Daniel as providing a happy ending to its narrative in its portrayal of a coming divine kingdom that puts an end to human ones, *The Sympathizer* pushes us to read the biblical writing's consistent focus on power, sovereignty, and empire from the perspective of someone with no power at all. Reading Daniel through the lens of *The Sympathizer* can make us ask how satisfying a solution to the abuse of imperial power this biblical book really provides and whether much more needs to be said about the future it foresees as dominated by yet another empire, because Daniel himself, a socially privileged figure just like all the other characters in the book, never really grapples with the way empires abuse the powerless. The narrator of *The Sympathizer*, however, inhabits a very different socioeconomic context and so has a much different perspective on the damage that imperial and even anti-imperial power inflicts on those subjugated by such forces.

Encountering Daniel after *The Sympathizer* can help those of us used to stories featuring protagonists with immense unearned social privilege, something that stems in part from the ways in which such characters benefit from the power exercised by European and American empires, to notice how subaltern perspectives are absent in Daniel's narrative of imperial conflict. Readers from privileged socioeconomic locations in particular can often be prone to overlook the suffering of those outside of particular racial and national boundaries, those whose well-being our empires decide is of little concern in comparison with maintaining the privileges of those at the imperial center. It can be easy for us to see Daniel's picture of the future as a happy ending because the right kingdom will be victorious,[5] but *The Sympathizer* points out that from the standpoint of those who never fit inside privileged imperial boundaries a mere transfer of power tends not to be what benefits the oppressed. Neither the human nor heav-

---

5. In fact, the study carried out by Greg Carey (2017) as to how the story of Daniel is told and taught to young and young adult white American evangelicals concludes that the educational materials used to do so almost entirely avoid any critique of the concept of empire.

enly characters of Daniel seem able to imagine an empire-less world (see Polaski 2004, 669), and after reading *The Sympathizer*, narrated from the point of view of a character who is accepted by no culture, let alone the imperial one, this lack of imagination in the biblical book can push us to ask if something else needs to be said about the problems of empire and its treatment of the powerless beyond what the characters in Daniel are able to envision.

Before we begin this reading, a brief explanation is in order as to the version of Daniel I will use, since multiple editions of the book appeared in the ancient world. The versions of Daniel in the OG and Masoretic traditions are fairly different, not only because the OG has two stories (Susanna and Bel and the Dragon) the MT does not, as well as a long poem in Dan 3 absent from the MT, but because even the stories the two traditions share in common are in a different order and their versions of them, especially those in Dan 4–6, are sometimes quite different.[6] Even apart from these chapters, the smaller differences between the MT and OG elsewhere in Daniel result in versions of stories with different emphases.[7] In some cases those divergences in the shared material can be explained through obvious changes made by copyists but more frequently reflect series of alterations in textual traditions long separated from each other, or at some points perhaps even two separate traditions that may have derived from common stories but not a common written text.[8] The emergence of the

---

6. These sorts of differences tell us, as the Dead Sea Scrolls do, that there was no clear line between copying and redacting in the late second temple period (Perrin 2021, 48). For Papyrus 967 as the best witness to a pre-Hexaplaric text of the OG, including the order of its stories in which Dan 7–8 comes between Dan 4 and 5, see the discussion in Finsterbusch and Bellantuono 2021.

7. For example, see the comparison of the OG and MT versions of Dan 8 in Young 2020 or the comparison of these two versions of Dan 7–12 in Beyerle 2006. And in a case like Dan 11, while the MT and OG assumably derive from a common written source, each underwent so much alteration as their copyist-redactors aimed to emphasize different things that it becomes very difficult to establish which version is closer to a hypothetical original or how to construct such an earlier text based on the evidence available to us (see, e.g., the discussions in Settembrini 2018 and Scolnic 2022).

8. To take Dan 4–6 as a brief example, Michael Segal (2017) argues that while some verses in MT Dan 5 not found in the OG were later additions to the Masoretic textual tradition, the MT's version of Dan 5 and that of Dan 4–6 in general is closer to the common core text that underlies both traditions. The OG varies so greatly from the MT in these chapters that Segal describes it as an instance of a rewritten Bible.

translation traditionally attributed to Theodotion may reflect yet another text of Daniel or perhaps is the result of a redaction of the OG toward the proto-MT.[9] There was no standard edition of Daniel in the ancient world, and Josephus's stories about Daniel, for example, reflect aspects of both the OG and Theodotion.[10] It is simplest, then, to see the MT, OG, and Theodotion as three different editions of Daniel (so also, e.g., Henze 1999, 38–49; Ulrich 2012; Segal 2016a, 5–6), each with its own particular collection, ordering, and wording of Danielic traditions and each with its own emphases,[11] rather than as three witnesses to the same text. To read Daniel after *The Sympathizer* demands choosing one of them, and I have settled on the Masoretic version of the book, if only because this text is shared by Judaism and at least one of the Bibles that Christians use. One could conduct the exercise of reading Daniel after *The Sympathizer* with the other editions, which would produce somewhat different results, but limits of space do not make that possible here.

Empire and the Powerless in *The Sympathizer*

The unnamed narrator of *The Sympathizer* introduces himself at the beginning of the novel as "a spy, a sleeper, a spook, a man of two faces" (1),[12] and we learn that he is writing a confession to someone he addresses as "my dear Commandant" (2). We soon discover as well that he is, or at least

---

Others disagree with Segal's analysis and argue that OG Dan 4–6 is closer to an original shared text (e.g., Albertz 1988, 13–42, 77–84, 113–28; Wills 1990, 144–52; Munnich 2015), but the MT and OG diverge to such an extent that it seems reasonable to conclude, as Ian Young (2016) does in regard to Dan 5, that these two textual traditions have no common written source, at least at this point, and stem instead from different writings that derive from similar oral versions of Danielic material.

9. See, e.g., the discussions in Collins 1993, 11; and McLay 2005, 322.

10. See Vermes 1991, 161. For a similar phenomenon in New Testament writings, see Collins 1993, 9.

11. For a discussion of the different emphases of these three textual traditions, given the different texts and order of material found in each, see Holm 2013, 301–15.

12. This line reflects the opening of Ralph Ellison's *Invisible Man*. *The Sympathizer* is full of allusions to other texts (for a partial list see Rody 2018, 398–400). Like the narrator of *The Sympathizer*, that of *Invisible Man* is a nameless person of color and his identity is continually defined by others, a problem of central concern for the narrators of both novels. For the subversive effect of some of *The Sympathizer*'s allusions to other writings—in the language of postcolonial theory, for the mockery of colonial thought they produce—see Kumamoto Stanley 2020, 288–90.

was, a Viet Cong spy who had received his undergraduate education in the United States in order to learn American ways of thinking (15–16). This makes him a more effective infiltrator into the South Vietnamese military, in which he worked as an aide-de-camp to the general in charge of the secret police during the last stages of the Vietnam War. This education has left him not only with a deep knowledge of American culture but with a flawless American accent when he speaks English: "If an American closed his eyes to hear me speak, he would think I was one of his kind" (8–9). Such fluency in American culture and language means he accompanies the General (which is how this character is always identified in the novel) when he meets with Americans, including Claude, the General's liaison with the CIA.

He has infiltrated the secret police so effectively, in fact, that the General takes him with him when he, his family, and his officers flee Saigon just ahead of its fall to the North Vietnamese army, allowing the narrator to continue reporting on the General's plans to the communist government of Vietnam after he has been resettled in California. As an infiltrator into the enemy's command structure, the narrator must play two roles on two opposing sides—the General's loyal officer and the Viet Cong's loyal spy. He cannot do only one of these jobs; if he is to remain undetected as a spy, then most of the time he must act out his role as a captain in the secret police trained by the CIA, which on occasion means arresting and interrogating other Viet Cong operatives. In one case he refers to his act of interrogating a captured Viet Cong spy as "what I was supposed to do and not supposed to do" (250). The true identity of a good spy must remain unknown to those on whom they spy, yet this is only possible if the spy sometimes acts in contradiction to that true identity, problematizing the question of what true identity even means in such a case. The novel can be read, as we will see in this part of the chapter, as the narrator's struggle to determine that true identity, to decide on which side he truly supports and sympathizes with, and whose beliefs he should truly adopt.

One way to describe a spy is as a sympathizer or at least the General does so when he says that sympathizers are "spies in our ranks. Sleeper agents" (76). Sympathizers' "friendly faces" are "only masks for calculating wills" (165), for from the point of view of those against whom they work their sympathy for the cause is only apparent, not real. Yet the narrator does sympathize with the character that he plays of a captain in the secret police, although he labors under the reality that his only mask is his face, something he cannot remove (178). It is a way of referring to the fact that it is difficult for him to determine what his true identity is. He is so sympathetic, in fact, that he uses the terms *we* and *us* instead of *they* and *them* when he refers to the South Vietnamese military, even though from the standpoint of his role as a spy that institution is the enemy, the *them*. His mother, he confesses, taught him that "blurring the lines between us and them can be a worthy behavior" (48). He can sympathize even with the Western bourgeois culture the communist leadership in Vietnam so steadfastly opposes and at one point provides a list of the aspects of life in the United States that he enjoys from TV dinners to the modernist novel to "that omnipresent American narcotic, optimism" (364–65). As another character says, "It's impossible to live among a foreign people and not become changed by them" (283), something dependent on developing at least some sympathy for them.

Sympathizers as spies pose a problem to those on whom they spy, for their sympathy allows them to better assimilate into that group. But they also pose a problem to those on whose behalf they spy, for true sympathy can make it difficult to refrain from becoming a collaborator, an issue that plagues the narrator (200). It is precisely the problem he refers to when he says that his interrogation of a Viet Cong prisoner amounts to doing "what I was supposed to do and not supposed to do." Spies are not true believers in the ideals of those on whom they spy, but collaborators are not true believers in the ideals of those on whose behalf they are purportedly spying. The difficulty of determining one's true identity and beliefs is such a problem for a sympathetic spy that is no wonder that in this confession of a former spy who felt strong sympathy for those he spied on there are so many references to beliefs, both political and religious, that different characters use to define their identities.

At different points the narrator recalls the catechism he memorized during his Catholic upbringing in Vietnam (e.g., 270, 322), and the political beliefs of those around him are often cast in religious terms. The General's belief in the French and Americans accompanies his belief in God, although as the North Vietnamese victory approaches, the narrator observes that the General's "faith in the *mission civilisatrice* and the American Way was at last bitten by the bug of disbelief" (3) as events undermine the Americans' promise of "salvation from communism" (15). A former professor at the American college where the narrator studied says that he had once been a communist but had become "a born-again American" who now promotes what he understands to be the civilizing mission of the West against the world's barbarism, something that he seems to believe necessarily involves armed force (132–34). When the narrator, along with some of the General's officers who fled with him to the United States, returns to Southeast Asia after the communist victory in order to conduct an armed mission into Vietnam that the General sees as the first strike in a larger insurrection, they find themselves under the command of an officer who compares their meager forces to Jesus and the apostles who relied on their faith and the word of God. "We are like those true believers," he says and tells the soldiers they are on a mission to save others just as the apostles were (382–83).

The narrator, however, says that he lacks the kinds of beliefs normally invoked when people aim to justify their roles in killing others, such as "the need to defend God, country, honor, ideology, or comrades" (129), which is perhaps why he says that he finds it difficult to participate in killing (105–6). The General, in fact, accuses the narrator of being "too sympathetic" to notice the danger posed by potential spies who must be killed (301–2). As far as the General and other powerful characters in the novel are concerned, the demands of belief, in particular the belief in original sin, must take precedence over sympathy for human life. When Claude, the CIA's advisor to the General, tries to soothe the narrator's conscience ahead of a mission he has been given to kill a suspected spy among the General's officers, he tells him that "we're all innocent on one level and guilty on another. Isn't that what Original Sin is all about?" (134). It is not only Christians from the West who invoke this belief to override sympathy for human life; Man, the narrator's childhood friend and Viet Cong handler, tells him at one point that his actions as a spy would lead to people being killed, "but they aren't innocent. Neither are we, my friend. We're revolutionaries, and revolutionaries can never be innocent. We know too much and have done too much" (145).

The narrator's struggle to determine where his true sympathies and beliefs lie—what his true identity is—is not made any easier by the fact that because of his multiethnic heritage neither side truly accepts him as one of their own, a problem faced by other characters in the novel as well. His mother is Vietnamese, but his father was a French priest, "and strangers and acquaintances had enjoyed reminding me of this ever since my childhood, spitting on me and calling me bastard" (25), an attitude to his racial background adopted even by his mother's family (183–85). After the United States government resettles the General and his men in California, the narrator strikes up a relationship with Sofia Mori, an American of Japanese descent whose experience living as an ethnic outsider in the country of her birth parallels his own. She says that she has been made to feel inadequate when she tells white Americans that she has no interest in traveling to Japan or learning Japanese. As much as she knows she is American, she says that "I've felt like a spy" (99–100). "It doesn't matter how long you've been here, Ms. Mori said. White people will always think we're foreigners" (157). She refers at one point to an uncle who refused to fight for the United States in the Second World War after the American government put his family in an internment camp. After the war he moved to Japan, where white people had told him all his life he should go, only to discover that he was not accepted there either (279–80). So it is not only the narrator who finds himself feeling like a spy, trapped between cultures that do not accept him and regarded like Ms. Mori and her uncle as "neither one thing nor another" (280).

The officers who flee to the United States with the General, however, do not need to struggle with their identity in this way. They do not experience the narrator's attraction to American culture, in part because of its rejection of them. As the narrator puts it, when Americans even bothered to notice the Vietnamese refugees, they regarded them "with ambivalence if not outright distaste" (153).[13] The General's men only begin to feel like true individuals rather than an undifferentiated mass in the white imagination as they don uniforms and begin to drill for the mission that the General sees as the first step in an eventual overthrow of the communist government of Vietnam (286–87). They yearn to return there, a place where they, unlike the narrator, had been fully accepted their whole lives. They have no interest in assimilating into a country that does not want them, and they harbor as much distaste for American culture as white America does for them. The fact that the General's eldest daughter, who had been studying in the United States years before the rest of her family fled Vietnam, has embraced American culture and become a pop singer

---

13. The Vietnamese characters in the United States are "surrounded by Americans so tall they neither looked through nor looked down on these newcomers. They simply looked over them" (123). As Evyn Lê Espiritu Gandhi (2020, 62) notes in an article on *The Sympathizer*, refugees challenge fundamental ethnic and racial categories of the modern nation-state, and so they tend to be excluded from the larger political cultures in which they find themselves. In some cases, Americans in the novel simply find it easier not to see those who do not fit their understandings of the way in which the world should be; when they find they cannot help but notice the Vietnamese refugees, however, they tend to experience their very presence in America as unsettling and distasteful.

fills her parents with anger. Her mother spits out the word "singer" when describing her with as much animus as she uses when pronouncing the word "communist" (158), as if her daughter were part of the enemy her husband still wants to fight. In the United States, the General's wife says, "We will not be able to protect our children from the *lewdness* and the *shallowness* and the *tawdriness* Americans love so much" (159), a very different view than the narrator's sympathy for Western culture.

As a result, the other Vietnamese characters regard American culture differently than Ms. Mori and the narrator do. Ms. Mori, who was born in the United States, tells one of the Vietnamese emigres that "you must claim America" by referring to himself as a Vietnamese American rather than as Vietnamese. "If you do not claim America, if America is not in your heart, America will throw you into a concentration camp or a reservation or a plantation" (357). Even if one believed that the mere attempt by persons of color to put America in their hearts would be enough to stop them from being consigned to internment camps or prisons, the refugees' continual experience of being treated as outsiders and the desire to return to their past lives in Vietnam means that they have no wish to assimilate. One of the General's officers says he knows perfectly well that he is unlikely to come back alive from a mission but that, from his point of view, "Hell's better than this shithole" (289).

The narrator, however, recognizes that the officers' dream to return to a place where they unconditionally belong, where their identity is never in question, is merely utopian. The clock in the restaurant in California that the General owns is set to Saigon time since, as the narrator observes, displaced people live in two times—the present and the past lives in their homeland. But in the impossibility of the return for which the General's men hope, "The open secret of the clock, naked for all to see, was that we were only going in circles" (259–60). The General and his men cling to a dream of belonging that can never be realized, their old lives in Saigon now forever out of reach. They are unwilling to even try to reach some sort of compromise with America, as Ms. Mori urges, and so never deal with issues of identity, belonging, and sympathy as the narrator must, since no group accepts him.

In order to assimilate or even just to survive in a nonnative culture, immigrants must study it closely, and the narrator says, "We were the greatest anthropologists ever of the American people" (337). His struggle to determine his own sense of identity, the beliefs and sympathies it should encompass, is linked to the fact that there are no people willing to accept him, and so he notices, as others seem not to, just how similar the warring sides claiming his loyalty actually are. They can adopt the tactics of their enemies, and for example, the General says, "We must think like the communists" and "live and work underground, as they did" (180). When the narrator survives the doomed incursion into Vietnam by the General's men, who are inevitably captured by the Vietnamese military, since the narrator in his role as a spy had informed them of the plan, he is sent to a reeducation camp to purge him of his Western sympathies and is questioned using techniques taken from the same CIA manual of torture and interrogation he had used when embedded in the secret police (447–50). Even more insidious than this, however, are the similarities the narrator sees between the slogans the communists and Americans and their Vietnamese allies use to express the beliefs that justify the slaughter and oppression in which they engage. Near the beginning of the novel, the narrator refers to his willingness to die for Ho Chi Minh's assertion that "nothing is more precious than independence and freedom" (36), yet the right-wing American congressman who supports the General's plan to launch an insurrection in Vietnam invokes precisely the same slogan to describe the ethos of the United States (338–39). At one point, the General and his pro-Western supporters chant the phrase "Vietnam forever!," but readers are told that the Communist Party uses the same slogan (156–57). "A slogan is just an empty suit," Ms. Mori tells the narrator. "Anyone can wear it" (157).

It eventually becomes clear to the narrator that these slogans and clichés really mean nothing when broadcast by Western imperial powers or, for that matter, by the Communist Party in Vietnam. Even before his return to Vietnam with the General's officers, a refugee who fled the communist takeover tells him that "before the communists won, foreigners were victimizing and terrorizing and humiliating us. Now it's our own people victimizing and terrorizing and humiliating us. I suppose that's improvement" (199). When both sides treat the powerless the same way, then their claims to act out of beliefs that result in independence and freedom are indeed "empty suits draped on the corpse of an idea" (480). It is perhaps easiest for those at home in no culture, those who are always excluded and powerless and who can say like the narrator that they "ranked among the meanest" (379), to see how meaningless such claims to belief are when anyone powerful speaks them. So while the narrator hears people on both sides of the conflict invoke a belief in original sin to justify the killing of their enemies, to those whose lives seem of little concern to the powerful, the phrase "original sin" is simply a set of words available to anyone who is powerful and who wants to use it to justify the killing and oppression of the powerless.

Whatever claims the powerful might make in the novel about their beliefs, they appear to evince little concern for those who rank among the meanest. As the General rallies his troops during one of their training sessions to prepare for the insurrection, he tells them that they will launch a revolution to free the people, but he shows no concern for "who the people were and what they might want" (287). The General approvingly quotes Marx in asserting that the powerless "cannot represent themselves; they must be represented" (189), an idea to which the novel continually returns. When the powerful represent the powerless then they will be, as far as the powerful are concerned, whoever the powerful say they are and will want whatever the powerful say they want.[14]

This power of representation is most vividly evident as the narrator is attached as a consultant to the filming of a Hollywood movie of a story set during the Vietnam War. The film helps to shape and create the reality of the war and of the Vietnamese as they would be construed by audiences around the world, a point explicitly made by its director, referred to as the Auteur. Long after the war itself is forgotten, the Auteur says, the movie "will not just be about the war but it will be the war" (233). Its Vietnamese characters are largely played by Vietnamese refugees in the Philippines where the film is shot, and their role is mainly to be killed (211–12, 228–29), although some of the extras play members of the Viet Cong who rape and torture innocent victims. The narrator comes to realize the movie is a work of propaganda, an American story told from an American point of view (205–6) in which the Vietnamese are extras largely present to play nameless characters who would be killed or barely human savages who fight for what the narrator refers to as King Cong, Hollywood's bestial version of the Viet Cong.[15] And because the powerless are represented

---

14. Sylvia Chong (2018, 371) suggests that the characters in the novel seem to understand this quote from Marx more as Edward Said reappropriated it, for Marx was referring to the political representation of small-holding peasants in France, whereas Said uses it to discuss the depiction in art and culture of what the West has created as the Orient in its cultural imagination. We could point as well to Gayatri Spivak's (2010a, 29–34) discussion of the passage in Marx where this quote occurs, part of her reflection on the problem of the subaltern voice as something the powerful can hear only in terms of their own representations of it.

15. In this way, notes Roberta Wolfson (2023, 60–64), the film participates in a broader American reframing of the conflict as one of the country's "good wars,"

by movies like this one, they can learn to identify against themselves. The narrator finally sees the complete version of the film in Thailand after traveling there with the General's men and along with the southeast Asian audience in the theater he sides with the American characters and cheers for the destruction of the Viet Cong (372–74).

Once the narrator and the surviving members of the General's raiding party are captured upon crossing the border into Vietnam, they are sent to a reeducation camp, and only then do readers realize that the narrator has been writing his confession—the first part of the novel, in other words—at the behest of the camp's commandant. When he is sent to be tortured, it is his old friend and handler Man who oversees this, although unwillingly; the commandant demands the torture, and Man hopes to save the narrator's life by complying with the order. Man does get the narrator to confess to a crime he committed, one that he appears to have suppressed and refused to confess even to himself: In his role as a member of the South Vietnamese secret police, he witnessed and did nothing to stop the torture and gang-rape by three policeman of a captured female Viet Cong agent whom he had helped arrest. The narrator's description of the rape (451–58) is long, gruesome, and hard to read. It is one of the most important points in his narrative where he fails to act on the sympathy that he has for others (Sillin 2019, 633).

The narrator also describes the rape of one of the fictional Vietnamese characters in a scene from the film on which he worked, and it is hard not to see a parallel between that and the rape in the novel, especially as the narrator says the room in which the female agent was raped was called the movie theater (451). Just as he suppressed the rape of the agent, the rape scene of the movie had been the only one that silenced the Thai audience in whose midst the narrator first saw the film (373; see also Chong 2018, 374–75). The narrator had tried to prevent the inclusion of the rape scene in the movie, but the Auteur had pointedly ignored his advice (212–13);[16] reading the narrator's description of the actual rape after that of the fictional one he watches on-screen helps us see that both reflect aspects of the representation of the powerless. As Amanda Gradisek (2020, 21–22) puts it, there can be no true representation of the oppressed if stories like the narrator's failure to act in preventing the rape of the agent are not told,

---

viewing it only from a white American male perspective as a struggle for civilization and freedom.

16. See also the discussion in Prabhu 2018, 392–93.

nor can the narrator truly understand his identity apart from the ways in which others have represented him until he deals with his guilt in this rape.[17] By doing nothing in that context, he had sided with the imperial representation of the colonized as those whose lives do not matter, the same message broadcast by the Auteur in a film seen by audiences around the world.

After having wrung this confession from the narrator, Man goes on to confirm what the narrator had heard earlier from the refugee: For the powerless, life under communist rule is not any different than it had been when Vietnam was controlled by Western imperial powers. As Man puts it, "Now that we are the powerful, we don't need the French or the Americans to fuck us over. We can fuck ourselves just fine" (472). The revolution in Vietnam, the narrator concludes, ended up traveling the same road as those in France and the United States, each beginning as a movement for independence and freedom and ending by depriving the powerless of exactly that (487). While torturing the narrator, Man repetitively asks him what is more precious than independence and freedom, a reference to Ho Chi Minh's slogan for which the narrator had once said he would die (36). "Nothing is more precious than independence and freedom," Ho had said, but the narrator comes to realize the slogan has two opposing meanings. The first is the one for which he said he would die, but it dawns on him that one can also take these words to mean that the phrase "independence and freedom" is less than worthless because it is used to motivate people to do horrible things to the powerless, and so even nothing at all is more precious than that (486–87). There is nothing, no true belief, behind this slogan used by both the Communist Party and the right-wing American congressman, only a desire by the powerful for more power, achieved by representing the powerless as those whose lives have no value. The powerful "are the ones who say nothing with great piousness, who ask everyone else to die for nothing, who revere nothing" (480), and so there is no point to the reeducation camps like the one where the narrator is tortured except to teach meaningless slogans that hide these facts (471–72).

In the end, the narrator does not choose to determine his identity by aligning with one of the two sides that both want him to be their loyal

---

17. The narrator is also accompanied in much of the novel by the ghosts of two men to whose deaths he directly contributed, and we can see their presence as symbolizing an unrecognized history, a failure to face up to the past in an ethical manner (so also Bosman 2019).

soldier and sympathizer, for as someone excluded as an outsider by every culture he can eventually see how alike and empty the slogans and statements of belief of the powerful are, even when they belong to opposing groups at war with each other. He decides to sympathize instead with the powerless, those who inhabit the same subaltern position as he does, something reflected in the book by his namelessness, which points to the lack of importance he has in the eyes of the powerful.[18] By the end of the novel, the narrator even uses first-person plural pronouns to refer to himself—or, we should say at this point, to refer to themself—a move that we could see as expressing solidarity with others who suffer oppression imposed on them by the powerful.[19] This new identity would not have been possible for the narrator had they not been forced to confront their complicity and lack of sympathy when doing nothing in the face of the agent's suffering as she was raped. The narrator does not know why so many people have chosen to believe in slogans that mean nothing and to kill and die for nothing but concludes that it is necessary to "sympathize with the undesirables among the undesirables. Thus magnetized by experience, our compass continually points toward those who suffer" (493–94). The narrator bases their new identity in solidarity with all who are powerless and excluded and says that "despite it all—yes, despite everything, in the face of *nothing*—we still consider ourselves revolutionary. We remain that most hopeful of creatures, a revolutionary in search of a revolution" (495).

By the end of the novel, it is still not entirely clear what such a revolution might look like, but as readers we have enough information to glimpse at least its most basic principles: Sympathize with "the undesirables among the undesirables"; reject belief systems that are merely lists of clichés; and refuse the powerful's representations of the powerless as a disposable mass whose role is to be killed for slogans and statements of belief that mean nothing. If time for the General and his officers in the United States moves in a circle, the utopian past for which they long forever out of reach, the same metaphor applies—if in a somewhat differ-

---

18. As Debra Shostak (2020, 183) argues, many characters in the book are identified not by their names but by their roles or rank (the General, the Auteur, etc.), which dehumanizes and impersonalizes them, but the narrator's namelessness is a way of showing how he is never truly recognized.

19. So Kumamoto Stanley 2020, 297. Nguyen (2018, 432) himself describes the narrator's use of a collective *we* at the end of the novel as "the collective 'we' of revolution and solidarity."

ent way—for both the communists and Western imperialists in the novel. Both believe they know the direction of history and the truth of progress,[20] but both follow the same path from revolution back to oppression, repetitively subjugating the powerless to what Man calls "the horrors of history" (439). Progress is something that can only be accomplished apart from empire and the powerful, and only through a dedication to the needs of those who suffer.

Sympathy, Spies, and Empire in Daniel

If we read Daniel immediately after *The Sympathizer*, we may be struck by similarities between the situation of Daniel and his three companions from Jerusalem and that of *The Sympathizer*'s narrator, seeing something like the rhyme Sechrest describes when she looks for parallels between the situations and contexts of biblical characters and contemporary communities disadvantaged by race, gender, class, and poverty. Like the novel's narrator, Daniel and his colleagues are torn from their homeland following a military defeat and are forced to migrate to a powerful empire. Once in Babylon, there is no sense that these Jewish characters will ever be able to return,[21] so like the narrator in *The Sympathizer* there is no culture fully willing to accept them as their own. Like the narrator, however, they are able to assimilate to some degree, and the character of Daniel, as we shall see, develops sympathy for the foreign kings whom he serves. Like the narrator, Daniel and his friends are educated in the powerful empire in order to absorb its culture and language (1:4), and they are even given Babylonian names (1:7). The story of their forced migration to and education in Babylon is told in Hebrew in Dan 1, but 2:4b–7:28 is in Aramaic, and there we see the Jewish characters abandoning their native language and interacting with imperial officials fluently in the language of empire,[22]

---

20. At one point, the narrator refers to Man's past teaching of Marxist theory in regard to the way capitalism monopolizes time, entirely controlling the timetable of workers. Marxism, however, sees the proletariat as ultimately in control of time, since in its view history inevitably moves to undermine capitalism (441–42).

21. Some of the stories and visions of Daniel are set in Babylon during the time of the Babylonian Empire (Dan 1–5; 7–8), but others take place there after Babylon falls under foreign rule (Dan 6; 9–12). The following chapter will discuss how in Ezra-Nehemiah Jewish exiles in Babylon are permitted to return to Jerusalem and Judah once foreigners take control of Babylon, but that is never raised as an option in Daniel.

22. While this fits the linguistic situation of the exilic period in which these sto-

paralleling *The Sympathizer*'s narrator's fluency in English. Insofar as the use of a particular language can say something important about one's identity, in the stories of Dan 2–6 we can certainly refer to the linguistic assimilation of the Jewish characters in the book.[23]

Unlike *The Sympathizer*'s narrator, however, the Jewish characters of Daniel are among the elite, for the Babylonian king Nebuchadnezzar takes only Judeans "of royal descent and of the nobility" (1:3) to Babylon following the destruction of Jerusalem so they can be educated in "the literature and language of the Chaldeans" (1:4) for three years, with the goal of making them fit to serve in the royal palace (1:5). Daniel and his friends may be foreigners forced to migrate to the imperial center, but they are elite foreigners who serve in the Babylonian court and that makes their experience in Babylon different in notable ways from that of *The Sympathizer*'s narrator in the United States. The main character of *The Sympathizer* is a subaltern and ultimately accepted by no culture, but Daniel and his friends could hardly be said to be "ranked among the meanest," with the result that the fate of the powerless remains almost entirely invisible to Daniel. We would not have to read the biblical book through the lens of *The Sympathizer* to notice its interest in the issues of sovereignty and empire, but this strategy of reading after the minoritized does turn our attention to the ease with which the character of Daniel in particular is accepted by and can sympathize with imperial power in the stories of Dan 1–6, the focus of this section of the chapter. It also allows us to read the accounts of the visions in Dan 7–12 as heaven's attempt to reeducate Daniel away from this sympathy, as the narrator of *The Sympathizer* was subject to reeducation upon his return to Vietnam, but as the next section of the chapter discusses these visions do not portray heaven as being any

---

ries are set, when Hebrew was spoken in Judah and Aramaic was widely spoken in the Neo-Babylonian Empire, in the mid-second century BCE, as the MT's version of Daniel coalesces, Aramaic was actually the language commonly spoken in Judea and Greek was the language of empire. Hebrew, however, appears to have been revived as a national language (and script) in the Hellenistic period, once scribal training in Aramaic ended with the fall of the Persian Empire, and knowledge of Hebrew, at least among the educated in Judea, became an important symbol of nationalism; see Schniedewind 2006 and Schwartz 2005, 68. In the second century, then, Hebrew rather than Aramaic would have been seen by some Jews as the language of Jewish heritage that they should speak.

23. See, e.g., Valeta 2007, 92. The use of Aramaic in Daniel reflects a complex identity in which Jewish life is intertwined with imperial rule; see Portier-Young 2010, 103.

more aware of or concerned with the powerless than Daniel is. This act of reading after, however, also allows us to look to *The Sympathizer* to imagine the growth of Daniel's character in ways that make it possible for us to picture him as someone with the potential to identify and sympathize with the oppressed, as the narrator of *The Sympathizer* eventually does, someone who could develop into "a revolutionary in search of a revolution" led by them.

In the first part of the book if Daniel is largely sympathetic to the kings he serves in Babylon, it is also clear that he and his companions from Jerusalem have no interest in complete assimilation to Babylonian culture. Just as some of the Vietnamese characters of *The Sympathizer* express radical distaste for American culture, Daniel decides right away that לא יתגאל "he would not defile himself" with the food and wine provided by the king (1:8) and asks that he and his companions be allowed to eat only vegetables and drink only water while living at court (1:12). The use of the verb גאל "to defile" suggests to some scholars that Daniel believes the royal rations violate the food laws of torah (see Lev 11; Deut 14:3–21),[24] while others argue that this does not explain Daniel's reluctance to drink the wine from the royal rations since torah does not label any kind of wine as illicit within the Israelite diet and that we see in Dan 1 an attempt on the part of the Jewish characters to maintain their cultural identity (e.g., Cristofáni 2005, 6–7). Had this been their intent, however, then we might imagine they would have been clear that they were going to conform to the food laws of torah, which would allow a different diet than simply vegetables and water. Perhaps it is easiest to see their request as an act of refusal, a rejection of the Babylonian food provided by the Babylonian king and an assertion that they would not entirely assimilate into Babylonian culture (so, e.g., Soesilo 1994, 444; Chia 2006, 178–79). Given their willingness to accept their Babylonian education and names, Daniel and his companions have less reluctance than most of the Vietnamese characters in *The Sympathizer* to accept imperial culture, and while that is likely related to the much higher status they are accorded within the empire where they find themselves, they

---

24. E.g., Sweeney 2001, 129. However, the Hebrew verb גאל never actually appears in either Lev 11 or Deut 14 and had the character of Daniel truly been thinking of those laws, we might expect him to use the root טמא "unclean," which those chapters repetitively use to refer to unclean food and the state into which Israelites enter when they eat such animals. For the use of גאל in late Second Temple period literature, see Seufert 2019, 650–52.

clearly reject the notion of the complete absorption of their cultural identities by Babylon.[25]

This is not the only refusal of complete assimilation to empire in the stories of Daniel and his friends, but before we turn to the others it is worthwhile to point out that this first one is quite limited in its rejection of Babylonian culture. If the four Jewish characters reject the king's food, they do not reject their new Babylonian names—after Dan 1, in fact, Daniel's three companions are called only by those names (Shadrach, Meshach, and Abednego), with only one exception (2:17)—nor do they refuse their three-year course in Babylonian literature and language. In the narrative surrounding their education, it appears to be important that the king be able to satisfy himself that they have become Babylonian enough to serve in his court, and the fact that Daniel appears to exhibit great wisdom is not enough for the king. We can see this once we notice that the story of Dan 2, in which Daniel alone among the sages of Babylon is able to interpret Nebuchadnezzar's dream, takes place in the second year of the king's reign (2:1) and in the midst of Daniel's three-year Babylonian education. Daniel's great feat of wisdom in that story is rewarded by the king with his elevation to a position over the other sages, and at Daniel's insistence his three companions are promoted as well (2:48–49). Yet they are all still required to complete their education and be interviewed by Nebuchadnezzar at the end (1:18–20).[26]

One might wonder why, following such a display of wisdom, the king still finds it necessary to determine their fitness for service to the crown, but this series of events in the chronology of the book makes sense if we see Nebuchadnezzar as concerned that these foreign additions to the imperial court assimilate to Babylonian culture. The king discovers that Daniel and his friends are far wiser than anyone else in the kingdom (1:18–20), and while 1:17 tells us that this wisdom comes from God rather than their Babylonian education, for Nebuchadnezzar it is not enough that they demonstrate wisdom, they must become culturally and linguistically like

---

25. John Ahn (2023, 324) suggests that Daniel and his companions reject the food because it consisted of rations given to Babylonian priests, and by rejecting the food they reject religious, if not political, assimilation.

26. The copyist of the Hebrew text behind the OG translation saw this as a problem and so altered the original date at the beginning of 2:1 (בשנת שתים "in the second year") to בשנת שתים עשרה "in the twelfth year." Like that copyist, some modern scholars see the chronology of events in MT Dan 1–2 as illogical; e.g., Collins 1993, 154–55; DiTomasso 2005, 69–70.

the Babylonians at court. So if we can read the food controversy of Dan 1 as resistance to complete enculturation, it is a resistance with somewhat limited effect, as Lim (2017) also argues, for they receive a long course in Babylonian literature and language that ends with them being Babylonian to an important degree.[27] Daniel and his friends, in large part because of their elite status, are able to assimilate into the culture of empire in a way that is not possible for the characters of Asian descent in *The Sympathizer* and seem more amenable to imperial culture than many of the characters in the novel.

Merely because Daniel and his friends have been promoted to important positions in the kingdom, however, does not mean that they are exempt from all of the dangers faced by outsiders brought to the center of empire. In Dan 3, Nebuchadnezzar demands that his officials worship a massive golden image he has constructed on pain of being thrown into a fiery furnace, but Shadrach, Meshach, and Abednego refuse. (Daniel is not mentioned in this story, so it is not clear if he worships the image.) The three Jewish characters, who are now Babylonian officials and called only by their Babylonian names in this story, do not explain why they will not worship the image, which they appear to equate with Nebuchadnezzar's god (3:18), even though they are not certain that the God whom they do worship will be able to save them from death (3:17). This story of a rejection of imperial religious culture finds a close parallel in the story of Dan 6, which takes place after Darius the Mede seizes control of Babylon in the book's narrative. Here, Daniel finds himself in a similar situation. In Dan 6, Darius decrees an unchangeable law that demands his subjects pray only to him for a thirty-day period on pain of being thrown into a lion's den, and like his compatriots in Dan 3, Daniel refuses to accommodate this order. In the MT's edition of Daniel, clear parallels in plot and vocabulary link the two stories,[28] but even in a cursory comparison of Dan 3 and 6 the similarities are evident: Jewish outsiders, who have been forcibly removed to the center

---

27. Lim reads Dan 1 in dialogue with short stories by Alfian Sa'at, a Malay author, set among the minority Malay population in Singapore. For this conclusion in regard to the effectiveness of the Jewish characters' refusal to eat the king's food, see Lim 2017, 674–76. Lim (2019, 110–14) also argues that, from a Confucian standpoint, the act of Daniel and his friends of concealing from the king their rejection of the royal rations (see 1:10–15) is objectionable, particularly because it is accompanied by compromises of embracing a new foreign identity and climbing the political ladder at court.

28. For a discussion of these parallels, see Segal 2018, 267–69.

of the empire, see limits to the amount of assimilation to imperial culture they are willing to tolerate and are willing to risk death rather than bend to that culture when it comes to the religion they practice. These are good limits to set, apparently, since divine power—the real power in the cosmos, according to the book—validates these decisions in both stories by miraculously saving these faithful worshippers of the God of Israel from death.

The fact that we see some resistance by Daniel and his friends against imperial culture in Dan 1–6, however, does not mean that these stories are monolithically anti-empire. We can see these chapters expressing some sympathy for the royal characters, for Nebuchadnezzar is never rebuked for erecting a statue for his subjects to worship (see, e.g., Coxon 1995, 88–89), just as Darius is never criticized for demanding that his subjects pray to him alone. Nebuchadnezzar may have forcibly relocated Daniel and his friends to Babylon, but that is the result of a divinely authorized victory (1:1–2) in which he unwittingly acts as God's ally (Chia 2006, 172–74). The king's dream in Dan 2, the interpretation of which God reveals only to Daniel, involves a statue with a head of gold. Daniel tells Nebuchadnezzar that he is the one whom the golden head represents, the one to whom God has given kingship over the whole world and the power to rule all humans and animals (2:37–38). It is not difficult, then, to see the golden statue Nebuchadnezzar erects in the very next story as reflecting that interpretation, a celebration of the fact that he rules the world by divine acclamation (see also Meadowcroft 2020, 22–23; Waller 2020, 340–41). Assumedly he has missed the real import of that vision, which is not that he is king but that God has made him one and so he must undergo the events narrated in Dan 4, prefigured by yet another dream that Daniel alone can interpret. Here, Nebuchadnezzar is driven from human society and made to live like an animal until he realizes that God alone is sovereign, but once he does so he praises God and is restored to his place as king, becoming even greater than before (4:31–33 [ET 34–36]). Certainly one way to understand stories like these is as communicating the message that there is nothing wrong with the Babylonian Empire or Nebuchadnezzar's rule, so long as the king is aware that imperial power is ultimately bestowed by God.

Nebuchadnezzar is largely a sympathetic character in Dan 1–4[29] and is really the main character of these chapters, or at least of Dan 2–4. He

---

29. See Davis Bledsoe 2014. For a very different reading of the king's character, however, see Valeta 2008, 120–22.

moves from acknowledging that the God of his Jewish subjects is a great revealer of secrets (2:47), a point at which he worships Daniel (2:46), to being so impressed by the power of that God to deliver Jewish worshippers that he decrees that any subject who speaks ill of God will be executed (3:29), to fully acknowledging God's complete sovereignty of the cosmos (3:31–33 [ET 4:1–3]; 4:31–32 [34–35]). By the time we reach the story of Dan 4, in fact, Daniel (who does nothing to inhibit the king's worship of him in 2:46) and Nebuchadnezzar seem fond of each other. Nebuchadnezzar summons Daniel—who in this chapter is more frequently called by his Babylonian name, Belteshazzar[30]—because he knows that "a spirit of the holy gods is in you" (4:6 [9]). Daniel's reaction to the dream the king has called him to interpret is exactly like Nebuchadnezzar's, for both are "terrified" (בהל) by it (4:2, 16 [5, 19]), and it is Belteshazzar/Daniel who expresses the wish that this terrifying dream foretell not the king's future but that of his enemies, while it is Nebuchadnezzar who attempts to calm his advisor's fears as to what might happen to the king (4:16 [19]). Daniel, it is fair to say, has developed sympathy for Nebuchadnezzar.

We see this sympathetic attitude on Daniel's part in Dan 6 as well, and in this story Daniel is so loyal to Darius that the king plans to set him over all his other officials (6:4 [ET 3]). The point of the king's administrators, as the MT of Daniel tells the story, is to prevent loss from accruing to the king (6:3 [2]), and so when the other high-ranking officials plot to remove Daniel, it is assumedly because his fidelity to the king and empire prevents them from using their positions of authority to defraud the kingdom.[31] Daniel is so faithful to the duties of his imperial office that the other offi-

---

30. The name Daniel appears twice in MT Dan 4 (4:5, 16 [ET 8, 19]), but Belteshazzar six times (4:5, 6, 15, 16 [8, 9, 18, 19]).

31. Their motivation is sometimes construed as jealousy sparked by Daniel's upcoming promotion (so, e.g., Fewell 1988, 144–45; Kirkpatrick 2005, 105–6), but the MT version of the narrative specifically states that the point of the three highest officials (סרכין), of whom Daniel is one at the beginning of the story, is to prevent the satraps, those who rank immediately below them, from taking advantage of their positions. The king's promotion of Daniel over the other two סרכין might cause those two individuals to be jealous, and in the OG's version of the story, which says nothing about the officials having any role in preventing the satraps from stealing from the king, it is only those two officials who plot against Daniel (OG 6:4, although see also Segal 2016b, 423–38 in regard to OG 6:14). In the MT's version of the story, however, the satraps would have no reason to be jealous, since Daniel's promotion does not alter their position in the imperial hierarchy, and so the fact that in the MT they as well as

cials find it impossible to accuse him of any sort of negligence in regard to his administrative work, and so their plot to remove him must focus on his religious practices (6:5–6 [4–5]), the only aspect of his life that he is now unwilling to conform to imperial culture. After those officials convince Darius to create the unalterable decree that ends with Daniel in the lions' den, however, we see the king struggle to rescue him, his sorrow when he cannot, and his joy when his faithful servant miraculously survives (6:15, 19, 24 [14, 18, 23]); the story of Dan 6, in fact, is largely one that follows events from Darius's perspective (Viviés 2005, 137). By this time, Daniel has adopted the standard phrase characters in the book use to address monarchs—"O king, live forever!" (6:22 [21])[32]—and he says that if he has acted in complete fidelity to God, he did so also in regard to the king (6:23 [22]). Daniel may be a foreigner in this kingdom administered from Babylon, but he is a more loyal subject than the empire's other high-ranking bureaucrats, the result of the sympathy he has for the kings he serves.

The fact that we can refer to Daniel as an imperial sympathizer, however, does not stop him from conveying heaven's messages about God's ultimate sovereignty even when, in a case such as the message revealed in Nebuchadnezzar's dream in Dan 4, Daniel only reluctantly transmits the bad news to a king he regards sympathetically. To be fair, Daniel is notably less sympathetic in his interaction in Dan 5 with Belshazzar. In the MT's version of this story, this son of Nebuchadnezzar is aware of what his father underwent to learn the truth of God's sovereignty but has decided to ignore that lesson (5:18–22), and Daniel does not hesitate to condemn him (5:23–28). Belshazzar's abuse of the Jerusalem temple vessels by using them in a festival honoring his gods (5:1–4) leads to his death and the transfer of the rule of Babylon to Darius the Mede (5:30–6:1 [ET 5:30–31]), and so this story is the most obvious criticism of the royal court in Dan 1–6 (see, e.g., Humphreys 1973, 211; Henze 2001, 14). We see in these chapters that the kings can make poor religious decrees accompanied by murderous punishments for disobedience (Dan 3; 6), and that they can act in ignorance of God's sovereignty (Dan 4; 5), while the court itself can seem full of disingenuous officials whose sole goal appears to be to enrich themselves at the empire's expense (Dan 6). In his role as someone

---

the other two סרבין plot against Daniel suggests that all of these officials believe he will stand in the way of their abuse of their positions for their own financial gain.

32. We see other imperial subjects using this phrase to open addresses to the king in 2:4; 3:9; 5:10; 6:7 [ET 6].

to whom God has given extraordinary abilities to interpret visions and dreams (1:17), Daniel repetitively relays to monarchs the divine messages that state God alone determines the fate of kings and empires (2:36–45; 4:16–24 [19–27]; 5:17–28), but outside of the case of Belshazzar, these are never total condemnations of the king, and the notion that imperial power in and of itself might be of dubious worth is never raised (so also Newsom 2017, 171–72).

Because of his high-ranking position, Daniel's criticisms of aspects of royal thought and behavior proceed from the center of earthly power itself (Sangtinuk 2010, 39). If he has an easier time living as a foreigner near the center of imperial power than the Vietnamese characters in *The Sympathizer* do, that is obviously because of his roots in a foreign nobility, an elite status that the empire recognizes. But Daniel and his friends are not merely absorbed into empire, their actions and interpretive work critique it on behalf of God. They are like spies to some degree who have infiltrated the human empires said to govern the whole world (so 2:38; 4:19 [ET 22]) even as they work for another power. Through that work, they manage to convince the kings—two out of three, at any rate—to acknowledge heaven's sovereignty. The ability God has given to Daniel to interpret dreams and the refusal of his three friends to worship the king's image so impress Nebuchadnezzar (2:47; 3:28) that they are important steps on his path to the recognition that God and not he is sovereign,[33] and Darius's reaction to Daniel's miraculous deliverance from the lion's den is similar (6:27–28 [26–27]). That acknowledgment can be seen as the apparent goal of the Jewish characters' metaphorical spycraft, bringing the kings and empire into alignment with the will of heaven. The outcome of each of the stories of Dan 1–6 is utopian (so Valeta 2005, 322–23) in the sense that it is a victory for the power that Daniel and his colleagues really serve, but Daniel is still able to accommodate human empire and have sympathy for it. He may be a kind of spy whose arrival in Babylon bends the will of kings to that of heaven, yet he also seems at home in the empire and happy to work for its benefit (Polaski 2004, 668) and in this sense is like the narrator of *The Sympathizer*, who also has sympathy for the different sides of the conflict in which he finds himself and an ability to blur the line between *us* and *them*.

---

33. For longer discussions as to how these actions influence Nebuchadnezzar, see, e.g., Fewell 1988, 81–82; Wills 1990, 81–83.

Empire and the Powerless in Daniel

The character of Daniel does not make a perfect parallel with *The Sympathizer*'s narrator because of the vast power he wields in the empires in which we could say he works as a spy. For that reason he does not seem to be able to take the final steps in character development and identity formation and come to the conclusions that the novel's narrator, who "ranked among the meanest," does in regard to the oppression exercised by the powerful against the powerless. The sympathy Daniel exhibits for the foreign kings and kingdoms, however, could be understood as the motivating factor behind the series of visions revealed to him in Dan 7–12, ones that portray those foreign empires in an entirely unsympathetic manner.[34] If there is a parallel with the story of the narrator of *The Sympathizer* here, it could be the point at which he is put into a reeducation camp to purge him of his pro-Western sympathies. Daniel has prospered within the Babylonian Empire ruled by Nebuchadnezzar and his son, even after he tells Belshazzar that God would bring an end to the kingdom he rules (5:29), and Darius the Mede places Daniel over all the other officials in the kingdom (6:4 [ET 3]). We read, in fact, that Daniel "prospered" in Darius's kingdom as well as in that of Cyrus the Persian (6:29 [28]), whose empire follows the Median one in the book's chronology. Daniel may have been heaven's spy in the midst of empire, but he has done very well for himself within the Babylonian Empire, accepting Nebuchadnezzar's worship of him without rebuking the king (2:46) and remaining conspicuously absent from the following story in which his three Jewish colleagues refuse to worship the king's statue.

The problem with sympathetic spies, in short, is that they can end up as collaborators, and as we read Daniel after *The Sympathizer* we can

---

34. The standard scholarly explanation for the decidedly more negative depiction of the foreign empires in Dan 7–12 is a historical one. As the notes in the chapter's introduction briefly discuss, the stories of Dan 1–6 are based on traditions that predate Antiochus IV's suppression of Palestinian Judaism in 167–164 BCE, while the visions of Dan 7–12 (or at least of Dan 8–12) were composed during that persecution and so portray foreign empires as dangerous and violent entities. For some scholars, then, there is an unresolved tension between the two main parts of the book; see, e.g., Collins 1993, 51–52 and Newsom 2012, 559. It is clear enough in this historical explanation of the composition of Daniel why the visions of Dan 7–12 would have been included in the book, but it is much less clear why Dan 1–6 with its more positive views of empire would have become part of Daniel also.

understand the visions of Dan 7–12, visions that appear only to Daniel and that he is told he must keep secret (8:26; 12:4), as designed specifically to benefit him alone, to remind him where his true loyalty should lie and what his true identity is. These visions of the latter half of the book that condemn human empires put Daniel in the same position as Nebuchadnezzar in the stories of his visions of Dan 2 and 4, for, like the king, Daniel does not understand them and needs an interpreter in order to make sense of them (7:15–16, 19; 8:15–16). He says that the vision of Dan 7 יבהלנני "terrified me" (7:15, 28), the same reaction he and Nebuchadnezzar had to the king's second vision (4:2, 16 [ET 5, 19]). Daniel has become so much of an imperial sympathizer that he reacts to visions that emphasize the evil of all human empires and their ultimate destruction with the same frightened response as one of those empires' rulers when the king learns of God's sovereignty. Heaven, it might seem, is concerned that Daniel is abandoning his true loyalty, beliefs, and identity to the power he is supposed to serve and is becoming a collaborator.

Yet while reading Dan 7–12 after *The Sympathizer* can help us see that these visions are meant to reshape Daniel's loyalty, the novel also helps us see that heaven's message in this last part of the book is insufficient. Having read *The Sympathizer*, we can regard Daniel as someone who must become more than heaven's partisan; he must also reshape his identity as he learns to see empire through the eyes of the powerless, to become "a revolutionary in search of a revolution" that they lead, something that demands more change than the mere shift in loyalty that heaven asks of him and something that demands that readers go further than the book's visions in imagining what heaven's own kingdom should look like.

The first of Daniel's visions involves a series of four beasts or monsters meant to represent four kingdoms, as Daniel is told in the interpretation (7:17). It reflects to some degree Nebuchadnezzar's vision in Dan 2 of the statue, the four parts of which also represent four kingdoms (2:37–41), and just as in that vision, the final human kingdom of Dan 7 is destroyed and replaced by an eternal one established with divine approval (cf. 2:44 and 7:23–27). Unlike the king's vision of Dan 2, there is no mention in Daniel's vision of any human monarch or empire receiving their authority to rule from God (see 2:37–38).[35] In Dan 7, the human kingdoms are

---

35. The monsters in Dan 7 arise out of "the sea," so it is not clear in the story of this vision as it might have been told before the formation of MT Daniel if they operate with divine sanction, as Nebuchadnezzar is said to do in 2:37–38 and the Medes

represented by monsters, uncanny and frightening animal-like creatures[36] that are associated with violence (7:5, 7), and the final one is described in the MT as "frightening and dreadful and very strong" (7:7). The interpretation of the vision emphasizes this beast's violence, and Daniel is told that it will make war with the "holy ones" (7:21), and will "trample," "crush," and "devour the whole earth" (7:23). Its reign does not come to an end until it is violently destroyed by a court (7:11) overseen by an "ancient one" (7:9). The fourth kingdom of Nebuchadnezzar's dream is also associated with violence (2:40), and Daniel says there that God will establish an eternal kingdom that will violently destroy all others (2:44). That earlier dream in which a kingdom appointed by God also annihilates the previous one, which is also the fourth in a series, helps readers see the court of Dan 7 as a heavenly one and the ancient one who oversees it on a throne as God.[37] When in Dan 7 eternal authority and kingship are said to be given to a figure described as "like a human being" whom "all peoples, nations, and languages" will serve (7:13–14), just as the "peoples, nations, and languages" were once ruled by the kings in Dan 1–6 (3:4, 7, 29; 3:31 [ET 4:1]; 5:19; 6:26 [25]), it seems simple enough to see this figure as a representation of the eternal kingdom authorized by the heavenly court, as this follows the same pattern of events in the vision of Dan 2. In Dan 7, a good

---

and Persians are in 5:28. For differing opinions on this matter, see, e.g., Frisch 2016, 117–18 and Merrill Willis 2010, 71. If we read MT Daniel as a unit, however, and interpret Dan 7 through the lens of Nebuchadnezzar's dream in Dan 2, then we would have to conclude that God has allowed these kingdoms to rule, albeit in the awareness of their monstrous natures.

36. As Heather Macumber (2015, 12–16) points out, monsters are terrifying precisely because they cross accepted boundaries, combining qualities or aspects in what are often seen as unnatural ways.

37. That is almost always how critical scholarship makes sense of this figure, although for a dissenting view see Fröhlich 2015, 114–15. Fröhlich's argument rests on the parallels between Dan 7 and 1 En. 14, part of the Book of Watchers (1 En. 1–36), yet even in that chapter the figure on the throne is clearly God. Whether the story of Dan 7 that the Masoretic tradition drew from was influenced by Enochic material or whether the influence ran in the other direction in the vision's current context, readers encounter the story after that of Dan 2 where God is specifically said to intervene in history and establish a new and eternal kingdom (2:44), the same role that the court and the ancient one play in 7:13–14, 26–27 (for competing arguments, see, e.g., Stokes 2008, 345–51 and Kvanvig 2005, 255–58). Even if an original version of Dan 7 drew from 1 En. 14, in its current literary setting the ancient one is most obviously understood as God.

political entity represented by a human-like figure replaces the evil ones represented by animal-like monsters,[38] as "the people of the holy ones of the most high" take possession of the world's kingship and authority, so that all other authorities will serve them (7:27).

It is possible that Daniel is terrified by this vision and its interpretation (7:15, 28) because of his sympathy for the empire he serves and with which he strongly identifies, but this reaction may be due instead to his realization that he might be working for the final violent empire of this revelation. The vision emphasizes that kingdom's violence, and Daniel is certainly aware of Nebuchadnezzar's war against Jerusalem and sack of God's temple there (1:1–2), as well as his various royal orders that command death for those who violate the king's decrees (3:6, 11, 29) or who merely are not as wise as the king wishes (2:5, 12–13). Since Daniel sees the vision of Dan 7 during the first year of the reign of Nebuchadnezzar's son (7:1), as far as he is aware at this point the Babylonian Empire might be a very good fit for the fourth beast that makes war against the "holy ones" (7:21). Daniel knows that Nebuchadnezzar finally does acknowledge God's sovereignty and laud God's eternal kingdom (3:31–33; 4:31–32 [ET 4:1–3, 34–35]; 5:20–21), but Daniel receives this vision after Nebuchadnezzar's death and during the reign of Belshazzar, the only king of Dan 1–6 whose rule is depicted as irredeemably evil. After seeing this vision and hearing its interpretation, Daniel might also believe that it simply does not matter if he has not been working for the fourth kingdom in the series he witnesses, for all human empires are

---

38. There is actually no consensus in scholarship as to how to identify this figure, and he is frequently understood as an angelic figure such as Michael, who appears later in the book (e.g., Koch 2007, 370–77; Joseph 2013, 274), perhaps a heavenly representative of "the people of the holy ones of the most high," who in 7:27 are said to receive the eternal kingdom (so, e.g., Segal 2014, 292–94). The context of MT Daniel up to this point, however, suggests a different identification for this figure. Nebuchadnezzar's vision of Dan 2 is of a series of four kingdoms, the final one of which is replaced by an eternal one; read in that light, the four monsters and the human-like figure of Dan 7 also represent kingdoms. While the interpretation of Daniel's vision initially refers to four kings in the discussion of the four monsters (7:17), the four kings are each founders of a kingdom represented by one of the monsters. The final beast does not represent a single king after all, because the individual kings who rule the fourth kingdom are represented by the beast's horns (7:24). The logic of the symbolism and of the earlier dream in Dan 2 dictates that the human-like figure also represents a kingdom, the one that "the holy ones of the most high" receive after the destruction of the previous one.

revealed here in their true form as monsters (Portier-Young 2010, 111–12), and even his sympathy for a king like Nebuchadnezzar starts to seem like collaboration. The vision represents human empires as bestial and evil entities, just as the movie on which *The Sympathizer*'s narrator works represents the Viet Cong as King Cong, a monster so evil that the audience should only hope for its destruction.

So even though the next vision of Dan 8, also revealed to Daniel during Belshazzar's reign (8:1), clarifies that he does not serve the final human empire, he does not appear to feel any better at the end of this new revelation saying that it literally sickens him (8:27). The vision and interpretation of Dan 8 also involve kingdoms represented by animals, but here Daniel is told the first animal he sees represents the kingdoms of Media and Persia and the second the kingdom of Greece. The final king of that final kingdom is described rather like the final king of the last kingdom in Dan 7, for both of them challenge heavenly power. The last king of Dan 7 speaks against God and "will plan to change seasons and law" (7:25), while the final king of Dan 8 attacks heaven and overthrows God's sanctuary (8:10–12, 25). If Daniel understands the first vision in light of the second, then the "seasons and law" of 7:25 most obviously refer to Jewish religious festivals and torah. The last king in both visions attacks the "holy ones" (7:21) or "the people of the holy ones" (8:24) and in both is ultimately destroyed (7:26; 8:25).

Since the last kingdom of Dan 8 appears to be the same as the fourth one of Dan 7, and since Daniel is told that the last kingdom of Dan 8 is Greek in origin, then he at least knows that he does not work for that final human kingdom that attacks heaven, overthrows God's temple, and attempts to change God's law. Yet even the Median and Persian kingdoms that precede the kingdom of Greece in Dan 8 are described largely in terms of their violence (8:4), and when at the end of the vision Daniel says he is sickened and yet returns to his work for Belshazzar (8:27), the evil king, perhaps his own collaboration with these violent monsters is what sickens him. It may be that he knows in his heart that if he is still alive when the Median and Persian kingdoms conquer Babylon that he will serve them as well, something readers know to be true because they have already seen in Dan 6 how loyally and sympathetically he serves Darius the Mede. At the end of this second vision and its interpretation Daniel says that he does not understand it (8:27), even though the geopolitical future its symbols are supposed to represent is spelled out fairly clearly in the interpretation of 8:19–26. Perhaps Daniel's claim at its conclusion in regard to his failure to understand may suggest that he simply cannot accept it, that its portrayal of empires as universally violent just does not fit into his basic worldview and understanding of imperial power and his place in it.

If we choose to read these visions in the light of *The Sympathizer* as a kind of reeducation of Daniel on heaven's part, then he is struggling and failing to come to grips with what the human empires truly are, although he has been serving them and sympathizing with them and their rulers. Heaven tells Daniel of the great violence associated with the Median Empire before Darius the Mede arrives in Babylon, but Daniel will serve him loyally anyway. Knowing what he knows about the Median Empire specifically and about human empires more generally, Daniel could hardly be surprised when Darius decrees a law that ends with Daniel being sealed in a lions' den, or when, following his miraculous salvation, the king decides to execute not only those who convinced him to create that order but their wives and children as well (6:25 [ET 24]). Daniel, like the narrator of *The Sympathizer* in the reeducation camp, is being forced to confront the question of his true identity, being asked to identify as either a true servant of heaven or of empire. Even after his second vision, however, Daniel does not modify his sympathies in the way heaven wants him to. Despite the fact that he is told that the earthly kingdoms are violent monsters and will be replaced by an eternal one supported by heaven, Daniel will later tell Darius after that king overthrows Belshazzar that he hopes Darius will "live forever" (6:22 [21]). Even after the first two visions, it seems Daniel does not side with heaven's understanding of the kingdoms as evil entities whose power will come to an end.

At the end of Dan 7, the language of the MT's edition of the book switches back from Aramaic (the language of empire) to Hebrew (the language of Judaism) as if heaven had originally decided that Daniel was so ensconced within the empire that his first vision of its ultimate evil and destruction had to be revealed in the language of imperial power, the language in which Daniel had been operating as an imperial collaborator. Given that Daniel says at the end of the first vision revealed to him in Hebrew (Dan 8) that he does not understand it (8:27), and given that the sympathy he expresses and enacts in regard to Darius in Dan 6 after he has seen the first two visions is hardly in accord with heaven's portrayals of the evils of earthly kingdoms, it would seem that visions and interpretations in neither Aramaic nor Hebrew appear to have convinced him to alter his identity and sympathies as heaven wishes. The narrative introducing his final vision of Dan 10–12 and revealed after the time of Darius in the book's chronology during the reign of Cyrus of Persia, however, insists that he understands it (10:1). To some degree that assertion seems surprising; near the end of that vision, Daniel says, "I heard, but I did not understand" (12:8). While that could be taken as a response only to the speech from a heavenly figure in 12:7, the dense and complicated symbolism of 10:20–12:4 is never interpreted, unlike that of the visions of Dan 7 and 8, and Daniel explicitly says he could not understand even the interpretation of that last vision. On the other hand, however, Daniel receives this final vision of the book in the third year of Cyrus, according to the MT's edition (10:1), and 1:21 says that he remained at court only until Cyrus's first year.[39] Perhaps heavenly visions and the violence of the kings he serves has taught Daniel to begin viewing these empires in the way heaven urges him to, causing him to abandon the court and his previous loyal service to those rulers, and indicating that he eventually learns to understand and agree with heaven's depiction of all human empires as evil.

Throughout this final vision, someone whom Daniel describes as "a man" (10:5), one with "human form" (10:16) having "human appearance" (10:18), says that he has been and will go on fighting "the prince of the kingdom of Persia" (10:13, 20) and says that Persian rule will be followed by Greek power (11:2–3). As this is the same series of empires described in Dan 8, such a revelation of imperial succession now seems straightforward enough, although if we are to understand Daniel's interlocutor in human form as a heavenly figure, then it would seem that heaven is at war with the human kings—or at least with representatives of them in the supernatural realm[40]—who precede and who rule the final human kingdom described

---

39. The text of MT 1:21 says ויהי דניאל עד שנת אחת לכורש המלך, paralleled in the OG and Theodotion. It indicates Daniel's presence "until the first year of Cyrus the king," and while this may refer to Daniel's presence in the kingdom (מלכותו is the final word of 1:20), in 10:4 Daniel is still in Mesopotamia in Cyrus's third year. Assumedly, then, 1:21 indicates that Daniel remained present before the king—in the royal court, in other words—which is where we see him in 1:18–19, until Cyrus's first year.

40. There is no scholarly consensus as to the basic identity of שר מלכות פרס "the prince of the kingdom of Persia" in 10:13, although since the same verse refers to Michael as אחד השרים הראשנים "one of the foremost princes," it might make sense to see the Persian prince as a supernatural representative of the Persian king and/or people; see, e.g., DiTomasso 2005, 213–14n521; Toepel 2005; Wasserman 2013; Fröhlich 2015, 124–25. As a result, when Daniel's interlocutor says that שר יון בא "the prince of Greece is coming" (10:20), we could see him as referring to a battle with a supernatural power who represents Antiochus; see, e.g., Walsh 2020, 175–78.

in Dan 7 and 8, including King Cyrus of Persia whom Daniel once served. In Dan 11, the human-like one goes on to describe a long and bewildering series of wars and alliances between "the king of the south" and "the king of the north" and their descendants (11:5–45), concluding with the reign of "one who is despised" (11:21) and who, like the final king of the visions of Dan 7 and 8, attacks the temple (11:31) and exalts himself over God (11:36).[41] Some even among the wise, those who are said (at least in the MT) to be able to lead others to righteousness (12:3), will be killed at that time (11:33–35), caught up in the final king's destruction of "the people of the holy ones of the most high" as described in earlier visions (8:24).[42] But like the final kings of Dan 7 and 8, the despised one of Dan 11 will be defeated (11:45), although in this vision his defeat is followed by an unprecedented "time of anguish" (12:1), as well as by the resurrection of some of those who have died either to "eternal life" or "eternal abhorrence" (12:2).

Readers are first introduced to Daniel as an outsider brought to the center of empire who must be taught Babylonian literature to serve in court, and we see him at the end of his story with "a true book" (10:21) brought by heaven that announces a long series of events that must be kept secret "until the time of the end" (12:4; see Polaski 2004, 649). In the visions revealed to him, heaven repetitively puts him in the position of

---

41. From the standpoint of historical study of the book, 11:5–39 relates the conflict between the Seleucid and Ptolemaic empires from the time of the death of Alexander the Great to Antiochus IV's persecution of Judaism. Whoever composed the chapter appears to have had a good knowledge of the geopolitical events in this region over this period of history, although they described these events using coded language, referring to Ptolemy I, for example, as "the king of the south" (11:5). See, e.g., Delcor 1993 and Scolnic 2014.

42. Critical scholarship disagrees as to the identity of the "holy ones" of Dan 7; some see the קדישׁין of 7:21–22, 25, and 26 as the Jews who suffer under Antiochus IV's persecution (e.g., Seow 2004, 236–40; Stuckenbruck 2006, 126–27), although some argue the term refers to heavenly figures who represent Israel in some way (e.g., Joseph 2013, 274; Segal 2014, 291–94). Another way to think of "the holy ones" and "the people of the holy ones" is that the former are supernatural representatives of the latter, such that what happens to the holy ones happens also to the righteous Jews, the holy ones' people suffering under Antiochus's persecution (see, e.g., Merrill Willis 2010, 77–78; Remington Rillera 2019, 773–74). The holy ones of 8:13 appear to be heavenly beings, but according to the MT's edition both the holy ones and the people of the holy ones are said to receive the eternal kingdom (7:22, 27), and the final evil king attacks both the holy ones (7:21) and the people of the holy ones (8:24).

Nebuchadnezzar in the first part of the book, using recondite symbolism to communicate to him that he owes his allegiance to the true power of the cosmos. If God intended Daniel to go to Babylon to communicate a message of divine sovereignty to human kings, Daniel has spent so much time there and has developed such sympathy for imperial culture that heaven seems to view him as a collaborator, and the fact that Daniel has difficulty understanding these visions only seems to support that view of him. Nevertheless, at the beginning of the final vision we are told that Daniel does understand it, and the fact that in the edition of Daniel we are reading he no longer works at court tells us that he has come to see imperial rule—or at least existing imperial rule—in the negative way heaven does. He is also told near the end of his final vision that some of the dead will be resurrected, and the last bit of information Daniel receives in this revelation as it appears in the MT's edition is that "you will rise for your lot at the end of the days" (12:13). Precisely what that lot will be is apparently up to him, depending on the degree to which he has absorbed the reeducation of the true book, allowing it to displace his sympathy for the literature, culture, and kings of human empires.

Like the state powers of *The Sympathizer*, heaven in Daniel has no room for those who sympathize with other cultures, authorities, and belief systems, so the entire second half of the book is devoted to convincing Daniel of the evil of the political entities for which he has exhibited sympathy. When we read Daniel in the wake of the novel, however, we might think to ask how the powerless would benefit from the final eternal kingdom endorsed by heaven. Perhaps the most important realization *The Sympathizer*'s narrator comes to is that it is the powerless who are most able to see how power is abused for nothing but more power, since they are the ones who suffer and who are represented and treated as if they were nothing. But Daniel is not powerless in the stories about him. He works as a kind of spy for heaven, and God is able to save him from certain death, while in his roles in the human kingdoms he is promoted until, by Dan 6, only the monarch is more powerful than he (6:4 [ET 3]). The novel's narrator ends up as "a revolutionary in search of a revolution" because their experience has led them to prioritize the alleviation of the suffering of the powerless, while simultaneously becoming aware that there is no political entity willing to join in such a revolution in more than just words. Unlike the narrator, however, Daniel is not "among the meanest" and remains unaware of the necessity of such a revolution. He may sympathize with both heaven and human empires and eventually come to believe that heaven's critique of human imperial rule as monstrous and violent is accurate, yet no entity in the book, including heaven, appears interested in privileging the powerless. Heaven wants Daniel's undivided loyalty, but read after *The Sympathizer* we can see that this demand is insufficient in and of itself, since the ethical question to ask is not which empire to support but how to "sympathize with the undesirables among the undesirables." Such powerless figures, however, are not present in the narrative, and none of the book's characters spends any time considering what they might want.

When we read Daniel with *The Sympathizer* in mind, we can see that, while the biblical book is focused on promoting one empire over another, it is not clear who will benefit from heaven's coming victory beyond its partisans, those who refuse to sympathize with human empires. Such partisans apparently include "the wise" who will be killed during the reign of the final king of Daniel's visions, although they will also shine "like stars forever and ever" (12:3) and so receive some sort of reward for their great suffering. Yet at no point does Daniel seem to notice that heaven has shown no interest in the fate of the powerless and those who suffer on a daily basis under imperial rule, nor are any such subaltern characters present in the narrative to speak for themselves.

As in *The Sympathizer*, no entity competing for sovereignty demonstrates any concern for the powerless; on the one occasion in which any character in Daniel does so it is Daniel himself, for as he interprets Nebuchadnezzar's second vision he tells the king that he should act "with mercy to the oppressed" (4:24 [ET 27]). Yet this assertion on Daniel's part seems entirely unrelated to the vision and to what happens to the king in this story (so also Fewell 1988, 99–100), for both the vision and its fulfillment in Nebuchadnezzar's temporary removal from his throne are directed solely to the imperative of getting him to acknowledge God's sovereignty, and nothing is ever said about any change in the king's treatment of his subjects who ranked among the meanest. At best Daniel's words in 4:24 [27] seem like a vague concern on his part alone as to the plight of the powerless, and at worst mere lip-service to such concern, which is never raised again in the book.

The book's lack of interest in the fate of those who suffer is often the kind of thing that those of us familiar with benefiting from the privileges of empire fail to notice, which might explain why Daniel does not recognize this as missing from his revelatory visions either. The truly powerless of the world are as absent from Daniel's world (both that of the character and the book) as they are from the worldviews of the powerful characters in *The Sympathizer*. The eternal kingdom authorized by heaven "will be given to the people of the holy ones of the most high" (7:27), but beyond the fact that this kingdom will not come to an end as the others do, there is no sense that it will be any different from the ones that have preceded it. There is certainly no indication that it will show any greater concern for the powerless than the ones Daniel helps administer. "All peoples, nations, and languages" will serve the people to whom this eternal kingdom is given (7:14, 27), just as the "peoples, nations, and languages" served the previous kings (3:4, 7, 31 [ET 4:1]; 5:19; 6:26 [ET 25]). But what if those peoples have no wish to serve the eternal kingdom? Will they be killed by the people of the holy ones of the most high just as Nebuchadnezzar said he would destroy "any people, nation, or language" that spoke ill of Israel's God (3:29)? It is unclear what would happen to the powerless of such a people, nation, or language, since they are not represented in a book that has a laser-like focus on empire, power, and sovereignty and are almost entirely invisible in its portrayal of the world. What happens to them is apparently of no concern, since they are absent and do not reach even the status of the nameless Vietnamese characters who are killed off in the movie for which *The Sympathizer*'s narrator acts as an advisor. The powerless clearly do not represent themselves in Daniel; they are not represented at all, in fact, as if they did not exist, which implies that no one needs to concern themselves with who they are or what they might want.

The Ethical Problem of Daniel

Reading Daniel after *The Sympathizer* exposes what seems to be a glaring ethical problem with the biblical writing, for this process allows us to see Daniel's focus on power, authority, and empire, something that never considers the powerless, as incomplete. No powerless figure ever appears in Daniel's narrative to ask how the coming eternal kingdom will actually make things better for those whose lives are not worthy of consideration in decisions made by earthly rulers. It is not only demographically privileged readers who can be prone to see a happy ending in Daniel in its portrayal of one empire's ultimate victory over another, despite heaven's utter lack of consideration for the oppressed; that is also, for example, Nancy Cardoso Pereira's (2016) reading of Daniel in the context of the suffering faced by the poor and powerless in such places as Latin America and Palestine. When one is suffering the ravages of empire, it may well be good news to hear that the empire will be destroyed by a different one, but that in itself is not enough.

One could argue that because it is God who approves the final eternal kingdom that Daniel can assume that it will show concern for the powerless and their suffering, since in the book it is God who miraculously rescues Daniel and his friends when they are condemned to death. As portrayed in the book, however, God does not seem concerned with human suffering. For example, the story of Dan 9 opens with Daniel reading Jeremiah, and he follows this reading with prayer (9:1-3). Daniel's decision to pray may have been prompted by his reading of Jer 29:12-14, which refers to the seventy-year punishment and tells those who have been taken into exile in Babylon—people like Daniel—to pray, something that would allow God to respond by returning them to Jerusalem.[43] Daniel's prayer of 9:4-19 reflects theological ideas that are at home in other biblical books: God has exiled the inhabitants of Jerusalem and Judah because they failed to keep torah and listen to the prophets; so God has merely done what the law of Moses promises God would do under such circumstances; and Daniel concludes by asking God to listen to his prayer, show mercy, and forgive (9:15-19).[44]

However, his prayer of repentance and plea for forgiveness are met immediately with a message conveyed by a heavenly figure who tells him that there will be no mercy or forgiveness, only many more centuries of punishment (9:24-27). Jerusalem's punishment will last not seventy years, as Daniel has read in Jeremiah, but seventy weeks of years, or four hundred and ninety years in total. Confessions of sin and pleas for forgiveness do not make any difference because God has already decided history's course, and it is one of suffering.[45] There is no sense that God is merciful or willing to forgive and to alleviate the suffering of the powerless, which is why a heavenly messenger must explain to Daniel that he has misunderstood Jeremiah or, to read 9:24-27 slightly differently, Jeremiah was mistaken in claiming that Jerusalem's punishment would come to an end after only

---

43. So, e.g., Segal 2011, 291-92. For a list of the parallels between Jeremiah's letter to the Babylonian exiles in Jer 29:1-23 and Dan 9, see Pfemmer De Long 2012, 221-26.

44. For the reflection of themes and vocabulary of other biblical books in the prayer of Dan 9, see Haydon 2014.

45. The central idea of Daniel's prayer is that God will respond with forgiveness to repentance, but this does not fit the larger theology of the book, as scholars often point out; see, e.g., Werline 2007, 30-31.

seventy years. In light of Dan 9, God's salvation of Daniel and his friends in the stories of Dan 3 and 6 appears to have been motivated not by mercy but by the divine need to demonstrate to human kings that ultimate power is exercised by heaven, not earthly monarchs.

Another way to try to deal with the ethical problem presented by the book's failure to consider the powerless is to argue that it is not really a problem at all, since the author was intending to focus on a different issue altogether—divine sovereignty—and there is no point in asking questions of Daniel that the author was not intending to answer. Let us set aside the matter of what authorial intention would even mean in regard to a writing with multiple ancient editions, no one of which is clearly an original version of which the others are variants, each one with different sets of emphases and each compiled from traditions about Daniel that were told and reworked over a very long period of time. The fact of the matter is that biblical scholars constantly ask questions about texts that their authors—whatever criteria we might use for defining authorship in the case of any given writing—do not seem interested in addressing, but these questions are normally historical in nature: When and in what ecclesial context were the Pastoral Epistles written? What were the stages of the composition of the Pentateuch, and when did they occur? In all cases we can only work with the evidence we have and interpret it through the series of questions we want to ask, which we have determined are important because of the particular hermeneutical approach to which our contexts and worldviews commit us. When faced with the specific hermeneutical context of reading the MT of Daniel after *The Sympathizer*, it is difficult to be overly positive as to the author's ethical concern for the powerless, and to say that their real interest is in describing divine sovereignty does not change that fact, since it is heaven's failure to express any concern for the powerless in the divine exercise of power that is at the center of the ethical problem I have identified.

As chapter 1 argues, there is no universal hermeneutical rule that demands we privilege authorial intention, and liberative interpretation is driven by questions and concerns that arise from minoritized contexts. Sometimes that will demand pointing to ethical dangers of particular biblical texts, the kind of reading often referred to as suspicious. For argument's sake, if we wanted to refer to some figure living in terror of Antiochus IV's persecution as the author of Daniel, we could certainly generate empathy for the terrible situation in which they found themselves and understand their focus on a divine victory over Antiochus, but our interpretation will still have to be driven by contemporary questions and concerns of the minoritized. In this specific case the questions and concerns have been raised by reading Daniel after *The Sympathizer*, and that has resulted in identifying an important ethical problem that we cannot ignore if we honestly want to pursue this hermeneutical process of reading after minoritized literature. A decision to always agree with the ethical intentions of biblical authors (again, even bracketing out the very difficult question of what one means by *author* in the context of many biblical writings) is not tenable within this hermeneutical approach, because it would frequently put us at odds with important ethical beliefs we already hold.

Interpreters approaching Daniel from a specifically Christian perspective could certainly decide to deal with the problem by reading Daniel intertextually with New Testament writings. In the tradition of Christian interpretation, in fact, this is a common hermeneutical approach,[46] which is unsurprising given that the New Testament also refers to an eternal kingdom sanctioned by heaven. As *The Sympathizer* points out, however, to the powerless one empire looks more or less like another, and it is not clear that New Testament writings always deal with the ethical problem Daniel poses better than Daniel does. In the Gospel of Mark, for example, Jesus teaches that only those who give away their wealth to the poor (10:17–31) or truly act out of love of God and neighbor (12:28–34) will be able to become a part of God's kingdom, and these teachings can certainly be understood as ones that privilege the powerless. As Tat-siong Benny Liew (1999, 7–12) points out, however, this gospel does not look toward an abolishment of imperial hierarchy and violence so much as it foretells the replacement of one empire with another. As someone who grew up in Hong Kong and witnessed both the deleterious effects of European colonialism and the reaction against it in Chinese communism, Liew writes that he is hesitant to idealize any power structure and so is suspicious of a solution to the problem of oppression that amounts to substituting the reign of one empire with a different one.

God's kingdom in Mark is one that looks to Jesus alone as lord (κύριος), but this does not seem overly different from the gentile and Roman empires with rulers who "lord over" (κατακυριεύουσιν) their subjects as Mark 10:42

---

46. See, e.g., Redding 2021, 157–231, which discusses Christian interpretations of Dan 7 from the Epistle of Barnabas to the Protestant Reformation; all of the interpreters mentioned here interpret this vision through the lens of Revelation and often other New Testament writings.

puts it (Liew 1999, 13–22). Mark does not describe a kingdom authorized by God that is more inclusive than the ones it will replace, just one that uses different criteria to define authority, privilege, and exclusion, an exclusion that will involve a violent destruction of those marked as outsiders who will undergo indescribable torture (9:42–48; 14:21). "The problem is that by defeating power with more power, Mark is, in the final analysis, no different from the 'might-is-right' ideology that has led to colonialism, imperialism and various forms of suffering and oppression" (Liew 1999, 26). Lynne St. Clair Darden (2015a, 145–55) makes a similar point in her reading of Revelation, arguing that, while John of Patmos stood against the Roman Empire, his attempt to critique it in Revelation only reproduced its imagery of power, such that the heavenly empire he envisioned does not seem much different from the oppressive power of Rome. Revelation, she writes, only "maintains the status quo and imagines a new world order founded on violence and bloodshed" (155). The narrator of *The Sympathizer* eventually develops the same sort of suspicion of the anti-imperial rhetoric he encounters in his story and concludes that anti-imperial power in and of itself is not a solution to the suffering of the powerless. The revolution they begin to seek at the novel's conclusion is one driven by sympathy for those who suffer and a refusal to represent them as disposable and of little value, rather than by a desire to replace one empire with another.

So if we are trying to find a solution to the ethical problem with which Daniel leaves us after we read it after *The Sympathizer*, then perhaps it lies in the hope that Daniel will undergo the same kind of character development as the novel's narrator does and become the kind of revolutionary into which the narrator evolves by the end of the novel, a partisan not of a new empire but of the powerless. As readers if we are convinced of the dangers of empire, then it is not enough to read the book of Daniel's critique of it; we must read beyond what the MT's edition of the book calls "the time of the end" (8:17; 11:35, 40; 12:4, 9; see also 8:19 and 12:13). Like the communists and Western imperialists in *The Sympathizer*, heaven in Daniel claims to know in what direction time and history are moving, and even foresees some sort of end to history as Daniel knows it. From *The Sympathizer*, however, we learn that from the standpoint of the powerless and the excluded time can seem like a circle, as one empire replaces another and then treats the powerless in exactly the same way as its predecessors, while in Daniel, despite God's absolute sovereignty, heaven can sometimes appear more interested in prolonging rather than alleviating suffering (e.g., 7:25; 9:26; 12:1).

We might hope, then, that Daniel will eventually learn that real revolution and progress do not correspond to an imperial timetable, and that it is not enough to see an ending simply because one empire defeats another. Readers with liberative aims can try to imagine beyond the time of the end to which heaven refers in Daniel to a truly revolutionary picture of what the divinely approved kingdom might look like if it is to be any different from the imperial monsters that precede it. We can, as Pablo Richard does (2000, 30–32), imagine it as a kingdom of the people, one in which "the wise" who will shine like the stars are not merely partisans of one particular empire but are teachers of justice and in which the time of the end is an end to a history of imperial oppression. Without such interpretive imagination, however, the kingdom authorized by heaven represents nothing but more imperial power.

Just as a slogan is a suit that anyone with power can wear in order to gain more power, a mere reference to a kingdom supported by heaven does not necessarily say anything about it except for the power that lies behind it. Any powerful figure or entity can appeal to this concept for any reason they choose, even when that involves the subjugation of the powerless. For Christopher Columbus, for example, the lands he encountered on his voyages became the final eschatological kingdom, a divine gift to his imperial patrons[47] who were about to conquer and decimate the populations of what Europeans would eventually refer to as their New World, while in the first extant Greek commentary of Revelation—a sixth-century work by Oecumenius—the final divine kingdom becomes largely identical with the Byzantine Empire (Villiers 2013). Neither heaven's demand that Daniel see the monstrous nature of the empires he works for nor Daniel's eventual recognition of that fact is enough, for heaven never explains what will make the coming kingdom it supports better than the ones it replaces. If, as readers, we hope that Daniel will decide to understand it in more concrete and specific terms, something like Richard's kingdom of the people, then the powerless will have to become visible to him; he

---

47. In a letter composed in 1500, Columbus writes of those lands in reference to Queen Isabela of Castile and Leon: "Of the new heaven and earth of which our Lord spoke through Saint John in the Apocalypse, after what was spoken through the mouth of Isaiah, he made me the messenger and showed me where it was. All were incredulous, but to the Queen my Lady he gave the spirit of intelligence and great exertion and made her heir of all of it like a dear and much beloved daughter. I took possession of all of this in her Royal name" (Colón 1892, 311; my translation).

cannot simply represent them as heaven's visions do, which is to say as entirely invisible and so of no importance at all.

In order to undergo the kind of character development *The Sympathizer*'s narrator does and recognize the priority of the powerless, Daniel will have to confront his role as an important administrator of the human empires and the suffering for which he was responsible, something that he, unlike the narrator, never fully grapples with. He has been the kings' loyal servant refusing to do them any harm (6:23 [ET 22]), even after he becomes aware of their empires' violence, something he did not need heavenly revelations to discover. In Dan 2, Nebuchadnezzar had wanted to kill all of the sages of Babylon because none of them could interpret his dream, but when the dream and its interpretation are revealed to Daniel, he intervenes on behalf of those men asking the king to spare their lives (2:24). By the time of Darius, however, Daniel does nothing to stop the king when he resolves to execute not only his other officials but their entire families (6:25 [24]), a sin of omission on the part of Darius's favorite courtier far worse than that of *The Sympathizer*'s narrator in the case of the rape of the female agent. Without taking the sort of responsibility the narrator does for having done nothing for the powerless in the face of oppression, Daniel will not be able to truly see who he is and has been or ever be able to understand that his true sympathy should be with "the undesirables among the undesirables." If, in fact, he cannot acknowledge his ethical failure in regard to his inaction in the deaths of the officials and their families or in any other sort of imperial violence in which his loyalty to empire has made him complicit, then the concept of a kingdom connected with heaven will never be more than an empty slogan "draped on the corpse of an idea" for him. If he saw such an admission as unnecessary in the new kingdom, he would clearly be expecting it to be yet one more political entity in which one can do nothing as the innocent are put to death, a tacit acceptance of monstrous imperial power.

If we were to imagine Daniel's story continuing, then we might hope that he would not see his identity as something limited by the binary choice heaven offers him in the visions of Dan 7–12 where the human empires are monsters, just as the Viet Cong become King Cong in the movie in *The Sympathizer*, with the result that Daniel is pushed to identify himself as a partisan of either one side or the other, which will assumedly determine the lot with which he is rewarded at the end of the days (12:13). Since, by 10:1, Daniel appears to have left the royal court, he has taken a first step to dissociate himself from the violent empires he once served. Those of us who read Daniel after *The Sympathizer*, however, would hope this is just the first step on a longer ethical journey that will lead him to acknowledge his participation in imperial evil like the narrator of *The Sympathizer* does. This first step would be something related to a new ability to see the powerless and to understand his identity as tied to the ethical need to "sympathize with the undesirables among the undesirables," so that he too can become a revolutionary in search of a revolution. That could include supporting and working with the subjugated to prioritize the revolutionary change they want to see, as well as imagining a heavenly empire as a kingdom of the people, something that privileges their well-being and allows them to represent themselves and their needs.

The central ethical problem that I have identified in this reading of Daniel is not one that would have occurred to me had I not read it after *The Sympathizer*. By using a new kind of text as a way to focus my reading, it should be unsurprising to find that I notice different things and come up with different questions as I read. Since *The Sympathizer* turns my attention to the plight of the powerless subjugated by empire, the failure of the book of Daniel to address the issue or to represent the powerless at all suddenly becomes a problem that I cannot ignore. It is true that, at this point, I have done very little to describe the sort of revolution that I would hope Daniel would eventually commit himself to, something that reflects the fact that the narrator of *The Sympathizer* refers only to general guiding principles that shapes their new revolutionary outlook at the end of the novel. Yet this can change as I read other biblical texts after other works of literature by minoritized authors, as the following chapters show. As chapter 1 mentions, we might see this picture of Daniel as a character on the brink of seeing the subjugated and being willing to privilege their revolutionary needs, someone whose growth reflects the kind of hermeneutical journey that mainstream biblical studies could be on. The mainstream of the discipline has largely acted up until now as if the work of our minoritized colleagues was not important enough to prioritize, and so that the experiences of subjugated groups were not important enough to foreground in our hermeneutical approaches. As I argue in chapter 1, however, it is perfectly possible for us to privilege those experiences, contexts, and goals in light of our ethical priorities. To do that we first need to see and hear those disadvantaged by socioeconomic structures and to listen to their stories so that we can look for ways to do our interpretive work in light of them. This may be necessary merely to notice the ethical problems in interpretation that arise when biblical texts such as Daniel ignore the subaltern altogether, but, as the following chapters demonstrate, once we pair other works of minoritized literature with other biblical writings, it allows us to highlight other challenges an ethical hermeneutic must grapple with as well.

3
THE HARD LAW OF LOVE:
COMMUNITY IDENTITY AND INCLUSION IN
ANGELS IN AMERICA AND EZRA-NEHEMIAH

Introduction

If one basic problem that interpreters aiming to contribute to liberative discourse must learn to avoid is the failure to notice the complete absence in biblical texts of subaltern characters, another closely related issue is the silencing of those characters when they do appear in biblical narratives. Unlike Daniel, the story of Ezra-Nehemiah does include figures whom we could describe as powerless, but the problem we see in this book is that they are entirely deprived of speech. We see and do not hear them as it were, and so they do not represent themselves but are represented by much more powerful characters in the story who portray them as dangerous interlopers into Israelite society who must be removed from the community's midst. Commentators often point out that Ezra-Nehemiah is a writing that reflects the concept of group identity, providing one particular definition of what the postexilic community settled in and around Jerusalem should be like and who should and should not belong to it (e.g., Esler 2003; Rothenbusch 2012, 247–428; Heckl 2016, 410–11; Laird 2016, 2; Tiemeyer 2017, 1). As this writing—or any writing or any group—draws boundaries that define and identify a people, these lines will both exclude and include. To be clear as to who belongs in one's community means, in part, specifying who does not. At a number of points important characters in Ezra-Nehemiah are quite clear as to which groups of people pose a threat to Israel and must be excluded as dangerous foreigners, as a cancer whose presence within the community could lead to the group's destruction. This chapter focuses on the ethical problems raised by a text that can seem so determined to use xenophobia and radical exclusivity in its depiction of the subjugated and in particular by the way in which it silences powerless characters, refusing to allow them an opportunity to represent themselves.

Readers who are privileged by the central social and economic locations they inhabit within their own cultures are the interpreters most likely to miss the way in which Ezra-Nehemiah silences the most vulnerable characters of its narrative world, because the conversations we normally have and the media we normally consume so rarely feature such voices, although we are not the only ones who can face this problem.[1] However, reading it after Tony Kushner's play *Angels in America*,[2] which is actually made up of two linked plays, *Millennium Approaches* and *Perestroika*, can make us aware not only of the silencing of the powerless in Ezra-Nehemiah but also of the way they are represented by the more powerful characters in the book as dangerous and impure foreigners who should have no place within the community. Engaging in the hermeneutical process of reading a biblical text after literature by an author disadvantaged by his sexual orientation and religion not only allows my interpretation to highlight this as a problem but also to envision one solution to it that might be of emancipatory use to some. While reading Ezra-Nehemiah after *Angels in America* draws my attention to the silencing of the powerless women in the biblical writing, it also pushes me to imagine what their speech would be like, for *Angels in America* is full of speech by characters excluded from full membership in American society, and who reflect on the notion of group identity as the powerful ones in Ezra-Nehemiah do. *Angels in America* is subtitled *A Gay Fantasia on National Themes* because it uses fantasy to address the failure of the United States to include vulnerable groups, especially the queer community, within the concept of what it means to be an American, and later parts of this chapter will make the case that *Angels in*

---

1. For example, Elelwani Farisani (2002, 633–34, 639–40) discusses the way a number of African readers of Ezra-Nehemiah have ignored the silencing of the subjugated characters in the book.

2. Specifically, I will be using a version of the play revised in 2013. Kushner completed the first draft of *Millennium Approaches* in 1988 and that of *Perestroika* in 1990 but made changes to both plays in subsequent years, although mainly to the latter. Some scenes were altered and others removed, and Kushner (2013, ix) wrote that *Perestroika* "is now closer to complete than it's ever been." Other references to page numbers from *Angels in America* will appear in the text of the chapter. Italicization and ellipses in quotations from the play are present in the original.

America can help contemporary readers think through the exclusionary understanding of identity that Ezra-Nehemiah presents.

To return to the particular way I am drawing on Sechrest's concept of rhyme, reading Ezra-Nehemiah after *Angels in America* allows me to notice first that both works include characters who are disadvantaged by the ways their societies are structured and who are caught up in exclusionary discourse about group identity. The socially central male characters in the biblical writing are clear that there are women who want to be part of their community but who should not be, despite the fact that they worship the God of Israel or have married and had children with community members. Sometimes there are good reasons why we might be concerned about individuals who are or who want to be part of a community we belong to; for example, they might hold racist or sexist views that we find profoundly problematic. But this is not the issue at stake in Ezra-Nehemiah as far as the main characters whom the book privileges with speech explain things; the community wants to define and guard its borders against particular groups of people not because those groups hold deeply unethical beliefs but because their very status as foreign makes them dangerous and impure. These figures assert that God's law has no allowance for intercourse between Israel and peoples outside of this community as they define it. They believe, for example, that foreign women who have intermarried with community members must be divorced and forcibly expelled along with their children, because their very nature as foreigners excludes them from ever becoming part of the community, and their natural impurity will always pose a danger if they remain within the community's borders. It is a way of creating and enforcing group identity that, to a Black biblical scholar such as Cheryl Anderson (2009, 47–48), seems uncomfortably reminiscent of the antimiscegenation laws that prohibited interracial marriages in parts of the United States until the 1960s.

This strategy of reading after minoritized literature, however, also allows me to notice that one of the ways Ezra-Nehemiah makes its exclusionary case for community identity is by silencing the most vulnerable characters of its narrative, the women branded as foreigners who are expelled from the group. That such women are unclean and dangerous and that God's law demands a physical separation between them and Israel because of their impurity are settled facts as far as the book's main characters are concerned. The women are not permitted even to voice their pain and shock when they are forced to leave their families and community, let alone to provide any kind of rebuttal to the ways in which they have been characterized or to articulate a different version of what this society could look like.

So as in the previous chapter, the process of reading a biblical text after a contemporary work of minoritized literature allows us to go further than simply noticing similarities between these two writings but to search as well for liberative lessons Kushner's play can bring to our interpretation of a biblical work. In *Angels in America*, American identity is contested by members of different groups who have been excluded from full membership in American society—gays, Jews, and Mormons (who in the nineteenth century were forced to flee the United States to what would become the Utah Territory)—and who grapple with exclusionary understandings of what it means to be American, particularly when powerful voices are intent on discarding and pushing them to the social margins. The characters of *Angels in America* provide no single way to deal with this exclusion, but reading Ezra-Nehemiah after the play does more for readers than problematize the exclusion of the characters who are disadvantaged by gender and ethnicity, readers who might see such exclusion as laudatory or entirely overlook the fact that these characters are not permitted any speech. It also provides us with ways to imagine how the voices of the powerless characters in that biblical story, whose suffering has been ignored and for whom no place in the community has been found, might create their own fantasia on national themes.

The idea of providing voices for these silenced characters is one that comes from contemporary minoritized interpreters of the book like Nāsili Vaka'uta (2011, 161–78), who uses the daily experiences of the *tu'a*, the Tongan lower class, to imagine such speech. Stories that arise from such experiences are not texts I know well enough to use as an interpretive lens, but reading Ezra-Nehemiah after *Angels in America* provides us with a similar interpretive strategy, helping us notice problems with the biblical book that we might have otherwise ignored, aiding us in imagining what the voices silenced by this writing might say if they had been allowed to speak, and helping us devise inclusive visions of community radically different from those articulated by the main characters. This interpretation of Ezra-Nehemiah, then, is one way of going beyond my reading of Daniel in the previous chapter, where the best I could do, with the help of *The Sympathizer*, was imagine how Daniel might become a revolutionary in search of a revolution by simply noticing the existence of the powerless and their concerns. Reading Ezra-Nehemiah after *Angels in America* allows me to imagine the vulnerable characters of this biblical book as revolutionaries aiming to rethink what community can and should be so that they can remake the exclusionary group of the book into one that will include them.

Before I turn to this reading, a brief word is in order about the development of Ezra-Nehemiah as a writing. Scholarly work in recent decades has argued that there were long processes of redaction behind originally independent components, such as the Nehemiah Memoir (e.g., Wright 2004), the material in Ezra 7–10 and Neh 8 associated with Ezra (e.g., Yoo 2017), and the book's opening chapters (e.g., Bortz 2018), each such argument reflecting the view that Ezra-Nehemiah was a work that ultimately took centuries to develop (so, e.g., Blenkinsopp 2009, 86–90; Burt 2014, 70). Whether or not this is true does not affect the interpretive work in this chapter, which examines the book's final form (insofar as we can determine what that is)[3] as a story set in the Persian period. More to the point perhaps is the matter as to whether we should consider Ezra-Nehemiah as a single composition or, as a small minority of scholars hold, Ezra 1–10 and Neh 1–13 originally made up two separate writings (e.g., VanderKam 1992; Becking 2011, 27–28; Amzallag 2018). There are good reasons to maintain, as scholarship traditionally has, that this is a single piece of literature: Ezra 4:8–23 refers to local opposition to the construction of Jerusalem's wall, a matter that is never otherwise discussed in Ezra 1–10 but that is resolved in Neh 1–6; the same genealogy appears in Ezra 2 and Neh 7; there are narratives about Ezra in the third person in Ezra 7 and 10 as well as Neh 8; in Ezra 7 Artaxerxes orders Ezra to teach the law, something we do not see him do until Neh 8 (see Karrer-Grube 2008, 139–42); the importance of avoiding marriages outside of the community is emphasized in Ezra 9–10 as well as in Neh 10 and 13; and both Ezra 9 and Neh 9 contain prayers focused on the consequences of the people's failure to keep the law. I will, as a result, treat Ezra-Nehemiah as a single unit, but it would not matter greatly for the reading in this chapter even if Ezra 1–10 and Neh 1–13 had each been composed individually. In such a case

---

3. The text of 2 Esdras (the OG of Ezra-Nehemiah) has been strongly influenced by the kaige translational tradition, and we have received an OG text that varies little from the MT of Ezra-Nehemiah (see Janz 2008). The most significant points at which we see differences between the MT and OG are in the lists of Neh 11 and 12; in these cases, the OG reflects shorter and older versions of the lists, which were expanded in the Masoretic tradition (see Fulton 2015). So by "final form" in this context, I mean a text of Ezra-Nehemiah that we could construct as lying behind the MT and OG.

these two pieces of literature would simply be like the two linked plays of *Angels in America*: Ezra 1–10, like *Millennium Approaches*, begins a story to which Neh 1–13, like *Perestroika*, provides a sequel.

Identity and Exclusion in *Angels in America*

The events in *Angels in America* take place in New York over a four-month period from late 1985 to early 1986, except for the final scene set in 1990. We are located, then, at the height of the AIDS crisis among the gay community in that city, and two of the play's main characters have the disease. In the context of this suffering experienced by a community excluded because of the sexual orientation of its members, *Angels in America* explores the concept of American identity and the struggles to contest it, both on the part of those who want to expand it to include the disadvantaged and those who want to put a stop to such progress and change. In the process we see what causes some characters to fear change and how suffering drives others to move forward, demand their inclusion in American society, and embrace responsibility for the vulnerable.

Both American identity and change are central themes of the soliloquy that opens *Millennium Approaches*, a eulogy for an elderly Jewish woman. The speaker, Rabbi Isidor Chemelwitz, who has "a heavy Eastern European accent" according to the stage directions (9), admits that he did not know the deceased, but says,

> She was ... *(He touches the coffin)* ... not a person but a whole kind of person, the ones who crossed the ocean, who brought with us to America the villages of Russia and Lithuania—and how we struggled, and how we fought, for the family, for the Jewish home, so that you would not grow up *here*, in this strange place, in the melting pot where nothing melted. Descendants of this immigrant woman, you do not grow up in America, you and your children and their children with the goyische names, you do not live in America, no such place exists. (10)

The concept of identity, and in particular the identity of a group historically relegated to the margins American society,[4] is a key part of the rabbi's

---

4. Contemporary scholarship has challenged the view that anti-Semitism in the United States has been exceptional and transitory (see Tevis 2021). It is important to remember that American anti-Semitism is not simply historical in nature; for example, the Federal Bureau of Investigation's summary of hate crimes in the United States in

eulogy. If it seems odd that he says "no such place exists" as America, his point would seem to be that insofar as one might think of the United States as a melting pot in which immigrant identity is subsumed into larger American culture that is simply not true from his perspective (Wahman 2017, 22–23). For the rabbi, "this strange place" is "the melting pot where nothing melted," something to which his accent and Yiddish-influenced syntax at other points in the monologue bear witness. This does not mean there has been no assimilation, however, for he speaks in English, not in Yiddish, and as he reads the list of the dead woman's descendants at the beginning of the eulogy he seems surprised by some of the "goyische names" of her grandchildren (9–10; see also Minwalla 1997, 106).

The Jewish identity Rabbi Chemelwitz discusses is related to movement and change, for he links it to Jewish migration from Eastern Europe to the United States. In the monologue this movement is more than physical but cultural and religious, for the woman he eulogizes "carried the old world on her back across the ocean, in a boat, and she put it down on Grand Concourse Avenue, or in Flatbush, and she worked that earth into your bones, and you pass it on to your children, this ancient, ancient culture and home" (10). This journey remains part of who her descendants and American Jewry are, the rabbi says: "You can never make that crossing she made, for such Great Voyages in this world do not any more exist. But every day of your lives the miles that voyage between that place and this one you cross. Every day. You understand me? In you that journey is" (10–11). As a result, this reference to movement is a rejection of change, since for Rabbi Chemelwitz the Jewish journey is one that refuses change and assimilation into "this strange place," and the American Jewish community of which he speaks is one that might as well still live in "the villages of Russia and Lithuania." As far as he is concerned, there is no American melting pot, but this exclusion of Jews from American identity does not concern him, for it allows his community to maintain their "ancient, ancient culture and home."

Other characters express even more strident opposition to change and movement, none more obviously than the angels of the work's title. The Continental Principality of America, the being who is normally referred to in the play simply as "the angel," brings a book of prophecy to Prior Walter,

---

2022 found that over ten percent of them were driven by anti-Jewish bias (Federal Bureau of Investigation 2023), even though Jews make up only about two percent of the population of the United States.

one of the two gay characters in the play with AIDS. The message that she and the other angels want Prior to deliver to humanity is one of complete stasis. God abandoned heaven, according to the angel, after becoming entranced with the constantly changing humans when they were created. The angels believe that if humans cease their movement and change that God will return to heaven, and they do not think heaven alone suffers God's loss. The angel connects that divine abandonment as well to the plague that has infected Prior:

> Before the boiling of blood and the searing of skin comes the Secret catastrophe:
> Before Life on Earth becomes finally merely impossible
> It will for a long time before have become completely unbearable.
> *(Coughs, then, with great passion and force:)*
> YOU HAVE DRIVEN HIM AWAY! YOU MUST STOP MOVING! (172)

There seems something insidious about this prophecy, however, and Prior is reluctant to accept it. The audience hears of this angelic annunciation in *Perestroika*, as Prior relates the story of the visitation to his friend Belize, a gay Black nurse. The audience sees Prior, the angel, and Belize on stage at the same time, witnessing both the heavenly address to Prior and Belize's critique of it.

> BELIZE: It's ... worse than nuts, it's—"Don't migrate"? "Don't mingle"? That's ... kind of malevolent, isn't it, 'cause—
> *(Continue below:)*
> PRIOR: I hardly think it's appropriate for you to get *offended*, I didn't invent this shit it was *visited* on—
> BELIZE *(Continuous from above):* —you know, some of us didn't exactly *choose* to migrate, know what I'm saying, some of us—But it *is* offensive or at least monumentally confused and it's not ... *visited*, Prior. By who? It *is* from you, what else is it? (175)

Belize does not believe the angel was real and connects the message of divine abandonment to Prior's anger and grief over the fact that his boyfriend, Louis, abandoned him when Prior was first hospitalized with severe symptoms of AIDS.

If the angel's injunction for humans "Neither Mix Nor Intermarry" (172) sounds rather like Rabbi Chemelwitz's view of things in regard to the Jewish community in the United States, the heavenly decree that humans not "intermingle" (170) sounds particularly offensive to Belize, the descendant of slaves brought to the Americas. One wonders if heaven chose Prior as prophet not only because of his first name, which refers to what has come before (see Foertsch 1999, 61–62)—the prophecy demands that humans cease their movement and progress so that things can go back to the way they were—but because of his elite heritage. Prior is wealthy enough that he is able to live off a trust fund (3), and Louis tells Prior's nurse that "Prior is an old old family name in an old old family. The Walters go back to the Mayflower and beyond. Back to the Norman Conquests. He says there's a Prior Walter stitched into the Bayeux tapestry" (53–54). Prior's economic security reflects his family's deep roots in the European colonization of America and, for that matter, in the Norman colonization of England,[5] and the fact that Prior is "long-descended" appears to have factored into heaven's choice of him as prophet (160).

The angels' prophecy, that is, is one that might find sympathy among those of Prior's privileged socioeconomic background, those who benefit from the status quo and who have no interest in change or progress, but Prior is also a gay man infected with AIDS. He is a pariah in 1980s America as he is a member of a minoritized community ravaged by an epidemic the Republican administration of Ronald Reagan pointedly ignored.[6] Heaven's prophetic demand that change and progress cease so that things can go back to the way they were is a philosophy associated with the political right wing of the United States, and even as we witness the angel deliver the prophecy to Prior it is clear that its vision of stasis is not an original idea. The message railing against progress is a restatement of a reactionary philosophy long associated with American conservatism, as is demonstrated by the fact that Prior and Belize (as he listens to Prior's retelling of the angelic visitation) already seem to know parts of it:

ANGEL: There is No Zion Save Where You Are!
If you Cannot find your Heart's desire—
PRIOR: —In your own backyard—

---

5. Allen Frantzen (1997, 139–41) argues that because the Bayeux tapestry did not include any Anglo-Saxon names, only those of the Norman conquerors, that Prior has hybrid Norman and Anglo-Saxon origins.

6. Donald Francis (2012, 299), who helped devise the Center for Disease Control's AIDS prevention plan for the United States in 1985, writes that "ignoring AIDS was not a passive endeavor. It was an active policy of the Reagan Administration."

ANGEL, PRIOR AND BELIZE: You never lost it to begin with.
(The angel coughs. Prior is disturbed and confused by the citation; she is confused and disturbed that humans know these lines. For Belize it's proof, of course, that this is a dream.) (172)

Unbeknownst to her, the angel has delivered a prophecy that quotes *The Wizard of Oz*,[7] but the point is that heaven's message seems less than imaginative. It has been spoken many times before by the American right and the country's elite, fearful of change that might threaten their privilege.

The notion that progress must cease, that the past—what is prior—is a golden age we must embrace once again is also the belief of Joe Pitt, who has moved from Salt Lake City to Brooklyn to work as a clerk for one of the justices of the federal appellate court in New York. Joe and Harper, his wife, are Mormons, descendants of another group who in the nineteenth century were a persecuted, minoritized community just as the gay men of the play are (see Savran 1995, 216–18). The situation of Mormons in America in the 1980s was, however, much more secure than had been the case in the previous century, which explains to some degree why Joe is a true believer in the Reaganite brand of conservatism that understands itself as returning America to its better past. "Things are starting to change in the world," he says to Harper. "Change for the good. America has rediscovered itself. Its sacred position among nations. And people aren't as ashamed of that like they used to be. This is a great thing. The truth restored. Law restored. That's what President Reagan's done, Harper. He says: 'Truth exists and can be spoken proudly.' And the country responds to him. We become better" (26). The change that Joe talks about is a restoration, a going-back, an end to what someone living on the margins of American society would understand as progress. So we see here another kind of response to American exclusionism: In the case where American society has changed to the extent that it is willing to include a once-excluded group, it can be easy to forget that earlier subjugation and how awful it can be.

Joe's own case is complicated, however, for, despite his beliefs in the ideals of the American right, he is also a closeted gay man who becomes attracted to Louis, Prior's boyfriend, who abandons him when it becomes clear how ill he is. Louis and Joe work at the same courthouse, and as the two of them begin their flirtation their conversation turns toward the

---

7. For a discussion of references to *The Wizard of Oz* in the play and *Angels*' use of camp in general, see Kilner-Johnson 2019.

Reagan family. "I mean, what's it like to be the child of the Zeitgeist? To have the American Animus as your dad?" Louis wonders. "What's it like to be Reagan's kid?" He answers his own question: "I think we all know what that's like. Nowadays. All of us ... falling through the cracks that separate what we owe to our selves and ... and what we owe to love" (74). Louis and Joe are at opposite ends of the political spectrum, but both agree that this sort of Reaganite freedom from responsibility and love for others is "kind of terrifying" and "heartless" (74). It reflects the ethos of Reagan's own family, at least as Louis describes it, a nonfamily shorn of obligations—of "what we owe to love"—in regard to others. Both Louis and Joe are, during this dialogue, contemplating the abandonment of their obligations to their partners who need them, since Louis will shortly abandon Prior because he does not wish to witness his suffering, and Joe will leave Harper, who struggles with mental illness.[8] To experience this kind of freedom from responsibility that their conversation connects to Reagan would be, Joe says, as if "overnight everything you owe anything to, justice, or love, had really gone away. Free. It would be ... heartless terror. Yes. Terrible, and ...Very great. To shed your skin, every old skin, one by one and then walk away, unencumbered, into the morning" (75). To act in freedom from such responsibilities, Louis observes, makes them "children of the new morning, criminal minds. Selfish and greedy and loveless and blind. Reagan's children." This is what life is like, he says, "in the land of the free" (77).

Embracing a Reaganite freedom from responsibility and love for his sick partner who needs him, however, is something Louis avoids in his discussion of his left-wing political principles. During a conversation with Belize, Louis derides conservatives' understanding of freedom and liberals' putative belief in tolerance for the gay community (94), but he tells Belize that true democracy in the United States is still possible because Americans are not wedded to their cultural and racial pasts as European nations are. As he puts it, "There are no gods here, no ghosts or spirits in America, there are no angels in America, no spiritual past, no racial past, there's only the political, and the decoys and the ploys to maneuver around the inescapable battle of politics, the shifting downwards and outwards of political power to the people" (96). It is a view of the nation strikingly at odds with that of Rabbi Chemelwitz, who sees only a Jewish community that still

---

8. For a discussion of the ways in which *Angels in America* emphasizes both Prior's and Harper's suffering and the stigmatization that results from it, see Byttebier 2011, 293–98.

exists in the religious and cultural past of "the villages of Russia and Lithuania," not in America, since for him "no such place exists." Belize finds Louis's view that the racial pasts of Americans have no bearing on national identity offensive, particularly as this involves the assumption that racism in America is of no significance in and of itself. By dismissing racism as a central aspect of oppression in the United States, Louis absolves himself of any ethical responsibility to address it. Belize suggests to Louis that his supposedly radical political speeches about the nature of democracy are a way for him to avoid the topic of his abandonment of Prior in his time of need, and so his abandonment of the responsibilities imposed by love: "I've thought about it for a very long time, and I still don't understand what love is. Justice is simple. Democracy is simple. Those things are unambivalent. But love is very hard. And it goes bad for you if you violate the hard law of love" (104).

"The hard law of love" stands in opposition to the freedom Louis and Joe desire, freedom as the American right understands it. That loveless and responsibility-less understanding of freedom is embodied in the play by Roy Cohn, a character based to some degree on the historical figure of the same name. The Roy Cohn of *Angels in America*, like the Roy Cohn of history, was an acolyte of J. Edgar Hoover and Joe McCarthy (58) and a key figure in the prosecution and execution of Julius and Ethel Rosenberg for sending American military secrets to the Soviets. The character of Roy, like the historical personage, also engaged in illegal ex parte communication with the judge during the sentencing stage of Ethel Rosenberg's trial to ensure that she would receive the death penalty (113–14), despite the fact that it is not clear that she actually participated in any acts of espionage at all (Clune 2016, 5, 29–30). (And, although it likely did not seem worthwhile to mention the fact when Kushner wrote *Angels* in the late twentieth century, the historical Cohn was also an important mentor to Donald Trump; see Ventura 2018, 317.) In the play, Roy hopes to become an ersatz father to Joe, to make him a part of the same far-right political lineage of which he is a member and to send him to Washington, DC to work in Reagan's Justice Department. Part of the "fatherly" advice Roy dispenses to Joe is that love and responsibility are traps (61), the same Reaganite view of freedom that Louis and Joe discuss. Roy's reason for adopting Joe into this "family" that lacks both love and responsibility is a selfish one: As a lawyer, he has illegally taken money from a client, and as a result the New York Bar Association aims to disbar him, so he wants Joe in the Justice Department to exert influence against the process (68–70).

The character of Roy, like the historical figure, dies of AIDS, and like Joe he is a closeted gay man. But while Joe will eventually enter a relationship with Louis, Roy refuses to admit that he is gay, a matter that he insists on when his doctor diagnoses him with the disease. When it comes to words like *homosexual* and *gay*, Roy says, "Like all labels they tell you one thing and one thing only: where does an individual so identified fit in the food chain, in the pecking order? Not ideology, or sexual taste, but something much simpler: clout." Roy has the ear of high-placed officials in the Reagan administration, whereas, he says, "Homosexuals are men who in fifteen years of trying cannot pass a pissant antidiscrimination bill through City Council. Homosexuals are men who know nobody and who nobody knows. Who have zero clout" (46). Roy defines himself by power and control, and so he will not identify with vulnerable groups in which he could claim membership, like the gay community, which is why he tells his doctor that "Roy Cohn is a heterosexual man, Henry, who fucks around with guys," and why he does not have AIDS, since "AIDS is what homosexuals have. I have liver cancer" (47).[9]

Both the queer and Jewish communities have been scapegoated by Americans in similar ways (see Solomon 1997, 121–23), so Roy takes no comfort in his Jewish heritage either, telling Joe that anti-Semitism is an important reason why "the genteel gentlemen Brahmin lawyers, country-club men" are trying to have him disbarred. To them, he says, he is "some sort of filthy little Jewish troll" (69).[10] Roy roots his identity instead in his status as a lawyer, which has brought him the clout that he believes he needs to survive as a gay Jewish man with AIDS who would otherwise be disadvantaged in America by his sexual orientation, ethnicity, and illness; he refuses to accept that minoritized status, believing that the mere exercise of power to selfish ends is enough to transcend and obscure it. He is wrong about this, however, for the characters in *Angels in America* know that he is gay just as they know he is Jewish, and at his disbarment hearing one of participants says to another, "I've hated that little faggot for thirty-six years" (253). It is no wonder, then, that Roy sees the world as a dangerous, awful place; at one point he says that he sees the universe "as a kind of sandstorm in outer space with winds of mega-hurricane veloc-

---

9. This is not the only point in *Angels in America* in which AIDS appears as "a signifier of disempowerment"; see Piggford 2000, 184–85.

10. For a discussion of the ways in which *Angels in America* refers and alludes to Roy's Jewishness, see King 2008.

ity, but instead of grains of sand it's shards and splinters of glass" (13). At another, he says,

> My generation, we had *clarity*. Unafraid to look deep into the miasma at the heart of the world, what a pit, what a nightmare is there—*I have looked, I have searched all my life for absolute bottom, and I found it, believe* me: *Stygian*. How tragic, how brutal life is. How false people are. The immutable heart of what we are that bleeds through whatever we might become. (210)

Roy's attempt to find a place for himself in America, then, is one that depends in part on his denial of his triply minoritized identity and in part on his ability to manifest selfishness and lack of responsibility for others in a drive to gain clout. The law is the tool Roy uses to survive and gain power, to protect himself and make his way in an America that has no place for the powerless. Lawyers, he says, are "the High Priests of America. We alone know the words that made America. Out of thin air. We alone know how to use The Words. The Law: the only club I ever wanted to belong to" (215). In Roy's view, however, this means that the law is something he can use to protect his own interests and to provide him with security in a country that would otherwise prefer he did not exist. "You want to be Nice, or you want to be Effective?" he asks Joe. "Make the law, or subject to it. Choose" (113–14). Roy has chosen, and he will not be subject to any law that he cannot make or bend to his purposes. In the America his character manifests, power used for protection and for selfish ends, not care for and the honoring of responsibilities toward the needy and suffering, is how one fights exclusion.

The result, however, is a character as evil as the universe he sees. He embodies the America that wants no part of the vulnerable people it pushes to its margins, an America that prizes a freedom without love and responsibility for those who suffer and distributes justice without concern for Belize's hard law of love. And while Louis may espouse political views far to the left of Roy's, Belize is not convinced that his beliefs are concrete enough to measure up to this law either, since they allow him to abandon his boyfriend suffering from AIDS and to claim that racism is not a problem he needs to concern himself with. All of Louis's talk about justice and democracy do not amount to anything more than "Big Ideas," he tells him at one point while they speak by the statue of the angel Bethesda in Central Park.

BELIZE: Louis and his Big Ideas. Big Ideas are all you love. "America" is what Louis loves.
(Louis is looking at the angel, not at Belize.)
LOUIS: So what? Maybe I do. You don't know what I love. You don't.
BELIZE: Well I hate America, Louis. I hate this country. It's just big ideas, and stories, and people dying, and people like you.

The white cracker who wrote the National Anthem knew what he was doing. He set the word "free" to a note so high nobody can reach it. That was deliberate. Nothing on earth sounds less like freedom to me.

You come with me to room 1013 over at the hospital, I'll show you America. Terminal, crazy and mean. (230)

In the play, America in its most pejorative sense is largely embodied by Roy, the occupant of room 1013 of the hospital ward where Belize works and the character in *Angels in America* who most unapologetically embraces the American concept of a selfish freedom with no regard for the suffering and minoritized, despite the fact that he himself is both suffering and minoritized. As he is dying of AIDS—"what homosexuals have," as he puts it—on Belize's ward, Roy demonstrates how well aware he is that there is no place for those who suffer in the conservative understanding of America that his character so prizes: "Americans have no use for the sick. Look at Reagan: he's so healthy he's hardly human, he's a hundred if he's a day, he takes a slug in the chest and two days later he's out west riding ponies in his PJs. I mean *who does that*? That's America. It's just no country for the infirm" (189).

Roy is not the only selfish character in the play, for both Joe and Louis abandon their partners struggling with illness. Both exhibit some remorse for their actions, but Joe as a conservative lawyer shares to at least some degree Roy's view of an evil and uncaring universe. In a conversation with Louis he criticizes the way Louis clings to his view of a world that can be perfected, that is not entirely unredeemable (202). "You have to accept that we're not put here to make the entire earth into a heaven, you have to accept that we can't. And accept as rightfully yours the happiness that comes your way" (203). Beyond the personal callousness that results from abdicating responsibility for making the world better, reflected in the selfishness of Joe and Louis, who abandon their partners who need them, it has resulted in Joe's role in and responsibility for drafting inhumane and antigay legal decisions. It is an open secret in the courthouse that Joe largely writes the decisions assigned to the conservative judge for whom he clerks—at one point he simply refers to them as "my decisions" (246)—and when Louis finally realizes what Joe has done with the law, he is able to see the evil for which Joe has been responsible and in turn how poorly Louis has acted in abandoning Prior. Louis refers to one of the decisions for which Joe was responsible as "an important bit of legal fag-bashing" (249). In another case Joe drafted a decision ruling against plaintiffs who were suing a company whose factory's pollution was blinding children, finding, as Louis puts it, that "the Air and Water Protection Act doesn't protect *people*, but actually only *air* and *water*" (247). Only now is Louis able to leave his relationship with Joe and eventually ask forgiveness from Prior (284), assumedly because he can see how much like Joe he had been acting.

The angels in heaven themselves, the audience discovers near the end of the play, share Roy's view of a frightening and dangerous universe. Prior eventually rejects the prophecy heaven has given him and wrestles with the angel, as Jacob does in Genesis, and just like Jacob, Prior demands a blessing from the angel, which in his case is to go to heaven and return the prophetic book the angel had originally given him.[11] There he encounters the Continental Principalities, seven angels, each associated with one of the continents, and they are "frightened and grief-stricken" (272) because they can see dimly into what they believe to be a disastrous future. When Prior states that he wants to return the prophecy, he must explain to them that it is impossible for humans not to move and change, and he says that the angels' desire to have God return has simply made them overlook divine culpability for the disasters on earth.

> PRIOR: If after all this destruction, if after all the terrible days of this terrible century He returned to see ... how much suffering His abandonment had created, if all He has to offer is death ...
> You should *sue* the bastard. That's my only contribution to all this *Theology*. Sue the bastard for walking out. How dare He. He oughta pay.
> *(All stand, frozen, then the Angels exchange glances. Then:)*
> ANGEL: Thus spake the Prophet. (275–76)

Prior in the end does deliver a prophecy, but to heaven, not earth. The angels offer him a chance to remain in heaven, where change and his suffering will cease, where he will not have to experience either earth's future

---

11. This is certainly not the only allusion to the biblical Jacob in *Angels in America*; see Lipschitz 2012.

horrors or the ravages of AIDS, but Prior instead opts to return to the land of the living, saying, "I want more life. I can't help myself. I do" (278). And he remains unconvinced of the angels' belief in a disastrous future, telling them they can only see what they are afraid the future will be, not what will actually happen (279).

Prior's view of the cosmos by the end of the play is one that has no room for an understanding of a God who has no concern for those who suffer, a being whose interest in caring for others is not, in the end, any greater than Roy's. It has no space for the angels' fear of the future and their certainty that it only brings more suffering and destruction, a view that is also just like Roy's. Without Prior's alternative vision of the way things are and could be, one is doomed to be like Roy and create a world that is "terminal, crazy and mean," a self-fulfilling prophecy of selfishness and evil. As James Corby (2010, 19–20) puts it, in *Angels in America* it is the far right's understanding of freedom that has created the world Roy believes in, one that wants to subjugate him because he is Jewish, gay, and suffering from AIDS, causing him to act in selfish ways that make things even worse.

The play offers an alternative to Roy's philosophy and his understanding of America, however, and key to it is the notion that things can change for the better by progressing forward rather than backward as Joe desires. Prior, suffering from AIDS, is abundantly aware of the suffering one can be forced to endure, but without a belief that things can change there is no recourse except the stasis of death, the angels' preferred solution, or profound selfishness, which is Roy's. Roy, "the polestar of human evil," as Louis puts it (229), does not change, nor does Belize, the play's moral center,[12] but all of the other main characters do to some extent, arguably none so obviously as the three main female ones.

---

12. That Belize is the ethical center of *Angels in America* while also being its most underdeveloped main character, according to some readers, is sometimes seen as problematic; see, e.g., Savran 1995, 222 and Ventura 2018, 330–33. Savran, for example, argues that Belize becomes the center of "a white imaginary." Ventura argues that the hopeful ending of *Angels* is belied by the fact that the HIV rate in areas of urban poverty in the United States remains very high, a result of racism viewers of the play can ignore because *Angels in America*'s one main Black character and moral center ignores this problem as well. Framji Minwalla (1997, 110–14) argues, however, that Belize is able to critique Louis's optimistic liberal views in regard to democracy in the United States because he is Black and because he can see how Louis is unable to

When we first encounter Harper, Joe's wife, she is as afraid of the universe as Roy; "Everywhere, things are collapsing, lies surfacing, systems of defense giving way" (16), she says in her first speech of the play. When Joe tells her he has been invited to join the Justice Department, Harper refuses to move from New York because she says Washington is "a giant cemetery" (23), yet she is also afraid to remain even in their Brooklyn apartment, since she believes "a man with a knife" haunts their bedroom (23–24). In the first part of *Angels in America* her only escape is through valium-induced hallucinatory travel, provided with the help of an imaginary figure named Mr. Lies.[13] Over the course of the play she changes, however, realizing that the travel she hallucinates with the aid of her medication will not truthfully make things better. To change and progress she will have to face the truth and take action, and she does, getting Joe to admit that for him she hardly exists at all—"Finally. The Truth," she says at that point (244)—which enables her to free herself from his selfishness. In *Angels in America*'s penultimate scene we see her on a true journey through space as she leaves Joe, voicing words of hope that seem key to the alternative the play provides to the American right wing's view of the world: "Nothing's lost forever. In this world, there is a kind of painful progress. Longing for what we've left behind, and dreaming ahead" (285). Like Prior, Harper suffers from illness and abandonment and like him suffering motivates her to fight for something better:

> I feel like shit but I've never felt more alive. I've finally found the secret of all that Mormon energy. Devastation. That's what makes people migrate, build things. Devastated people do it, people who have lost love. Because I don't think God loves His people[14] any better than Joe loved me. The string was cut and off they went. Ravaged, heartbroken, and free. (263)

---

understand the insidious power of racism, even though Louis is himself minoritized because he is gay.

13. Mr. Lies is a member of the International Order of Travel Agents or IOTA (4), which perhaps gives some idea of the very limited amount of comfort his hallucinatory services can provide; see Kilner-Johnson 2019, 215. On pages 107–8 of the play, we see that this sort of travel can bring some sort of solace to Harper, but it is at best a temporary solution (106).

14. The reference to God's people in this context is an allusion to the Mormons of the 1830s and '40s, a persecuted group whose early vision of progress and communitarianism forced them to flee the United States to what later became the Utah Territory (see Savran 1995, 216–18). On pages 189–93 of the play, we encounter

There is more than one response to suffering and evil in *Angels in America*, and Harper's change and progress that evolves out of her reaction to suffering is shared by other characters. Joe's mother Hannah also changes over the course of the play; we first encounter her in Utah when Joe calls to tell her that he is gay (79), and she then travels to New York so that, she says later, she can take him back to Salt Lake City (197). That explanation, however, does not make sense of the fact that she has sold her house in Salt Lake City, the place that another Mormon character calls "the home of the saints, the godliest place on earth"; that same character warns her, in fact, that "every step a Believer takes away from here is a step fraught with peril" (86). It is a view of Salt Lake City much like the angels' view of heaven: Since paradise exists there is no point to movement, change, or travel away from it. It encapsulates the American far right's insistence that progress must stop and the needs of the subjugated must be ignored so the United States can return to a past golden age, the Reaganite view Joe expounds with such rapture. But the fact that Hannah sells her house in Utah suggests that she is primed for change, and the care she shows Harper, whom her son has abandoned, and Prior, whom at one point she must take to the hospital, shows her acting out of a compassion that confounds Prior's expectations. She is the one who tells him to reject the prophecy he has received, wrestle with the angel, and demand a blessing (241–42, 259), and so she is key to his ultimate rejection of heaven's message that sounds so much like that of the American right.

Hannah manifests what Belize seems to mean when he talks about the hard law of love, compassion for the suffering and vulnerable. This law must also involve forgiveness, something exhibited by the ghostly figure of Ethel Rosenberg,[15] who has reappeared on earth to see Roy suffer not only the disbarment that occurs immediately before his death but the terrible pain he suffers as he is dying from AIDS (253). That she might revel in the agony of the man who was instrumental in her execution is understandable, yet, as he approaches death and the disease appears to disorient him, he acts as if he were a frightened child who

---

Harper and Prior in the Diorama Room of the Mormon Visitors' Center in New York, which tells a story of the Mormon exodus.

15. The play never actually describes Ethel as a ghost or clearly explains what kind of numinous being she is; see Barnett 2014, 134. She claims to have the ability to walk through walls, but on page 188 of the play also has to take the train to get to Roy's disbarment hearings.

believes Ethel to be his mother and so she sings to him, transforming her hatred into compassion (253–54). Belize is also able to extend forgiveness to Roy, despite the hateful, racist way Roy treated him while a patient on his ward (e.g., 151, 187). Belize calls Louis to say the Kaddish, the Jewish prayer for the dead, for Roy after he has died. "He was a terrible person," Belize says. "He died a hard death. So maybe … A queen can forgive her vanquished foe. It isn't easy, it doesn't count if it's easy, it's the hardest thing. Forgiveness. Which is maybe where love and justice meet. Peace, at least. Isn't that what the Kaddish asks for?" (265–66). And when Louis cannot remember the Aramaic words of the prayer, Ethel's ghostlike figure appears one last time to provide them (266–67). Roy would not accept his identity as a gay Jewish man and inflicted great suffering on the world because of his refusal to embrace these parts of himself, but they are posthumously restored to him through Belize's and Ethel's acts of unselfish forgiveness, where justice is leavened by love.[16]

The final scene of *Perestroika*, the second of the two plays, takes place four years after the rest of *Angels in America*, and here we see Prior, Louis, Belize, and Hannah gathered together under the statue of the angel Bethesda in Central Park. The scene opens with this new family engaged in good-natured squabbling about the geopolitical consequences of perestroika, the political restructuring of the Soviet Union that led to the end of the Cold War. "Remember back four years ago?" asks Louis. "The whole time we were feeling everything everywhere was stuck, while in Russia! Look! Perestroika! The Thaw! It's the end of the Cold War! The whole world is changing! Overnight!" (287). "They're making a leap into the unknown," he continues later in the scene. "You can't wait around for a theory" (288). His words here reflect the opening scene of *Perestroika*, a soliloquy by "the World's Oldest Living Bolshevik" that parallels that of Rabbi Chemelwitz at the beginning of *Millennium Approaches*. The Bolshevik speaks of "the

---

16. Roy cannot escape his horrific view of the universe, but whether this leaves his character unredeemed (so Omer-Sherman 2007a, 16–17) depends on how one understands redemption in this context. Belize and Ethel cannot force Roy to accept the minoritized aspects of his identity he has rejected, but in his death they can act as representatives of the communities who would have accepted him had he been willing to look at the world and act differently. So if one can understand redemption as something that can happen posthumously, Roy receives it. In the end, says Minwalla (1997, 108), *Angels in America* does not allow Roy merely to be a villain because we are forced to see him through Belize's and Ethel's redemptive eyes.

Classic Texts" that "gave us Praxis, True Praxis, True Theory married to Actual Life." Despite the power of those classic Marxist-Leninist texts, he admits that "we must change," but he refuses to do so until someone can "show me the theory": "Show me the words that will reorder the world, or else *keep silent*" (138). Like the rabbi, the Bolshevik can only believe in the certainties of the past and cannot see a way to progress and move forward, despite the fact perestroika was necessary because the Classic Texts failed to provide what their authors had hoped.

The final scene of *Angels in America* responds to the two scenes that open the two plays. Unlike Rabbi Chemelwitz, the family at the end of *Angels in America*, its members disadvantaged by sexual orientation, gender, race, religion, and disability, thinks about ways to transform America instead of accepting their status as those excluded from the social center as the preferred solution. Unlike the Bolshevik, they believe there can be no change for the better if we cannot make the same sort of leap into the unknown that perestroika did. The ending of the play has sometimes been criticized for ignoring differences in race, ethnicity, and class, and concluding only with vague liberal pieties with no clear plan as to how to realize a vision of America different from that of Roy's and the American far right's.[17] One can read the play's ending rather differently, however, noting first that its final words, which come from Prior as he breaks the fourth wall and speaks directly to the audience, provide not closure but a beginning:

> This disease will be the end of many of us, but not nearly all, and the dead will be commemorated and will struggle on with the living, and we are not going away. We won't die secret deaths anymore. The world only spins forward. We will be citizens. The time has come.
> Bye now.
> You are fabulous creatures, each and every one.
> And I bless you: *More Life*.
> The Great Work Begins. (290)

---

17. See, for example, Savran 1995, 223–24 and Ventura 2018, 324–26, 329–30. Ventura and Savran differ, however, in their views as to which minoritized groups are excluded in this final scene. Savran concludes that *Angels in America* ignores oppression based on class for identity politics that privileges race, gender identity, and sexual orientation, while Ventura says a triumphant queer liberalism at the end of the play ignores differences in race and ethnicity.

With these words Prior repeats the opening of the angelic annunciation at the very end of *Millennium Approaches*: "The Great Work begins: / The Messenger has arrived" (125). While for Charles McNulty (1996, 93) this ending of *Angels in America* in *Perestroika*'s final scene is "hard to accept," especially because the play "hasn't provided any convincing evidence to suggest the state of emergency has let up in the least," the key issue in Prior's concluding words is that the play only provides a beginning.

Prior had to reject the prophecy with which heaven provided him, and so it could not serve as a beginning of a Great Work, as it was based on a worldview that is too frightened of the future to allow for progress. A very different Great Work must begin after the audience leaves the theater (so Solomon 1997, 132), and it must begin in communities like the one we see in its final scene, those with intimate knowledge of what it means to suffer because of the ways that dominant sociopolitical forces have excluded them and who know the value of the hard law of love that privileges responsibility and care for the suffering. Prior does not claim that the state of emergency has come to an end or that "we"—the excluded—are truly recognized by America as citizens, only that they will be. Change must come from the outside, from those pushed to the social margins, because it is the exclusive center of America that needs reform, and it is not a coincidence that the ideal of reform's genesis in the play comes from America's enemy during the Cold War, an ideal that by 1990 was already leading to the war's end. As a result, the play ends with an insistence that the groups excluded by American society be included in the polis so they can become a true part of the political system. As Louis puts it, "That's what politics is. The world moving ahead. And only in politics does the miraculous occur" (288; see also Kornhaber 2014, 737–38). This is a very different view of the need of the minoritized to fight for the inclusion of their voices in the shaping of American society than that of Rabbi Chemelwitz who refused to even acknowledge America's existence.

Angels in America is, as it is subtitled, *A Gay Fantasia on National Themes*, and it uses fantasy to broaden the American political imagination (Scapp 1997, 92–93), a fantasy that provides a place for the Great Work to begin and points in the direction in which this movement can progress. Once the excluded can fight their way into the political scene and truly become citizens of America they can push for a political vision of heaven as Belize describes it to Roy. It is a vision so inimical to Roy's beliefs as to what the world should be like that he listens to Belize virtually without interruption only because he is so strongly under the influence of morphine at this point during his hospitalization. Belize's description of heaven—or, we could say, his utopian view as to what America could be—portrays it as a city like San Francisco, with

> Piles of trash, but lapidary like rubies and obsidian, and diamond-colored cow-spit streamers in the wind. And voting booths.
> ROY: And a dragon atop a golden hoard.
> BELIZE: And everyone in Balenciaga gowns with red corsages, and big dance palaces full of music and light and racial impurity and gender confusion.
> *(Roy laughs softly, delighted.)*
> And all the deities are Creole, mulatto, brown as the mouths of rivers.
> *(Roy laughs again.)*
> Race, taste, and history finally overcome.
> And you ain't there. (222–23)

If there are concrete steps to realize this kind of American identity, they will not arise out of a fear of progress and the future, nor out of a view of the law that understands it as something that should be turned to the selfish desires of the powerful—those who would prefer to be dragons atop golden hoards—and excludes those who most need its protection. *Angels in America* provides no direct roadmap that allows the new families of those pushed to the social margins to begin with their experiences of suffering and move "ravaged, heartbroken, and free," as Harper puts it, toward the inclusive vision of American identity Belize describes, but one cannot wait for a perfect theory to begin the journey. The perestroika of the play is a leap into the unknown, a "painful progress," as Harper says, "longing for what we've left behind, and dreaming ahead."

Community Identity and Exclusion in Ezra-Nehemiah

Ezra-Nehemiah, as I have already mentioned, has in common with *Angels in America* an interest in defining group identity, although as we will see in this section of the chapter, its main characters come to very different conclusions in regard to the matter than the new family of the minoritized in the final scene of *Perestroika*. Nor is this the only topic both works explore, for Ezra-Nehemiah is also interested in how one should conceive of change, movement, progress, and intermingling; whether the point of the law is to protect oppressive social structures or those subjugated by them; how frightened one should be of the future; what one's community owes to the vulnerable and minoritized; and what might appease an absent God. Reading it after *Angels in America*, however, throws into stark relief the fact that Ezra-Nehemiah's main characters are largely privileged ones; there are powerless figures in this story, but they are not given a voice in the narrative that would allow them to represent themselves. After encountering *Angels in America*, readers of the book might be more prone to notice the stark exclusivism of Ezra-Nehemiah that the main characters rely on as they represent the powerless and articulate their views of community identity in order to exclude them. As we will see in the final section of this chapter, however, reading the book through the lens of *Angels in America* can help us imagine how some of the powerless characters with no voice in the book might have described things such as intermingling, progress, the law, God, and community identity if they had been allowed to speak and how they might have pointed to the shortcomings of the ways in which the main characters represent them and exclude them from a place in the community.

Ezra-Nehemiah opens at the end of the exilic period as the Persian king Cyrus announces that "all the kingdoms of the earth YHWH, the God of the heavens, has given to me" and that this God has commanded him to rebuild the temple in Jerusalem (Ezra 1:2) that Nebuchadnezzar destroyed when he captured the city. Readers encounter no direct speech from God in Ezra-Nehemiah, although Cyrus will not be the only character who will make claims about the divine will and certainly no one challenges his understanding of it in the opening of the story. This new ruler of the earth goes on to choose those who belong to the people of this God to carry out the task of rebuilding the temple (1:3), and he personally goes to a Babylonian temple to bring the gold and silver implements Nebuchadnezzar had looted from the temple in Jerusalem and returns them to the members of the Judean community in exile who are about to travel to Jerusalem to carry out the construction project (1:7–11). But while the book opens in Babylon, its narrative does not linger there long as the exiles—or some of them, at any rate—are set into motion to make the journey to Jerusalem to carry out a divine order overseen by the Persian king.

Despite the fact that most of Ezra-Nehemiah's story takes place in Judah, with only short narrative returns to the diaspora, the work repetitively refers to the community at its center as "the exile" with its origins in "the captivity,"[18] almost as if they had never left Babylon at all. This emphasis on the group's connection to the exile appears to be an important part of community identity in the book, a focus of this writing that is apparent almost as soon as the group is introduced. They are "the people of the province" according to Ezra 2:1–2, a small part of the vast world empire ruled by Cyrus, as well as "the people of Israel" and "the ones going up from the captivity of the exile" according to these same verses that introduce a long list of the ancestral houses, the basic social grouping of the Jewish community in Babylon,[19] who send some of their members to Jerusalem (2:3–63). The final verses of this list tells readers that there were a handful of such houses who could not prove their Israelite lineage through written genealogical records (2:59–63), which implies that such records existed—at least in the narrative world of Ezra-Nehemiah—and could validate the Israelite descent of the vast majority of this group.[20]

This list of Ezra 2 is just one of the many parts of Ezra-Nehemiah that has led commentators to conclude that an important focus of the writing as a whole is to define and defend the identity of this community in Judah,[21] to make it clear what it means when one wants to define oneself as an Israelite, at least as that term would have been understood from the standpoint of the book's main characters. The sum of these migrants, Ezra 2 says, is "all Israel" (2:70) and "all of the assembly" (2:64), two more terms that appear frequently in the work to refer to the community. The book does include the diaspora in Babylon within its understanding

---

18. Ezra-Nehemiah refers to the community as "the exile" in Ezra 1:11; 2:1; 4:1; 6:16, 19, 20, 21; 8:35; 9:4; 10:6, 7, 8, 16; Neh 7:6. It links them to "the captivity" in Ezra 2:1; 3:8; 8:35; 9:7; Neh 1:2, 3; 7:6; 8:17.

19. For the בית אבות "ancestral house" as the basic social group of the Judean exile and postexilic Judah, see Weinberg 1992, 49–61; Williamson 2003, 477–78; Janzen 2017a, 39–47.

20. In 2:59–63 we encounter ancestral houses who were unable "to make known [in regard to] their ancestral house and their seed if they were from Israel" (2:59), and 2:62 refers specifically to a written genealogical record. Since 2:61–63 is concerned with the particular problem of priests being unable to prove their priestly descent, it is not clear if we should read 2:59–63 as a whole as saying that all of the exiles with a relatively small number of exceptions could turn to written genealogical records. But if not, then the verses imply that in the narrative world of Ezra-Nehemiah there were at least well-accepted oral genealogies to prove Israelite lineage.

21. And Jonathan Dyck (2000), for example, makes precisely this point in regard to Ezra 2.

of "Israel,"[22] but the definition of the word in Ezra-Nehemiah does not extend beyond the exiles taken to Babylon and their descendants. Readers of the book are clear right away as to who this community is: They are Israel, a term limited to those who can trace their descent to the people whom Nebuchadnezzar exiled to Babylon, some of whom now migrate to Jerusalem and Judah under a royal command that is itself a response to a divine order that the temple be rebuilt. This community can also be said to be defined by their loyalty to their God and the Persian king. They offer sacrifices to God and observe religious festivals as soon as they arrive, "according to what is written in the law of Moses" (3:2).[23] They also act upon the רשיון "order, permission"[24] of King Cyrus when they get to Judah as they gather supplies to begin the temple construction project he is overseeing (3:7).

And if readers become aware early on in Ezra-Nehemiah as to what defines the identity of this community, they also soon learn who they are not. As soon as they arrive in Judah we read that they are afraid of עמי הארצות "the peoples of the lands" (3:3), and although we do not immediately learn who these peoples are or what threat they pose to the group, it is a term that the book uses to refer to groups living in the region who cannot be considered as part of the community, at least from the perspective of the main characters. Once temple construction begins, the exiles are approached by עם הארץ "the people of the land" (4:4), who are now defined as the community's "adversaries" (4:1). Attempts to define group identity must exclude as well as include, since not everyone can be a part of the community around which one is drawing a boundary, and "the people(s) of the land(s)" are clearly not part of the assembly of exiles at the center of Ezra-Nehemiah's narrative. This is not because the people of the land are inherently hostile to the exiles and the temple; in fact, they first come into contact with the community when they ask if they can join in the work of temple construction, explaining that "like you we worship

---

22. The group is called "the assembly" in Ezra 2:64; 10:8, 14; Neh 5:13; 7:66; 8:2, 17; 13:1. It is called "Israel" in Ezra 2:2, 59, 70; 3:1; 4:3; 8:29; Neh 2:2; 7;7, 73, and in many other places. "Israel" is also used to refer more broadly to the exiles in Babylon as well as their kin in Palestine in such places as Ezra 6:21; 7:7, 10, 28; 8:25, 35; Neh 1:6.

23. Reading ככתוב בתורת משה with the MT; the OG reflects Hebrew ככתובים בתורת משה "according to the things written in the law of Moses."

24. רשיון is a *hapax legomenon*. In 2 Esdras the word is translated as ἐπιχώρησις "permission," although the less literal 1 Esdras uses γραφέν "written order" (5:53).

your God" (4:2). The exiles reject this offer, however, because they say King Cyrus commanded them alone to build (4:3). These characters know that the people of the land worship the same God as they do, but this does not make them Israelites, at least not as they define the term, since the people of the land are not descended from those exiled to Babylon but from people relocated to the area centuries before by an Assyrian king (4:2). No character in the book offers any critique of the ways in which the people of the land worship the God of Israel; they are excluded from the temple project because they have the wrong ancestors and as far as the central community in Ezra-Nehemiah understands things Cyrus has ordered only those who can trace their descent to the exilic community in Babylon to be involved in the rebuilding project.

The people of the land do nothing in this narrative that could be seen by the exiles as adversarial until they are prohibited from joining the reconstruction of the temple, but once that happens we read in 4:4–5 that they paid Persian officials to impede the work. The story does not explain why their desire to see a rebuilt temple for God in Jerusalem is replaced by opposition to it, but one obvious rationale for this change of heart is to understand them as reacting against a place of worship for their God founded on exclusionary principles. The exilic community does complete the temple, however, and when they celebrate the festival of Passover soon after, those who participate in it include only "the descendants of Israel, the ones returning from the exile, that is, all who separated themselves from the impurity of the nations of the land to them" (Ezra 6:21).[25] One of the important aspects of the temple as it appears in Ezra-Nehemiah is that it can be used as a way to distinguish between the true Israel as characters in the book define this group and the other peoples who live in the region including those who also worship the God of Israel, since those peoples may not help build or participate in worship at the temple. By

---

25. One could also translate בני ישראל השבים מהגולה וכל הנבדל מטמאת גוי הארץ אלהם as "the descendants of Israel, the ones returning from the exile, *and* all who separated themselves from the impurity of the nations of the land to them" (see, e.g., Lau 2009; Kessler 2010, 333–34). Both translations are grammatically correct but given the sustained distinction between the community and the people of the land in Ezra 3–4, an inclusivist reading of 6:21 in which nonmigrants join the exilic community in order to participate in the worship the text associates with the completion of the temple does not appear to be the better understanding of the verse. For a longer discussion, see Thiessen 2009.

the end of the story of the temple's reconstruction in Ezra 1–6, we can see that descent, loyalty to God and the Persian monarch, and participation in community worship as something that must exclude "the impurity of the nations of the land" are ways of distinguishing between the true Israel and those who should not be considered as members of this community.

The group at the center of the book interprets Cyrus's order that anyone who belongs to God's people "may go up to Jerusalem, which is in Judah, and build the house of YHWH, the God of Israel" (1:3) as meaning that the exilic community alone is responsible for and associated with the temple, and so this group claims an exclusive relationship to the kings of Persia, since as they see it Cyrus sent them alone to build. In Ezra-Nehemiah's narrative they alone of all the peoples in the region work with and for the king, and they alone reap the largesse of these kings who provide massive amounts of money and resources to construct the temple and even on occasion pay for the sacrifices offered within it (Ezra 6:8–10; 7:15–24; 8:25–27). The Persian king also provides the resources to rebuild the wall around Jerusalem that the Babylonians had destroyed (Neh 2:7–8), the construction of which allows the city to be reinhabited once more (11:1–24). There are, in short, certain perquisites that accompany the claim to be the king's loyal subjects in the region. By using their association with the temple as one manifestation of their group identity that excludes all others in the area, the exilic community actually drives the people of the land to oppose its construction, and so makes them seem like disloyal subjects of the king who has ordered the temple to be built and of the God who has given this command to the king.

The story of the temple construction in Ezra 1–6, then, goes a long way to help readers see who is truly a part of this community associated with the temple and who is not. We find more emphasis on defining community identity as we move to the story of Ezra 7–10, where the narrative jumps ahead some generations to the seventh year of the reign of King Artaxerxes,[26] who sends Ezra, a priest and scribe from the Babylonian

---

26. For the purposes of this chapter, it does not matter if the historical Ezra was active during the reign of Artaxerxes I (see, e.g., Janzen 2021a, 34–38) or Artaxerxes II (e.g., Lemaire 2014, 417), since our interest here is in the character of Ezra as he appears in Ezra-Nehemiah, not in the historical figure, and in the book Ezra is present in Judah at the same time as Nehemiah, since he teaches the law in Neh 8 after Nehemiah leads the rebuilding of Jerusalem's wall but before our last glimpse of Nehemiah in the thirty-second year of Artaxerxes I.

diaspora, to Jerusalem. Part of the king's command to Ezra is that he is to convey massive royal donations to the temple (7:15–24), but Artaxerxes also tells him that he must establish legal reforms in the region based on "the law of your God" (7:25),[27] a reference to torah. Ezra is ordered to teach these laws to all who do not know them, and Artaxerxes emphasizes that those who do not obey "the law of your God and the law of the king" will be subject to punishment (7:26). Soon after Ezra arrives in Judah, however, he is told that the exilic community is not following the law of their God, because men from the exiles have married women from outside of the group with the result that "the holy seed has mixed itself with the peoples of the lands" (9:2). From the standpoint of a character like Ezra, it has not taken much time for a community once loyal to its God and divine law to begin ignoring its true identity and breaking down the boundaries that are supposed to separate it from the surrounding peoples. This breach of community identity, says Ezra in his prayer of 9:6–15, is a violation of God's law that the king has ordered him to teach (9:10–12), and he may have in mind laws like Exod 34:11–16 and Deut 7:1–4, where God insists that the Israelites not intermarry with the Canaanites after the conquest; Ezra's prayer "basically" quotes Deut 7, writes Bob Becking (2011, 53–54). Because of the particular language Ezra uses in his rebuke of the community, including his references to the נדה "uncleanness," תועבות "abominations," and טמאה "impurity" of the peoples of the lands (9:11), scholars sometimes also understand him as referring to laws that use similar vocabulary in Lev 15:19–33; 18:24–30; 21:1–5; and 22:2–3 (e.g., Klawans 2000, 44–45; Hayes 2002, 27–28; Olyan 2004, 5; Clauss 2011, 128–30; Southwood 2012, 136–40; Harrington 2012).

Ezra is afraid not of the punishment Artaxerxes has promised for those in violation of "the law of your God and the law of the king" but of the divine retaliation that will result from such disobedience, something that he believes will lead to the complete destruction of the exilic community around Jerusalem. Israel has always been guilty of violations of torah, he says in his prayer, and it resulted in destruction (9:7). The earlier generation of the exilic community in Ezra 1–6 makes a similar point, explaining

---

27. Because both the OG and the parallel verse of 1 Esd 8:23 reflect Aramaic דת אלהך rather than the MT's דתי אלהך, there are two independent translations reflecting a text that differs from the MT. For a brief discussion of 1 Esdras as a translation independent of that of 2 Esdras and as translating a text largely corresponding to yet somewhat different than proto-MT, see Bird 2012, 9–10.

that they were rebuilding the temple because the original edifice had been destroyed when their ancestors angered God, who sent Nebuchadnezzar to exile them to Babylon (5:11–12). While God has allowed Israel to return to Jerusalem and rebuild the temple, Ezra says now (9:8–9), the community's current violation of torah in marrying women from the peoples of the lands may result in its annihilation (9:13–15). After hearing his speech, the larger community shares his terror of the consequences of such intermingling with foreigners, and they agree that to act "according to the law" these women and the children they have borne must be driven from their midst (10:1–4). Ezra tells the assembly of the exiles that has gathered in response to the crisis that they have "rebelled" and augmented "guilt upon Israel" and that they must now resolve to return to following divine will (10:10–11), and the community agrees that they must force these women out of the community if they are "to turn aside the burning anger of our God" (10:14).

The hostility on the part of characters in the book to those whom they see as outsiders is linked to their fear of what God might do to their community, and their general view of the past is one in which their ancestors repetitively disobeyed the divine will as articulated in torah, resulting in horrific acts of punishment. When, for example, the narrative first introduces Nehemiah, we encounter him praying about Israel's sin and the destruction that resulted from their failure to keep the law of Moses (Neh 1:6–8). After Nehemiah reconstructs Jerusalem's wall he aims to repopulate the city, but before the community takes any steps in that direction, Ezra returns to the narrative scene in Neh 8 to teach the law, something that results in communal weeping (8:9) apparently because the people are aware they have been in violation of it. The teaching of the law is immediately followed by a communal confession of their sin and that of their ancestors (9:2), which leads to a public prayer by a group of Levites[28] in Neh 9:6–37 that emphasizes this failure on Israel's part to keep God's law from the moment God gave it to them at Sinai. Israel's habitual rejection of torah, the Levites say, was met with divine patience and beneficence for

---

28. The OG opens the speech in 9:6 with "and Ezra said," words that are missing in the MT, with the result that in MT 9:6–37 it is the Levites introduced in 9:4–5 who are the speakers. The additional words in the OG are likely a later addition to that textual tradition, however, as a scribe altered an earlier version to make Ezra, the important figure who teaches the law in Neh 8, the same character who now reflects on its significance in 9:6–37.

many years (9:16–25) until God finally began to punish the people with foreign invasions, rescuing them when they would cry out and instituting punishment once they inevitably abandoned the law yet again (9:26–30). If God decided not to completely annihilate Israel, the Levites say, that is due only to divine mercy (9:31), and the fact of the matter is that the exiles still suffer under foreign rule and are עבדים "slaves" in the land God originally gave to Israel, ruled now by yet another foreign power because of their sin (9:36–37).

Ezra-Nehemiah's repetitive identification of the community in Judah as the exiles from the captivity, even though they no longer live in Babylon, maintains readers' focus on the fact that divine punishment for sin as manifested in the destruction of Jerusalem and the exile has never really ended or at least has been lifted only temporarily. The community accepts the Levites' understanding of Israelite history, one of constant disobedience to torah followed by divine punishment, and so they resolve to make a written agreement that that they will follow the law from that point forward (Neh 10:29–30 [ET 28–29]). In the document they draw up they highlight four aspects of torah in particular that they agree to keep, assumedly because they believe violations of these specific laws are most likely to incite divine anger: They will not intermarry with "the peoples of the land" (10:31 [30]); they will not trade with them on the Sabbath (10:32a [31a]); they will remit debts every seventh year (10:32b [31b]); and they will supply all the material goods that the temple needs to function (10:33–40 [32–39]). In this way, then, the future wrath of God and complete destruction can be kept at bay, and perhaps the community's current experience of punishment as "slaves" to a foreign monarchy might be brought to an end, although that is not something the Levites' prayer directly requests.[29] With this more positive view of the future rooted in the community's resolve to adhere to the law, members begin to move into Jerusalem (11:1–24) as the city is now protected by the rebuilt wall constructed by Nehemiah. As readers near the end of the book, in short, they

---

29. In the broader context of Neh 8–10, it is not entirely clear what the community hopes to gain from swearing fidelity to torah, but at a minimum it is to avoid divine annihilation. It is not difficult to imagine some of the characters in this story believing that such obedience might bring an end to Persian rule, but there is largely no sense among the book's characters as a whole that Persian rule is a bad thing; for a reading of the Levites' prayer that fits this larger picture of Persian rule in Ezra-Nehemiah, see Oeming 2006.

find that the temple and city Nebuchadnezzar destroyed as punishment for their ancestors' sins have been reconstructed.

Ezra-Nehemiah, however, ends on a less positive note, for after Nehemiah returns from a trip to Babylon, where he had met with King Artaxerxes (13:6), he finds that the community has abandoned virtually all the parts of the law they had sworn to keep: They have intermarried with foreign women (13:23–27), and even a son of the high priest has done so (13:28); they are trading with foreigners on the Sabbath (13:15–18); and they have not supplied the temple personnel with their rations with the result that temple worship has been abandoned (13:10–13). Of the four laws the community swore to uphold, the only one of which Nehemiah does not find them in violation upon his return is the command to forgive debts every seventh year, and potentially that is only because the odds he would return in such a year were only one in seven. Despite the community's agreement to keep the law, they are no better at it than the earlier generations of Israel whom God repetitively subjected to punishment, something that culminated in the exile and Nebuchadnezzar's destruction of Jerusalem and the temple, punishments that have only recently been reversed. Nehemiah acts to correct the violations of the law he finds in Jerusalem on his return from Babylon, but the conclusion of the book can leave readers with a dire sense of foreboding. The community's written agreement to keep torah has not stopped them from violating it, and there is no guarantee that there will always be leaders like Nehemiah to force them to act in compliance with it (see Janzen 2017b). Even the high priest, after all, did not prevent his son from marrying an outsider woman, and given that Ezra and the Levites have described a God who needs little provocation to utterly destroy the community, a sentiment Nehemiah echoes in Neh 13:15–18 where he says God originally destroyed Jerusalem because Israel traded with foreigners on the Sabbath, such destruction hardly seems to be out of the question by the time we reach the end of the book.

The Inclusive Community:
Reading Ezra-Nehemiah after *Angels in America*

Not all interpreters have to read Ezra-Nehemiah after a writing like *Angels in America* to notice the book's exclusivism and other ethically disturbing ideas and themes. Minoritized readers in particular have been sensitive to the ways in which it draws communal boundaries in a manner that excludes and marginalizes those who are most vulnerable. As the first section of the chapter mentions, for example, Anderson (2009, 47–48) has pointed to a comparison between the story of the divorce of the foreign women in Ezra 9–10 and antimiscegenation laws in the United States, and Makhosazana Nzimande (2011, 290–92) has made a similar comparison with such laws in apartheid-era South Africa. Willa Johnson (2011, 96) points out, in fact, that Ezra 9–10 is still used in the United States to support racist behavior and oppose interracial marriage. One of Nehemiah's objections to marriage with women from the peoples of the lands is that some of their children are unable to speak the exilic community's language (Neh 13:23–24), and Jean-Pierre Ruiz (2011, 109) writes that diatribes like that against the presence of foreigners in what someone is defining as the true community sound "frighteningly familiar" to Latin American immigrants in the United States, who are often excluded from definitions of what it means to be an American because of their inability to speak English fluently. For women who struggle against exclusion in every aspect of life, says Elisabeth Cook Steike (2010, 16), Ezra 9–10 will be read only as a reflection of their own life experiences as powerless figures who are nonetheless viewed as dangerous contaminants of a "true" community.

There is, however, no universal hermeneutical rule which says that readers of biblical texts must agree with the main characters' or narrators' beliefs about God, Israel, the law, and the community's relationship to foreigners, and the problem we encounter as readers of Ezra-Nehemiah is that the powerless characters who might object to those views have no voice at all. A benefit of reading it through the lens of *Angels in America*, then, is that Kushner's play can help us imagine what those voices might sound like. While it is not only readers from very privileged contexts who can fail to recognize that the foreign women, the excluded characters in Ezra-Nehemiah, are permitted no speech at all, we are the ones who are least likely to be exposed to the speech, experiences, and stories from minoritized contexts and least likely to notice that the powerless foreign women do not represent themselves in the writing and are not allowed to speak about any other topic either. Only more powerful characters get to articulate views about what these women are like or about the concepts of appropriate kinds of change, the future, the point of the law, and God.

Reading Ezra-Nehemiah after *Angels in America* is not the only interpretive strategy available to those of us who would like to hear the foreign women speak to represent themselves and offer radically different perspectives on those issues, but it is one that challenges the other characters' monolithic and unnuanced depiction of the cosmos as something that is as frightening as the one envisioned by Roy and the angels in *Angels in America*, something those privileged with speech in Ezra-Nehemiah connect to their portrayal of the women as impure and dangerous. From the protagonists' standpoint, even the smallest communal misstep in regard to torah such as marrying foreign women or engaging in trade with foreigners on the Sabbath might result in utter annihilation, a point Ezra makes when he tries to put a stop to the former activity (Ezra 9:10–15) and that Nehemiah makes when he acts to impede the latter (Neh 13:15–18). This link they see between interaction with foreigners, and foreign women especially, and the disastrous future they fear is connected to the portrayal of God they imagine. This God may be absent from the narrative scene, just as God is in *Angels in America*, but in the minds of characters such as Ezra, Nehemiah, and the Levites who speak in the prayer of Neh 9, God is more than willing to visit annihilation on the exilic community because of the presence of these women, something that these central characters believe violates God's law. There are no powerless voices in the book to provide any opposing portrayals of the divine, and so the understandings of what the cosmos, the future, and God are like or what the point of the law is or what the community owes to the subalterns in its midst are ones articulated only by the powerful characters in the book, and this results in the maltreatment of the community's most vulnerable members.

Reading Ezra-Nehemiah after *Angels in America* does not only help us see the problems inherent in the silencing of the minoritized, something that produces a story that prioritizes the sorts of dangerously unethical worldviews held by characters like Roy and Joe, but also helps to clarify the dangers of the ways the main characters of Ezra-Nehemiah act. Given the cosmos the book's central figures imagine, one can try to amass power or clout as Roy does, hoping to use this power to protect oneself and advance one's own interests, regardless of whom this might harm. One can call for progress to stop as the angels do, part of a belief that the only acceptable change is to return to the way things were, the Reaganite worldview articulated by the angels and Joe. The main characters of Ezra-Nehemiah adopt both of these approaches. Like Roy they aim to align themselves with power, in their case with the kings of Persia, the most powerful figures on earth in the book's narrative, and claim an exclusive relationship with them among all the peoples in their region. They alone, they say, have been chosen by the Persian crown to build God's temple, despite the fact that Cyrus's command in Ezra 1:3 that the people of the God of Israel should rebuild the temple could be understood to include anyone who worships that God.[30]

As a result, the exilic community alone becomes the beneficiary of the great royal largesse shown to the temple and those associated with it at various points in the narrative. And like Joe and the angels, they want to stop change that is occurring and return things to the way they were. The men of the community themselves have chosen to marry women from outside of their group, and what characters such as Ezra, Nehemiah, and the Levites want is for this intermingling and change in the composition of the community to cease and for those women and their children to be sent away so that things can go back to the way they were when the first exiles moved from Babylon to Judah to rebuild the temple. That group, whom readers see in action in Ezra 1–6, was a better, more perfect version of Israel from the standpoint of the book's main characters, for they lived during a time when the community needed no one like Ezra to teach them the law or like the Levites to remind them of the consequences of Israel's long disobedience of it or like Nehemiah to force them into compliance with it. They remained loyal to their God and the kings through whom God works and knew that there was no question of allowing the peoples of the land to have any share in rebuilding the temple—and never even considered intermarrying with them—regardless of the fact that those peoples also worshipped Israel's God.

One of the benefits of reading Ezra-Nehemiah after *Angels in America*, however, is that the play provides us with scope to imagine how an exclusivist view of community identity is experienced by those who are excluded, and with the help of the play, which is *A Gay Fantasia on National Themes*, we can create fantasias of our own and imagine new families forming on the margins of Ezra-Nehemiah's central community, rather like the one we see in the final scene of *Perestroika*, ones that are paradigms of intermingling and that together make up a new and inclusive community. Such a family might include one or two or several women whom the main characters in Ezra-Nehemiah would consider to be foreign but who worship

---

30. In Ezra 1:3, Cyrus says that מי־בכם מכל־עמו "whoever among you from all his people"—where עמו refers to the people of YHWH—may participate in the construction of the temple. This does not define that group with a degree of specificity that would exclude Yahwists already living in Judah and its surrounding area, however, especially given that this phrase appears in a decree that Cyrus circulates throughout his whole kingdom (1:1) and not just in Babylon.

the God of Israel and who married members of the exilic community who bowed to community pressure and divorced them, forcing them from their homes along with their children. It might contain a figure from the community's elite, such as the son of the high priest who married a foreign woman (Neh 13:28) and who rejects the way others in the assembly understand the boundaries of the group. Since there were other men who, according to Ezra-Nehemiah, did not agree with the decision to force the foreign women from their midst (Ezra 10:15),[31] we could even imagine some of them as members of the families in this new community, preferring ostracization from the book's main group to abandoning the women and children they love. These families might contain figures like Hannah from *Angels in America*, women from the book's privileged group who eventually find it an ethical necessity to care for the suffering and disadvantaged around them because they have daughters-in-law and grandchildren who have been forced to leave that dominant group, causing them to now see their identities as linked to a new community of people who no longer seem like foreigners to them.

New families like these, we would imagine, could envision community very differently than the main characters in Ezra-Nehemiah do when, for example, they think about the role of the law in defining group identity. For a protagonist like Ezra, torah clearly excludes all non-Israelites from the community, and the foreign women are no more a part of Israel as Ezra defines it, regardless of which God they worship or whom they have married, than gay men are a part of America as Roy understands it. In both the play and the biblical book, the law is an extremely powerful tool in the creation of national identity. In *Angels in America*, it is so important for Roy to defy the disbarment committee and remain a lawyer until he dies because, he says, "Lawyers are … the High Priests of America. We alone know the words that made America. Out of thin air. We alone know how to use The Words" (215). One can either choose to make the law or

---

31. MT 10:15 refers to four men who עמדו על זאת "stood against this," but the OG has read a Hebrew text with עמדי על זאת "were with me concerning this." The OG's reading, however, makes little sense, given that Ezra 10 is a third-person narrative and we have no sense that this verse is the direct speech of any of the characters in the chapter who would refer to themselves at this point in the first person. The parallel verse of 1 Esd 9:14, which says that the men ἐπεδέξαντο κατὰ ταῦτα "approved of these things," is likely based on the same Hebrew text behind the OG but translated so that it fits the third-person context of the narrative here.

subject oneself to it, as Roy says, and we can see figures like Ezra and the Levites creating a postexilic Israel with their control of The Words of the law, shaping it and Israelite identity through their interpretation of torah. Yet one need not read the law of Moses as characters like Ezra and the Levites do, and we can imagine the new families forming on the margins of Ezra-Nehemiah's Israel speaking as they represent themselves, emphasizing different aspects of the law in order to create new understandings of who the community can be. Their reading of torah is one done through the hermeneutic of Belize's hard law of love and so understands it not as a basis to enforce exclusion and stasis but to move the community forward to include them as integral members of it. In our fantasia, their Great Work begins as they insist, like Prior at the end of *Angels in America*, that "we are not going away" and that "we will be citizens."

This fantasia imagines a new community challenging the interpretation of torah by Ezra and the other powerful figures in the book who believe that the law demands that the women whom they view as foreign be driven from the community, even if they are Yahwists and have married community members. Our new families could point out that Exod 34:11–16 and Deut 7:1–4, the passages in torah that both warn of the dangers of intermarrying with foreign peoples and that provide lists of proscribed nations from which Israel may not take marriage partners, collectively name the Amorites, Canaanites, Hittites, Perizzites, Hivites, Jebusites, and Girgashites. As a result, this new and inclusive community could argue that none of the women whom Ezra and others have determined are illegitimate marriage partners actually are, since none of them would have understood themselves as belonging to any of those nations; as far as we can tell, these were not ethnonyms used by anyone in the region in the postexilic period.[32] More to the point in the context of the narrative world of Ezra-Nehemiah, the ancestors of "the people of the land" whom we first encounter in Ezra-Nehemiah were not originally from Canaan (Ezra 4:2), just as, according to torah, Israel's ancestors were not, and so the members of our new community can point out that the women are not descended

---

32. It is not clear that all of the groups named in those chapters actually existed outside of Judean traditions about the past. But even to take the Hittites as an example of a people named in torah and well-known from other ancient Near Eastern writings, there is virtually no archaeological or inscriptional evidence that would suggest Hittites ever lived in the areas encompassed by the Iron Age kingdoms of Israel and Judah and certainly none from the Persian period (see Gilan 2013).

from any of the peoples named in Exod 34 and Deut 7. Torah never issues a blanket prohibition on the marriage of foreigners, regardless as to what Nehemiah appears to believe (Neh 13:23–27), and never refers to "the people(s) of the land(s)" when identifying groups into which Israelites must not marry. Moreover, our new families could argue that when Ezra and other community leaders imply that torah forbids marriage to "the Ammonites, the Moabites, (and) the Egyptians" (Ezra 9:1), they are simply twisting divine law in an exclusionary fashion, because these groups are never named in torah's lists of proscribed nations for marriage partners.[33]

From the standpoint of our new families hoping to guide Israel's reading of torah through a compassionate and inclusive hard law of love, Ezra's reference to the "uncleanness," "abominations," and "impurity" of the peoples of the lands (Ezra 9:11) that in his eyes demand that "the holy seed" of Israel have nothing to do with them appears as another misunderstanding or deliberate misinterpretation of torah, since at no point does the law describe non-Israelites with such terms (see Clauss 2011, 128; Harrington 2012, 11–12). Ezra's understanding of the law, God, and the way God will respond with destruction to the marriages of the foreign women convinces the community members of Ezra-Nehemiah that to act "according to the law" they must force all foreign women from their midst (Ezra 10:3). The new families could rightly point out that torah actually provides no guidance as to what to do even in the case when Israelites intermarry with individuals from the nations named in Exod 34 and Deut 7 (Japhet 2006, 141–51). As much as the community leadership might claim otherwise in Ezra 9–10 (or Neh 10 and 13, for that matter), they neither think nor act according to the law when it comes to the question of marriage to women whom they define as foreign, and this is certainly true if one wants to read torah as a hard law of love.

And if we use *Angels in America* to help us imagine how our new community of families might do more than just critique the ways in which Ezra and other privileged characters in Ezra-Nehemiah have chosen to

---

33. In this imaginary political discourse, our new families would have to deal with the objection that Deut 23:4 [ET 3] forbids Ammonites and Moabites from entering the assembly; in our context, the real question in such a case would then be whether a woman from one of these groups who married an Israelite man could then be considered an Israelite or Judean herself. Nonetheless, at no point does torah list the Ammonites and Moabites (or Egyptians) among the proscribed nations of illegitimate marriage partners.

read the words of the law, we can go further and picture them using torah in a more ethical and inclusive way to define community—a way that models Belize's hard law of love and so creates space and acceptance for them within Israel. We can imagine them, then, as beginning their reading of the law by referring to the command in torah to love one's neighbor as oneself (Lev 19:18), and point out that, even if one believes that some of the members of these new families are foreign because they are not descended from the Babylonian exiles and that the term "neighbor" in this context is synonymous with "fellow Israelite," torah includes laws that assume not only that foreigners can live within Israel's midst but that Israel also has a particular obligation to care for their well-being (e.g., Exod 22:20 [ET 21]; Lev 19:33; Deut 24:17).[34] Torah states, in fact, that foreigners may participate in some Israelite religious activities, including some that take place at the temple (e.g., Exod 12:19; Lev 22:18–20; Deut 16:11, 14). As the families we envision rethink what the law has to say about Israel and foreigners, then, they can argue that worship at the temple should not exclude them and that the temple itself should not stand as some sort of monument to the community's exclusivist vision of its identity.[35]

The law of Exod 12:48–49, these families could point out, actually allows any family of foreigners within Israel who wish to celebrate Passover to become "like a native" through the ritual of male circumcision and participate in that religious festival. If this does not make such resident aliens precisely the same as Israelites, it also indicates that they are welcome to participate in the worship of the God of Israel and that as far as torah is concerned foreigners are not somehow naturally impure with no right to live among Israelites and worship Israel's God.[36] And even aside from that particular commandment, torah insists that the same law

---

34. To be clear, my point is not that torah broadcasts a monolithic portrayal of how Israel should treat the גר but that it is possible to make the sort of argument that I am sketching out when reading torah as a whole. For perspectives on the changing status of the גר (and נכרי, תושב, and זר) in torah, see, e.g., Zehnder 2005, 311–401; Albertz 2011; Nihan 2011.

35. *Angels in America*, as Ranen Omer-Sherman (2007b) points out, puts the AIDS victim in the place of the vulnerable outsider whom the biblical prophets—and, as I have noted here, the biblical laws—insist that it is the community's responsibility to include.

36. The Hebrew word אזרח "native" appears in the Bible only in contradistinction to גר "resident alien," and in Num 15:29 it refers specifically to Israelites. (MT Ps 37:35 also uses אזרח but given the context and the witness of the OG, which uses the word

applies both to the natives of and aliens in Israel (so Exod 12:49; Lev 24:22; Num 9:14; 15:15–16, 29); as Lev 19:34 puts it, the foreign inhabitant and native within Israel must be treated the same way, and so "you will love the resident alien as yourself."

Important characters in Ezra-Nehemiah's story act as if such laws do not exist, however, and in the book the powerless are never given the chance to represent themselves or to explain what The Words of the law say about intermingling and what Israel owes to the powerless. The worldviews of some readers might predispose them to see the socially powerful main characters of a biblical narrative as heroes, but reading Ezra-Nehemiah after encountering *Angels in America* can lead us to understand them very differently. We might now think of them as villains or antiheroes, rather like Roy in *Angels in America*. If anyone in the play could be described as a villain he would seem to qualify, but it helps to know that he too is minoritized. It seems in part his awareness of how America has treated gays, Jews, and the disabled that has driven him to see a dangerous cosmos that he believes forces him to act selfishly and cruelly, siding with the same sociopolitical forces that benefit those who despise him because he is minoritized. In Ezra-Nehemiah, figures such as Ezra, the Levites, and Nehemiah live in an understanding of Israel shaped by the vast destruction Babylon visited upon Jerusalem, and this has become their key to understanding God, torah, and the future. Yet even Roy finds redemption of a sort in the play through the forgiveness Ethel and Belize offer him after his death, an acceptance of him as a gay Jewish man that he could not allow himself. Forgiveness, as Belize puts it, is "where love and justice finally meet" (266), and if there is no place for Roy's loathing of humanity and of himself in the vision of heaven or a utopic America that Belize articulates—"You ain't there," he tells Roy as part of this description (223)—there can at least be some understanding of why he became the sort of person he did. And forgiveness means that there is room in the new family at the end of *Angels in America* for someone like Louis, who abandoned Prior when he needed him most but who eventually realized how much a child of Reagan he had become and who acted to make amends and ask for forgiveness.

Those vulnerable to the depredations of dominant groups can see the importance of a hard law of love precisely because of the lack of such love

---

κέδρους, the MT has a copying error for an earlier ארז "cedar.") See also Kaminsky 2009, 6; Kelly 2013.

that has been shown to them; as Harper says, suffering and devastation can move people to change and migrate and build things, "ravaged, heartbroken, and free." We can imagine, then, the new families forming at the margins of Ezra-Nehemiah's main group using their experience of suffering and exclusion to reconstruct community as one that will include them because they make it into one that sees torah as constructed around the principle of the hard law of love that emphasizes support for the powerless. We might see them as modeling this law not only in their care and responsibility for each other but also in the understanding and forgiveness they are willing to show the members of Ezra-Nehemiah's main group, at least the ones who want to make amends and ask for forgiveness, so as to join them in this Great Work of rebuilding an inclusive community.

Nonetheless, their utopic political vision would steadfastly oppose important aspects of the ways those characters as portrayed in Ezra-Nehemiah see the world. The reconstructed inclusive community, for example, will have to talk about the future and the ways in which humans and God might choose to shape it very differently than the characters who speak in the book. God is no more present in Ezra-Nehemiah than in *Angels in America*, but characters in both works have a fair bit to say in regard to what they think God is like. For Prior a God who has abandoned the world to dreadful suffering is not a God worth contemplating. So perhaps we can imagine our new families objecting in a similar fashion to claims that God is willing to enact a vast destruction of Israel because some of its men have married women from outside of the community or because some of its members trade with foreigners on the Sabbath. They can imagine instead a God who gave a law to Moses commanding care for foreigners who dwell in their midst and who allow such people to worship the God of Israel along with them. They can point out as well that no matter what sort of command Cyrus has given as to who should construct the temple or how one chooses to interpret his words in this regard, the community has no religious or ethical obligation to allow an imperial monarch to define who can and cannot be associated with that place of worship.

In our liberative imagination sparked by reading Ezra-Nehemiah after *Angels in America*, then, we can envision the book's powerless characters forming their own visions of community identity and beginning a Great Work that aims to transform the group we see in Ezra-Nehemiah as they model a hard law of love based in responsibility and care for the suffering. Even if, for the time being, they can remain only on the margins of this postexilic society in Palestine, we can picture them as aiming to make themselves citizens of a new and better community they will have transformed, one in which they are truly citizens, "dreaming ahead" to better understandings of God, the future, and the law. Like Harper as we last encounter her in *Angels in America*, they may long for the families they left behind, even though their husbands refused to stand up to the community's pressure to divorce them and send them away, but they might also experience such devastation as providing them with energy to create new and better families and to transform the dominant community on whose behalf Ezra, the Levites, and Nehemiah speak. Political change like this might seem difficult to envision, but our new families could work with Louis's belief that "you can't wait around for a theory" to begin a Great Work of perestroika that restructures community in an inclusive way.

Someone could object that the result of such a reading in which we imagine the powerless characters of Ezra-Nehemiah as representing themselves only avoids the problems raised by what the book actually says, replacing this text with what we would like it to say, but that is not really true. This is a reading that takes seriously the claims of the main characters about things such as God, the nature of community, and the law of Moses and then, thanks in important part to reading the book after *Angels in America*, rejects them as inadequate. Many biblical characters and narrators say and do things with which we have ethical objections, and in the end it is up to us to evaluate such words and actions. We will always read biblical texts through the lenses of other texts—which will include those of our own worldviews and experiences—and when our acceptance of those other texts commits us to ethical action for liberation, we have an obligation to create interpretations of biblical literature that do not contribute to the problem of oppression. One could object as well that the work in this part of the chapter has ended up with a scholar from the demographic center of biblical studies speaking for or in place of powerless characters in a biblical story, and while that is obviously true, I am not speaking in the place of actual readers from disadvantaged contexts.

In reading after authors from minoritized social locations, I can make no assumptions as to how such readers might regard my interpretive work, as much as I might hope that it will prove to be of emancipatory value to some of them. Readers from other contexts who use different texts to read Ezra-Nehemiah—including those of their own experiences and worldviews—can come to conclusions in regard to the significance of this biblical writing that sound like the one in this chapter or that might be rather different, so this particular work of reading Ezra-Nehemiah after *Angels in*

America will not necessarily be useful in some contexts of emancipatory struggle. For example, Roger Nam (2019) sees in the speech of Ezra-Nehemiah's dominant characters the same sort of concern to preserve a certain view of community that Korean repatriates manifest in their attempts to maintain their culture, while Nzimande (2011) notes that even though African women are often portrayed like the foreign women of Ezra 9–10, the postapartheid Black community of South Africa can still identify with the sort of fear expressed by the main characters of Ezra-Nehemiah that their unique culture might disappear. These readings do not ignore the exclusionary rhetoric of the book's main characters, but such interpreters also empathize with them insofar as their own communities' trauma and displacement lead them to echo Rabbi Chemelwitz's concern to preserve an "ancient, ancient culture and home."

Other minoritized interpretations of Ezra-Nehemiah can sound more like the one in this chapter, and this gives me some confidence that my own interpretive work has liberative potential. Wil Gafney (2011), for example, discusses the dangers inherent in the ways the narrative voice and main characters of the book privilege imperial power, while Vaka'uta (2011, 122–31) points to the problem posed by Ezra's description of the "impurity" and "uncleanness" of the people of the land, something that reflects the way some European colonizers described the peoples whose lands they appropriated. Their work, in short, emphasizes the dangers of allowing the powerful to characterize and speak for the powerless, a problem that my interpretation recognizes and addresses with inspiration from *Angels in America*. My reading of Ezra-Nehemiah shares important similarities with that of María Andrade Vinueza (2017), and she argues that while Ezra 9–10 dehumanizes the foreign women of the story we must acknowledge the fear of communal destruction that motivates the more powerful characters to order the divorces. To deal with this issue, she also suggests reading the book in dialogue with other pieces of literature, although she specifically mentions other biblical texts that are more accepting of foreigners. I have done that here by turning to laws in torah that portray Israel as a community inclusive of foreigners, but it is my reading of Ezra-Nehemiah after *Angels in America* that allows me to imagine the subaltern women themselves seizing upon The Words of the law to forge an inclusive community.

When my interpretive strategy allows me to see some of the same problems in a biblical writing that some of my colleagues from minoritized contexts do and even to arrive at similar solutions as some of them, then it seems more likely that some might find it to be of potential emancipatory value, even though that will obviously not be the case for every minoritized context, and individual disadvantaged readers would have to decide if it provides a kind of reflection and imagination that could be put to practical use in their specific situations. The reading of this chapter at least has the benefit of focusing readers' attention on the problem of the silencing of the book's subaltern characters, a problem that interpreters from demographically dominant social locations who are often not used to hearing minoritized voices can fail to notice. Attending to this issue raises interpretive problems similar to those in Daniel that are the result of the absence of any powerless characters in that narrative, but the reading of this chapter allows me to go further than I did in the previous one in terms of envisioning an emancipatory response to the absence of powerless voices, something that was possible because *Angels in America* is somewhat more specific than *The Sympathizer* as to the direction the subjugated characters of its narrative world can take in response to their suffering. It can help privileged readers like me find liberation from an interpretive tendency to see the socially central characters of biblical narratives as heroes, even when their exclusionary visions of community can sound like those of racists in the contemporary world, enabling us to side with the subalterns of the story when the book permits them no voice at all. If we can see the character of Daniel as I construct him in chapter 2— someone who is poised to notice and listen to and follow the revolutionary lead of the powerless—as a model for the beginning of the hermeneutical journey mainstream biblical scholarship should be on if it wishes to engage in ethical interpretation, then this reading of Ezra-Nehemiah after *Angels in America* gives us a concrete sense of what one further step on this interpretive path can look like.

4
THE GRACE THEY COULD IMAGINE: SUFFERING AND THE SUBALTERN COMMUNITY IN *BELOVED* AND LAMENTATIONS

Introduction

Reading Ezra-Nehemiah after *Angels in America* has allowed us to ask about the extent to which we should agree with the views about God and community voiced by the major characters in that book, ones who identify a group of powerless women in their society as a kind of cancerous presence that must be cut out and removed from the group. Because the subalterns in Ezra-Nehemiah are not allowed to speak and are represented by the book's more powerful characters, reading it after *Angels in America* provided us with an avenue to imagine how some of those figures, identified and derided as foreign by those in the book privileged with speech, might have represented themselves and described community, the law, and God in inclusive rather than exclusive ways. Lamentations, in contrast, is made up in large part of the voices of speakers who have suffered unimaginable trauma, having survived the Babylonian destruction of Judah and Jerusalem in the sixth century BCE,[1] witnessed the great

---

1. Lamentations never directly mentions Babylon or any specific historical event but clearly reflects the destruction of Jerusalem and an exile of some of its population and is largely dated by scholars to the decades after the Babylonian devastation of the city; for this consensus see, e.g., Middlemas 2005, 178; Boase 2006, 3-4. There is no strong evidence that would suggest that more than one author is responsible for Lamentations (see the arguments in this regard in Assis 2009), and since Second Isaiah appears to respond to issues raised in all five poems of Lamentations (see the extensive study of this issue in Willey 1997; as well as Tiemeyer 2011, 352–60), it is a work of the

slaughter that accompanied it, and experienced rape, starvation, and torture in its aftermath.

Most of the characters who speak in the book are obviously subalterns as Mignolo (2005, 382–83) defines the term, the *damné(e)s*[2] whom dominant forces understand to be less than human and who are treated as if their lives have no value. Perhaps the defining characteristic of subalterns, those whose humanity is invisible to the powerful, says Nelson Maldonado-Torres (2007, 255–57), is their embeddedness in social locations that force them to confront the possibility of their death on a daily basis, the situation described by the voices of Lamentations. These figures, like those privileged with speech in Ezra-Nehemiah, work with particular assumptions as to what God is like and how God plans on treating their community, and just as in Ezra-Nehemiah, there is no divine speech to validate or contradict that which we see in the book. There is, however, much more variety in the ways the subaltern voices of Lamentations understand things such as God and the future than is the case for the characters who speak in Ezra-Nehemiah, and while speakers in Lamentations sometimes sound as if they largely share the worldview of the main characters of Ezra-Nehemiah, that is not always the case.

All of the speakers of Lamentations' five poems attempt to greater and lesser extents to come to grips with or explain the anguish of Jerusalem's survivors. Sometimes, as we will see, they can advance the sort of justifications found in other biblical books such as Kings, Jeremiah, and Ezekiel— or, for that matter, Ezra-Nehemiah—that make sense of the destruction of Judah and Jerusalem by placing the blame on the victims, who according to such writings suffer the just consequences for their sin and that of their ancestors at the hands of a God who has rightly punished them with slaughter and terror. After reading Daniel, which ignores the powerless, and Ezra-Nehemiah, in which the main characters conceive of them as a dangerous presence, we may be troubled by a biblical writing that allows subalterns to represent themselves but that sometimes has them speak as

---

exilic period. See also the arguments on linguistic grounds for a date of the book in the exilic period in Dobbs-Allsopp 1998.

2. Mignolo borrows the term *damnés* from the title of Frantz Fanon's book *Les damnés de la terre*, or *The Wretched of the Earth*. Fanon (1963, 250) uses the word to describe the identity of the colonized as created in colonialism, which resulted in "a furious determination to deny the other person"—non-Europeans, in the context of this discussion—"all attributes of humanity."

if they deserve the slavery, starvation, slaughter, and rape their community suffers and do not deserve to be treated in accordance with the most basic aspects of the dignity inherent to all humans. Lamentations, however, refuses to come to a clear and authoritative conclusion about these and related issues, such as whether God can be defined by more than violence or whether we should think of the lives of Jerusalem's survivors as things that matter or whether that community might envision a future that is more than their current suffering.

This chapter approaches that variety of perspectives in Lamentations after *Beloved*, a novel by the African American Nobel laureate Toni Morrison, which follows the lives of Black characters during and after slavery in the United States and privileges vulnerable voices speaking from a traumatized community whose experiences of slavery, torture, hunger, and rape are not dissimilar to those articulated by the speakers of Lamentations. What might be most helpful for many readers who feel compelled to draw some sort of conclusion from the speech of the voices in the biblical book is seeing how the characters of *Beloved*, like those of Lamentations, are confronted by justifications of their suffering that are rooted in dominant cultural explanations that disregard the value of the lives of the members of a subjugated group. Just as some speakers in Lamentations blame the traumatized survivors of Jerusalem for their suffering, as other biblical books do, the Black characters of *Beloved* have endured similar horrors because of a dominant white culture in the United States that views and treats them as subhuman. In both writings, what we might understand to be the characters' central problem lies in finding ways for them and their communities to imagine a future for themselves that is more than simply a mode of survival through their present suffering, something that demands envisioning a world in which they can understand themselves as valuable enough to be worthy of such a future. *Beloved* can help readers see the difficulty in claiming, as many biblical books do, that horrific communal suffering is the result of divine punishment and thus that it is the victims' fault.

It may be readers who come from places of great socioeconomic privilege who would find it most difficult to hear the voices of Lamentations as those of subaltern characters, since it would be more difficult for them than for readers in other social locations to imagine the pain of repetitively being told that one's community is treated as if its members' lives do not matter because they deserve no better; it may not even occur to some of us whose identities lie at dominant intersections of power that this is in fact the message of biblical writings that blame victims who have survived massive traumatic events. Reading Lamentations after *Beloved*, however, helps make it clear that much of the book's poetry is being spoken by characters who have been told this, and this reading strategy can allow us to hear the ways in which these subaltern speakers try to imagine a future that is more than just constant pain. In the novel, as we will see, such attempts involve the effort on the part of the Black characters to value and love themselves, an effort of imagination that must overcome the ways in which white American society portrays them and that in this story can only be accomplished with community support. They are generally, although not always, more successful in this regard than the speakers of Lamentations, who often struggle to see themselves as humans whose lives matter enough to be worthy of humane treatment.

Reading the biblical book after *Beloved* allows us to see Lamentations as an unfinished conversation in which we can ask how the voices of that ancient community might go as far as some of the characters in the novel in imagining a future for themselves where, despite what other biblical writings might say, they can understand the lives of their members as things of value, an idea that demands imagining a God who believes that as well. But *Beloved* also cautions readers not to ignore the continued debilitating effects of massive trauma on communities and individuals, which does not entirely disappear even for characters in the novel who do imagine and enact better and more hopeful lives for themselves. As the final section of this chapter will discuss, it can be difficult for privileged readers in particular to hear subaltern characters whose suffering is rooted in deeply established socioeconomic structures. Those of us who benefit from such structures can impose clear and happy endings over subaltern speech that is actually much more open-ended and ambiguous, an act that allows us to avoid noticing how ethically problematic those structures are.

I have suggested that Daniel, as I make sense of the character in chapter 2, could serve as a model for the beginning of a more ethical hermeneutical journey on which the mainstream of biblical studies could embark; in my reading Daniel is someone ready to notice the absence of the oppressed and any concern for them. He is ready, in other words, to prioritize the people and experiences and interests to which he, the empires for whom he labors, and even the heavenly messages he receives have paid no attention. Readers of biblical texts from dominant social locations, like their counterparts in biblical stories, do not always instinctively listen for voices of the powerless and are not always able to hear them articulating positions about the value of their lives that those readers do not expect to hear. One of the most basic things biblical scholars should learn to do is to notice the absence of those disadvantaged by things such as gender identity, race, poverty, class, indigeneity, disability, and sexual orientation—whether characters in biblical narratives or fellow scholars whose work the discipline's mainstream largely treats as superfluous—since a further step on an emancipatory hermeneutical journey demands listening for and noticing their voices when they do speak. In the case of subaltern biblical characters, we will sometimes have to read after the minoritized just to notice that they are present and to find liberative ways to make sense of their speech in its fullness and ambiguity.

Community and the Imagination of Grace in *Beloved*

Beloved opens in 1873 at a house in Cincinnati the novel calls 124, named after its street address.[3] Its inhabitants in that narrative present are Sethe, who we soon discover escaped from slavery in Kentucky eighteen years previously (8),[4] her daughter Denver, and the ghost of a baby who died before she was two (5). "124 was spiteful," the narrator tells us at the very opening of the novel, "full of a baby's venom" (3), the spirit's anger the result of having had her throat cut (5–6). It surprises none of the Black characters of *Beloved*, all of whom survived slavery or live with those who did, that a ghost should haunt a house with Black inhabitants. Sethe's mother-in-law, Baby Suggs, who lived at 124 until her death eight years before the events of the narrative's present (8), tells Sethe that there is "not a house in the country ain't packed to its rafters with some dead Negro's grief. We lucky this ghost is a baby. My husband's spirit was to come back in here? or yours? Don't talk to me" (6). Denver, born on the Ohio River as Sethe fled slavery, is said to have "lived all her life in a house peopled by the living activity of the dead" (35). Ghosts, literal and metaphorical, pursue the characters from the beginning of the novel to its end, and in a real sense *Beloved* could be said to be about characters striving to create a

---

3. Some readers see particular kinds of numerology at work in the house number; see, e.g., Washington 2005, 175; Ng 2011, 233.

4. Morrison 2004. The first edition of the novel was published in 1987. Page numbers from the book are cited in the text. Italicization in quotations from the book is present in the novel.

future made up of more than the suffering that is constantly present as the spectral-like pain from the past.

Whether in the form of the ghost or in bursts of memories, the traumatic past of slavery constantly intrudes on and dominates the lives of the novel's characters. The narrative is continually interrupted by horrific memories and stories of the past that force their way into the characters' present.[5] Readers learn early on that Sethe was pregnant when she fled slavery in Kentucky and that immediately before she escaped two nephews of the farm's white manager, called schoolteacher, raped her by taking her milk from her breasts and then whipped her to the point where she was left for the rest of her life without feeling in the skin on her back (18–21). She can still be taken by surprise, the narrator tells us, by the vision of "boys hanging from the most beautiful sycamores in the world" (7). She recalls at one point the memory of a woman from the plantation where she was born informing her that she was her mother, a woman whose body Sethe later encountered as so badly mutilated that she could not recognize her among the pile of Black corpses where she lay (72–73). Paul D, who had been enslaved with Sethe on the same farm in Kentucky and had not seen her since her escape eighteen years earlier, arrives at 124 near the beginning of the novel with his own storehouse of traumatic stories, revealed slowly over the course of the book. His memories from before, during, and after the Civil War include ones of

> Negroes so stunned, or hungry, or tired or bereft it was a wonder they recalled or said anything. Who, like him, had hidden in caves and fought owls for food; who, like him, stole from pigs; who, like him, slept in trees in the day and walked by night; who, like him, had buried themselves in slop and jumped in wells to avoid regulators, raiders, paterollers, veterans, hill men, posses and merrymakers. Once he met a Negro about fourteen years old who lived by himself in the woods and said he couldn't remember living anywhere else. He saw a witless coloredwoman jailed and hanged for stealing ducks she believed were her own babies. (78)

Here, as is so often the case in the novel, larger summaries of Black suffering during and after slavery are interspersed among personal accounts of the characters, such as Paul D's memories of prison in Georgia where the

---

5. See, e.g., Finney 1990; Brandt 2017, 400–405. For a discussion of this aspect of *Beloved* as a reflection of trauma, see Wyatt 2021.

Black inmates were raped daily by the white guards (126–27) or the story of a character by the name of Stamp Paid who was forced to hand over his wife to his owner's son so he could rape her whenever he chose (217–18); as in the passage above, many of the characters' own horrific experiences have been widely shared by Blacks elsewhere.

The Civil War, which the narrator tells us had "short, flashy results" (201), has not greatly lessened the terror experienced by the Black characters in the novel. As Paul D left Alabama at the war's end, he saw twelve dead Blacks including women and children in the first eighteen miles of his journey (317). He recalls being in a city after the war and seeing "five women arriving with fourteen female children. All their men—brothers, uncles, fathers, husbands, sons—had been picked off one by one. They had a single piece of paper directing them to a preacher on DeVore Street. The war had been over four or five years then, but nobody white or black seemed to know it" (62–63).[6] And in the novel's narrative present, Stamp Paid reflects that

> whitefolks were still on the loose. Whole towns wiped clean of Negroes; eighty-seven lynchings in one year alone in Kentucky; four colored schools burned to the ground; grown men whipped like children; children whipped like adults; black women raped by the crew; property taken, necks broken. He smelled skin, skin and hot blood. The skin was one thing, but human blood cooked in a lynch fire was a whole other thing. (212)

It is no wonder, then, that the characters try so hard not to remember the past. After escaping from prison, Paul D "had shut down a generous portion of his head" (49) and kept his memories "in that tobacco tin buried in his chest where a red heart used to be. Its lid rusted shut" (85). For Sethe, "the future was a matter of keeping the past at bay. The 'better life' she believed she and Denver were living was simply not that other one" (51). It is no simple thing to keep the past at bay, however, not only because whites continue to visit the past horrors associated with slavery upon Blacks but also because of the power of past traumatic events to shape the present

---

6. As Kimberly Chabot Davis (1998, 246) notes, there are few references in *Beloved* to historical events, like the end of the Civil War, as such things made little difference in the characters' lives. In the novel, she writes, history is more "an amalgamation of local narratives."

of the traumatized, something Sethe refers to as "rememory" and that is much more powerful and corporeal than memory, since it is something others can see. As she explains the concept to Denver,

> someday you be walking down the road and you hear something or see something going on. So clear. And you think it's you thinking it up. A thought picture. But no. It's when you bump into a rememory that belongs to somebody else. Where I was before I came here, that place is real. It's never going away. Even if the whole farm—every tree and grass blade of it dies. The picture is still there and what's more, if you go there—you who never was there—if you go there and stand in the place where it was, it will happen again; it will be there for you, waiting for you. (43–44)[7]

One reason why the past can seem inescapable to those who have survived the traumatic events associated with slavery has to do with the way they warp one's understanding of self, family, and communal life. Slaves were torn from their families,[8] and Baby Suggs, for example, gave birth to seven children, all of whom were taken from her. When it came to the birth of her youngest, "It wasn't worth the trouble to try to learn features you would never see change into adulthood anyway" (163).[9] Nor had she been allowed to know herself much better than her children, because her life had been so closely circumscribed by terror: "Could she sing? (Was it nice to hear when she did?) Was she pretty? Was she a good friend? Could she have been a loving mother? A faithful wife? Have I got a sister and does she favor me? If my mother knew me would she like me?" (165). Forced separation from family and friends was so frequent and horrific that Paul D, who had seen one of his friends driven mad in slavery (80–83) and another burned alive (266–67), concludes that it is risky for Sethe to

---

7. For a discussion of the concept of rememory in *Beloved*, see Perez 2014, 196–97. As Melanie Anderson (2013, 67) says, rememory in *Beloved* is "an obsessively repetitive trauma."

8. An important aspect of the novel, in fact, is its reflection of the many ways in which slavery interfered with the ability to form healthy familial relationships; see King 2014, 161.

9. To say that Baby Suggs denies her love for her children (so Putnam 2011, 38) is to miss the complexity of her story, which describes the tragedy of being denied the opportunity to know them and, as discussed below, the problems the novel raises about the very concept of love in the context of slavery.

love Denver as she does. "The best thing, he knew, was to love just a little bit; everything, just a little bit, so when they broke its back, or shoved it in a croaker sack, well, maybe you'd have a little love left over for the next one" (54). Ella, a member of the local Black community, had been repetitively raped as a slave by a white father and son and had allowed the child born of the rape to die (305); it is not surprising to learn that "she considered love a serious disability" (301).

The perversion of human relationships and growth of self that result from slavery and racialized terror, then, is one way in which the past maintains its tenacious hold on the characters' lives. Sethe's description of rememory sounds like the way in which victims of posttraumatic stress disorder do not remember but relive traumatic events through things like fugue states and hallucinations (see Kolk 2014, 66–69), but the past also invades the present in an even more concrete way twenty-eight days after Sethe's escape from Kentucky in 1855 when schoolteacher arrives at 124 to return her and her children to slavery. Black lives are subject to the whims of white hatred and violence even outside of slave states and, for that matter, even after the Civil War, because whites regard them precisely the same way that they did before 1865; the military victory of one white state over another has not changed that. That is not to say that the novel portrays all white characters as alike; the white family who owns 124, for example, supported the abolition of slavery, but from the perspective of the Black community this just means that "they hated slavery worse than they hated slaves" (162).

At the root of this white hatred, reflects Stamp Paid, is their belief that Blacks are not human but dangerous animals: "Whitepeople believed that whatever the manners, under every dark skin was a jungle. Swift unnavigable waters, swinging screaming baboons, sleeping snakes, red gums ready for their sweet white blood."[10] This belief makes whites "bloody, silly, worse than even they wanted to be, so scared were they of the jungle they had made. The screaming baboon lived under their own white skin; the red gums were their own" (234). Baby Suggs's view of whites is similar: "Even when they thought they were behaving, it was a far cry from what real humans did." When Sethe argues that not all whites are the same, Baby Suggs tells her that "there's more of us they drowned than there is all of

---

10. For a discussion of the background and context of the theme of cannibalism in portrayals of Blacks in the Africana experience, see Rice 1998.

them ever lived from the start of time. Lay down your sword. This ain't a battle; it's a rout" (287). When schoolteacher arrives to manage the farm where Sethe and Paul D were enslaved, he teaches his two nephews a racist pseudoscience that involves classifying the animal and human characteristics of the Black slaves (227–28); it is no wonder, then, that those nephews rape the pregnant Sethe by taking her milk from her breasts "like I was the cow, no, the goat, back behind the stable because it was too nasty to stay in with the horses" (237).

So it is not only white control of power and violence that keeps the past of slavery alive in the present, it is also their control of language that defines Blacks as animals whose lives are of no more value than those of expensive livestock. After a slave explains to schoolteacher why killing and eating a stoat caught on the farm does not amount to theft, which is how schoolteacher views the act, "schoolteacher beat him anyway to show him that definitions belonged to the definers—not the defined" (225). It was his intention to educate not only his nephews but to "reeducate" Blacks who believed they were human (259) instead of "gelded workhorses whose neigh and whinny could not be translated into a language responsible humans spoke" (148).

Given these factors, merely escaping slavery or living in post–Civil War America does not amount to freedom in its fullest sense. Nonetheless, upon arrival at 124 in the first month after fleeing Kentucky, Sethe begins to build real relationships with family and the larger Black community in Cincinnati: "Freeing yourself was one thing; claiming ownership of that freedom was another" (111–12), the narrator explains at that point. At the time, Baby Suggs spoke in Black churches and in warmer weather acted as "an unchurched preacher" in an outdoor space called the Clearing. Her spiritual leadership consists of what Stamp Paid calls "the Word" (210), and it does not involve homilies about God or sin or forgiveness but calling on the Black community to laugh, dance, and cry (102–3). To live in freedom demands imagining and accepting a different world than that spoken and enforced by whites; the only grace they could have, Baby Suggs says, "was the grace they could imagine."

> "Here," she said, "in this here place, we flesh; flesh that weeps, laughs; flesh that dances on bare feet in grass. Love it. Love it hard. Yonder they do not love your flesh. They despise it. They don't love your eyes; they'd just as soon pick em out. No more do they love the skin on your back. Yonder they flay it. And O my people they do not love your hands. Those

they only use, tie, bind, chop off and leave empty. Love your hands! Love them. Raise them up and kiss them. Touch others with them, pat them together, stroke them on your face 'cause they don't love that either. *You got to love it, you!*" (103–4)

Without this grace, this communal will to think of themselves with words and ideas different from the ones used by whites, without being able to value themselves as humans to whom love is due, there could be no future for them that is more than just survival.

But Baby Suggs's Word cannot entirely displace white words and violence that also aim to define the reality of the novel's Black characters. As Sethe learns upon arrival at 124 to claim ownership of her freed self within the Black community of Cincinnati, a spontaneous party and feast take place at the house, but afterward the community is "furious" that they had gathered there to share such "reckless generosity," seeing it as "uncalled-for pride" (162). One way to understand such anger directed at Baby Suggs for a celebration to which they contributed and in which they participated is anger at themselves—even if they cannot admit that—for acting as if they were free and could celebrate as if they had a future ungoverned by white terror.[11] It is one thing to be told to love and value oneself but quite another to accept that Word when even self-love is a dangerous thing, as "anybody white could take your whole self for anything that came to mind" (295). The rage the community directs toward 124 results in their refusal to warn the household of the approach of schoolteacher and three others only a week after that celebration (185), and as a result these four apocalyptic horsemen arrive and confound Sethe's developing sense of freedom and the love she had been experiencing for her children, who had, with the help of the underground railroad, successfully escaped slavery just before she did. "I couldn't love em proper in Kentucky because they wasn't mine to love" (190), she says, and in an attempt to spare them the horror of slavery tries to kill them as soon as she sees schoolteacher in front of 124. "I took and put my babies where they'd be safe" (193), she tells Paul D, although she managed to kill only her two-year-old daughter who would

---

11. Jonquil Bailey (2017) also argues that the community's reaction here is a rejection of Baby Suggs's preaching, as Bailey sees them refusing a view of the world they understand to be impossibly utopic. Bailey herself understands Baby Suggs as proclaiming a message that does not move far enough away from white racism as supported through white theological language to meet the community's needs.

return as a ghost. Her act causes the community to abandon the inhabitants of 124, and Baby Suggs to abandon her preaching in the Clearing, which she believes "had been mocked and rebuked by the bloodspill in her backyard. God puzzled her and she was too ashamed of Him to say so" (208). She, like Sethe, could no longer have the grace they had been able to imagine, since that imagination did not stop the terror of slavery, driven by a white culture that does not view Blacks as human, from finding them.

Paul D exorcises the ghost on his arrival at 124 eighteen years after the killing (21–22), and at the point where he, Sethe, and Denver seem as if they might form a family that renews 124's ties with the community (56–59), Beloved, a young Black woman, appears at the house. Readers disagree as to the precise nature of Beloved's identity,[12] but to at least some degree she is a reincarnation of Sethe's dead daughter, the same age she would have been had she lived. She bears the name Sethe put on the tombstone (5) and knows a song Sethe composed and sang only to her children (207). Near the end of the novel, Denver says Beloved was her sister but also that "at times I think she was—more" (314). Precisely what this "more" might encompass is not entirely clear and for some readers it seems best to say that her full identity is impossible to define (e.g., Anderson 2013, 74) or that she is "an excessive character that mobilizes and accumulates meaning after meaning as the narrative unfolds, becoming identified not only with Sethe's shameful and painful rememories but also with the collective and disremembered shame and trauma of the slave experience" (Bouson 2000, 152).

In Beloved's portion of a series of consecutive monologues spoken by Sethe, Denver, and herself, she has memories—or, in the context of the novel, rememories—of the horrors of the Middle Passage: A dead man lies on top of her; they are brought barely enough water to remain alive; they are packed into a space too tight to move; a pile of bodies is thrown into the water; they are rocked by storms; and so on (248–52). To some extent, then, she reflects a collective and generations-long experience of Black suffering during and after slavery,[13] a suffering that never stops because time

---

12. For some summaries of the suggestions in this regard, see Holden-Kirwan 1998, 418–22 and Marks 2002, 66–69.

13. So also, e.g., Wyatt 1993, 474; O'Reilly 2004, 86–87. Beloved's very name points to a corporate Black identity, since it is the same one that Sethe put on the gravestone of her otherwise unnamed daughter, and she takes it from the opening of the preacher's address at the beginning of the funeral, when he refers to those assem-

never advances for her, as we can see in her speech that seems to relive the experience of the slave ship: "All of it is now   it is always now   there will never be a time when I am not crouching and watching others who are crouching too   I am always crouching" (248).

Beloved herself appears to be at least something like Sethe's understanding of a rememory (so Carden 1999, 410), in which past trauma becomes physically present, and to an important extent she embodies the past. Beloved has a "bottomless" desire for Sethe's stories about the past, and despite the fact that "every mention of her past life hurt" and that she could normally only provide "short replies or rambling incomplete reveries" when asked about it, Sethe finds herself enjoying the act of telling those stories to Beloved (69). And once Sethe identifies Beloved with her dead daughter, she becomes obsessed with explaining to her why she killed her (284, 295–96), just what she was trying to justify to her daughter's ghost at the opening of the novel (4–6). We can see Beloved as, in part, the power of the traumatic past, whose presence forces Sethe to continually relive the trauma of being driven to kill her own daughter and for whom the trauma of slavery and the Middle Passage "is always now." She appears just as Sethe considers that a future life with Paul D might be possible and begins to literally fall apart as he and Sethe grow closer together (157–58),[14] as if Sethe's ability to forge a future that is made up of more than the pain of the traumatic past is antithetical to Beloved's very existence, which is in important part an incarnation of past suffering. She feeds off Sethe's stories of the past (69) and her explanations for her killing of her child, explanations that Beloved never truly accepts (295–96). Beloved also relives the rape associated with slavery—when "ghosts without skin stuck their fingers in her and said beloved in the dark and bitch in the light" (284)—with Paul D, telling him that "you have to touch me. On the inside part. And you have to call me my name" (137). Paul D had also been raped as a slave or at the very least had witnessed the rape of fellow slaves on a daily basis (127), and rape is a common experience of characters in the novel (see Barnett 1997). Paul D feels incapable of not having sex with Beloved, "humiliated" since "there was nothing he was able to do about it" (148), and this causes the memories of the past that he had sealed away in the "tobacco tin" to flood to the surface (137; see also Carden 1999, 412–15).

---

bled as "Dearly Beloved" (5). The name, in other words, is a way of referring to the entire community (see Rody 1995, 104).

14. For the motif of dismemberment in the novel, see Travis 2010, 233–34.

In the belief that her dead daughter has returned, Sethe abandons her life outside of 124, quitting her job to live entirely in what she thinks of as the "no-time" of the house (225). This results only in her consumption by Beloved, the manifestation of past Black suffering that takes away Sethe's life as slavery did. The more attention Sethe pays to her and explanations she offers, the healthier Beloved becomes, while Sethe wastes away (294–95). Near the end of the novel, Beloved appears as if she is pregnant (308), as Sethe was when she escaped slavery, but whereas the story of the birth of Denver at the Ohio River as Sethe is about to cross to (temporary) safety in 1855 is accompanied by an image of hope for a future generation,[15] Beloved has no interest in a future. Beloved cannot give birth to a hopeful future, only to Sethe's repetitive suffering of a past that is continually present and that itself functions as a kind of slavery (so, e.g., Schmudde 1993, 131; Caesar 1994, 119), as Beloved feeds off Sethe's suffering and appears to be in the process of killing her. In the same way, the sex Beloved has with Paul D, which he experiences as a humiliation he is unable to resist, makes him relive the trauma of slavery and wonder if schoolteacher had been right in viewing him as more animal than human (148).

It is the Black community who saves Sethe from Beloved as the killing rememory of the traumatic past.[16] When Denver forces herself to leave 124 to ask for food once all of Sethe's savings have been spent, the community women become aware of what Beloved is doing to her, and they return to 124, which they had abandoned eighteen years before when Sethe killed her daughter. The community had not supported her with song when she was arrested for the killing (179), and in the novel they are "supportive and necessary, yet divisive and petty" (Page 1992, 32), sometimes ignorant of the ways in which they scapegoat their weaker members.[17] Now, however, they act in defiance of their earlier indifference to Sethe's suffering (see

---

15. At Denver's birth, the narrator refers to bluefern spores floating along the riverbank, "seeds in which the whole generation sleeps confident of a future. And for a moment it is easy to believe that each has one—will become all of what is contained in the spore: will live out its days as planned. This moment of certainty lasts no longer than that; longer, perhaps, than the spore itself" (99).

16. In *Beloved*, writes Daniel Batt (2021, 162–63), the community as a whole can be seen as the novel's hero.

17. So also Hinson 2001, 148. On page 176 of the novel, even schoolteacher in his racist way is able to see that his nephews' rape of Sethe is related to her killing of her daughter, although he accepts no culpability of his own, but the Black community in the novel never seems to blame anyone but Sethe (see Schmudde 1993, 123–25).

Spargo 2002, 117), and as thirty women come to confront Beloved and sing outside of 124, Sethe feels "as though the Clearing had come to her" with a song "that broke the back of words," and she "trembled like the baptized in its wash" (308). Her baptism or rebirth through a renewal of the grace that the community could provide her, that of which Baby Suggs spoke in the Clearing, could be said to break the back of the words she and Beloved had been speaking to each other, which trapped her in a fixation to past suffering.

Sethe is not entirely torn from the grip of the past, however, for at that moment, as she and Beloved stand in the doorway of 124 before the women, she sees a white man driving a cart on the road and experiences it as a rememory of schoolteacher's arrival. Yet this time events unfold differently, and instead of trying to kill Beloved, Sethe runs to kill the man (308–9), while on this occasion the community women are present to prevent her from harming anyone (312). She does relive the past to some degree, but she and her community, who failed to warn and save her from schoolteacher's arrival at 124 in 1855, are also able to act differently this time, such that Sethe does not entirely reenact the past event. Beloved, who experiences the appearance of a white man with a whip as a repetition of the trauma of the Middle Passage,[18] disappears at this point, so perhaps she can only manifest herself in corporeal form insofar as she as well as those around her remain fixated to and relive the traumatic suffering of the past.

In the end, it is not impossible for the community to imagine grace for themselves and to love, value, and support each other in mutual aid. The origin of their abandonment of 124 lay in the celebration hosted by its inhabitants soon after Sethe's arrival, the community's anger a reaction against their own momentary experience of liberation from the past and present terror perpetrated by whites. Yet as the group of women approach 124 to save Sethe from Beloved, the first thing they see is a rememory of that event eighteen years previously, one that involved not trauma but a

---

18. In Beloved's traumatic rememories of the Middle Passage, she has lost and feels abandoned by a woman who was assumedly her mother and who appears to have died on the voyage (250–51), and she refers to "men without skin" (251), her way of describing whites in this context. Near the end of the novel, as Sethe runs toward the white man in the horse-drawn cart, Beloved experiences this as her mother "leaving Beloved behind. Alone. Again." She sees a man as well "with a whip in his hand, the man without skin, looking. He is looking at her" (309).

communal celebration (304). It is not possible for that community to live in complete freedom from the horrors of past and present, but it is necessary to provide themselves with the grace and love they can imagine in order to help each other do more in the future than just survive. Denver, for example, is frightened to leave 124's yard, knowing the outside world only as the source of terror and rememory so horrific that it causes mothers to kill their own children, yet she leaves anyway to reestablish ties with the community to save Sethe from starvation and the debilitating attention Beloved pays to her. She overcomes her fear in dialogue with a spectral appearance of Baby Suggs, who refers allusively to her own suffering and who urges Denver to leave the yard, despite the knowledge that there is "no defense" against white terror. "Know it," her grandmother says to her, "and go on out the yard. Go on" (288).[19] It is the grace the community can imagine for the inhabitants of 124, something that values them as humans who cannot be left to the destruction Beloved is visiting upon the house, that allows for the salvation that Denver could be said to experience at the end of the novel. Raised in a household haunted by the past that taught her to fear the outside world, by the end of the novel she has a job and resumed her education with the help of community members, one of whom hopes to send her to college (314), thus making her a member of a new generation receiving a new education that can replace the one enforced by schoolteacher (Krumholz 1992, 405).

It is less certain, however, that Sethe has a hopeful future by the end of the novel (see, e.g., Carden 1999, 420–21; Fulton 2005, 192); readers last encounter her in the same bed to which Baby Suggs retired to die, and Denver tells Paul D that she is afraid that she has lost her mother (314). When he asks Sethe if she plans to die, she says only that "I don't have no plans" (320) and bemoans the disappearance of Beloved, "my best thing" (321). There is no future for herself that Sethe can see, and her "best thing" is an embodiment of intergenerational Black trauma. Like Baby Suggs, who died in the same bed in which Sethe now lies, Sethe could be said to be "suspended between the nastiness of life and the meanness of death," as "her past had been like her present—intolerable" (4). There can be no

---

19. Whether one wants to understand the Baby Suggs with whom Denver converses here as a ghost or as the creation of Denver's imagination, the passage rehabilitates the character, who spent her final years in bed in 124, having given up on grace and hope. The Baby Suggs with whom Denver speaks here sounds much more like the one who led meetings in the Clearing before schoolteacher's arrival.

future for Sethe if she can only live in her past suffering, but her story ends with at least the possibility of one in the community of family formed with Paul D, who says to her, "me and you, we got more yesterday than anyone. We need some kind of tomorrow" (322). And when Paul D tells her that it was not Beloved, the manifestation of her dead daughter and a whole history of Black suffering, that is Sethe's "best thing" but Sethe herself, he imagines grace for her as the community women had done earlier. Whether she is able to accept this grace, this love of herself as a true and valuable human and something that would allow her to make a future in family and community, is not a question that the novel resolves.

Grace in *Beloved* allows for a future for the Black community in which the present is more than just survival and a repetition and continuation of past suffering, although it is never something individuals can entirely accomplish by themselves. A whole culture is arrayed against the notion that Blacks are fully human and should be treated as such, and in the novel it is only with the power of community that the characters might hope to really imagine the kind of grace of which Baby Suggs spoke in the Clearing, in which they can truly value themselves as humans should. It is not something that will banish the trauma of the past, but it is something that offers a future beyond that trauma, something that prevents suffering from being "always now" and one's "best thing." It is something that replaces the sorts of words written and taught by schoolteacher and white culture with the Word that Baby Suggs speaks in the Clearing, one that acknowledges a painful past and present and yet imagines the possibility of a different future, one that privileges the vulnerable.[20]

It is also a grace dependent on the stories told by the characters to themselves and each other, ones that can replace those told by schoolteacher and other whites that reflect their beliefs about the sub-humanity of Blacks.[21] The speech of the novel's characters gives them agency even in the reality of great suffering, and Baby Suggs and Stamp Paid, for example, tell stories of the ways in which they abandoned the names given to them by slaveowners and claimed new ones that reflect identities they forge themselves (166–68, 217–18; see also Hamilton 1996, 430–31). When the narrator says that Paul

---

20. As Matthew Smalley (2018, 34, 38) notes, Baby Suggs's preaching in the Clearing begins by calling the children, reflecting Jesus's call to them in the synoptic gospels (Matt 19:14; Mark 10:14; Luke 18:16) as a way of privileging the powerless.

21. For a discussion of the ways in which *Beloved* demonstrates how language itself contributed to the enslavement of Blacks, see Linehan 1997, 303–5.

D wants to put his story next to Sethe's (322), his desire parallels her conviction expressed earlier that "her story was bearable because it was his as well" (116).[22] If Sethe is to have any future, it will be one in which she can tell her own stories of the past to a family and community who can hear and accept them and provide her with the assurance that she can reject and replace those that schoolteacher told about her and that she can become a definer of herself rather than the defined.[23] The community women have at least made such a future possible for Sethe, with support voiced through a song "that broke the back of words," but new words will have to be found to replace the old ones.

The novel's short epilogue says at a number of points that "it was not a story to pass on" (323–24), a claim that can seem paradoxical as the novel itself has just passed on a story (so, e.g., Page 1992, 38). The phrase is ambiguous, however,[24] and from the perspective of the novel's characters we could see it as referring to Beloved's story—or Sethe's or Paul D's or that of any of the Black characters—and so as the kind of story that one does not want to pass on because it is so painful. The community forgot Beloved, the narrator tells us, since "remembering seemed unwise" (324). Yet if Beloved disappears at the moment when the community arrives at 124 and makes a future possible for Sethe, her absence is still a kind of presence: "Down by the stream in back of 124 her footprints come and go, come and go. They are so familiar. Should a child, an adult place his feet in them, they will fit. Take them out and they disappear again as though nobody ever walked there" (324). The characters may not want to tell Beloved's story of multigenerational Black suffering and so they forget it, but while whatever future they may have will depend on the stories they can tell and the grace they can convey to themselves and each other, such stories will be incomplete without Beloved's. These grace-full stories that allow them to define themselves anew as human beings who deserve futures, educations, families, and celebrations would not be entirely honest if they omitted the story of Beloved that they prefer to forget, for their stories still fit hers, to some degree, as their feet fit her spectral footprints.

---

22. Sethe and Paul D have, in fact, similar stories of the past; see the comparison in Daniels 2002, 350.

23. John Allen (2021, 294–95) sees in *Beloved* a struggle on the part of characters aiming to tell their stories in a way that can give them some freedom from the past that opens up a more hopeful future.

24. For some of the ways in which it could be understood, see Durkin 2007, 553–54.

Beloved is full of stories the characters are unable or find too painful to tell (see Lee 1994, 577), just as Sethe finds her past to be "unspeakable" and something she tends not to clearly articulate (69). The arrival of schoolteacher and the rest of the four horsemen at 124 may be apocalyptic in nature, but there is no final apocalyptic judgment or release from history in the novel, no escape from Beloved's story of communal Black trauma (Jesser 1999, 327). "Beloved" is the novel's final word, a past that can return (Davis 1998, 251), but this need not mean that her story is the last word in the characters' lives, even if they cannot avoid it or stories like it as they create and retell their own. By imagining grace for themselves and each other within a supportive community, the possibility of a future exists for them, something that was not possible for Beloved, whose story could never change.[25]

Imagination and Its Failures in Lamentations

To return again to the way I am drawing on Sechrest's notion of rhyme, it is not difficult to draw comparisons between the experiences of the Black characters in *Beloved* and those of the voices who speak in Lamentations. Like the former, the latter, who have survived the Babylonian destruction of Jerusalem, have also experienced slavery (Lam 1:1; 5:13),[26] desperate hunger (e.g., 1:11–12, 19; 2:12, 19; 4:4), rape (e.g., 1:8, 10; 5:11),[27] torture (5:12), and witnessed mass killings (e.g., 1:20; 2:21). In both texts, in fact, we encounter women who feel as if they have to kill their own children (2:20; 4:9–10), as well as characters who can be understood as personifications of communal suffering, and in both works those who suffer are subalterns treated as if their lives do not matter. As the narrator of the poem of Lam 4 puts it, "the precious children of Zion" may have been

---

25. And in that sense, her story was not one to pass on because it cannot go on or progress but can only repeat past Black trauma (so Moglen 1993, 36–37).

26. One of the first aspects of Jerusalem's suffering that we read about in the book is the מס "forced labor" to which Jerusalem's inhabitants have been subjected (1:1), and we can read 5:13 in the same light, especially since 5:8 refers to the community as being ruled by slaves who put them to forced labor.

27. For the Hebrew of these and other verses in the book as referring to rape, see, e.g., Guest 1999, 417–19; Dobbs-Allsopp and Linafelt 2001. The figure of Daughter Zion is a rape victim, writes Juliana Claassens (2013, 75–78), and Rhiannon Graybill (2021, 116–18) says that we can see all of Lamentations, and particularly Lam 1–2, as a rape story.

"worth their weight in refined gold," but are now "valued as clay pots, the work of a potter's hand" (4:2). While readers from minoritized groups such as Deryn Guest (2006) can find in Lamentations voices that echo their communities' pain,[28] interpreters from dominant social locations in particular might be prone to overlook the way that the book devotes so much space for the powerless, whose lives are valued as nothing, to speak of their suffering and to try to find ways to forge a future despite that.

This section of the chapter, then, focuses on the different and conflicting reactions these subaltern speakers have to this suffering. In Lamentations the response to great national anguish is sometimes quite different from that of other biblical writings, and to some degree this points to yet another similarity with *Beloved*: Both works provide us with attempts to find a language of grace that values the members of a subjugated group as fully human and that can see a future for them, something along the lines of the Word of Baby Suggs's preaching that rejects claims that the suffering of the powerless is what they deserve and a necessary reflection of who they are, the kind of idea communicated in the words and actions of schoolteacher's lessons. The characters of *Beloved*, however, are often more successful in creating such a language than the speakers of Lamentations. In the final section of the chapter, I will use the novel as a basis for imagining how the speech of Lamentations' subaltern voices might continue so the speakers could understand themselves as humans worthy of a future and could picture a God who sees and treats them that way as well. To do so, however, will demand actually listening to the suffering and ambiguity expressed in that speech and acknowledging that it would be hermeneutically problematic to speak for those characters in imagining an unambiguous and entirely happy ending to their dialogue.

One reason why Jerusalem's survivors who speak in Lamentations have such difficulty valuing and thus imagining grace for themselves and their community is a deeply entrenched understanding in Israel, Judah, and the ancient Near East as a whole that the destruction of kingdoms and cities is

---

28. Guest (2006) refers specifically to the way Lamentations reflects the widespread queer experience of abuse and betrayal and the way in which its imagery can be used to address the community's suffering and bereavement in connection with AIDS. We could refer here as well to the work of Wil Gafney (2017a, 206), who looks at biblical lament in general as a kind of prophetic voice and sees Black Lives Matter protests as "performance prophecy accompanying proclamation prophecy, reading all as lament."

the manifestation of the divine punishment of their inhabitants, especially for cultic failings. As early as the late third millennium BCE, for example, the Curse of Agade links the destruction of Akkad to its king's cultic missteps;[29] the Weidner Chronicle (*ABC* 19), known from Neo-Assyrian and Neo-Babylonian copies (Grayson 1975, 43, 145), says that kings who do not maintain cultic norms are punished with national disasters. By the thirteenth century BCE Assyrian royal inscriptions begin to claim that the conquest, destruction, and exile of peoples by the Assyrians was the result of the inhabitants' evil behavior that had so angered their gods that they had abandoned them, leaving the people to the punishment enacted by Assyria.[30] So when Esarhaddon, for example, on numerous seventh-century BCE inscriptions justifies his father's destruction of Babylon, he characterizes the city as full of lies, murder, dishonoring of parents, social injustice, oppression of the poor, abandonment of the proper worship of the gods, and theft of temple property (e.g., RINAP 4.104.i.18–33; 108.i.1–16). This made Marduk so angry, the king writes, that the god destroyed the city and exiled its inhabitants, something that incited so much fear in the other gods of Babylon that they fled to the heavens (e.g., 104.i.34–ii.1; 106.i.10–ii.3; 108.ii.2–iii.14). Given this broader cultural context, it is no wonder that ancient Judeans would understand the destruction of Jerusalem and the Babylonian exile as the result of divine punishment for their actions. Moreover, the Neo-Assyrian treaty format is rooted in the notion that the divine world punishes those who violate the treaties they have sworn to uphold. As this is an important part of the cultural background in which the biblical concept of covenant develops, it is common to see biblical writings explain the Babylonian destruction of Jerusalem, not to mention other national disasters, by referring to the evil of the people and their kings as failures to behave as God's covenant with Israel demands.

For our purposes it does not particularly matter to which historical disaster Lamentations responds, but since there is a consensus that it was written in the decades after the Babylonian destruction of Judah and Jeru-

---

29. See in particular lines 100–175 of the Old Babylonian version in Cooper 1983.

30. The motif of divine abandonment had been used before this time in the ancient Near East but only as the explanation of the defeated to explain their defeat; the first known use of this motif from the standpoint of the victor comes in the thirteenth-century inscriptions of Tukulti-Ninurta, who claims that he could defeat Babylon because the Babylonian gods abandoned the city (see Machinist 1976, 464). For the appearance of this idea in Neo-Assyrian inscriptions, see Trimm 2017, 602–3.

salem, a very brief survey of other biblical writings that provide explanations for this event can help us get a sense of how deeply rooted in Judean thought the notion was that the destruction of Jerusalem was caused by the sin of the very people who died in and suffered from that disaster, as well as by the sins of their ancestors. The book of Kings, for example, says that King Manasseh caused Judeans to partake in his cultic sin—something that, the narrator says, was merely a continuation of the way Israel had always acted (2 Kgs 21:15)—leading to the divine decision to destroy Jerusalem (21:1–16; 23:26–27; 24:2–4), while Chronicles portrays the people's sin as building up over a long period of time until God reacted by slaughtering Jerusalem's population by means of the Babylonians (2 Chr 36:15–17). In a similar way, Ezra-Nehemiah portrays Israel as a generally sinful people whose iniquities led to Jerusalem's destruction and exile (Ezra 5:12; 9:7; Neh 9:26–30), and Deut 28:15–68, with notable parallels to Neo-Assyrian treaties,[31] also portrays the destruction and exile as a general failure on Judah's part to keep divine commandments. Other biblical passages focus more specifically on Judah's cultic sins, as Kings does—and, for that matter, as Esarhaddon tends to when he refers to the sins of Babylon (e.g., RINAP 4.105.i.27–37; 110.ii.13–23; 111.i.3–9; 113.11)—and so, for example, Jeremiah and Ezekiel use the prophetic marriage metaphor to explain the annihilation of Judah. In this literary device the people as a group are portrayed as God's wife, and their worship of other deities is described as prostitution, so that God's actions of inflicting destruction, mutilation, and execution are justified (e.g., Jer 3:6–10; Ezek 16:35–43; 23:9–10, 22–35, 46–49) or at least they are if one assumes that this is the sort of thing husbands should do to women who have extramarital sex.[32]

---

31. Carly Crouch (2014, 108–17) rightly argues that Deut 28 reflects a broad tradition of ancient Near Eastern curse material rather than that found specifically in a single known Assyrian treaty such as the Vassal Treaty of Esarhaddon. Her point that there is not enough evidence to argue that the chapter reflects that particular treaty is well-taken, yet Judah was a client to Assyria for about a century and would have been sworn to such a treaty. Deuteronomy 28 certainly reflects aspects of Esarhaddon's vassal treaty (SAA 2.6) among others; useful comparisons with Deut 28 include SAA 2.6.418a–c, 428–430, 449–450, 519–520, 530–532, 547–550, and 599–600. This is not evidence that parts of Deut 28 were taken from that treaty, but it does show that the curses of this chapter for disobedience to the covenant were like ones used in Neo-Assyrian treaties to describe divine punishment for their clients' failures of loyalty.

32. See the discussion of the prophetic marriage metaphor in Weems 1995. In this sort of metaphor God is presented as innocent and patient (64–67), and the violence

Carleen Mandolfo (2007, 14–15) refers to biblical explanations like these for great suffering as a "master narrative" because of the widespread notion in biblical literature that massive destruction as experienced in Israel and Judah is the fault of those who suffer and die as a result of it and often the fault of their ancestors as well. Given that national disasters as grave as the destruction of Jerusalem would commonly be understood in this way, we can see how difficult it would be for the speakers of Lamentations to avoid such explanations and how easy it would be to see themselves as deserving of their great suffering, in which they have been and are being treated as humans should never be. We should not be surprised if these speakers have great difficulty in imagining grace for themselves or in conceiving of a God who believes their lives matter, nor should we be surprised to find that the language of Mandolfo's master narrative is present in Lamentations. Mandolfo (2007, 59–65) refers to that master narrative as speaking through what she calls a Didactic Voice, something that appears at points in the book, as speakers repeat this master narrative to the survivors of Jerusalem's destruction, who include starving children, rape victims, and the traumatized who have survived but witnessed the mass slaughter of family and compatriots.

Readers from privileged social contexts who have never been treated as if or told that they belong to a group whose lives matter less than those of other humans may not always notice the ethical difficulties raised by texts like Jeremiah, Ezekiel, or Ezra-Nehemiah that blame the survivors of destruction, slaughter, starvation, and rape in attempts to justify their suffering. Having read *Beloved*, however, we can see that there is a comparison to be made between the master narrative of the Didactic Voice in many biblical books and the schoolteacher's lessons that for him and other whites justify their treatment of the Black characters in the novel. The parallel is not exact, because in *Beloved* it is whites' racial hatred that leads them to view Blacks as animal-like, as beings whose suffering matters no more than that of animals, while the Didactic Voice that appears in Lamentations explains the suffering of Jerusalem's survivors as the result of divine punishment for communal sin, and these two justifications for the mass infliction of pain are obviously different.

---

directed against the victims, personified as women, is portrayed as a demonstration of divine love (92–93). The passages from Ezekiel are clearly meant to explain the exile; for the argument that this is also true for the prophetic marriage metaphor in Jer 3, see Crouch 2020.

Yet in the end, horrific suffering is horrific suffering, no matter how one chooses to justify it. The rape, slavery, starvation, and torture experienced by the survivors of Lamentations is simply not the sort of thing reasonable people think humans should have to endure and so not something we think that anyone should ever try to justify. We would, after all, see as ethically problematic the argument that the sort of suffering undergone by the Black characters of *Beloved*, which is much like that experienced by the speakers of Lamentations, is the result of divine will. To try to justify that suffering in any way is to dehumanize the victims, to assert that they can be treated as humans should not be because their lives do not matter to the degree that human lives should. Reading Lamentations after *Beloved* helps us to see what the characters who speak using the Didactic Voice must assume about what God is like and how little value the sufferers' lives must have both for God (in the way that Voice portrays divinity, at least) and for those willing to adopt the explanations of the Voice's master narrative.

Lamentations, however, contains the speech of a number of characters, and the Didactic Voice is not all we hear. Both the poems of Lam 1 and 2 open with the speech of a narrator, and their words alternate with those of a personification of Jerusalem—a female character normally called Zion or Daughter Zion (e.g., 1:6, 17; 2:6, 8), sometimes Jerusalem or Daughter Jerusalem (e.g., 1:7; 2:13, 15), Judah or Daughter Judah (1:3; 2:2, 5), Israel (2:3, 5), or "the daughter of my people" (2:11),[33] and who to some degree can seem like a parallel to the character of Beloved insofar as she embodies the suffering of an entire group of people. As the narrator and Zion speak in Lam 1–2, we can see some of their perspectives changing in regard to suffering and its explanation and their confident, even if anguish-filled, articulations of the Didactic Voice in the first poem of Lam 1 disappear by the second. We see alterations of explanation and understandings of suffering in the words of the speaker of Lam 3,[34] who introduces himself

---

33. The personification of the city as a woman was an aspect of some city laments from Mesopotamia (see Dobbs-Allsopp 1995; Berges 2002, 110–17). In 1:17; 2:2, 3, however, the narrator merges the female character of Zion with the male figure of Jacob. In 1:17, for example, the narrative refers to Zion stretching out ידיה "her hands," and equates her with Jacob while discussing צריו "his enemies." See also Floyd 2012 for arguments that בת ציון should be translated as "daughter (of) Zion" and understood as a personification of Jerusalem.

34. Scholarly opinion as to the number of speakers in Lam 3 varies, in part because the first-person singular speech in 3:1–39 and 48–66 is interrupted in 3:40–47 by speech in the first-person plural (see, e.g., Heim 1999, 160–61; Lee 2002, 168). Only

as "the man" in 3:1 and who articulates more than one point of view about the suffering he and his fellow survivors endure. In the two poems of Lam 4 and 5, we encounter two more speakers, a narrator and a community of survivors, and the two voices do not entirely agree as to how to respond to the community's trauma or as to what kind of future they may have.

The variety of perspectives we find in the characters' responses to the horrific and widespread suffering Lamentations describes leaves the book without any single message as to how to make sense of the traumatic events that lie behind it or how to envision a future in the midst of such pain (so also, e.g., Middlemas 2012, 52; Bier 2013; Rong 2013, 167–70). So while we come across examples of speakers using Mandolfo's Didactic Voice, we encounter other responses as well. Reading Lamentations after *Beloved* can allow us to see the speakers as belonging to a vulnerable community whose lives are valued as nothing and who have been forced to endure great anguish as a result, which means that like the Black community in the novel they simply do not always agree with a master narrative that claims their lives and their pain do not matter and that the suffering they endure can be justified. To use terminology Graybill (2021, 12–14) has adopted for discussions of biblical rape narratives, Lamentations is fuzzy, declining to clearly categorize or definitively explain Jerusalem's destruction, and it is messy, failing to provide a coherent story that adheres to an accepted narrative line, with the result that there is no clear resolution to the speakers' pain (15–16) that can be tidily summed up by the Didactic Voice's master narrative.

The speech of a narrator opens the book in 1:1–9b, and they refer to Zion's sin (1:5, 8) as explaining the terrible change in her fortunes: Once "princess among the provinces," she has become a slave (1:1); her old friends and companions[35] deceived her, showing themselves to be enemies (1:2) who "laughed over her annihilation" (1:7) and "despised her" (1:8); a once-populous city now seems largely abandoned (1:1, 4); and Zion's splendor has disappeared along with her leaders (1:6). "Her downfall was extraordinary," the narrator says (1:9). Their explanation of such suffering through reference to Jerusalem's sin tells us we are encountering an instance of the

---

one speaker is ever introduced in this chapter, however, and we can understand the man as speaking on behalf of his community in 3:40–47.

35. The use of the terms אהבים "friends" and רעים "companions" in 1:2 suggests the narrator is referring to nearby kingdoms who were previously Judah's allies (see Olyan 1996, 215–17).

Didactic Voice, although the narrator's use of it is not as strident as it is in other biblical writings, for in these verses they spend much more time discussing Zion's experience of pain than explaining it by focusing on the city's iniquities, the specifics of which they never spell out (see, e.g., Parry 2007, 144), and so they can seem moved by her suffering (so Salters 2000, 300–1). And once Zion herself begins to speak, first in 1:9c (only to be interrupted in 1:10–11b by the narrator, whose speech returns with more descriptions of her pain), and then again in 1:11c–22 (although the narrator interrupts again in 1:17 to speak of Zion's suffering), her focus on her anguish is complemented by her imitation of the narrator's didactic claims as to her sin, and she expends more energy discussing that than the narrator does. God "made her suffer for the greatness of her iniquities," the narrator says (1:5), but Zion puts much more specific emphasis on divine responsibility for her pain and how her sin stands at the root of this suffering God has caused, referring to "my iniquities" (1:14, 22) and her disobedience to God's word (1:18, 20).[36] Zion refers to God's responsibility for her suffering nine times in 1:12–15 using a variety of metaphors, and so she can appear even more devoted to—or trapped by—the master narrative that victims are responsible for the horrors that have been inflicted on them than the narrator is.

It does not seem possible in this poem for Zion to imagine a God who is not primarily defined by violence, and she quickly abandons her calls to God to see and give heed to her pain in 1:9c and 11c, turning instead to descriptions of the suffering God has inflicted. Her speech in the book's first poem culminates in 1:20–22 with her request that God act violently against her enemies; it would seem, at this point, that there is nothing else Zion wishes to request from God since she cannot imagine God as doing anything except causing more violence. The Didactic Voice, whose words Zion speaks, assumes not only that the people have sinned but that God punishes them, thereby justifying whatever suffering they endure. And because it is not clear here that Zion can imagine a God who does anything but cause suffering, her conception of God is hardly a comforting one; she agrees with the narrator that she has no "comforter" (1:2, 9, 16, 17, 21) in the midst of her great anguish, someone who would be able to restore her life (1:16). She is alone, the very first observation the narrator makes about

---

36. In 1:20, however, the OG reflects a text equivalent to Hebrew מרר מרתי "I am very bitter" rather than the MT's מרו מריתי "I have surely disobeyed" (see Seow 1985), and in 1:18 the OG has read a form of מרר "to be bitter" while the MT has a form of מרה "to disobey."

her (1:1), as her friends have abandoned her and become her enemies who rejoice in her annihilation (1:7, 21). There is no one she or the narrator can think of who could create any community with her or who could comfort her, no one with whom she might forge a better future or who might call upon her to imagine enough grace for herself so that she could understand herself and her people to be worthy of humane treatment and to conceive of a God willing to provide it. As a result, there is no future she can imagine that is different than her present anguish.

Reading Lam 1 after *Beloved*, we might be struck not only by the fact that much of the chapter is spoken by a personification of a people who have endured slaughter, slavery, and exile, rather like the character of Beloved when she speaks as if she is in the hold of a slave ship in the Atlantic, but also by the debilitating effects of living without community. The narrator describes what has happened to Zion but is not the comforter who could restore her life, and God, as Zion imagines divinity, is unable to play that role either. The narrator and Zion do not even directly address each other in this poem, although that does not mean that they are not affected by each other's speech (see Lee 2002, 160; King and Venter 2009, 259). By the poem of Lam 2, the narrator appears to have listened to her, and their words are now dominated by references to the suffering God has caused her, as Zion's speech was in Lam 1. Neither the narrator nor Zion, in fact, uses the Didactic Voice to link Jerusalem's sin to its destruction in the second poem.[37] It is not just that the narrator focuses on God's responsibility for Zion's suffering in their speech of 2:1–19 (or 2:1–20);[38] God is the subject of twenty-nine of the thirty-one verbs in 2:1–8 (Dobbs-

---

37. One could see 2:14 as the sole exception to this claim, for there the narrator says that Zion's prophets received visions that were שוא "empty, false" and "did not reveal your iniquity." The focus of this verse, however, is not on drawing a link between Zion's sin and her great suffering, a connection both the narrator and Zion make in Lam 1, but on the fact that her prophets were prevented by God from receiving visions that would reveal her wrongdoings so that she could alter her actions and avoid destruction. The point of 2:14, that is, better fits the theme of God as Zion's enemy rather than that of sin as leading to justly earned punishment. In the narrator's speech of Lam 2, as noted below, God is motivated by enmity and anger directed against Zion rather than by justice, and in 2:14 the narrator is not using the Didactic Voice to make a point about Zion deserving her punishment but is making one of Lam 2's numerous references to God as destroyer.

38. It is not entirely clear whether the narrator or Zion is speaking in 2:20; see below, as well as Parry 2007, 152.

Allsopp 2004, 34), verses that refer to Zion's utter destruction, and there are six references to divine anger in this section, which portrays God as Jerusalem's "violent destroyer," as Elizabeth Boase (2008a, 35) puts it. The narrator's consideration of Zion's speech in the first poem allows them now to describe God as Jerusalem's true enemy (2:4, 5), and while the city's human enemies mock her and claim responsibility for her downfall saying, "We have engulfed them (בלענו)" and "this is the day we hoped for" (2:16), the narrator says at a number of points that it is actually God who "engulfed" Zion (2:2, 5, 8) on "the day of his anger" (2:1). It was God who "made your enemy rejoice over you" and "exalted your adversary's horn" (2:17), the narrator says, now addressing Zion directly.

The narrator not only abandons the claims of the Didactic Voice in Lam 2 by portraying God as like a human enemy rather than a just judge but is now also clearly moved by the suffering they see. Like Zion in 1:2 and 16, the narrator now weeps (2:11), and like Zion in 1:20, the narrator now says that חמרמרו מעי "my bowels churn" in response to Jerusalem's pain (2:11). The two are now lamenting together (so, e.g., Conway 2012, 117; Bier 2015, 98), and it is no longer enough for the narrator to state that Zion has no comforter, as they did in the first poem of Lam 1, for they now ask what they can do to fill that role (2:13; and see O'Connor 2002, 99–101). It is precisely in this verse, in fact, that the narrator ceases to simply talk about Zion's suffering and begins to speak directly to her, and so we note a small step toward community here in Lam 2, something that in *Beloved* is a necessary aspect of the grace that might allow the characters to imagine a future different from a past and present defined by suffering. We notice as well an abandonment of the words that might trap the narrator and Zion in a belief that this suffering can be explained through some unspecified sin, a claim that would assent to the notion that Jerusalem's slavery (1:1), the starvation of its children (2:11–12), the rape of its inhabitants (1:3, 8, 10, 13; 2:8–9),[39] and the slaughter of its young people (2:19) are justified, an idea that would make sense only if individual lives have less than human value. In Lam 2, we might say, it is God's behavior rather than Zion's that the speakers portray as problematic (so O'Connor 2002, 34), particularly since God in the narrator's imagination here is motivated by enmity and anger, not justice. The narrator is, however, able to call upon

---

39. For the Hebrew of 1:3, 8, 10, 13; 2:8–9 as referring to rape, see n. 27 above; and see Graybill 2021, 117–18.

Zion to imagine a God who might bring her suffering to an end and near the conclusion of the poem suggests that her weeping might draw divine attention that would end the starvation and slaughter in Jerusalem (2:19). So closely does the narrator in their new role as comforter empathize with her that it is unclear if 2:20 is part of their direction as to how Zion should appeal to a God who might be able to act out of concern for her pain or part of her cry to the divine that closes this poem.

Yet this slight movement toward community, as the narrator empathizes and speaks with Zion, and away from justifications of Jerusalem's suffering is not some sort of mass arrival of Zion's companions in a larger and fuller restoration of community. It is not equivalent to the gathering of community women at 124 near the end of *Beloved* as they assemble to save Sethe from the trap of endless past suffering embodied by Beloved, although just as Sethe felt that the women's singing "broke the back of words," we can see something similar in Lam 2 as the narrator and Zion abandon the words of the Didactic Voice and refuse to blame her for her horrific trauma. Zion's appeal to God, which she undertakes at the end of the second poem at the narrator's suggestion, indicates that she and her comforter are able to believe that there is some sort of divine action that might create a future that is more than just anguish, but neither appears overly confident in this regard. Both now understand God to be Zion's true enemy (see Hens-Piazza 2021, 29–31), and Zion tells God that "in the day of your anger," when God killed her inhabitants, "you butchered them (טבחת)[40] and had no pity" (2:21). When Baby Suggs dealt with trauma at this level as she spoke in the Clearing, she called upon the community to mourn and celebrate themselves rather than instruct them about sin and repentance. If we can see the narrator in Lam 2 as becoming Zion's comforter as they mourn with her, then at least one step toward community and the support it provides in the face of great suffering has been taken, although it is a small one.

God, however, does not speak here or anywhere else in Lamentations.[41] It is uncertain how much trust either the narrator or Zion has that God

---

40. The verb טבח is sometimes used in the Bible to refer to the killing or butchering of animals (e.g., Exod 21:37 [ET 22:1]; Deut 28:31; 1 Sam 25:11) but is often applied metaphorically to human slaughter (e.g., Isa 34:6; Jer 11:19).

41. Technically, the speaker in Lam 3 refers to a time in the past when, he says, God told him, "Do not be afraid" (3:57)—we would consider this to be a reference to a past event, at least if we decide to understand אמרת in that verse as referring to the

will ever act to alleviate her suffering or how much trust that God is any different from the violent entity Zion has so far imagined God to be. Perhaps, like Baby Suggs after schoolteacher's arrival at 124, an event that shattered her belief in a future for the Black community that could move beyond the pain of the present, Zion and the narrator are puzzled by God—or at least by their understanding of God—and too ashamed to say so. The abandonment of the Didactic Voice by the two speakers in Lam 2 can allow us to see this poem as an indictment of divine actions that create great suffering with no explanation and no divine response to cries for mercy (so Dobbs-Allsopp 1997, 38–39), and it suggests the speakers are trying to look beyond the master narrative of the Didactic Voice to deal with Zion's trauma. Perhaps, given enough time, they would be able to articulate something like Baby Suggs's Word and imagine the lives of Jerusalem's survivors as valuable and worthy of love rather than as like those of animals that are beaten and killed, and perhaps they might be able to imagine a God who could act as a comforter defined by mercy and love for humans rather than by violence, enmity, and anger.

Whatever further steps they might take in an ongoing conversation, however, are left to readers' imaginations, for the third poem of the book introduces a new speaker, who refers himself in 3:1 only as הגבר ראה עני "the man who has seen affliction,"[42] a phrase that links his situation to that of Zion, who also suffers affliction (1:3, 7) that she wants God to see (1:9). But while Zion and the narrator appear to be listening and responding to each other, the man of Lam 3 has no one to talk to, and no one who could function as his comforter, although he certainly seems to need comfort, since in 3:1–20 he describes personal anguish in a way that sounds much like Zion's in the previous two poems. He depicts God as his powerful enemy who has made him suffer, just as the narrator and Zion describe God earlier. God "bent his bow" against him (3:12), the man says, which

---

past rather than construing the verb as a precative perfect (see below)—but no divine speech is recorded as responding to the catastrophe of Judah and Jerusalem's present suffering.

42. Attempts to identify the man as a specific individual known from other biblical writings (see the suggestions summarized in Hecke 2002, 265–66) or even more generally as a personification of the soldiers in the defeated Judean army (e.g., Owens 1990, 83) miss the point that the poet could have identified this speaker with greater specificity had they wanted to. The pain he articulates in the opening section of this poem suggests that this suffering is what defines him and that we can see him as one of Jerusalem's traumatized survivors.

is precisely what the narrator says God did to Zion in God's role as her enemy (2:4). Like Zion in 1:13, the man says God has made him שמם "desolate" (3:11); like her, he has been humiliated by God before others who laugh at him (1:7; 2:15–17; 3:14); and like her, he suffers עני "affliction" and מרוד "homelessness" (1:7; 3:19).[43]

In light of Zion's situation in the earlier two poems, we might be struck by the man's isolation; not only does he not have someone else to even notice his pain as Zion has the narrator, but he emphasizes how God has walled him away and cut him off from communication with anyone else including the divine (3:5–9; and see also Eidevall 2005, 136). Lacking any comforter who might, as Zion puts it in 1:16, restore his life, the man must comfort himself, and although he says in 3:18 in the midst of his description of his pain that his תוחלת "hope" in God has been destroyed, he maintains in 3:21 nonetheless that אוחיל "I will have hope," and from this point until 3:41 the tone of his discourse changes markedly. This middle section of the poem of Lam 3 could indeed be understood as comforting, at least by those who are comforted by the Didactic Voice, which the man adopts here.[44] He begins to refer to God's steadfast love, mercy (3:22, 32), and faithfulness (3:23). One should have hope, he repeats (3:24–26), and in 3:21–41 he maintains that his community has sinned and that their suffering is the punishment they deserve. Nonetheless, the man says, a future without suffering is possible for them, because while God may have caused their anguish, God did not desire to do so and will have mercy (3:31–33), and the community must return to God if this is to happen (3:40–41).

Readers searching for hopeful messages in Lamentations often focus on the man's words at this point,[45] the central part of the book's central poem. Of course, for the man to be able to comfort himself with words that speak to the possibility of a future different from his present that is dominated by suffering, he finds himself saying in 3:21 that he has hope, even though three verses earlier he had claimed that his hope in God was destroyed. And the hope he can articulate with standard theological ideas

---

43. For a full list of the aspects of Zion's suffering in Lam 1–2 that the man repeats here, see Korzec 2021, 640–41.

44. His words at this point in his speech are often said to be influenced by so-called wisdom literature, reflecting the kind of ideas one can find in Proverbs. See, e.g., Kalmanofsky 2007, 60; Boase 2008b, 463–64; Thomas 2011, 215.

45. See the discussion of this tendency in scholarship in Linafelt 2000, 5–13 and Bier 2014, 147–49.

of the Didactic Voice seems to disappear as suddenly as it arose; the man says in 3:40–41 that his community's solution to their great pain is repentance for their sin but then immediately claims in 3:42–44 that God has not forgiven and is not listening to prayers—one of the points he had made in the first part of his speech (3:8)—making repentance useless. With no community or comforter to dialogue with and provide him with solace, it is perhaps easy to lose hope. God does not speak to provide him with any, and so the man turns to weeping to draw divine attention (3:48–51), which is what the narrator had urged Zion to do (2:18–19). There is no evidence in Lam 1 and 2 that weeping and recitations of one's anguish motivate God to respond or act, and yet in the last part of the poem the man appears to regain his hope. He turns in 3:52–62 to an incident from his past in which God saved him and told him not to be afraid when his enemies attacked him חנם "for no reason" (3:52)[46] and moves directly from describing that past suffering and the beneficent divine response to it to his present situation, asking God to destroy his current enemies and repeat the act of rescue the man experienced in the past (3:63–66).

The man's understanding of God changes at different points throughout the poem, as does his hope for a future somehow different from his current suffering. God is at first his enemy who has made communication with others, including God, impossible; then God is the just judge who awaits repentance in response to the punishment righteously but unwillingly inflicted on the man's community; then God is, again, the uncommunicative agent of suffering; and finally God is the just judge once more, who in the past rescued the man from those who made him suffer "for no reason" and, the man expects, will inflict violence on his enemies now. There is, in short, no stable view in Lam 3 as to what the man believes God or his future might be like: Does God listen or not? Can God offer mercy, or only more violence and suffering, whether

---

46. The argument is made on occasion that we can read the verbs in the perfect in 3:56–61 as precative perfects and thus as referring not to a past event but to what the man hopes God will do for him to alleviate his present suffering (see Stone 2021 for a defense of this position). It is unlikely that they should be read this way here (see, e.g., Gladson 2010), although since the man seems to fuse that past event with his present situation (see below), he expects God to act in the future as God acted in the past. In other words, even if one reads the perfects in 3:56–61 as referring to past events, by the end of the poem the man seems to firmly expect that God will act to provide him a better future.

directed against the man and his people or others? Does the man truly believe his community to be guilty and to deserve the anguish God has imposed on them as he says in 3:21–41 or is he an innocent figure as he was in the past when his enemies made him suffer "for no reason" as he claims in 3:52–66?[47] It is possible in the middle of the poem for the man to imagine a future different from his present, which is defined by pain, and it is possible for him at the end even to reject the notions that his suffering can be justified and that God is responsible for it, even if at that point he once more seems to only imagine a God who is primarily defined as an agent of violence. In his internal debate God is sometimes culpable and sometimes innocent, sometimes absent and sometimes present, sometimes defined by mercy and sometimes by violence (see Dobbs-Allsopp 1997, 48–49; Gericke 2012, 173–74).

As at the end of Lam 2, readers can only imagine how the speech of this poem might continue, because Lam 4 contains the voices of two new speakers, a narrator whose words dominate the poem of this chapter and a community of sufferers who use the first-person plural in their speech of 4:17–20. The narrator seems like a different figure than the one who speaks in Lam 1 and 2, who eventually abandoned charges of disobedience against Zion and moved to become her comforter instead. The narrator of Lam 4 speaks with the Didactic Voice and emphasizes the community's sin (4:3–4, 6, 13–16), although their words also focus on many of the same aspects of Zion's suffering articulated in the book's first two poems: starvation (2:11–12, 19–20; 4:4, 9–10), which is so severe that it reaches the point of cannibalism (2:20; 4:10); the community's desolation (the root שׁמם appears in 1:4, 13, 16; 4:5); the burning of Jerusalem (2:3; 4:11); the exile of the people (1:3, 5; 2:14; 4:22); and the destruction of the city (the root שׁבר appears in 1:5; 2:9, 11, 13; 4:10). Yet the narrator of Lam 4 goes further than any other speaker in the book in proclaiming a future for the community that will entirely alter their current situation and in 4:21–22 at the conclusion of the poem says that divine violence will be directed against the community's enemies, just what Zion and the man hoped would happen (1:21–22; 3:63–66), while also claiming that the community's own punishment has already come to an end.[48]

---

47. On this final question, see O'Connor 2002, 56 and Janzen 2019, 110–11.
48. This is the sense in which תם עונך in 4:22 is normally taken, although it is not

The community, however, seems much less sanguine about their future in the poem, and they do not adopt the narrator's Didactic Voice that blames them for the suffering they experience, in which those killed by the sword are better off than the survivors who are currently starving (4:9). When they speak in 4:17–20, they say nothing about their alleged sin nor do they call upon God or anyone else to witness their suffering as Zion had done in 1:9, 11, 21–22; 2:20–22 or as the man did in 3:42–51, 63–66. They can only describe it here and do not share the narrator's confidence in the brightness of their future, saying instead that "our end has drawn near, our days are fulfilled, for our end has come" (4:18). They cannot accept the narrator's surety of a different future for the community, and if they believe at this point that God controls what happens to them, there is no indication that they expect divine action on their behalf. In the light of *Beloved*, in which the community can act to provide grace to their members, it might seem to be a positive development at this point in Lamentations that we finally hear the speech of a communal voice, but they do not offer each other support or even signal that they see any future for themselves at all. We might, in fact, be reminded of the Black community in the novel when they were enraged by their own participation in the celebration of their freedom and future soon after Sethe's arrival at 124, the result of their failure to imagine lives in which they truly believed in and could claim such freedom. The mere existence of community is not enough to create a future that is more than just continued suffering if its members cannot imagine or accept it.

That being said, however, the community does not repeat in Lam 4 the narrator's words that blame them for their suffering, just as a character like Sethe in *Beloved* rejects schoolteacher's lessons as to why Blacks should suffer as slaves. And in the book's final poem of Lam 5, the community alone speaks, and here we can see that if they have not wholeheartedly embraced the narrator's claim at the end of the previous chapter that God acts on their behalf, they also have not entirely abandoned the possibility of that idea. Their final speech opens in 5:1 with a call to God to give heed (הביטה) to their pain, repeating the request Zion and the man had made (1:11; 3:63), and Lam 5 is dominated by the

---

impossible to read this phrase as saying that the punishment will come to an end in the future (see Middlemas 2005, 205–6).

descriptions of their suffering that they want God to notice. They refer to the starvation (5:6, 9–10), rape (5:11), and torture (5:12) they suffer and emphasize that they no longer control the land they live on (5:2).[49] "Slaves rule us" (5:8), they say, with the result that they are treated like slaves (5:13) by rulers who apparently have no concern for their anguish. The community is, in passing, now willing to accept earlier iterations of the Didactic Voice, and they say they suffer for their ancestors' sin (5:7) and that "we have sinned" (5:16).

In the end, however, the community who speaks this final poem, a group subject to mass killing, slavery, rape, and starvation, cannot imagine much of a future for themselves beyond such suffering. They still are not able to entirely muster the grace that would have them believe they do not deserve the pain they experience, nor is it clear that they have much ability to imagine a God who might treat them differently. They may open Lam 5 with a call to God to remember their suffering (5:1), but by 5:20 they say that God has still forgotten them. They call upon God to "restore us" and "renew our days" in 5:21, but the very next and final verse of the book leaves it ambiguous as to just how likely they believe such positive divine action to be. The opening words of 5:22 are כי אם, a phrase that could be translated a number of ways each giving the community's final words a somewhat different nuance and there is no scholarly consensus as to how to make sense of them in this context.[50] In those final words, they may be calling upon God to restore and renew them "even though [כי אם] you have utterly rejected us, are exceedingly angry with us," but it is also possible to understand them as saying, "but rather [כי אם] [than restoring and renewing us], you have utterly rejected us, are exceedingly angry with us." They may be asking God to restore and renew them "unless [כי אם] you have utterly rejected us, are exceedingly angry with us," but yet another way to make sense of that last verse is as an uncompleted thought that trails away into silence: "if [כי אם] you have utterly rejected us, are exceedingly angry with us ..." (Linafelt 2001). In that last case the community might seem unable to imagine words that could accommodate a future that goes beyond a past and present that are, like those of Sethe and Baby Suggs, intolerable.

---

49. For a full list of the aspects of suffering from earlier chapters repeated here, see Janzen 2019, 116.

50. For a survey of the proposed options and the strengths and weaknesses of each, see Salters 2010, 373–75.

Imagining Grace in *Beloved* and Lamentations

I pointed out in chapter 2 that none of the characters in Daniel has any concern for the subaltern and in chapter 3 that the subaltern characters of Ezra-Nehemiah are silenced, but I have been proposing here that in Lamentations we are able to hear subaltern speech. Am I right about that? Gayatri Spivak, after all, made the claim in the original version of "Can the Subaltern Speak?" that "the subaltern cannot speak," since the powerful will only hear subaltern voices in ways that benefit dominant interests, ignoring what the powerless actually intend to say. In a later edition of that essay, however, Spivak (2010a, 63) refers to that conclusion as "an inadvisable remark," which seems a prudent reworking of her earlier position, given that the specific example of subaltern speech that she discusses in the essay is something that she claims to understand (62–64) and thus is something she claims to hear.[51] Yet in both editions of the essay, a key aspect of subaltern speech as Spivak understands the concept is that it needs a true listener, someone willing to hear and recognize it as a poor fit for accepted narratives that justify the worldviews of the powerful. Hearing the subaltern speech in Lamentations, then, means encountering it in all of its messiness and fuzziness, to use Graybill's terms again. It both adheres to and rejects dominant Judean explanations of horrific disasters, as voices that contradict each other and themselves are unable to reach any resolution that could explain Jerusalem's destruction and their great suffering. As a fuzzy and messy work, Lamentations has no clear resolution and provides no obvious catharsis, and if speakers question the Didactic Voice's master narrative, they are also willing to embrace it at times.

If readers from privileged social locations are to hear this speech, then we will have to be prepared for it to be messy and fuzzy, particularly insofar as it often does not sound like the master narrative that appears else-

---

51. Spivak's specific example of unheard subaltern speech is the suicide of Bhubaneswari Bhaduri, an Indian woman who hung herself in 1926 following her inability to carry out a political assassination. The act, says Spivak, was Bhaduri's own rewriting of the *sati*-suicide text, even if members of her own family could not understand this (2010a, 62–63). Spivak (2010b, 228) says that she does understand the speech of the suicide, however, and hears it as an attempt "to erase the axioms that endorsed *sati*" from an ethical standpoint different than the British colonial one that legally abolished it as part of a colonial narrative in which white men saved brown women from brown men (see Spivak 2010a, 48–57).

where in biblical texts justifying horrible suffering by blaming subaltern victims and does not provide a tidy narrative resolution that allows us to stop thinking about the ongoing suffering of the powerless. Working with the assumption that subaltern narratives that relate their suffering have clear and even happy endings means that privileged readers need not ever be fundamentally bothered by those stories, since they always seem to work out. What the privileged hear in that kind of listening or reading is not subaltern speech but their imposition over it of their own understanding of the world as a fundamentally good place insofar as it maintains their privilege in an ethically unproblematic way. Reading Lamentations after *Beloved*, however, can help those of us not used to looking for or hearing the subaltern in biblical literature to recognize that at many places in this biblical book we are encountering subjugated speakers attempting to represent themselves and can help us become good listeners or readers, willing to allow this speech to unsettle rather than justify our understandings of subaltern suffering. This interpretive strategy can also provide us with inspiration to ask in this final section of the chapter how we might envision the characters of Lamentations continuing their speech as they imagine grace for themselves, just as readers of *Beloved* might want to ask what kind of future Sethe faces, something that demands imagining how she might interact with the other characters in the traumatic context of her past and continued suffering.

As a result, we can only pursue this final part of our reading process when we remember that the character of Beloved is a manifestation of intergenerational trauma that never entirely disappears, something that all of the characters must grapple with and something that is not always done successfully. If we want to be good listeners of the speech of Lamentations while also asking how it might continue beyond the bounds of the book as these characters imagine grace for themselves, we cannot assume that this will simply erase the suffering these voices describe, in which the dead can seem better off than the living. That sort of erasure on our part would merely repeat assumptions of the Didactic Voice as embodied by the narrator of Lam 4, who claims at the end of their speech that the community's suffering is over. That claim is not, after all, something that the communal voice speaking in Lam 4 and 5 can accept, and to ignore their rejection of it is to ignore the messiness and fuzziness of subaltern speech in the book by insisting that it arrives at a clear and cathartic conclusion that allows privileged readers to assume that such speech never fundamentally challenges any important aspect of the world as they understand it.

Imagining how Sethe's story might continue beyond her final appearance in *Beloved* in a way consistent with the novel's narrative means that we cannot simply ignore her suffering, but it also means that we must take into account the support that her community, Denver, and Paul D can offer her. Similarly, in our role as good listeners of subaltern speech in Lamentations, if we cannot ignore the pain these voices have expressed, we can also notice the ways in which the speakers have already imagined some sort of grace for themselves in which they can see a future that is more than their present anguish, as messy and fuzzy as that imagination might be. The man of Lam 3, for example, seems to be moving toward a more hopeful view of the future in 3:21–41, although this part of his speech that imagines a forgiving and merciful God is part of a claim that the pain his community experiences and the traumatic events that caused it are justifiable. The narrator of Lam 4 confidently claims the punishment of the community has come to an end, even though that position is abandoned in the communal speech of the following poem. The case is also, as we have seen, that it is not always possible for the speakers to imagine a God who might be characterized by anything more than a propensity for violence and enmity, which is how the community's final words at the end of the book can be read, as can those of Zion at the end of Lam 1 and those of the man at the end of his poem. The best future some of the book's characters can imagine is one in which their understanding of a perpetually violent God makes others suffer with them. Yet the basis for imagining a better future rooted in a view of the suffering community as human and worthy of humane treatment and in an understanding of a God who would never be responsible for the sorts of horrors they have suffered are already present in the book.

Looking to *Beloved* as inspiration for how such speech could develop, it is important to remember that in the novel any hope in regard to a future defined by more than just pain is found in the mutual support of a community of fellow sufferers, something we see most obviously when the women of the Black community save Sethe from the tyranny of past trauma embodied by Beloved. Community in such a context is more than simply the presence of other people but is a network of support that allows the group to acknowledge and survive suffering while also imagining, striving for, and celebrating a future in which more than just survival is possible. The narrator of Lam 1–2 is able to act in this kind of supportive way for Zion; those two poems use the verb נחם "to comfort," including the participle מנחם "comforter," six times (1:2, 9, 16, 17, 21;

2:13), and the narrator slowly adopts the role of comforter there insofar as they empathize with Zion's pain and in Lam 2 abandon attempts to justify things such as the starvation of her children and the slaughter and rape of her inhabitants. The narrator can eventually see how much the lives of the survivors matter and so stops trying to insist that it is right for them to be treated in ways humans should not be. If survivors cannot imagine that they do not deserve to suffer, then it becomes difficult for them to envision or try to create a future that is more than an extension of their mere act of survival in the present. Perhaps this is why Zion says a comforter would be able to restore her life (1:16), and we eventually see the narrator try to do just that.

The man of Lam 3, however, has no comforter, and while he refers to life in a larger community in 3:40–51 and uses first-person plural language in that part of his poem, the other community members never speak and so do not seem interested in engaging him in conversation. But this does not mean that he is entirely unable to imagine grace for himself, and at least at the end of his speech he draws a parallel between his current situation and that of his past where he bore no responsibility for the pain his enemies inflicted on him. If in the final section of the poem he cannot imagine a God who does anything except act violently against others, he at least can move beyond a belief that he is somehow to blame for or deserves his suffering. But because the ways in which he conceives of things such as his pain, the future, and God change numerous times throughout that poem, it is unclear as to what sort of stable conclusion, if any, he might arrive at regarding such ideas if his speech continued. The narrator of Lam 4 appears to want to act as a comforter for the community, and while this largely amounts to functioning as a channel of the Didactic Voice, blaming the community for their pain, the narrator also insists the community's punishment has come to an end. The communal voice in Lam 4 and 5, however, is unable to accept that attempt to comfort them, and they also clearly have difficulty imagining how they will even survive—let alone have a future any different from their present—for their understanding of God does not seem to permit that.

Some readers of Lamentations see a progression from hopelessness to hope as one reads through the book, a movement from despair to an explanation for the horrific traumatic events the community has undergone, something that allows for a developing sense of group identity (e.g., Conway 2012; Boase 2016; Cataldo 2020). This position seems like a way of avoiding the messiness and fuzziness of the real pain present in this subaltern speech, however, and it is difficult to justify in light of the diverging and conflicting perspectives of the various speakers of the book, when even the opinion of the same voice can change (e.g., Rong 2013, 167–70; Williamson 2015; Bier 2015, 29–37). Because there is no single viewpoint or authoritative voice in Lamentations, particularly because God never speaks to validate one view of things or to provide a different picture than those advanced by the speakers, the question as to who God is, what God is like, and how that should affect their understanding of their suffering and future is entirely up to the imaginations of Lamentations' characters. For them it matters greatly whether God can largely or entirely be defined through enmity and violence or through concern for the community manifested as a willingness to treat its members as humans whose lives actually matter, such that their future can be more than their present suffering. The book acknowledges the existence of the powerless, as Daniel does not, and allows them to speak, as Ezra-Nehemiah does not, but the speakers of Lamentations have not yet been able to clearly and firmly imagine grace for themselves that could allow them to envision a God who is not responsible for and rejects justifications of their slaughter, slavery, starvation, and rape. Nothing has yet entirely broken the back of the dehumanizing words of the Didactic Voice that justifies their trauma.

In *Beloved* the name of the eponymous character is the novel's final word, but this does not make the suffering she embodies the final word of the community's story of self-understanding, even if it is not something they can banish from it. For the traumatized community of Lamentations as well, the suffering they have experienced will continue to shape their lives, but that does not mean that it need be the final and deciding word. If we could picture the community imagining a more hopeful future for themselves, perhaps one as bright as Denver's at the end of *Beloved*, then they would need to break the back of the words of the Didactic Voice that blames them for their anguish and insists that mass slaughter, rape, torture, and the starvation of children are all part of the divine will. They would need to imagine grace for themselves such that they can conceive of their own lives as valuable, the belief Paul D urges Sethe to adopt at the end of the novel, and envision a God who believes that as well. And just as picturing Sethe's future beyond the end of the novel involves imagining how she might interact with Paul D and other characters, envisioning a developing imagination of grace on the part of characters in Lamentations is something that depends on the whole panoply of voices in the book: the narrator of Lam 1 and 2, who does not flinch from acknowledging

Zion's suffering and who can thus empathize with her and become her comforter; Zion, who is clear as to her need for a comforter who could restore her life; the man of Lam 3 who maintains, at least sometimes, that God can be defined by mercy and concern for the suffering; the narrator of Lam 4 who insists that things will be better, even if they offer no evidence or divine word to support that belief; and the community of Lam 4 and 5 that, at least at first, will not accept the blame the narrator attributes to them for their distress, and at points is willing to believe that God could notice their pain and save their lives.

The mere existence of a community of subalterns who has suffered the same set of traumas is not a panacea, as *Beloved* shows, but it is possible that it can provide the support its members need to create a different future, and so it could be a hopeful sign that Lamentations closes with the community speaking together. At this point, they would largely appear to be unable to imagine the kind of future Denver has at the end of *Beloved*, since with the help of her community she has begun to create a different life, something that will involve an education that can allow her to replace schoolteacher's old lessons with new ones. They cannot yet imagine a character like Baby Suggs, at least as she was before schoolteacher's arrival at 124, who could understand the need for and the power of communal grace to shape a future. If we were to compare the community in Lam 4 and 5 to any character in *Beloved* it might be to the figure of Sethe near the end of the book, who feels as if she has no future left to plan for but for whom a real future in community is still a possibility. Based on the speech in Lamentations, the same seems to be true for that community. The epistemological resources for imagining a real future are present among the characters who speak in the book, but there is no guarantee that the community can accept those aspects of the speech and imagine grace for themselves.

We need not conceive of a desire to imagine a continuation of the characters' speech simply as a need for readers to impose some sort of resolution that avoids the writing's messiness and fuzziness, something that would make us poor listeners of subaltern speech, but as a recognition of a basic structural principle of Lamentations that the community's speech is not yet completed and that space is still open for them to tell different stories about who they are, as characters in *Beloved* do. The structural element in question is that of the alphabetic acrostic present in the first four poems of the book, in which consecutive verses start with words beginning with successive letters of the Hebrew alphabet; for example, 1:1

starts with the word איכה, which begins with the letter *aleph*, while 1:2 starts with the word בכו, which begins with *bet*, and so on, until the last verse of the first poem starts with a word beginning with *tav*. The poems of Lam 2 and 4 are structured the same way, and Lam 3 offers an extended variation of this sort of acrostic, but the community's speech in the book's final poem is exempt from this structure.[52] For some readers the acrostic signals a sense of completion, in which all necessary information from *aleph* to *tav* (or from A to Z) has been provided (e.g., Johnson 1985, 60–61; Owens 1990, 77), although given the variety of shifting opinions in successive poems with acrostic structures it seems unconvincing, since even the same poem can offer competing viewpoints.

However one wants to understand the point of the acrostic structure of the poems in Lam 1–4,[53] it does function to distinguish each of the book's poems from the others, since verses that start with words beginning with *tav* mark the end of each. As a result, one way to read the disappearance of the acrostic order in the community's speech in Lam 5 is to see it as allowing for speech and reflection about God and themselves that go beyond the bounds of the book. There is no *tav*, no final letter, that signals an end, however arbitrary, to their reflections about what they, God, and the future are like and no pattern of language or words that need repeat in how they decide to conceive of such things. And because their speech in this final poem is not closed off by a decisive end to an alphabetic acrostic structure, we can envision it continuing as the community imagines themselves as a group who deserves to be treated as all humans should and merits something better than suffering and pain, since there is no justifica-

---

52. In the poem of Lam 3, each series of three verses has each verse start with a word beginning with the same letter, and so all of the verses in 3:1–3 start with words beginning with *aleph*, all of the verses in 3:4–6 start with words beginning with *bet*, and so on, until in 3:64–66 we encounter three verses that each start with a word beginning with *tav*. Attempts to see the final poem, or at least a part of it, as an acrostic are unconvincing and so have not been widely accepted; see, e.g., Bergler 1977 and Guillaume 2009. Even if one were to accept that there is some sort of acrostic message in Lam 5, however, it is not an alphabetic one that comes to a definitive end with the final letter of the alphabet and puts a stop to a discussion that one can imagine going beyond the bounds of the book.

53. Other readers see the acrostic structure as alluding to a fate as implacable and inevitable as the order of the alphabet (Pyper 2001, 62–63) or as providing order where there is no clear progression of thought (Hillers 1992, 27) or simply as an aesthetic device (Westermann 1994, 99).

tion for being treated as if their lives were not of human value. They may yet be able to imagine themselves as a group made up of members who should not constantly be threatened with slavery, death, rape, starvation, and torture and who exist in relationship with a God who sees them as valuable creatures whose lives matter.

So if in Lam 5 the community does not entirely abandon the Didactic Voice, it is still possible to see the absence of acrostic structure to that poem as signaling the possibility of future and better communal speech and as allowing readers to imagine what this might sound like. *Beloved* helps us with this act of imagination, and reading Lamentations after the novel can allow us to notice that voices in the biblical book have already articulated the basic elements of this better speech: an acknowledgment of Zion's great pain; a willingness to listen to survivors and act as comforter; descriptions of a God who offers mercy rather than violence; a rejection of the notion that the survivors are to blame for their suffering; and the ability to picture a future that is more than just survival. The speakers we encounter in Lamentations cannot sustain these ideas consistently, but they are able to articulate them in some form nonetheless. We can imagine future speech from the community speaking in the first-person plural at the end of the book that combines and develops those ideas so as to entirely reject justifications of the horrors to which Jerusalem's survivors have been subject. Readers who may never have thought much about the ethical problems raised by tacitly accepting the words of the Didactic Voice can, with the aid of *Beloved*, see the importance of abandoning the Voice's claims that tell a powerless and suffering community that there are perfectly just reasons for the slaughter, starvation, rape, slavery, and torture that has been inflicted on them—perfectly ethical reasons, in short, for why they are being treated in ways humans should never be treated—and that this sort of dehumanizing suffering is God's will.

This is, perhaps, as far as good listeners of subaltern speech can go with this project of imagination; unlike my reading of Ezra-Nehemiah, where I invented subaltern speech because there was none available at all, the presence of such speech in Lamentations requires a different approach if we truly believe the subaltern characters of the book who have already spoken should be heard. To truly listen to these voices, this project of imagination does not avoid the messy and fuzzy speech already present in Lamentations with its emphasis on suffering and disagreements as to how to make sense of it. It does not go so far as to generate future speech and dialogue for the characters we have encountered in the book, but it does draw upon some of the things they have already said and some of the ways they have acted toward each other. This means, of course, that this project cannot guarantee that all of the speakers would eventually resolve all of the book's disagreements in regard to understandings of suffering, God, and the future, just as in *Beloved* we cannot know with certainty if Sethe will be able to imagine grace for herself in a better future with her community and Paul D. To claim otherwise, whether in the case of Sethe or that of the voices of Lamentations, would be to pretend as if their traumas had only minor impact on their lives.

As in the interpretation of Ezra-Nehemiah in the previous chapter, the case is not that this reading replaces the text of Lamentations with what we would like it to say, it simply acknowledges that the book's structure can be understood as inviting readers to imagine how the voices we encounter in the discussion might develop ideas they have already touched on and arrive at conclusions not rooted in an immoral master narrative that blames them for their suffering. As readers trying to be good listeners of subaltern voices, then, we can see an ethical imperative for this aspect of our reading of Lamentations, which recognizes that the subalterns have their own resources to challenge unethical narratives deeply rooted in their cultural contexts. If they did not and were entirely unable to argue against the Didactic Voice's master narrative, they would end up like the community of Ezra-Nehemiah as it is represented by the dominant characters of that book. Those speakers, who appear in Jerusalem and Judah long after the events experienced by the characters of Lamentations, are part of a postexilic community so frightened by their understanding of a vengeful and violent deity that they feel compelled to demonize the most vulnerable members of their community, whom they designate as dangerous outsiders, just as white culture in *Beloved* imagines Blacks as a group who are so dangerous that they must be subjected to slavery and a whole host of terrors.

But this chronology of biblical narratives, in which the community of Ezra-Nehemiah appears in Jerusalem after that of Lamentations, also provides us with the warning that the Didactic Voice does not simply disappear. Perhaps this changes how we should conceive of the continuing conversation of Lamentations' speakers and lead us to understand it as something that allows the Didactic Voice to dominate. On the other hand, perhaps we can imagine a conclusion to that dialogue in which more hopeful views prevail and produce a community that can challenge the views of the main characters of Ezra-Nehemiah. Having paid attention to the subaltern speech of Lamentations, we can admit that both of these outcomes are possible, as are more ambiguous options in which the community arrives at no definitive agreement as to how to understand themselves, their suffering, God, and the future. An important hermeneutical lesson of the messy and fuzzy subaltern speech of Lamentations we encounter when reading it after *Beloved* is that there is no tidy and cathartic conclusion to it that might lead privileged interpreters to assume that it only validates the way we already look at the world.

5
AS LIMINAL AS POSSIBLE: HUMAN IDENTITY AND RELATIONSHIP WITH THE DIVINE AND NONHUMAN IN *FRESHWATER* AND GENESIS 1–11

Introduction

The word *genesis* points to beginnings, and a chapter about the beginning of Genesis might at first glance be understood as one about the importance of origins. Genesis 1–11 is indeed a narrative—or narratives, as I will discuss—of human beginnings, and as origin stories are sometimes understood to be explanations as to why things are the way they are, some read these chapters as accounts of how human origins explain important aspects of human identity. Within many Christian theologies, for example, stories from these chapters are understood to explain why humans are sinful creatures in need of divine redemption, since in such readings Gen 2–3 provides a narrative of a fall into sin that affects all of humanity; in Christian literature, we encounter this notion as early as Paul (Rom 5:12; 1 Cor 15:21). We see it as well in Jewish writings by the late Second Temple period (e.g., Sir 25:24; 4 Ezra 3.21; 4.30; 7.118; 2 Bar 48.42; 54.19), while rabbinic literature would go on to develop the Second Temple-era belief that an evil inclination drives humans to sin, an idea rooted in the reference in Gen 6:5 and 8:21 to the human יצר "inclination" as רע "evil."[1] In a related manner, origin stories are also sometimes interpreted as establishing norms for identity and action, and for some readers of faith, for

---

1. For the appearance of this concept in the literature of the Second Temple period, see, e.g., 4Q422 I, 12; 4Q436 I, 10; T. Asher 1.8; 3.2. For the appearance of יצר הרע in rabbinic texts, see, e.g., b. Yoma 69b; b. Ketub. 51b; Sif. Deut. 45; Gen. Rab. 9.7.

example, the stories in Gen 1–11, and those in Gen 1–2 especially, are understood to demonstrate that only heterosexual intercourse is acceptable, that heterosexual marriage should be a sexual norm, and that the traditional Western binary distinction between male and female should be the only acceptable way to conceive of gender (e.g., Dresner 1990; Murphy 2017; Patterson 2019).

When texts are frequently read in oppressive and exclusive ways, it can be difficult to imagine them as having liberative value. Certainly not all interpreters read the opening of Genesis as a condemnation of those who do not conform to the cisheteronormativity of Western culture,[2] but those of us with unearned social privilege due to our sexual orientation and gender identities may often find it difficult to produce readings of these chapters with potential emancipatory value for LGBTQ+ communities. In order to do so here, I read Gen 1–11 after *Freshwater*,[3] a novel by the Nigerian-born transgender author Akwaeke Emezi. *Freshwater* is not the story of creation and the development of human civilization that we see in Gen 1–11, but like that piece of biblical literature it foregrounds the relationship between the human and divine, or at least between one human and her relationship with various divinities. Ada, the central human character of the novel, is a Nigerian who moves to the United States, and she must struggle to establish a sense of who she is in relationship with the gods who live within her, who are themselves suspicious of the more powerful deities who have locked them within Ada's body. These different *ogbanje*, or "godlings" as the beings who live within Ada call themselves at one point (6), take turns narrating the bulk of the novel, providing different and at times conflicting accounts of events in Ada's life and their relationships with her. The novel is a story of a human's struggles and growth in relationship with divinities who eventually learn to change in response to her evolution; in the end neither the human nor the gods are who they were at the novel's opening, for their identities and relationships mature over time.

Gods do not live within the humans in Gen 1–11, but the humans in those stories are godlike—in the divine image according to one narrator

---

2. Some argue, for example, that the narratives of creation in Gen 1–2 portray humans who are originally androgynous and so see them as validating much broader gender and sexual norms; see, e.g., Rosen-Berry 2008; Reay 2009, 162; West and Walt 2019, 112.

3. Emezi 2018. Further references to the novel will be indicated by page numbers cited in the text. Italicization in quotations from the book is present in the novel.

(1:26–27; 9:6) or simply "like gods" (3:5) according to the other. We could read the opening chapters of Genesis as the origin story of godlike humans who are told to subdue and rule other parts of creation (1:28) and whose mistake lies in wanting to be more like God than they were originally created to be or, to put that another way, to ignore the categories of identity established for them at the beginning. In this interpretation they deserve the suffering imposed on them by God, who at one point goes so far as to kill virtually all of them in a reaction against their desire to locate their sense of identity outside of the one that God had expected to be the norm. This sort of reading is one that would sound familiar to many LGBTQ+ people, not only because they have been told repetitively that a failure to identify within "normal" categories of sexual orientation and/or gender identity violates the divine will, but also because they suffer harassment, poverty, imprisonment, and violence at extremely high rates for not being the sorts of persons the cisheteronormative world would prefer.[4] Read after *Freshwater*, however, Gen 1–11 can be seen not just as a tale of how humans and their relationship with God begins but also of how they and God change in both positive and negative ways as the stories progress; as in the novel, the humans and divine in these chapters of Genesis can be seen as evolving and maturing in relationship with each other.

Part of this developing sense of human identity and relationship with God involves notions of gender and sexuality that change, as I will dis-

---

4. To consider only data from the United States in this regard, an update to the Department of Justice's analysis of hate crimes in the United States in 2021 found that 20.4 percent of them were motivated by the victims' sexual orientation or gender identity; in comparison, hate crimes motivated by religious identification constituted 15.1 percent of all such incidents (United States Department of Justice 2023). An academic analysis of the National Crime Victimization Survey from 2017 to 2019 concluded that LGBT people in the United States were nine times more likely to be victims of violent hate crimes than cisgender and straight people (Flores et al. 2022). The largest survey of transgender people in the United States found that nearly half of them reported being sexually assaulted at some point in their lives and that 29 percent were living in poverty, compared with 12 percent of the US population as a whole (National Center for Transgender Equality 2015b, 3); the same study found that transgender persons were more than twice as likely as the general population to be imprisoned and that Black transgender women were more than nine times as likely to be incarcerated (National Center for Transgender Equality 2015a, 5). A 2021 study concluded that almost half of LGBTQ workers in the United States experience unfair treatment and/or harassment in the workplace because of their sexual orientation or gender identity (Sears et al. 2021, 1).

cuss in the fourth section of this chapter. In *Freshwater*, Ada eventually realizes that she is among the ọgbanje herself, and ọgbanje, she says, "are as liminal as possible—spirit and human, both and neither" (225–26). And, as we discover, the ọgbanje "brothersisters," as the novel calls them, do not adhere to binary categories of gender any more than they do to a categorical distinction between human and spirit, and so as Ada evolves in her self-understanding and identity with the ọgbanje, she also grows into a liminality in terms of her gender and sexuality. Reading Gen 1–11 after *Freshwater* can help readers, particularly ones who are privileged by existing binary categories of sexuality and gender, to see the liberative potential of this biblical text that has so often been used in oppressive ways. It allows us to see the human characters in these stories as liminal figures who abandon binary understandings of their identity and so who become queer, insofar as the queer is what troubles that which is considered to be normal and respectable (Marchal 2019, 8–10), and trans, insofar as the humans locate their identity in ways that transcend the categories of being established in the early chapters.[5] The original binary categories of human and divine we encounter near the beginning of this biblical material have been superseded by the time we reach its end, as humans have developed into liminal spaces between them. When read after *Freshwater*, we can be more apt to notice the shifting notions of gender and sexuality in Gen 1–11, leading us to see that the character of God who emerges in some of these stories is one who eventually accepts that the original binary distinction between human and divine is inadequate and who appears open to liminality or queerness in other aspects of human existence as well.

Reading Gen 1–11 after *Freshwater* allows interpreters who have never been regarded as less than authentically human because of our sexuality and gender identification to be able to read these biblical stories as throwing "normal" categories of sexuality and gender into question, and so to encounter this as a text with liberative potential, particularly as it presents human identity in general as trans or queer. With this reading strategy, readers can see these narratives as portraying a God

---

5. If it is most common to use "trans" as a prefix when thinking of concepts related to gender and sexuality, that is certainly not the only way we can use it, given scholarly inquiry into things such as trans-species literature (e.g., Hsu 2023) or the trans-corporeal, a reference to the bonds between humans and nonhuman entities in the natural world (e.g., Yoon 2023).

who values the lives of the queer and genderqueer, despite the fact that these chapters are so often read as justification for their minoritization in claims that the text portrays God as irrevocably establishing binary categories of male and female gender identification that are linked to a cisheterosexual norm. Without encountering a text such as *Freshwater* first, it simply might not occur to some of us that we could even search for such a liberative significance to these chapters or to understand the human characters of these texts as inhabiting liminal or queer identities, but in light of the novel we can see in Gen 1–11 a God who evolves and matures as the narratives progress and who grows to accept an identity for humans that transcends the binary categories established early on in the story.

In such a reading, then, the opening of Genesis is not about the importance of origins but about the change and maturity that both humans and God undergo. To look at these chapters otherwise is to understand them as a kind of ending, in which everything that needs to be said about gender and sexuality has already been said, and to regard the biblical material that follows as a series of appendixes to the conclusions reached in that regard in Gen 1–11. What we find instead when reading after *Freshwater* is the beginning of a story that emphasizes change that transcends and queers original categories of identity and relationship; in fact, as the final section of the chapter will discuss, if this approach can help us see humanity as queer, it helps us notice as well as the lack of clear distinction in this biblical text between humans, nonhuman animals, and the divine. Some interpretations of Gen 1–11 have been used to justify worldviews that understand the natural world as something humans can exploit for whatever purposes we choose, a view of things that has led to ecological crises that include global warming, a planetary disaster with far more dire consequences for the poor and the Two-Thirds World than for the wealthy and the countries most directly responsible for it. Extending our reading of Gen 1–11 as guided by *Freshwater* in this fashion means encountering a biblical text in which human, animal, and divine identities cannot clearly be distinguished from each other. The natural world as portrayed in these chapters cannot then be seen as full of nonhuman animals of a lower status of being than humans, which means in the logic of Gen 1–11 we are not free to damage and destroy them and their habitats at will, a portrayal of humanity's relation to the natural world with liberative potential for the disadvantaged groups most vulnerable to crises such as global warming.

The Coevolution of Human and Divine in *Freshwater*

Ada, the central human character of *Freshwater*, is born in Nigeria, but from the moment of her birth is different from virtually everyone else, as she is the daughter of "the god Ala, who is the earth herself, the judge and mother, the giver of law." Ada has human parents, but "the child of Ala is not, and can never be, intended for your hands" (9). The powerful god Ala is not a prominent character in the novel, but the *ogbanje* with whom Ada shares her body are, and they narrate most of *Freshwater*. At first there are two of them, the narrators of most of the first part of the novel, and they say that they, like Ada, are children of the gods (6) and refer to themselves collectively as "a god" (20).[6] Their relationship with Ada is complicated; when she emerges from the womb of her human mother, the *ogbanje* say, "We were at once old and newborn. We were her and yet not" (5). They are not sure where Ada stops and they start, they admit at another point (43). It is the struggle for Ada and the *ogbanje* to create a relationship with their independent yet united identities that drives the novel. What is at stake is Ada's very sanity and existence, and for much of *Freshwater* it appears that its central question is one the *ogbanje* ask: "How do you survive when they place a god inside your body?" (207).[7]

The *ogbanje* say that before Ada was born they were independent and could move in and out of her human mother's womb (1–3) but that upon Ada's birth they found themselves locked within her body against their will (4). They did not belong there, they say, or at least they should have been "asleep inside her membranes and synched with her mind" when she was born (5). The gates between human life and the noncorporeal world

---

6. Emezi largely avoids explaining Igbo cosmology in Western terms in *Freshwater*, with the result that Western worldviews are decentered and do not take on the role of what everyone is expected to know and what is necessary to know in order to define everything else (see Schindler 2023, 232). The *ogbanje* who inhabit Ada in the novel are characters who conform to the Igbo understanding of such beings as part human and part spirit, torn between remaining in the human world and desiring the death of their human host so they can return to the *ogbanje* cohort in the spiritual realm (Okonkwo 2008, 8–10).

7. In a later work, Emezi (2021, 56) writes that an *ogbanje* is not a spirit possessing a human since there is no distinction between the two. The difficulty Ada and the *ogbanje* face in *Freshwater*, however, is the failure to erase the distinction between them, and so throughout the novel they struggle to establish an identity of unity and healthy mutual dependence.

of the *ogbanje* should have been closed to prevent their consciousness of their origins, but they surmise that the gods somehow forgot to do so in this case. The more powerful gods are careless, the *ogbanje* say (5), and as a result it seems clear to them that Ada is destined to be driven mad (6), the inevitable result of gods trapped inside a body becoming aware of their identity. Over time the *ogbanje* begin to understand who they are; at age three Ada and the *ogbanje* within her see a python, the corporeal symbol of Ala (11–13), and that is the first time after Ada's birth that the *ogbanje* realize that their true parent is not Ada's human mother (1). Some years later, at a masquerade ceremony at which other *ogbanje* are present through their representation in masks worn by human participants, the two within Ada become fully awakened to their true identity by their *ogbanje* brothersisters who recognize their presence within her (17–20).

Perhaps Ada would not have been driven mad, the *ogbanje* hypothesize, if they had never realized their divinity (20); all madness, they say, derives from gods sealed into bodies when they remember they come from a different world. This contaminates the human realm, but the gods often do not care enough about humans to always close the gates of remembrance when divinities slide into bodies. Sometimes the human hosts are driven insane, sometimes the gods within them use the human bodies to do "atrocious and delicious things to torn people." Some *ogbanje* were excited by the damage they could do in the human world: "They took it too far. They took it only a god's length" (34). So the two *ogbanje* inside Ada are aware they pose a danger to her, saying that "she was contaminated with us, a godly parasite with many heads" (41). They do feel close to Ada (43) and want to protect her (37) but are also angry because they are "subject to decisions made around what was just a vessel" (47). In fact, they always refer to Ada as "the Ada," making her seem like an object rather than a person,[8] and as much as they claim they want to help her navigate a life they believe is doomed to insanity, they do not do a very good job of this. Because they see her as "just a vessel" and "the Ada," they can seem just as selfish and careless when it comes to her well-being as are the more

---

8. Contra Magaqa and Makombe 2021, 28, who argue the definite article emphasizes Ada's compound identity of numerous beings. It is not clear how calling her "the Ada" points to her as embodying different beings, and it is not an expression Ada or any other character uses to refer to her, even when she realizes she exists in identity with the gods who inhabit her. Given the *ogbanje*'s description of her as a vessel, the phrase more clearly indicates the status as a mere object she has from their perspective.

powerful gods whom they accuse of leaving them with self-awareness in a human body.

As a result, they do not stop Ada when, at age twelve, she begins to cut herself to provide them with sacrificial blood: "First duty, feed your gods," is their appreciative comment (41). When she is sent to the United States to attend college, they cannot understand why she misses her family and friends in Nigeria, since as gods they lack empathy for humans, and so they simply cut those feelings out of her (48–49). This failure to understand who she is as a human means that they do not allow Ada to try to mature by attempting to struggle with, adapt to, and overcome emotions associated with unhappiness. Later on they will refer to other acts of cutting they performed in her mind when she was younger, sectioning off memories of a neighbor who sexually abused her and of the beatings her older brother gave her. While this seems to the *ogbanje* like protection from "a terrible and wicked" world, as they put it (208), it also unmoors her from a sense of true identity, making her unsure of who she truly is, something that to her "felt like a developing madness" (210). At one point, Ada wishes to give herself completely to a man whom she loves, only to arrive at the devastating realization that this is not possible because the *ogbanje* had cut so much out of her (159–61). The pain and madness Ada experiences is directly attributable to the *ogbanje* and to what they do to her in misguided attempts to help and protect her, the result of their failure to truly understand her.

And although the *ogbanje* never admit it, they are at least partially responsible for the repetitive rape of Ada by Soren, her first college boyfriend. They are fascinated by Soren's "nightmare childhood trauma anger" and "by the ease with which he slipped into his rages" (55–56). At one point, Ada realizes that, although she and Soren have just had sex, she cannot remember the sex itself, whether she had consented to it, or even if they have had sex on previous occasions (57–58), and this failure of memory seems difficult to explain without the *ogbanje*'s interference, given what we know of their ability to section off parts of Ada's memory. Their interest in Soren's anger, something they manifest without the least interest in or sympathy for the nightmares and trauma that have produced it, would explain why they keep Ada so close to him and his abuse, despite the fact that he has raped her and that she is at times so frightened of him that she has to physically hide from him (56). The *ogbanje* apparently believe they can protect her simply by removing memories of his rape of her from her mind, and so it is only three years later when Ada reads a definition of rape online that she can finally realize what the ọgbanje allowed to happen to her (174).

So the ọgbanje's claims to be Ada's protectors and saviors (209) ignore some of their obvious failures to truly act as such, failures born of the fact that as gods they do not entirely understand or care to understand the full range of human emotions or to empathize with human suffering; gods can love humans, the ọgbanje say, but such love is accompanied by "a taste for suffering" (37). Moreover, ọgbanje are by nature "malicious spirits" (31), and in the case of the two who initially inhabit Ada's body, matters are even worse, since their brothersisters are angry that they were "born incorrectly" (89) with consciousness of their divinity. They want them to return to the noncorporeal realm, which can happen only when Ada dies, and in an attempt to push her toward suicide, the brothersisters have her mother abandon the family while Ada is a child (27–32), yet the two ọgbanje within Ada do nothing to oppose those actions. It is, in fact, their failure to protect Ada from Soren that results in terror so great that Ada's screams attract yet another divine presence to lodge within her (58), the one Ada would later name Asụghara (70–71), the figure responsible for about half of the novel's narration. Over time it becomes clear to readers and to Asụghara herself that she too is ọgbanje. At one point she is visited in Ada's mind by two ọgbanje brothersisters who make her aware of her true identity (127–32); assumedly these are the two who inhabited Ada's body originally, since they had earlier realized that Asụghara was "just one of us" (87). Upon her arrival in Ada's mind, Asụghara sees it as her job to protect Ada from Soren; he had "made Ada a gibbering thing in a corner," Asụghara says, "but he would never hurt her again" (65). Ada loves her, Asụghara says, "because I hated that boy," and "because I was strong and held her together," and she says that she loves Ada as well (70–71).

Asụghara's love for and protection of Ada, however, are as questionable as that of the other ọgbanje no matter how much she claims otherwise. Asụghara may hate Soren, but she continues to have Ada—or at least Ada's body—have sex with him. The protection Asụghara provides is to ensure that Ada is not consciously present during the sex, and when using Ada's body in this way, Asụghara says, "I expanded against the walls" of her mind, "filling it up and blocking her out completely. She was gone. She might as well have been dead" (64). Like the other ọgbanje within Ada, Asụghara believes that she will save her human host (61–62), but her use of Ada's body to have sex with Soren, even though Ada is not consciously present, does not seem overly different from the rape of Ada to which the other ọgbanje assented and hardly seems like salvation. Asụghara, like them, accepts the sacrificial blood Ada offers as she cuts herself (71), and after Asụghara has Ada break up with Soren, she uses Ada's body to have sex with other men. Asụghara refers to herself as "a weapon" (120),[9] "unforgiving and petty and vindictive" (116), and as "a little beast, if you like, locked inside Ada" (70). Much of what Asụghara does, particularly in the way she uses Ada's body for sex, is done for her own pleasure, her enjoyment of having a body to use as well as an existence separate from the interconnected mass of the ọgbanje brothersisters (62). At one point, she uses Ada's body to sleep with the brother of one of Ada's close friends because "he felt good" (76), knowing that, should the family find out, they would refuse any further communication with Ada (78) and knowing that sleeping with the brother made Ada feel "ashamed" and "dirty" (82). "Ada was right," Asụghara admits later on, "I found pleasure in evil" (145), her actions being evil because she hurts Ada and others to indulge herself.

Unlike the other two ọgbanje within Ada, Asụghara takes great delight in finding herself within a body, and she often takes control of it. She has Ada cut off her hair so she more closely resembles the way Asụghara envisions herself (66–67) and has her lose a dangerous amount of weight as well, an "experiment" to "see how close to the bone I could get Ada down to" (69). "It wasn't important anymore, what happened to her body," (69), Asụghara maintains, and perhaps to assuage her own conscience she asserts at times that she and Ada are really the same. "We were one," she insists at one point, although this is part of her explanation that she was ruining Ada's relationship with a man she loved (114). "I'd contaminated her too much," Asụghara says, with the result that Ada was now "an impostor; she was now me" (119). And since Asụghara's brothersisters want her to return from the human realm, she concludes she must drive Ada to suicide, something she rationalizes as a way to protect her, since it would end her suffering (134–36). At this point, Asụghara simply cannot see or will not admit to the selfish sophistry of this plan, based in important part on ending suffering for which Asụghara herself is largely responsible. She uses Ada's body to have sex only with "cruel men, men who cheated and lied," and she admits that she drags her "through unprecedented filth in

---

9. The chapter that introduces Asụghara, and the first one she narrates, opens with the (untranslated) Igbo sentence, Ọbịara egbum, gbuo onwe ya (61), which means, "Take a weapon, kill yourself" (Cobo-Piñero 2023, 290), an allusion to Asụghara's character and what she will try to make Ada do.

the name of protection" (141). When Ada seeks out therapy, Asụghara refuses to allow her to talk about the *ogbanje* within her, causing a massive migraine that creates so much pain that Ada does not return to the therapist (146–50). "I needed her to rely only on me," she says, "so I could take her home and we could be with our brothersisters again" (150).[10]

Asụghara's plans for Ada's suicide end in failure—the very final words of the last section of the novel she narrates are, "I had lost" (183)—and as the other two *ogbanje* resume control of the narration, they say it was a foolish plan, "taboo to Ala," and one Ala would never have allowed to succeed, since Ada is her child (184). Asụghara, Ada, and the other two *ogbanje* must all find a way to coexist in the same body, despite the damage these gods have done to her in what they have considered to be their attempts to save her from a cruel world and their presence within her. While Asụghara now seems to play much less of a role in Ada's life, the other two *ogbanje* decide "to accept that this body was ours too" (187), which seems like progress of a sort, since at least Ada ceases to appear to them as a corporeal prison. They "want to change the Ada into us," they say, to have Ada's body physically represent who they feel they are as Asụghara had, and for the *ogbanje* this means that they want to have Ada undergo breast reduction surgery to better reflect the liminal gender space they occupy (187); they are suspended, they say, "between the inaccurate concepts of male and female" (193). Their desires appear to overlap with Ada's in this regard (189–90), even though they do not appear to consult with her in making the decision to have the surgery.

We could understand her acquiescence to have her body manifest the *ogbanje*'s sense of gender liminality as part of Ada's growth in self-understanding, something that instinctively feels to her like a natural reflection of her true nature, even if she has not yet entirely realized what that is.

---

10. The assertion that, in seeking therapy, Ada treats her madness through a Western framework of mental health and so recolonizes herself (Harlin 2023, 316–18; for a similar position, see Ukwueze 2023, 73–74) creates a binary view of Western and Igbo culture that is not entirely borne out in the novel. In the end, Ada's healing derives from steps she takes and from her encounter with a Yoruba priest (see below), but there is no sense in *Freshwater* that therapy in the context of a Western understanding of mental health could not be beneficial for her, even if it would be insufficient in and of itself. As Rocío Cobo-Piñero (2023, 290–91) points out, on page 189 of the novel, Ada uses a therapist to help her find a language to make sense of her gender and sexual identities, so the fact that Asụghara initially prevents Ada's return to therapy is simply another manifestation of her selfishness and intent to drive Ada to suicide.

Part of Ada's process of determining that she too occupies the same liminal space as the ọgbanje within her—a space between human and divine, "spirit and human, both and neither" (226)—is her growing awareness of the liminal space of gender and sexuality that she occupies. Asụghara may have used Ada's body to have sex with men, but the other ọgbanje tell us that she arrived in Ada accompanied by a figure Ada names Saint Vincent. The ọgbanje do not believe that he is divine, and he is not able to control her body as Asụghara does, but he makes Ada feel more male or at least more the way her body felt before puberty (121-24). As a prepubescent, the ọgbanje say, "The Ada felt like a trickster, which felt right. She could move between boy and girl" (123). Under Saint Vincent's influence, Ada explores the possibility of having sex with women (124-25), and an important part of her maturity that she reaches toward the end of the novel involves her recognition of the different liminal spaces in which she exists. The liminal ground between divine and human that she occupies is related to her gender and sexual liminality, something that seems natural to her—it is possible, the ọgbanje admit, that Vincent had been inside of her all along (122-23)—but also something influenced by the gods within her as well. She can in the end only truly understand her own identity once she is able to say that "I am my others; we are one and we are many" (226).

In order to arrive at this self-understanding, however, Ada is not the only one who has to change and mature; the ọgbanje must also, and their acceptance of Ada's body as theirs is only one step, inadequate in itself, in their growth. The ọgbanje and Asụghara learn from Yshwa, yet another god who inhabits Ada; at her baptism as an infant, the Christian priest kept referring to "some christ, another god," as the ọgbanje put it, and he "walked over, scattering borders," accepting the girl being offered to him (8). Yshwa loves humans, they say, although "he loves them as a god does, which is to say, with a taste for suffering" (37). After Soren, Ada had stopped trying to reach Yshwa, at least according to Asụghara, who says that "he was never there for her, not like me" (83). If Asụghara claims she can block Yshwa from reaching Ada, saying that he just makes her feel worse, she also says that Ada had become too broken to hear him (84-85). Yshwa, though, insists that Ada is constantly talking to him and that Asụghara is the one of whom Ada is ashamed (85-86). Only later in the novel, in a section narrated by the other two ọgbanje, do we discover that Ada and Yshwa had been conversing far more than Asụghara ever knew or admitted (195). By that point, all three of the ọgbanje begin to listen to him, accepting him as a brothersister who had also experienced life as a divinity within a human body. They admit that his gentleness and love amount to "a good code," albeit an unnatural one, since they experience humans and their world as "cruel" (196).

Despite this interaction among the gods within Ada, the ọgbanje appear to remain selfish beings, and even their acceptance of Ada's body as their own only leads them to use it along with Asụghara to trick humans and break their hearts, making Ada suffer (197). Yshwa's teachings are not enough to stop them from acting that way, and so it is Ada herself who begins to limit the damage they do. The ọgbanje have cut memories out of her, making her feel as if there are different versions of her, "a developing madness," and so she makes the decision to tattoo her body with these different memories and versions of herself, as well as with a picture of the ọgbanje. "She never cut herself again after that. We had all evolved," the ọgbanje say (210),[11] but this is an evolution based on actions Ada chooses. Her growth continues as she meets a priest in Nigeria, who is able to speak to her and to the ọgbanje. He "pulled the Ada out into the light," they say, and he "called her by all of our names." It is because of their interaction with him that they realize Ada "is not ours, we are hers" (215). It is painful when the priest departs, but the ọgbanje no longer section off Ada's unhappy memories (216), so they now leave her with the sadness of his departure as part of herself, something she must deal with and incorporate into her evolving sense of identity.

In the end, it is Ada who supplies the answer to the question the ọgbanje say she herself poses: "How do you survive when they place a god inside your body?" (207). She begins to realize that she is not weak, as the ọgbanje had assumed, a false conclusion that led to their selfish and misguided attempts to protect her. Ada takes over the narration at the end of the novel, taking it back, we could say, from the ọgbanje and so demonstrating how she has now taken control of her own story. On one of the

---

11. There is a parallel between the tattooing and the "benign bodily incisions" made in Igbo culture on an ọgbanje child to anchor them to the human world and prevent an early death (Okonkwo 2008, 11; and see Emezi 2021, 198–99), and there is a qualitative difference between this tattooing and the cutting of herself Ada had done since she was a child, as the ọgbanje appear to recognize. The tattooing enables Ada to deal with her fragmentary and compartmentalized senses of self in a healthy way, whereas her earlier acts of cutting merely reflected the "developing madness" of that fragmentation. Kate Harlin (2023, 318–19) argues as well that Ada's breast reduction surgery can be seen as a parallel to the Igbo ritual cutting of ọgbanje children.

very few pages of Ada's own narration that occurs earlier in the novel, she says that what the *ọgbanje* relate about her "will be the truest version" of any story that involves her, "since they are the truest version of me" (93). But following the meeting with the priest, the last part of her story told by the *ọgbanje*, she understands that she is Ala's child, and so she evolves into the liminal identity that was hers all along and says that she is "letting go of being human" (225). In the end it is prayer to Ala that helps her realize that she is not really human but is, or has become, one of the brothersisters. "Ọgbanje are as liminal as possible—spirit and human, both and neither," says Ada in her narration that closes the novel. "I am my others; we are one and we are many" (226). The question Ada's "others" thought she posed was not entirely the correct one to ask, because Ada was never entirely the weak human they believed her to be, and so they are not the truest part of her, as Ada had once assumed, and they had to learn the truth about her evolution beyond what they had all assumed to be her original identity. Their attempts to save her from the cruel human world and her own weakness misconstrued who she was, or at least who she was in the process of becoming, and so the pain they caused her and those whom she loved stemmed from their own selfishness that led them to ignore Ada's developing identity as a brothersister, a being as powerful and liminal as themselves, a being who exists to be in identity with them.

Ada's true salvation from madness is one that results in her wholeness and recognition of herself as someone living in some sort of identity with divine beings and is the acceptance of a sense of self that places her in a space that is "as liminal as possible," both human and spirit, both male and female, and at the same time none of these. The *ọgbanje* could not save her from the world—they appear too selfish for that—nor from their presence in her body. While at first they have a need to control her for what they convince themselves is her own protection, in the end they can admit that Ada "was easier to control when she thought she was weak" (215); once she understands that she is not, she is able to take her place in a relationship of identity with them.

The Coevolution of Human and Divine in Gen 1–11

At first glance it might not appear that the stories of Gen 1–11, which focus on the beginnings of the world and humanity and their early development, have much in common with *Freshwater*. It is true that there are references to multiple divinities in these chapters, just as there are in the novel: At one point, the main divine figure in Genesis says, נעשה אדם בצלמנו כדמותנו "let us make humanity in our image, according to our likeness" (1:26); this figure admits at another point that האדם היה כאחד ממנו "humanity has become like one of us" (3:22); and near the end of these chapters calls upon the other deities to respond to the human act of building a city and tower by saying, נרדה ונבלה שם שפתם "let us go down and let us confuse there their language" (11:7). Biblical Hebrew does not use plural verb forms and pronominal suffixes to indicate a plural of majesty (Clines 1998, 2.459–60; Joüon and Muraoka 2006, 347n7); the God who speaks in these verses converses with other gods. Nonetheless, we do not see in these chapters the multiplicity of divine figures who are named and who act in *Freshwater*, figures who are even responsible for the bulk of the novel's narration, for while there may be more than one divine figure present in the stories in Gen 1–11, only one of them ever speaks or takes center stage in these narratives. And while it is true that the humans of Genesis become like gods according to one of the narrators or were originally created in the divine image and likeness according to the other, this is not entirely the same situation as *Freshwater* in which gods live within Ada.

Nonetheless, having read a novel in which a human and "godlings" must come to grips with her evolution into a liminal space that makes her "spirit and human, both and neither" as they all grow in their self-understanding and identity with each other, we can see Gen 1–11 as a set of stories less about the importance of origins than about the developing relationship between human and divine and recognize that the different sorts of identity that each has evolve throughout the course of the narratives in these chapters. Reading Gen 1–11 after a work like *Freshwater* makes it easier for those of us whose social privilege means that we have never been forced to suffer because of our sexual or gender identity to see narratives in these chapters that portray human identity as in flux rather than immediately established as a rigid status quo. Moreover, as we will see in the next section of the chapter, this process of reading a biblical text after a work of literature by an author at a minoritized intersection of race, gender identity, and culture allows us to see the character of God as evolving in some of these stories to the extent that we can imagine this figure accepting as fully and authentically human those who identify outside of cisheteronormative binary categories of gender and sexual orientation.

We should note at the outset of this reading that Gen 1–11 has multiple narrators, just as *Freshwater* does. We might be used to describing narrators like the ones we encounter in this part of Genesis as omniscient, which is to say as truthful and all-knowing figures in the world of the text, but the two narrators of these chapters disagree with each other in some important ways and provide us with conflicting and at times contradictory accounts of some of the events they relate, a case somewhat like that of *Freshwater*, where the *ogbanje* narrators do not always agree in their accounts of Ada's life or provide readers with accurate assessments of it. In Genesis this is the result of redactional activity, and regardless as to how one wants to explain the steps in the composition of Gen 1–11, it is possible to separate the material in these chapters into Priestly and non-Priestly sections. One need not follow the explanation for the redactional development of these chapters as the Documentary Hypothesis conceives of it in order to conduct the sort of reading I do here, but for the sake of convenience I will borrow the Documentary Hypothesis's nomenclature and refer to one of the narrators as P and the other as J. To be clear, I do not mean to link my use of these sigla to any theory of composition but am only using them as names for the two different narrators whose voices I identify in these chapters.[12]

It is the narrator P who opens Genesis with an account of creation by a being referred to only as אלהים or God, who encounters some form of the earth at the beginning of this creative activity covered by water that P describes as תהו ובהו (1:2), a phrase that portrays the earth in its watery precreated state as hostile to life.[13] God, however, begins to establish order,

---

12. Even scholars who believe the Documentary Hypothesis provides the best explanation for the composition of the Pentateuch will disagree at points when it comes to assigning particular verses or passages to one of the Hypothesis's sources; within this group of scholars, however, assigning specific verses in Gen 1–11 to Priestly (P) and Yahwistic (J) sections is largely uncontroversial. For those who argue the Hypothesis fails to adequately explain the composition of Genesis and the following books—and who would distinguish between P and non-P material, rather than between P and J—there is still broad agreement as to where we can locate Priestly material in Gen 1–11, and distinctions between P and non-P verses and passages among this group tend not to differ greatly from the traditional distinction between P and J here, even though the competing theories as to how this non-P material was collected and added can differ greatly (see, e.g., Otto 1996; Kratz 2005, 248–99; Carr 2020, 223–49). The process of composition does not affect my reading here, however, for it depends only on the notion that I can find two contrasting and at times contradictory narrative voices, regardless of when and in what order the non-P material was composed and added.

13. For discussions of this phrase, see Tsumura 2005, 22–32 and Walton 2011, 140–44.

on the first day of creation making light to separate day and night, and on the second day a dome God calls heavens to separate the preexisting waters on earth from those in the heavens, and on the third dry land called earth, which produces vegetation. The next three creative acts correspond to the first three, filling the spaces that have already been created: the celestial bodies are made on the fourth day, slotting into the spaces of day and night created on the first day; on the fifth day birds are created to fly in the heavens created on the second day, and fish to swim in the earthly waters that were separated from the heavenly ones; and on the final day land animals and humans are created to fill the earth that appeared on the third day.[14] It is not clear why this God wants to create; given the story's apparent interest in order, such that spaces are made on the first three days to accommodate the things created on days four through six that will fill them, perhaps God simply wishes to replace the תהו ובהו with an order hospitable to life, but because we are given no statement of motivation, to some degree God appears as unknowable as the great gods, like Ala, whom the ogbanje discuss in *Freshwater*.

It is not until 1:26 that we get the sense that other divine beings are present beyond the one responsible for creation up to that point, and here the God who has alone been acting up until this point addresses the other deities, urging the creation of humanity "in our image, according to our likeness." No more is heard about those other gods in this part of the story, however, and in 1:27 the narrator again refers only to the single God in charge of creation, said in this verse to create האדם "the human," both male and female, "in his image."[15] Perhaps we should understand the use of words such as "image" and "likeness" as referring to some sort of physical resemblance between the gods and the male and female human, as some have argued (e.g., Moore 1996, 93–95; Garric 2008), since P's narrative in 5:3 will refer to Seth as in the "image" and "likeness" of his father.[16] If that is the case, then the fact that humanity is specifically created as both male and female may imply that the God who creates them is androgy-

---

14. For a more detailed discussion of the long-recognized correspondence between the first and final three days of creation in Gen 1, see Crawford 2018, 571–75.

15. The OG version of Genesis has no equivalent to בצלמו "in his image," but the word appears in the MT and SP, so it was assumedly omitted by the copyist of the Hebrew text behind the OG through homoioarchton with the following בצלם.

16. For references to some of the passages in the Hebrew Bible that refer to God's physical appearance, see Kirova 2020, 3n10.

nous (e.g., Gudbergsen 2012). Others have pointed out that the Hebrew word צלם "image" and comparable words in the languages of the ancient Near East refer to statues understood to represent the presence of gods and rulers (e.g., Schüle 2005, 10–11; Herring 2008) and that the use of the word here suggests that the humans will represent the divine in the new creation (e.g., Quine 2015, 298–99; Crouch 2016, 9–10). God, after all, tells the humans that they are supposed to subdue (כבש) the earth and rule (רדה) the animals (1:28), verbs used elsewhere in the Bible to refer to subjugation that is sometimes violent,[17] thereby suggesting that the humans will actualize divine rule on earth by enforcing the divine order God has created (so, e.g., Dube 2015, 243; Haynes and Krüger 2017, 679–80), at least among the animals, although God provides no instructions as to how they would go about doing that. As Theodore Hiebert (2019, 266–67) points out, the imperfect וירדו in 1:26 follows the volitive נעשה, forming a purpose clause; that is, God proposes creating humanity in the divine צלם "so that they might rule." In P's story, both humans and animals are created as vegetarians (1:29–30), since apparently to kill fellow animals for food would be considered a violation of the created order, so given the sparse information we have here, it seems most likely that the humans are to rule the animals as divine representatives, with the specific goal of ensuring that such violence does not occur. This is an issue to which I will return in the discussion of this narrator's version of the flood story, but we can note at this point that, as it is not clear how humans might put a stop to all interspecies killing, one wonders how well God understands them.

Whatever precisely the word *image* might mean here, it does suggest that humans are in some way like the divine beings in whose image and likeness they have been created, but this account of the original relationship between human and divine in P's narration is not shared by J, as I am calling the other narrator in Gen 1–11. We are alerted to the presence of a different narrative voice providing a different picture of creation once we reach 2:4 and the following verses, where we find a figure called יהוה אלהים or YHWH God, who begins to act in a precreation setting where there is land but no rain, vegetation, or humanity (2:5). Clearly this does

---

17. In the Bible, the verb כבש generally has the sense of violent subjugation; see, e.g., Num 32:22, 29; Josh 18:1; 2 Sam 8:11; Zech 9:15; 1 Chr 22:18. The verb רדה is often used in the sense of rule over slaves or areas conquered by warfare; see, e.g., Lev 25:43, 46; 26:17; Num 24:19; 1 Kgs 5:4 [ET 4:24]; Isa 14:2; Neh 9:28. See also, e.g., Schüle 2011, 8–9; Möller 2011, 19–21.

not chronologically follow the account of creation in 1:1–2:3; it is instead a different creation story, one that is clearly incompatible with P's version in some ways. The use of the name YHWH points to the new narrator's interest in this particular figure among the אלהים, and according to J this God's first creative act is to form האדם "the human" from a combination of ground and divine breath (2:7), although in this story there is only one human at first. YHWH puts the human into a garden where this God has planted trees that provide food, as well as one called "the tree of life" and another called "the tree of the knowledge of good and evil" (2:8–9). YHWH warns the human not to eat of the latter tree, since "on the day you eat of it you will certainly die" (2:17).

The point of the human is לעבד "to work" or "to care for" the garden this God creates (2:15),[18] although J does not explain why this God wants a garden in the first place. After the creation of the human, YHWH believes it is not good that it should be alone and resolves to make "a helper corresponding to it" (2:18).[19] The case appears to be that God is not only concerned by the idea that the human might be lonely; YHWH does not only want to create a being "corresponding to" the human but one who can also function as a helper, and since the only task the human has been set has to do with the care of the garden, then assumedly the helper will participate in this work. YHWH, however, does not entirely understand the human who has just been created and tries to fill the perceived lack by creating animals, which the human names (2:19–20), but when this process fails to produce a helper corresponding to the human, YHWH then takes one of its צלעות "side parts"[20] to create a new being that the human apparently

---

18. One can see עבד as emphasizing agricultural work here (so, e.g., Batto 2013, 80–81) or the care and service the human is to devote to the garden (e.g., Habel 2013, 97), although these two ideas are certainly compatible with each other (e.g., Hiebert 2022, 82–83).

19. It is not entirely clear how to translate Hebrew כנגדו, which I have rendered as "corresponding to it"; for this translation, see Bechtel 1993, 112–13. See also Schüle 2005, 15, who argues that כנגדו points to "a unique level of correspondence." Since נגד generally refers to spatial relationships, another possibility for the translation of כנגדו here is "alongside of it" (see, e.g., Greenstein 2002, 237), emphasizing a spatial proximity between the אדם and the helper and emphasizing a divine concern for the loneliness it may be experiencing.

20. The noun צלע is often understood to mean "rib" in 2:21–22, but since this word never has this specific sense anywhere else it appears in the Bible, it is safer to use a more general term in translation (see Deutschmann 2017, 261).

decides does correspond to it (2:21-22). The human continues its work of naming here and calls this new being אשה "woman," and it—or by this point, since we now see a usage of vocabulary reflecting a distinction in gender, we can say he—now names himself: איש "man" (2:23).

J's understanding of creation contradicts P's, not only on the basic level of fact—such as what is present before creation begins, or in what order things are made, or how humanity is created—but in terms of J's depiction of the creator. God's order and forethought implied by P's story of creation—where a place is created for everything in days one through three, and everything made in days four through six goes into its prepared place—is absent in J's narrative. P's God so frequently describes the results of the creative acts as "good" (1:4, 12, 18, 21, 25, 31), assumedly because of divine foresight and the order it produces, that one could hardly imagine P's God saying, as J's YHWH does, that "it is not good for the human to be alone" (2:18). Perhaps P's God would, unlike J's YHWH, never be so careless as to leave a tree within the reach of humans that apparently will kill them upon the consumption of its fruit, although P's God in 1:28 is careless enough to order humans to rule the animals without giving them any instructions as to how. P and J also have very different understandings of what humans are when they are created. In P's narrative, they have been created in the image of the אלהים—in the image of God and the gods, in other words—which suggests they are like those divine beings in some sense, perhaps especially as they are to rule the animals in some unexplained way.

This is not the case, however, for the human in J's story in Gen 2; it may name the animals there, but like the human they are created from the ground and also described as נפש חיה "living being(s)" (2:7, 19). At the end of this creation story the two humans, like the animals, are naked (2:25). The humans can speak, but so can the snake we encounter in the following verses (3:1-5), and so it is not clear that there is much to distinguish the humans and the animals upon their creation in J's narrative. The very fact that YHWH originally believes that nonhuman animals would function as beings "corresponding to" the first human, a role that only another human can fill, also points to the close similarity between human and animal identity here. Since J's narrative of creation follows P's, we can read it as a response, in which case J indicates a disagreement with important aspects of that first description of creation and presents the animals and humans as largely kin when they are made (so, e.g., Gnuse 2021, 169-70; Middleton 2022, 290). The humans YHWH creates in J's story in Gen 2 are not the godlike masters and subduers of the world and of animals that they are—or at least are supposed to be—in P's version of events.

Humans do become godlike in J's story, however, although it is clear that this narrator does not believe their adoption of such an identity was YHWH's original intention upon their creation. The change comes about only because of the conversation in 3:1–5 between the snake, said to be ערום "wise, prudent" (3:1),[21] and the woman. Questioned by the snake as to the trees from which God has permitted them to eat, the woman expresses some knowledge, albeit imperfect, of the divine prohibition from 2:17 against eating from the tree of the knowledge of good and evil, an act that as far as she knows would lead to death.[22] The serpent directly contradicts YHWH's words in the original command and says that "you will certainly not die" upon eating from the tree and that instead "your eyes will open and you will be like gods (אלהים), knowing good and evil" (3:4–5). YHWH can appear as careless here as the powerful gods the *ọgbanje* describe and seems as little aware of what the humans might want or feel as the *ọgbanje* in *Freshwater*. YHWH apparently did not want the humans to eat of the tree but seems unaware how desirable it would prove to them once they had been told the truth of the results of eating from it.

In J's narration YHWH originally created the humans to be unlike gods, as beings without the knowledge of the difference between good and evil; this suggests, when we look to Deut 1:39, which refers to children as those who "do not yet know good and evil," that they are not what we would consider to be mature since they lack adults' knowledge of right and wrong (see Kawashima 2004, 488–89). As such, if one wants to construe YHWH's command not to eat of the tree as a test (so, e.g., Mettinger 2007, 23), it demonstrates YHWH's failure to understand the humans, since they lack the adult ability to distinguish between good and evil that they would need to pass it. The case is clearly not that the humans were created with

---

21. Hebrew ערום can be used in a pejorative sense (e.g., Job 5:12; 15:5), but the word is not inherently negative and can also describe those who are wise or prudent (e.g., Prov 12:16, 23; 13:16; 14:8); that is certainly how the LXX translator understood it when using the lemma φρόνιμος "sensible, prudent, wise." Arthur Walker-Jones (2008, 281) argues ערום simply indicates the snake's intellectual abilities.

22. In 2:17 YHWH commands the human not to eat from the tree of the knowledge of good and evil, "for on the day you eat of it you will certainly die." The woman had not been created when that command was given, and she tells the snake that God had forbidden eating or even touching the tree "lest you die" (3:3).

no knowledge.²³ They can speak, and the woman can judge for herself that eating the tree's fruit would make one wise (3:6), which tells us she has some sense of discernment,²⁴ but their knowledge at their creation is limited.

As the most עָרוּם, wise or prudent, of the wild animals created by YHWH (3:1), the snake is both like and unlike those animals—it may be a nonhuman animal but exceeds all others in its wisdom—and both like and unlike the humans. Like them and YHWH, the snake can speak, but the snake is wiser than the humans, for unlike them it is aware of the true results of eating from the tree (Brett 2000a, 86), possessing knowledge that otherwise only the gods have or that perhaps only YHWH does.²⁵ Upon eating the fruit "the eyes of the two of them opened" (3:7), precisely what the godlike snake told the woman would happen, and they do indeed become like the gods, as YHWH says to the other divine beings (3:22). In J's narrative, then, the humans evolve to become like gods against YHWH's wishes, and after they eat of the tree they make חֲגֹרֹת "loincloths" for themselves once they realize that they are naked (3:7). This specific realization is sometimes understood to be a reflection of the fact that with new knowledge and wisdom the humans are now aware that they had not been living any differently than the animals, and so this is often seen as the first step toward human civilization in J's narration, as the humans mature from animal-like children to wise and godlike rational adults (e.g., Korte 2011, 149–50; Turner-Smith 2015, 443–45; Alderman 2020, 110–11). The clothes the humans make at this point, which distinguish them from the animals, will soon be followed in J's narrative by the inventions of agriculture, religion, the city, and other trappings of civilization. Others have pointed to the fact that the clothes in question here are loincloths, things that cover only their genitals and something that points to their new awareness of sexual reproduction (e.g., Humphreys 2001, 38), and such knowledge also seems to play an important role in the evolution of humans and their relationship with the divine in J's story.

---

23. Some argue that the phrase "good and evil" in this context should be understood as a merism and that eating from the tree provides the humans with knowledge of all things in general (e.g., Rad 1972, 86–87), but that does not make much sense in this story, where the humans have some knowledge to begin with.

24. Kimberly Russaw (2015), in fact, sees the portrayal of the woman in this part of the story as reflecting characteristics of the wise individual in biblical texts.

25. Arthur Walker-Jones (2008, 287–88) argues the snake appears more divine than the anthropomorphic YHWH does in Gen 2–3.

On the other side of the human-divine dynamic in J's narration, YHWH can seem "an inexperienced, naïve, even bungling creator" (Batto 2013, 80). YHWH's statement in 2:17 that eating the fruit of the tree would result in certain death has proven false, and so at worst we can see this God as a liar (so, e.g., Rooke 2007, 162–64), although more charitably we might decide that YHWH had simply uttered an empty threat to keep the first human away from the tree. In this latter reading, YHWH does not understand the humans well enough to know that this would not stop them from eating from the tree—and does not even seem to understand them as well as the snake, whose conversation with the woman leads the humans to violate the divine command—and decides not to make good on the threat after they consumed its fruit. At this point in J's narrative, YHWH is clearly opposed to human maturation and their attainment of knowledge, and so divine retaliation follows their choice, although that reprisal does not result in death. The snake is cursed (3:14–15), although it did nothing but tell the truth. The woman and man will both experience עצבון "pain, hardship, toil," she in pregnancy and childbirth and he in farming, and the woman is now told that she will have desire for the man and that he will rule over her (3:16–18).

YHWH reacts like a threatened monarch who sees an unquestioned rule under attack, a divinity who had hoped to reserve true knowledge for the gods alone, says Frank Yamada (2009, 108–10). YHWH does not even bother to justify the hardship imposed on the woman, and the explanation of the man's—"you listened to the voice of your woman"—is telling, says Deborah Rooke (2007, 170–71), since it suggests that YHWH had wanted to exercise complete authority over the man, whose fault in divine eyes here is that he followed the woman's lead instead of a divine order motivated by an opposition to human maturity and reason (Kalmanofsky 2017, 28–46). Of the two of them, it was the woman who took the initiative in bringing wisdom and civilization to humanity, something YHWH finds threatening, and so something that results in the divine insistence here that the less ambitious man rule over her. At this point, YHWH reminds humans of their mortality (3:19) and expels them from the garden specifically so they do not eat of the tree of life and become entirely like the gods in the attainment of eternal life (3:22).

In J's narrative world, YHWH originally intended a clear distinction between the divine and human realms and is threatened by the humans' decision to abandon the identity with which they were created. J's portrayal of YHWH as selfish and somewhat careless would fit within the picture of the divine world of *Freshwater*. The *ogbanje* refer to themselves as "malicious," and one could apply the same adjective to YHWH in J's story, where God retaliates against humans for making a decision that they did not have the maturity to understand. This hardly seems fair, and in this regard YHWH again seems much like the divinities of *Freshwater* who, as readers are told, are not fair (199) and are careless with human lives and well-being (e.g., 5, 33, 83). YHWH, like the *ogbanje* who refer to their contamination of the human world by their presence within Ada, believes that the human and divine worlds should not mix. And like the *ogbanje*, YHWH does not entirely seem to understand humans.

But as humans mature and change in J's story, YHWH changes and adapts to their evolution, as the *ogbanje* do in response to Ada's growth in the novel. In both cases there are positive and negative divine responses; as an example of the former, in Gen 3 YHWH at least makes the humans "garments of leather" (3:21) before expelling them from the garden, which suggests a willingness to accept their choice for civilization to some degree, since God creates more elaborate clothing for them than they were able to make. The humans' choice to become like gods has now led to a kind of liminal status for them, existing neither as the animal-like humanity YHWH creates at the beginning of J's narrative nor as immortal gods; they are, to paraphrase Ada's expression near the end of *Freshwater*, god and human, both and neither. They have transcended the identity that they had been told they should inhabit, choosing new understandings for who they are and could be. If we want to describe them as trans in that sense, we could also say they have queered the original categories of creation and that from the standpoint of the world YHWH seemed to have in mind at the end of Gen 2 they have moved outside of originally distinct categories of creation into a kind of liminal borderland of ambiguous or queer identity. The queer, as Gloria Anzaldúa (1987, 19) puts it, manifests the failure of "an absolute despot duality that says we are able to be only one or the other" and that "claims that human nature is limited and cannot evolve into something better."

The man reacts to the divine retribution or at least to YHWH's insistence in 3:19 that humans will return to the dust from which they were formed by continuing his earlier work of naming. The one he had earlier called אשה "woman" he now names חוה "Eve" because, J explains, "she was the mother of all living [חי]" (3:20). Eve, of course, is not actually the mother of all living beings—in J's story, as we will see, she is not even the ancestress of all humans—but perhaps the man's exaggerated belief in regard to her procreative abilities reflects not only the humans' new awareness of sexual reproduction but also the concomitant knowledge that YHWH is not the only being in the cosmos who can create life (so also, e.g., Wolde 1994, 8–9; Humphreys 2001, 51–52). We can see a somewhat similar response on Eve's part in 4:1, where she gives birth to Cain (קין), a name that reflects her statement that "I have created [קניתי] a man with YHWH." Unlike the man, she acknowledges the fact that her ability to create life depends on the good will of the divine world, but she too expresses her awareness that she is a necessary part of creative activity (see Rooke 2007, 167–68). This will not be the last time in J's story that the humans understand their own creative ability, an understanding that results from the knowledge they now have in their new liminal or queer existence, as something that can respond to divine retribution.

As J's narrative continues in Gen 4, we see further developments in human knowledge and creativity, as well as a changing relationship between them and YHWH. In this chapter, readers see that the second generation of humanity, at least as it is embodied in Eve's two sons, has already developed at least some aspects of agriculture (4:2) as well as a form of religion—both Cain and his brother Abel offer sacrifices to God from their produce (4:3–4), apparently without divine prompting. YHWH, however, has regard only for Abel and his sacrifice, not for Cain and his, and provides no reasons for this disregard of Cain. While this has not prevented readers from trying to guess what they might be,[26] one imagines that if YHWH's rationale for rejecting Cain and his offering mattered to J, then it would appear in the narrative; the fact that there is no explanation just makes it seem as if YHWH is as careless and capricious as the divinities in *Freshwater*,[27] unable to treat—or perhaps simply uninterested in treating—all humans equally. One might conclude that YHWH, following the experience of the humans eating from the tree of knowledge, simply wants humanity to learn to unquestioningly bow to unexplained divine choices (so Humphreys 2001, 55–56). Whatever the explanation, YHWH's disregard for Cain certainly lies at the root of the latter's anger (4:5) that leads to the murder of his brother (4:8).

---

26. Perhaps, some have argued, YHWH just prefers Abel's animal sacrifice to Cain's grain sacrifice (e.g., Levin 1979) or prefers sacrifices with animal blood to ones without it (e.g., Hobbs 1986) or is put off by the fact that Cain farms the אדמה "ground" (4:2), which YHWH cursed in 3:17 (e.g., Jørstad 2016, 709).

27. For the depiction of YHWH as capricious at this part of J's story, see, e.g., Lohr 2009a, 492–94; Zucker 2020, 15–16.

Perhaps Cain kills Abel out of jealousy (so, e.g., Kawashima 2015, 265; Twersky 2017, 282), but since his anger is caused by YHWH's unexplained rejection of him and his sacrifice, we can also see the killing as an attack directed primarily against YHWH by doing away with the human God prefers, a murderous response to divine capriciousness and injustice (so, e.g., Ramírez Kidd 2015–2016, 33; Gossai 2019, 213–14). YHWH can sense Cain's anger before the murder occurs, but the attempt to address it amounts only to telling him that something crouches in wait for him at "the door of sin" and that Cain must learn to rule over this (4:7).[28] This cryptic statement about some sort of vague but menacing threat[29] that Cain must master does not assuage his anger or cause him not to kill his brother, any more than the threat about the tree of the knowledge of good and evil in 2:17 stopped the humans from eating its fruit. YHWH, like the gods of *Freshwater*, appears unable to fully understand and empathize with humans and their emotions and does not even seem to care enough about Abel to ensure his protection. Divine caprice and the failure of divine intervention lead to murder (so, e.g., Habel 2007, 83; Byron 2008, 3–4), and if YHWH does not kill Cain in response—YHWH, in fact, ends up providing Cain with protection from those who would kill him (4:13–15)—that may reflect YHWH's acceptance of some culpability for what has happened (so Gossai 2019, 213–14). Cain's punishment is thus limited to being driven from the ground—he can no longer practice agriculture, in short—and from the divine presence (4:10–16).

Yet Cain like his mother goes on to create after receiving divine punishment, and he fathers a son and builds a city (4:17), thereby furthering the development of civilization. J does not explain how it is that other people are present to build and fill a city or to bear children for Cain; there simply appear to have been other divine acts of creation that have taken place that our narrator does not care to mention, including the creation of humans not descended from Eve. The focus of the narration remains

---

28. This reads לפתח חטאת רבץ with the MT and SP. The OG here reflects a Hebrew text that has been altered somewhat (changing לפתח to לנתח, for example) in order to create an easier reading that explains the divine favoritism for Abel; see the discussion in Brayford 2007, 251–52. For the interpretation of לפתח חטאת רבץ as "at the door of sin is a crouching thing," see Schlimm 2012.

29. While YHWH does not provide the identity of the רבץ "crouching thing" at the door of sin, the verb is often used in the sense of menace, frequently that posed by wild animals (see Gatti 2017, 57).

instead on the development of civilization following divine punishment, and a short genealogy in 4:18 connects Cain to his descendant Lamech five generations later and to Lamech's children, who devise the arts of raising livestock, playing musical instruments, and constructing metal tools (4:20–22). YHWH may have banished Cain from farming the ground, saturated as it was with his brother's blood, but the divine claim that this would force Cain to become נע ונד "a nomad and a wanderer" (4:11–12) is not ultimately borne out, for Cain becomes a city dweller; ironically, וישב בארץ נוד "he settled in the land of Wandering" (4:16). Cain worries that being forced from the divine presence means that "anyone who finds me may kill me" (4:14), and so YHWH says that Cain will be protected by the threat of vengeance that will be taken seven times over on anyone who kills him (4:15). In the end Cain provides his own protection by building the first city,[30] so becoming a key founder of human civilization. His descendant Lamech, the father of other founders of civilization, also learns to protect himself and kills someone merely for wounding him, claiming that if YHWH would have taken sevenfold vengeance for Cain, any damage done to him will be repaid seventy-seven times over (4:23–24).

Having been banished from the land and YHWH's presence, Cain adapts and with his descendants builds a civilization, reflecting and continuing the work of the first human couple. Pushed even further away from the divine world, they use the creative ingenuity that accompanies the human choice to abandon their original animal-like existence and live within the liminal space between the original categories of human and divine that YHWH established at the beginning of J's story. They are not as weak as YHWH might have supposed when offering Cain protection, just as the *ọgbanje* eventually realize Ada is much stronger than they ever knew. Lamech's threat of violence projects strength but hardly qualifies as positive human change, although as he explicitly sees it as inspired by YHWH's promise to protect Cain he perhaps also understands it as a godlike thing to do. It is because humans decide to identify within this liminal or queer space and become godlike and rational adults that they can act with such creativity and make their own way in the world. Humanity has changed and adapted to divine actions and retaliation in ways YHWH could not foresee, rather like Ada toward the end of *Freshwater*, and they appear to be stronger and more resourceful than YHWH anticipated. And

---

30. For a somewhat similar view, see Lohr 2009b.

somewhat as Ada grows into a sense of self that involves an identity with the *ogbanje* within her, the godlike humans of J's narrative do not want to live without communication with the divine. Despite the divine banishment of Cain, the very last thing we read at this point in J's story before it is interrupted by P's narration is that humans began to call on YHWH (4:26). As self-sufficient as these descendants of Cain seem to be, they do not wish to live apart from the divine presence as Cain was forced to do any more than Ada ultimately wants to live apart from the *ogbanje*.

It is at this point that P's story resumes, and just as J had provided an account of creation that conflicts with P's, we might think of P as interrupting J's narrative to register disagreement with it. The material of 5:1–28, 30–32 (5:29 is J's own interruption of P's interruption) consists of a long linear genealogy, moving from Adam and his son Seth in 5:1–5 to Noah and his three sons in 5:32, ten generations later. Some of the names in this genealogy or very close variants of them also appear in 4:17–24, part of J's narration, as descendants of Cain rather than of his brother Seth: Enoch (4:17–18 and 5:18–24); Lamech (4:18–24 and 5:25–28, 30–31); Methushael (מתושאל) in 4:18, who appears as Methuselah (מתושלח) in 5:21–27; and so on.³¹ And if J incorrectly assigns the ancestry of these figures to Cain rather than to Seth—according to P, at any rate—what else could J be wrong about? For one, P claims (yet again) that God created humanity in the likeness of the אלהים (5:1–2), just as Seth, the son of Adam, appeared in the "likeness" and "image" of his father (5:3), statements that insist that J's story of a human evolution into a queer identity between original categories of human and divine is simply wrong.

P instead suggests a parallel between Adam's relation to Seth and the divine's relation to humanity, making the humans seem as if they are the gods' children at their creation, rather than the animal-like beings who appear at the beginning of J's story. There is no hint in P's narrative of a changing humanity who creatively works its way around divine retaliation to build civilization and care for itself, and we find instead in Gen 5 P's repetitious genealogy that names fathers and sons in a direct line from Adam to Noah's children. This has been interpreted both as pointing to a "failing lineage" that for P will justify the destruction of the world in a flood (Bauks 2019, 188) and as the depiction of a line of righteousness running from Seth to Noah (Brett 2000b, 40), but the

---

31. For more details, see Hoopen 2017, 180–81.

general lack of characterization and description of human action in this genealogy[32] does not allow us to say much more than that one lineage is seen to be more important than others, although P provides no more insight as to the significance of this particular line of descent than J does in the failure to explain YHWH's preference for Abel over Cain. At any rate, there is no sense at this point in P's story that either humanity or God has changed at all.

After P's interruption of J's narrative, something that rebuts J's version of human growth and evolution, J's voice returns and recounts a story of how בני האלהים "the divine beings"[33] had sex with human women (6:1–2), causing YHWH to state that human lifespans would no longer exceed one hundred and twenty years (6:3). J's YHWH appears to accept to some degree that the humans no longer are as they were created but clearly does not want to allow them to become more like gods than they already have, although the other divine beings in the story seem to have different thoughts on the matter. We might see this story, and in particular YHWH's reaction of limiting human lifespans, as J's response to P's genealogy, in which the age of every figure before Noah is listed. They are all said to live for centuries, which may fit P's assertion that the humans were godlike creations in the first place, but that from the perspective of YHWH's concerns in J's narrative seems uncomfortably close to immortality. In J's story, where YHWH is worried the humans might live forever and become exactly like gods (3:22), YHWH tries to reestablish a boundary between human and divine by limiting the length of human lives, even though other divine beings now seem to see little if any difference between themselves and the humans. P, however, presents a picture of a primeval world in which, at least at this point, there appears to be no change in the identity of humans, and so its narration contradicts J's portrayal of a boundary between divine and human that is continually in flux because

---

32. If there is a possible exception to this in the genealogy, it is the notice in 5:21–24 that Enoch "walked with God"—P says the same about Noah, whom the narrator describes as "righteous" and "perfect" (6:9)—but these verses say nothing specific about Enoch's life and actions (see Hoopen 2018). Even if we were to assume that this comment pointed to P's approval of Enoch's conduct, that would still be the exception that proved the rule, since no other part of P's genealogy in Gen 5 provides any reflection on the righteousness (or lack thereof) of the figures named here.

33. The juxtaposition of the phrases בני האלהים (literally, "the sons of the gods") and בנות האדם ("the daughters of humanity") rather obviously suggests the former are divine (so, e.g., Vervenne 1995, 25–26; Day 2012, 427–28).

of the liminal status of the trans humans who have moved outside of the category of being in which they were originally created. As a result, in P God exhibits no qualms with the extraordinary length of human lives, and in P's genealogy of 11:10-32 humans after the flood continue to live for centuries.

In J's account, on the other hand, humans feel forced to respond creatively to divine reactions against their choices to become more godlike, and in the case of YHWH's limitation on lifespans, it is the human Nephilim,[34] described as "warriors" (6:4), who have devised a way to deal with this new boundary meant to distinguish divine identity. While YHWH has already prevented humans from literally living forever, the Nephilim are described as אנשי השם "people of name," or famous people (6:4), and their fame, assumedly created through their martial deeds, allows their names to live on after their deaths (so Kawashima 2004, 392-93), a metaphorical if not literal immortality. Cain had managed something like this in naming his city after his son in 4:17 (Clines 1998, 1.343-44), and in a later story in J, humans will attempt to make "a name for ourselves" through the construction of a different city (11:4).

J's YHWH appears to struggle with how to adapt to the ways in which humans are changing, a reflection of the fact that the world we see in J's story is one reminiscent in *Freshwater*'s, where Ada occupies liminal space between the human and divine spheres, where we see concern on the part of the gods that the divine world is contaminating the human one, and where sometimes the divine world actively aims to destroy humans. Sometimes, as in *Freshwater*, this appears merely to be malicious, as in the divine reprisal of 3:16-18, a reaction to a decision made by humans when they were not adult enough to know the difference between good and evil; yet this decision was possible because YHWH's lack of understanding of them resulted in the failure to see that the warning of 2:17 not to eat of the tree of the knowledge of good and evil would not be enough to dissuade them from doing so. And by 6:5, YHWH appears to change the divine mind yet again about the humans and their evolving identity, for there J claims that YHWH sees such evil on the part of humans—"every inclination of the

---

34. The Nephilim of 6:4 are sometimes understood as the offspring of the divine beings and human women (see, e.g., Hamori 2008, 123; Routledge 2015, 40), but since 6:4 also says the Nephilim were present on the earth after the flood, they do not appear to be the divine beings' children, as no sexual liaisons between gods and humans are mentioned in J's postflood material.

thoughts of their hearts was only evil, constantly"—that YHWH believes it is necessary to destroy them by flooding the world (6:5–7). The focus of humans' inclinations and thoughts in J's narrative largely has to do with becoming civilized and more godlike, dedicating themselves to maturity and growth, for such stories of a transcendence of original boundaries have dominated J's narrative up to this point. Assumedly this is the "evil" YHWH deplores, a reversal of an earlier acceptance—to at least some degree—of the developing sense of who humans are.

P's narrative also contains a version of the flood story, although here God determines that "all flesh" and not just humans have "ruined" (שחת) the earth through their violence, causing God to decide to "ruin" the earth with a flood (6:11–13). P's narrative of human and animal existence up to this point, however, contains no examples of violence. To work with the very limited amount of evidence we have from that story, since in P both humans and animals are created as vegetarians (1:29–30) and since P's God indicts both humans and animals for violence here, it is assumedly the violence of interspecies killing—something humans have been unable to prevent in their original godlike role in P as the rulers of the animals—that is to blame for the flood as far as P is concerned. By the end of P's flood story, as a new start is made to creation, God repeats part of the blessing of humans when they were originally created—"be fruitful and multiply" (1:28; 9:1, 7)—but omits the original command to rule the animals, apparently stripping the humans of the role they have been unable to perform. The fact that they were created in the divine image now serves to distinguish them from nonhuman animals only insofar as it remains illicit to kill humans (9:5–6).[35]

The flood story of 6:5–9:17 is a mix of J's and P's narration, and while they provide conflicting details at points,[36] the outlines of their stories are

---

35. Stephen Wilson (2017, 272) maintains that in 9:1–6, humans continue to act as divine representatives, although now not insofar as they are to rule the animals but rather as those who must avenge human bloodshed, a much-reduced role.

36. The argument that there is no coherent flood story in the non-P material of Gen 6–8 (made by, among others, Ska 2009, 1–22) does not really work, at least not insofar as my reading of Gen 1–11 is concerned. If we follow Ska's division of the story and identify the non-P passages as 6:5–8; 7:1–5, 10, 12, 16b–17, 22–23; 8:2b, 6–12, 20–22, there is a complete and noncontradictory story with details that at points conflict with those in the Priestly version; for example, in non-P the flood lasts forty days (7:4, 12, 17; 8:6), but in P one hundred and fifty days (7:24; 8:3), and in non-P seven pairs of all clean animals come aboard the ark (7:2–3), but in P only one pair

the same: God spares Noah and his family from the flood that kills all other humans, making them the new founders of humanity; and at least one pair of each kind of animal is rescued in the ark inhabited also by the chosen human family. But as horrifically negative as YHWH's response to human change and civilization is in the flood narrative, what we see at the end of J's version might be considered as yet another change on YHWH's part in the developing divine-human relationship; immediately after smelling Noah's postflood sacrifice that produces a ניחח "restful odor," J's God resolves never again to curse the ground or destroy the earth because of humans, reasoning that "the inclination of the human heart is evil from their youth" (8:21), even though YHWH had originally caused the flood because "every inclination of the thoughts of their hearts was only evil, constantly" (6:5). Humans once again have responded in a creative way to divine retribution, for Noah has developed a kind of sacrifice that saves the world from future annihilation, a notable advance in religious technique produced by civilized humans. If YHWH still thinks of the human recognition that they exist within a liminal state as evil, at least God is willing to rethink this sort of violent retaliation in response to human choices for civilization. That being the case, perhaps the reference in 8:21 to the divine resolve to never again curse the ground—an allusion to the curse of it in 3:17–18—suggests that YHWH is willing to rethink that first divine reaction against a human decision to queer original categories of creation and transcend them. In 3:17, speaking to the אדם, YHWH had said, ארורה האדמה בעבורך "cursed is the ground because of you"; now, in 8:21, YHWH says, לא אסף לקלל עוד את האדמה בעבור האדם "I will never again curse the ground because of humanity." The YHWH we encounter after the flood is one who seems willing to overturn that curse, just as YHWH now firmly rejects the earlier divine decision to annihilate the earth for the humans' decision to understand themselves differently than YHWH originally did.

In J, YHWH changes because humans change. YHWH never had a good reason to curse the ground or to make pregnancy and childbirth painful; that seemed less like punishment than a divine maliciousness

---

of each kind of animal is saved (6:19). Regardless as to how one wants to explain the origins of the non-P material, it does create a coherent flood narrative; it is true that it contains no account of the construction of the ark, but in my reading—in which the narrators continually interrupt each other—my narrator J would not need to provide such a story, since in 7:1 they are interrupting P, who has already had God tell Noah how to build the ark.

similar to the kind the *ogbanje* of *Freshwater* describe. The *ogbanje* eventually begin to react positively to Ada's growth and maturity, as they themselves become more mature, and we can see something similar in J's portrayal of YHWH. And while P's story avoids the notion up until the flood narrative that humans and their relationship with the divine can change, even P allows that God's attitude to humans alters somewhat after the flood. Given P's sparse narrative up to this point, which contains no depictions of violence until God destroys the world, the easiest way to make sense of the violence on the part of "all flesh" that leads to the flood is to conclude that it is interspecies in nature, as the humans have failed to exercise their role as divine representatives who were to rule the animals and maintain a created order in which they and other animals were to be vegetarians.

P is more uncomfortable than J in referring to flaws in divine action, but assumedly the flood in P would not have been necessary if God had not created humans and animals as prone to whatever acts of violence caused God to initiate the flood or if God had explained how humans were supposed to rule the animals to prevent violence or given them the power to do so. For P it is only at this point that God realizes that humans are unable to prevent animals from killing each other, and in 9:2–3 God recognizes carnivorism as legitimate for the first time, a tacit recognition on God's part that this cannot be prevented. In P the humans fail to be the godlike rulers created at the beginning of that story, and so, rather as in J's narrative, they now exist outside of the category in which they were created. In P the humans are no longer the godlike rulers of the animals because they have been demoted from that position in the cosmic hierarchy; unlike the situation in J, they have become less like gods and more like animals, their nature now reflecting that of the nonhuman animals in the desire to kill and eat other species as they now indulge in the very violence they were created to prevent in their original role as divine representatives.

Humanity spreads abroad on the earth after the flood, and in Gen 10, which is a mix of narration from J and P, we see lists of the world's peoples and the lands where some of them live. But J tells one final story in 11:1–9 set earlier than the widespread cultural diversity of Gen 10. Here humanity still functions as a single group after the flood, speaking one language, and they resolve to build a city with a tower that reaches to the heavens—an impressive new development in the construction of cities—a process that would not have been possible had humans not invented the means to build them, as J emphasizes in 11:3. The point of the city, the humans say, is to "make a name for ourselves" so that they do not end up "scattered upon the face of all the earth" (11:4). They are once again employing their creativity to advance human civilization in response to punitive divine action—the flood, in this case—a key manifestation of their godlike nature in J's story. That, certainly, is how this situation is understood by YHWH, who says at this point that as one people with one language לא יבצר מהם כל אשר יזמו לעשות "nothing they plan to do will be thwarted" (11:6), which is reminiscent of the conclusion Job eventually draws about God: כל תוכל ולא יבצר ממך מזמה "you are able to do anything, and no plan of yours will be thwarted" (Job 42:2).

As we reach the end of J's story in Gen 1–11, the humans as a group are very much like a god, and YHWH essentially sees humanity as one of the אלהים. This is as close as human development gets in this story to moving out of a liminal state and fully into the status of divine. Individual humans are not immortal because YHWH acted before they could eat of the tree of life, but as early as 6:4 immediately after God puts a specific upper limit on human lifespans in J's narrative the Nephilim become "people of name," their fame keeping their names alive after their death. And here in 11:1–9, humanity acts as a united whole, a group that will not die, since YHWH responded to Noah's culturally advanced sacrifice by deciding to never again destroy the earth. By building a city so advanced that its tower extends to the heavens, the humans believe it will keep them united, a single godlike group who will last forever, immortalized in the city and the reputation of their name with a tower that would even allow them to ascend to the heavens and commune with the deities there.

But unlike the divine beings of *Freshwater*, J's YHWH is not reconciled to the godlike status of the humans at the center of this story. No matter how divine they may seem, YHWH does not wish to allow them to evolve beyond the liminal or queer civilized status they have already attained. So in J, just as YHWH spoke with the other deities to deal with the issue of the humans becoming godlike (3:22–23), YHWH now urges them to act together to confuse the humans' language (11:7), effectively stopping them from being a single people that could be considered as the equivalent of a god and thereby ending their building project and forcing them to scatter across the earth (11:8–9). YHWH is willing to accept some of the humans' choices for civilization, something that makes them like gods but not entirely so, and just as the *ogbanje* acknowledge Ada's strength near the end of *Freshwater*, YHWH can now admit that the humans are as powerful as gods. YHWH has changed in the ways in which the divine is willing to regard and relate to humans, but in the end will not accept humanity as a deity or relate to them on that basis and prefers them in the queer state into which they have grown.

In J's narrative in Gen 1–11, YHWH comes to accept—in fits and starts, at least—the human choice to mature and transcend the identity God originally imagined would define them. While YHWH does not permit them to become fully divine, this God does allow them to live in the liminal or queer space between or outside of the original categories of human and deity; to put that another way, the humans in J have developed and inhabit a new understanding of human identity. J's narrative places much more emphasis than P's on a changing relationship between a divine world and humans who have chosen to aspire to a divine-like existence. J's YHWH, like *Freshwater*'s gods, can seem careless and lack understanding of and empathy for humans, leaving a tree of knowledge of good and evil within reach of the originally animal- and childlike humans, not seeming to understand that they might want to eat of it. *Freshwater* helps us read Gen 1–11 as providing pictures of a God who is not an infallible being, who does not get everything right the first time, and who must learn how to coexist with humans as they grow in their self-understanding.

This is even true for P's narrative, where humans are created to subdue the world and rule the animals without receiving any instructions as to how to do so, with the result that God eventually decides that "all flesh" have ruined the earth with violence, for the humans have apparently been unable to be the rulers God wanted to govern the animals and prevent that violence. In both J's and P's narratives, then, God learns to accept that the humans are not entirely who they were created to be, and if in J they become godlike, in P they seem to become less so—permitted to participate in the interspecies killing toward which the rest of the animals seem to be drawn by their nature—rather than acting as representatives of the divine who could rule the animals and prevent that violence. God's reaction to this change is not always positive, and in both J and P God wipes out almost all life, a far more horrific act than any for which the gods in *Freshwater* are responsible. Yet the humans in Genesis, rather like Ada in the novel, respond with their own kind of strength using the creativity and maturity they develop to protect themselves from and respond to divine reactions against their choices and creating their own queer identity—a trans identity, insofar as they have decided to cross and defy clearly established categories—to which God is eventually reconciled.

Human Liminality in *Freshwater* and Gen 1-11

Ada's evolution in *Freshwater* concludes with her acceptance of an identity with the ọgbanje who live within her—"I am my others; we are one and we are many" (226)—and they are finally able to acknowledge her strength (216), the strength of a divine-like being. Ada says that "it was very hard, letting go of being human" (225), but also says that, as ọgbanje, she is "as liminal as possible—spirit and human, both and neither" (225-26). This liminal identity applies to her understanding of her gender and sexuality as well, for she appears to have no objections when the ọgbanje, having accepted her body as their own, have her undergo breast reduction surgery since they and their brothersisters are neither clearly male nor female. They combine Ada's new and somewhat more masculine body with feminine clothing, just as before the surgery they preferred binding Ada's chest to hide her breasts and wearing stereotypically masculine clothes (192-93). Ada's eventual awareness of the liminal space she occupies between human and divine accompanies the liminal place between binary gender categories where she eventually feels most at home, something that also corresponds to a liminal sexual identity outside of a heterosexual norm that she explores under Saint Vincent's influence.

Freshwater is a story of Ada's character development and growth that inevitably involves the divine beings within her and her relationship with them. In the end Ada becomes a very different figure than the ọgbanje ever believed possible; they had driven her mad, they claim at times (e.g., 6, 20), because they are gods who against their will are conscious of their divinity while locked in a human body. They lack the understanding of and empathy for humans to see what Ada truly is until she fully understands herself and grows into her mature identity that accompanies her realization that she does not belong within traditional categories of gender and sexuality. And her growth is only possible because the ọgbanje within her change as well, for only after they see her as powerful are they able to stop hurting her in their vain and selfish attempts to save and protect what they wrongly believe to be a weak human contaminated in its contact with the divine.

Read after *Freshwater*, we can see that if Gen 1-11 is a story of origins, those origins are not determinative. Put another way, it is a story in which both the humans and God change; if this is especially obvious in J's narration, where YHWH grows to accept the liminal status the humans have chosen—a rejection of the original binary distinction between humans and gods that exists at the beginning of J's story—it is true as well for P, where God eventually becomes reconciled to the humans' inability to rule the animals as divine representatives. Reading Gen 1–11 after *Freshwater*, we can feel driven to ask if J's and P's understandings of God are ones in which the divine would also be willing to support other kinds of human liminality, such as those Ada manifests in regard to her gender identification and sexuality, and we might note in light of the novel that in J's narrative, conceptions of human gender and sexuality undergo change just as human nature in general does. The אדם or human originally appears in J's story as a sexless and genderless creature (see Trible 1978, 15; Bal 1987, 112–13; Batto 2013, 78); gender and sexual differentiation can only exist once there is a distinction between male and female, and there is none until the woman is created in 2:21–22.[37] As we see gender identity start to develop in J's narrative, we find that it is the woman who goes on to perform what we would consider to be the stereotypically male role of leadership in the human decision to eat of the tree of the knowledge of good and evil, while immediately after the creation of woman J says that the man leaves his parents to "cling to his woman" (2:24).[38]

It is only in 3:16–18 that YHWH changes this relationship in which the woman is more active and dominant, a divine response to the humans' decision led by the woman to abandon the animal-like nature with which they had been created and queer the original categories of human and divine, inhabiting a trans state as they move beyond those categories. God now institutes what we would understand to be more stereotypical or

---

37. As Karalina Matskevitch (2019, 9–10) puts it, the gender of the אדם is constructed as the narrative of Gen 2 progresses. If one wanted to see the original אדם of 2:7–20 as male, as some readers do (e.g., Jobling 1986, 41; Kawashima 2006), then we can see the individual created from his (rather than its) "side parts" in 2:21–22 as a trans woman (Valentine 2020, 516–17), a woman who emerges from what some believe to be a man. But there are no categories to distinguish human gender in the story before the woman is created, since categories exist only to classify different things; when there is a category with only one being in it, that category cannot be subdivided. Before the woman is created in 2:21–22, the category "human" contains only one being, and so we cannot classify it within a subdivision of the category—such as "male" or "female"—before another human exists, and it is not at all clear in this story that there will ever be another human until 2:21–22.

38. George Heider (2012, 41–43) concludes in his study of the expression דבק ב- "cling to" in the Hebrew Bible that its use in 2:24 points to the woman as superior to the man.

"normal" gender roles: The man will rule over the woman; the woman's central role will be to bear children; and the man's central role will be to provide food through agriculture (see also Adam 2020). It is no wonder, then, that in later stories in Genesis it is always women who leave their families when they are married (Warner 2017, 281–82). Included in the divine retaliation of 3:16–18 is the imposition of a heterosexual norm, as Ken Stone (2006, 64–65) notes, since only at this point is the woman told that "your desire[39] will be for your man." YHWH, however, does not impose a reciprocal mandate on the man, so the obligatory heterosexuality here applies only to women, who now have less sexual freedom than men and whose desire God does not limit to a single gender.

If the woman is to be subjugated to her husband because of her leadership in humanity's evolution into its new, queer existence, then we can see how, given J's portrayal of YHWH, this "normal" gender hierarchy is something open to change in the logic of this story, as would be the other aspects of the divine reaction in 3:16–18 against the humans' choice, including the mandatory heterosexuality for women. Since YHWH eventually ends up assenting to this choice for liminal existence, one can easily imagine J's God as rethinking the hardships imposed on humanity as part of the initial divine reaction against it. In J's flood story YHWH's reaction against human "evil" can also be seen as a rejection of this human decision for liminality, as discussed in the previous section of the chapter, yet following Noah's postflood sacrifice, YHWH decides to accept the identity humans have chosen. In fact, in resolving in 8:21 to accept human "evil" and reject the earlier divine decision to destroy the world because of it, YHWH refers back to the curse of the ground in 3:16–18, as if already in the process of also revisiting that initial retaliation against a human choice to which God has now adapted. In the character of YHWH created in J's narrative, the God who can eventually accept a queer humanity who exists between the original categories of human and divine would also be open to existence outside of what we would consider stereotypical gender hierarchies and "normal" heterosexual relationships, because these

---

39. Reading תשוקתך with the MT and SP rather than תשובתך as reflected by the OG's ἀποστροφή σου ("your turning, recourse, refuge"). The Hebrew behind the OG was likely altered to correspond to the following assertion that the woman's husband "will rule over you"; as a result, a copyist decided, he will be the object of the woman's "turning."

binary norms are imposed in reaction against a human choice to which God eventually assents.

And if it is not difficult to imagine J's God as eventually deciding that men should not rule women, that women should take on leadership roles, and that heterosexual desire should not be imposed on women, we can also imagine this God accepting humans who wish to identify outside of the genders of male and female created in Gen 2, not only because YHWH in J is open to human growth and change outside of categories established at creation, but also because there is never any sense in J's story that there would be something illegitimate with not identifying as either male or female. Of course, we do not actually see YHWH do away with the hardships imposed on the humans in 3:16–18 or expressly accept those who do not identify within binary gender and sexual categories; the point here is that, given the character of YHWH created in these stories, it is simple enough to imagine this God acting in these ways. By Gen 12 the attention of both J's and P's narratives shifts from God's relationship with humanity in general to one with a single family in particular, but this does not mean that readers cannot rely on their impressions of how YHWH has interacted with humanity through Gen 11 to conclude that, had J's focus remained more general, we could eventually have seen a divine embrace of human liminality that extends to gender and sexuality.

The possibility of such growth and acceptance on God's part in P's narration remains far less obvious, in part because far less happens in it—if we exclude P's genealogies, then in Gen 1–11, P provides only stories of creation and the flood[40]—but even in P God adapts to human change to some degree, accepting after the flood story that it is not possible for humans to act as godlike rulers of the animals, since they are unable to prevent them from doing violence to each other. As mentioned above, the humans in P's account no longer fit the category of the human that was originally prescribed, since after the flood they no longer occupy the category of creation they were intended to fill; not only are they no longer rulers of the animals, but they now in fact seem like nonhuman animals themselves in their desire to kill and eat other species. P's God is willing to accommodate this new identity for humans, one that transcends the original category

---

40. This is true even when we consider the material in Gen 10 from P (10:1a, 2–7, 20, 22–23, 31–32), which, while it refers to different peoples and lands, is couched in the form of a genealogy of descent from Noah's sons. For a discussion, see Carr 2021, 305–9.

in which they were created as representatives of the divine with authority over the animals. In P's story God affirms after the flood that humans are still in the divine image (9:6), even though they are now much like the animals with whom they share the desire to eat other species rather than installed in some sort of governing hierarchy over them.

Yet when asking if it is possible to envision the God of P's narrative accepting humans identifying outside of cisheteronormative categories of gender and sexual orientation, we do not even need to appeal to the valorization this God bestows on a transformed humanity after the flood. Even though P's creation story says that God creates האדם "the human" as male and female (1:27), one could argue that this act immediately involves divinely approved change and development in human gender. It is certainly possible to read 1:27—"in the image of God he created it (אתו), male and female he created them (אתם)"—as describing a process that begins with an original creation of an androgynous human, one who contains within themself both male and female and is then divided into two beings (see, e.g., Culbertson 2009, 7). Not only does this sound very much like J's story of the creation of humanity, which begins with one human who is then separated into two, but it also can be understood as a story in which an androgynous human is one created in the divine image. As a result, we need not understand 1:27 as claiming that being human demands identifying as either male or female; the verse says simply that God creates humanity as both "male and female," and both male and female is precisely how some transgender people understand their identity (Valentine 2020, 516–17).

Moreover, P's narrative articulates no clear gender or sexual norms in Gen 1–11; humans are to be fruitful and multiply according to P (1:28; 9:1, 7), but this obviously does not demand that all adults have heterosexual intercourse. P's narrative is so sparse that we have little sense as to how this narrator might understand gender roles, although it is worthwhile noting that P's genealogies of 5:1–28, 30–32, and 11:10–32 mention only males (except in 11:29–31), as if the main role of men is to produce children, a gender role stereotypically associated with females. So while there is not remotely as much reflection on human identity in the parts of Gen 1–11 from P's narration, what little there is does not directly conflict with J's openness to human liminality, maturity, change, and divine character development. P does not challenge a portrayal of a God who would accept those who identify outside of what we would consider to be stereotypical categories of gender and sexual orientation.

Because we would applaud those who work to counteract the hardships YHWH places on humans in 3:16–18, who strive to make childbirth safer and less painful and agriculture easier for all involved in the process, and who fight against the subjugation of women to men and the universal enforcement of heterosexual norms, it is not difficult to imagine the objection that I am replacing the text of Gen 1–11 with what I would like it to say. As in the cases of my readings of Ezra-Nehemiah and Lamentations, however, that is not true. My argument about the portrayal of God in this part of Genesis is one reliant on a close reading of the way the narratives portray God as acting and relating to humans in these chapters, depictions of the divine that make it easy to imagine the divinities portrayed by both J's and P's narratives as ones who accept human choices to identify outside of what Western culture considers to be "normal" categories of gender and sexuality.

For those of us who are also privileged by our location within those categories, however, creating this kind of interpretation is not always easy to do, even when we also have ethical commitments to contribute to fights for emancipation whenever that is reasonably possible. Our privilege exists because of the ways our societies have decided to categorize the world and whom they have chosen to subjugate when doing so, and sometimes groups will enforce those categories by using interpretations of parts of Gen 1–11 to insist that women who take on leadership roles or people who identify as members of LGBTQ+ groups defy the divine will in their queer and liminal understandings of their sexual orientation, gender, and gender roles. A real benefit of *Freshwater* is that it pushes readers to consider who gains from a binary system of gender and sexuality (Talabi 2023, 339). It can push those of us who do benefit from dominant binary thinking about such aspects of identity to reconceive our hermeneutical approach to a text like Gen 1–11 when we read it after the novel, helping us create interpretations with liberative potential for a text so often used to enforce subjugation.

Trans-Species Liminality in Gen 1–11

Freshwater can help us go further in challenging interpretations of Gen 1–11 that look to this text to justify hierarchical binary categorizations that have been used in damaging ways, especially when we think of readings of these chapters that have been used to support human activities that have resulted in environmental destruction. Lynn White (1967), for example, argued in the middle of the twentieth century that Western thought has long used Gen 1:28, where God commands humans to subdue the earth and rule the animals, as justification for a belief in human transcendence over the natural world, an idea fundamental to the ecological crises produced by the industrial revolution.[41] If these crises affect all of humanity, they are also not distinct from issues of social justice; the Intergovernmental Panel on Climate Change (2022, 447),[42] for example, concluded that planetary warming of 1.5°C beyond the preindustrial average will "disproportionately affect disadvantaged and vulnerable populations" and that there is "high" scientific confidence that its worst impacts will be experienced by "indigenous people, children and the elderly, poor labourers, poor urban dwellers in African cities, and people and ecosystems in the Arctic and Small Island Developing States." The Panel noted as well that there is "very high" confidence within the scientific community that global warming of this level will "worsen existing poverty and exacerbate inequalities, especially for those disadvantaged by gender, age, race, class, caste, indigeneity and (dis)ability" (451).

As a result, interpretations of Gen 1–11 (or any other part of the Bible, for that matter) driven by ecological concerns are potentially of important liberative use for many subjugated groups. The one I provide in this final section of the chapter continues to read after *Freshwater*, a strategy that allows us to see the nonhuman animals in these chapters as kin to humans, liminal or queer in the same ways that humans are. In the light of the novel, we can see that the animals of Gen 1–11 transcend any kind of categorization that would clearly distinguish them from the human and the divine, which means that they cannot be placed in some sort of hierarchical view of the world that would understand them and their habitats merely as objects to be exploited by humans.

Western hierarchies of being that conceive of animals as inferior to humans also organize reality to privilege particular genders, races, and ethnicities, as Mmapula Kebaneilwe (2015, 698–700) notes. Ken Stone

---

41. For a discussion of White's argument and its reception, both positive and negative, by scholars in different academic fields, see Whitney 2015.

42. The IPCC is an intergovernmental body that provides the scientific input for international climate change agreements, and the document cited here was delivered to the United Nations Framework Convention for Climate Change in preparation for the Katowice Climate Change Conference (COP24) of 2018 (Intergovernmental Panel on Climate Change 2022, vii–viii).

(2018, 11–12) points out that environmental philosophers like Matthew Calarco have sounded similar warnings when arguing that the Western liberal focus on rights and rationalities has created hierarchies that justify the exploitation of both humans of non-European descent and animals. In such worldviews both can be denied rights because they are categorized as less than fully rational humans. A key aspect of the European understanding of the world in the first centuries of modern colonialism, writes Sylvia Wynter (2003, 300–3), was the concept of the Chain of Being, which structured Nature from most rational, a position occupied by European males, to least, and it justified colonialism by ranking populations of the colonized, understood to be gravely deficient in rationality, at the bottom of the Chain with nonhuman animals. This coloniality of being that justified a coloniality of power was thus codified in conceptions of race that continue to dominate Western thought (see, e.g., Grosfoguel 2007; Quijano 2024, 256–302). A reading of Gen 1–11 that focuses on a trans or queer portrayal of animals, then, is one guided by the same emancipatory impulses that have pushed me, under the influence of *Freshwater*, to see these chapters as transgressing binary distinctions of gender and sexuality, since similar sorts of hierarchical categorization have been developed to subjugate LGBTQ+ people.

In *Freshwater* we can see a kind of "tranimality," says Marta Sofía López (2022, 83–84), a portrayal of the animal world that does not adhere to a hierarchical binary categorization of nature that understands the nonhuman as of a lower status of being than humanity. Reading Gen 1–11 in the wake of the novel helps us see not only that the distinction between the human and divine continually shifts and is unstable, but also that the same can be said for the categories of nonhuman, human, and divine. An inclusive reading of Gen 1–11 with liberative potential for LGBTQ+ groups, then, is closely connected to one which could be described as a trans-species reading of these chapters, one that sees a kinship between humans and nonhuman animals. Such a reading can compel us to rethink capitalist conceptions of the natural world as full of nonhuman beings that humans can treat in whatever ways they choose because they are categorically inferior, a worldview that has resulted in the exploitation of nature that disproportionately harms a broad range of communities who are already vulnerable because of their social locations.

To return once again to *Freshwater*, we see in the novel one animal of particular significance. The first two ọgbanje narrators tell us that the python is the "flesh form of Ala" (9), and when Ada finally realizes that she is Ala's child, she also identifies as the snake: "I had forgotten that if she is a python, then so am I" (224). Ala's being is not limited to the corporeal form of the python, but the animal is also clearly more than one with only physical existence; the ọgbanje narrators say that "before a christ-induced amnesia struck the humans, it was well known that the python was sacred, beyond reptile" (9). The python is a being through which Ala can have physical embodiment and communicate with the world, and the ọgbanje's narration that opens the novel begins with a story of their encounter with Ala as a python three years after Ada's birth, when they had forgotten their true identity as ọgbanje and children of Ala (1). When they see the snake, they say, "Through its eyes Ala looked at us, and through Ada's eyes we looked at her—all of us looking upon each other for the first time" (11). The python, then, is a being who is simultaneously animal and divine, reflecting the tranimality to which López refers, and a conduit of revelation to the ọgbanje that begins a journey that soon brings them to their full awareness of their divine nature.

When we think of the snake of J's story in Gen 3 after having read *Freshwater*, then, it can be difficult not to see it as somewhat like the python in the novel, certainly insofar as it is a being not easily categorized as animal in distinction from the divine or human. It is described, as mentioned above, as wiser than any of the other animals (3:1). Its ability to speak makes it like the two humans and YHWH at this point in J's story, and if the snake is wiser than the other animals, it is also clearly wiser than the humans, at least when it first appears on the scene. Unlike them, it already has divine knowledge, and can tell the woman in 3:5 what "God knows" will happen when they eat of the tree of the knowledge of good and evil; as a result, it seems to be both animal and godlike at the same time. As Cameron Howard (2008, 24) points out, we could see the snake as providing the woman with a kind of divine revelation at this point, even if this is hardly knowledge YHWH wants communicated to them. The snake, in short, is much like the python of *Freshwater*, transcending any simplistic attempts to categorize it as "only" an animal in some category of being inferior to that of human, given its wisdom and its ability to possess and reveal divine knowledge.[43]

---

43. Readers familiar with Gloria Anzaldúa's work might be reminded of her discussion of Coatlicue, a Mexica (or Aztec) goddess associated with snakes (the Nahuatl word *coatl* means "serpent"). For Anzaldúa (1987, 46), Coatlicue functions as "a rupture in our everyday world," and what she calls the Coatlicue state is the awareness—or

As a narrator, J never directly explains the snake's motivation for initiating the conversation with the woman and revealing divine knowledge about the truth of the tree. The very little J does tell us about the snake is that it is "wiser" or "more ערום than all the wild animals YHWH God had made" (3:1). Given that this is the only description of the snake the narrative provides, we can see it as a character who wants to commune with the beings in the garden who have the potential to be as wise and prudent as it is, beings who already seem wiser than the other animals, since at least they are able to speak. To begin such a relationship with potential intellectual equals, however, the snake needs the humans to become more like gods themselves and to transcend the identity with which they were created, and so it sets the humans off on a path in which they can become like the gods, which means becoming like the snake. No such relationship between the humans and the snake ever develops, however, in part because YHWH's retaliation for the eating the fruit of the tree of the knowledge of good and evil begins by targeting the snake and involves placing "enmity" between it and humans (3:15). It is as if YHWH is aware of the snake's motivation for initiating the conversation that moved the humans to eat of the tree and aims to make it impossible for such a close trans-species relationship to develop. YHWH is not the only figure to blame for this outcome, however, since, as Howard (2008, 25) points out, we can understand the woman's disingenuous claim in 3:13 that the snake deceived her as a betrayal, an abandonment of the being who has helped her become godlike as she tries to steer divine retaliation to the snake and away from herself.

This failure to establish a close trans-species relationship, however, does not alter how alike the snake and humans are once the latter eat of the tree of knowledge of good and evil. If in doing so the humans have transcended the original category of identity that YHWH creates for them at the beginning of J's narrative, this shift into a queer state of being is not the only aspect of J's story that troubles a facile understanding of the categorization of the different aspects of creation at the beginning of its narrative. The appearance of a godlike snake obviously also transgresses or queers boundaries between the human, nonhuman animals, and divine, since the snake and human both are godlike once

revelation—of the oppression that prevents the subjugated from realizing their potential and that allows one to begin to understand the world in different ways and begin the process of change from subjugation to completeness (48–51).

the latter eat of the tree. We should remember as well in this regard that humanity at its creation in J appears much like the other animals, since both are created from the ground, both are described as "living being(s)" (2:7, 19), and both are naked.

This original kinship between humans and animals does not disappear in J's story, for even if the former develop a queer nature and become godlike, adopting clothing and other aspects of civilization, they do not cease existing as living beings like the nonhuman animals. And, in fact, the story of a brief amicable relationship between the snake and the woman points to the possibility of a kinship between humans and nonhuman animals that extends beyond some sort of abstract sharing of essence as "living beings"—for if the snake was more ערום (wise or prudent) than the other nonhuman animals, then that description implies there is some sort of wisdom or prudence among the other nonhuman species, even if of a lesser degree than that possessed by the snake. Other species do not lack wisdom in J's narrative, reflecting a point made numerous times in Proverbs where even very small animals such as the ant and locust are described as חכמים מחכמים "wise, well taught" with important lessons to teach humans (Prov 30:24–28).[44] So this reading of J's story points to the possibility of humans forming relationships with their nonhuman kin on the basis of this shared wisdom, even if those relationships would have to be somewhat different in nature than that which the snake might have envisioned at the beginning of Gen 3. In the end there is no clear distinction between the human and animal worlds in J's story, which helps to explain why, as mentioned above, YHWH initially believed in 2:18–19 that the animals could take a role in relationship with the first human that in the end only another human could fill.

P's story in these chapters has no nonhuman figure like J's snake that so clearly seems to transcend distinctions between animal, human, and

---

44. The second of these two words in Prov 30:24 is in the *pual* and has the passive sense of the verb חכם in the *piel*, where it is used to refer to making others wise or teaching wisdom. In that sense we might understand it as referring to these animals' skills in their work; see Fox 2009, 879. The OG had the same consonantal text as the MT but read the second word as a noun and so understood the whole phrase as referring to these species as "the wisest of the wise." For a discussion of 30:24–28 and the wisdom of the individual species described there, see Forti 2008, 108–18. Also see Forti 2008, 103–7 for a discussion of Prov 6:6–8, a passage that depicts the ant as a model for emulation that can make humans wise and of the longer version of 6:8 in the LXX that praises the wisdom of the bee.

divine. In P's narrative, of course, God originally commands the humans to rule the animals (1:28), an idea that has played an important role in justifications for a Western worldview of human dominance over the natural world that has contributed to contemporary ecological disasters, as White (1967) has argued. As we have seen previously in the chapter, however, the original human role in P as representatives of the divine who rule the animals in place of the gods collapses by the time we reach the end of P's flood story. It is worthwhile in this regard, in fact, to reflect on how similar humans and animals are in P, despite the original divine command to the humans in 1:28 to rule the animals. Both humans and animals are created as vegetarians in this story (1:29–30) with the result that the narrator presents an original creation in which no animal, human or otherwise, can legitimately kill another. If it is interspecies violence that appears to motivate God to destroy life in P's flood story, as discussed above, the end of that story also allows humans to kill animals for food, demonstrating that they appear to share the violent instincts of nonhuman animals in that regard. By 9:5–6, near the end of P's flood narrative, the original creation of humans in the divine image serves to distinguish them only insofar as this means it is illicit to kill humans, and it no longer functions as part of a hierarchical ordering of humans as the rulers of nonhuman animals.

One could argue that 9:1–6 does enforce some kind of animal/human hierarchy in P's narrative, since God now allows nonhuman animals but not humans to be killed for food, but it is not a hierarchy that we could surmise P's God is pleased with, since the divine plan in P's creation story is for an absence of any violence at all by any species of animal, including humans. As a result, while God permits humans to kill animals in 9:2–3, this may only be done for the purposes of consumption. God demands, in fact, that humans not consume animal blood, which appears to represent animal life in some fashion (9:4), as if each time humans drain blood from an animal they have killed for food, they are to be reminded that such life does not ultimately belong to them.

So in P's narrative, as in J's, distinctions between humans and animals do not remain the same as these stories progress. Humans become more like nonhuman animals in P, stripped of their original role as rulers and eventually depicted as driven by the same instincts as nonhuman animals to kill other species, while J contains a story of a snake who appears to have divine wisdom before humans do and refers to all animals as possessing some kind of wisdom. In J the animals, like humans, are queer, since they are liminal beings who do not exist in categories that clearly distinguish them from humans or even, in the case of J's snake, from the divine. And this liminality disturbs attempts to create clear and stable hierarchies of being in which the human, often implicitly understood as the white cisheterosexual male (López 2022, 78), is superior to all other creatures. In P, on the other hand, it is the trans nature of humans as they abandon their place in a hierarchy of governance over animals that queers the distinction between the categories of human and nonhuman animal. By the end of P's flood story, both seem driven by a shared nature to kill other species for food, and if the killing of humans remains illicit, the killing of nonhuman animals is tightly controlled, and the life of animals is not something that belongs to humans nor are animals beings that humans can kill for any reason they choose. Humans evolve in P into a trans space outside of the category of godlike rulers in which they were originally created and realize a kind of kinship with the nonhuman.

In neither narrative, in short, is the natural world something entirely other or different from the human one, some kind of inferior realm open to untrammeled human exploitation that harms not only nature but humans as well, disadvantaged ones in particular. This reading of Gen 1–11, then, complements the discussion of human liminality in regard to gender identity and sexual orientation earlier in the chapter, as both interpretive steps have been taken in light of the evolution of Ada into liminal spaces of identity in *Freshwater*. As in the previous chapters, reading after minoritized literature opens new paths of interpretation, ones that are hopefully of liberative use to those in minoritized social locations and ones that are particularly important when dealing with biblical texts like Gen 1–11 that have often been used to subjugate vulnerable groups in different ways.

6
CONCLUSION:
THE HERMENEUTICAL PROCESS OF READING AFTER MINORITIZED LITERATURE

I argue in chapter 1 that since textual meaning is produced through interpretation, the age of the biblical writings does not demand that the field of biblical studies must prioritize historical study. As a result, given that there are hundreds of millions of people disadvantaged by their social locations who look to the Bible as a potential resource in movements that resist structures of subjugation in their contexts, biblical studies as a community of scholars could decide to privilege an ethical commitment to support such movements in our professional work and place the interests and concerns that arise from such struggles for social justice at the heart of the discipline. After all, the field's overwhelming focus on historical questions is not a necessary aspect of the academic study of the Bible but is simply what we have chosen to prioritize. The meanings we create in our interpretations depend on the interests and questions we have, so if we hold an ethical commitment to support liberative struggles whenever that is reasonably possible, then we will want to prioritize questions in our research and teaching with that ethical interest in mind. The decision to privilege historical questions in our research also reflects a particular ethical stance. Even if it is unintended, it is one that assumes that resistance movements that fight oppression are not ones of immediate importance, since they must always be subordinate to scholars' primary interest in history.

There are many different interpretive strategies members of the field can pursue if we wish to create a better and more ethical discipline, as I point out in chapter 1, but all of them must begin with the contexts and experiences of those disadvantaged by structural forces and their interests and questions. This is the basic hermeneutical principle of interpretive work that reads for liberation, because the minoritized alone know their specific contexts and needs well enough to decide on the strategies and resources that would be most useful for their emancipatory struggles and because they must be the agents of their own liberation if it is actually to be liberation and not a process in which people with more socioeconomic privilege than they tell them how and what to think, the situation the subjugated are already in. If biblical scholarship is to do research with the potential to be of emancipatory use in movements that resist subjugation, then it must be work that is based in the experiences of those in the communities involved in those movements. As a result, all of us committed to such a hermeneutical goal, no matter what social locations we may inhabit, can stand to gain from exposure to a variety of contexts of minoritized resistance, a project that will broaden our liberative imaginations. Of course, in the process of any such exposure we must be aware that we could never have the same level of awareness as the members of a group different from our own as to what it means to live in their context and to face and resist the specific humiliations, depredations, and terrors of structural oppression they encounter. When we are not members of a community about whom we hope to discover more, we are not in a position where we can read biblical texts with them, especially when we belong to demographically dominant groups, since this can often result in reading for others as we impose our questions and concerns in interpretation.

This hermeneutical concern, however, should not prevent us from reading after those in minoritized contexts different from one's own, listening silently to a variety of experiences so that we can broaden our liberative imaginations as we aim to create work that could spark useful imagination, vision, and reflection in the contexts of resistance movements against structural forces. Reading after those in a disadvantaged context different from one's own, however, demands a recognition of one's epistemologically inferior position, since hearing such stories hardly conveys the same knowledge of the context that those living in it have. This is why, Sechrest writes, any attempts on the part of readers at dominant intersections of identity to engage in emancipatory biblical interpretation must proceed with a profound sense of epistemic humility. It is important to point out, then, that if one needs to experience the effects of subjugation inherent to life in an Asian context to do Asian interpretation or in a woman's context to do feminist interpretation or in a Black woman's context to do womanist or Black feminist interpretation or in a queer person's context to do queer interpretation, then the interpretations of the preceding chapters could not be said to be located in any of those hermeneutics, because I have the wrong sorts of experiences for that to be the case.

Reading biblical texts after contemporary literature by minoritized authors, however, has allowed me to look for something like the rhyme Sechrest refers to, as I have searched in those chapters for similarities in the contexts and situations of characters in contemporary minoritized literature and those in biblical texts. It is an interpretive strategy that has made it possible for a straight white male middle-class scholar like me to see enlightening similarities and differences in the experiences of characters and communities in biblical texts and in contemporary literature by authors from disadvantaged social contexts, including those of a Vietnamese immigrant to the United States and the story of Daniel or those of women and gay men in the middle of an AIDS crisis and the excluded women of Ezra-Nehemiah or those of African Americans traumatized by white racial hatred and the community in Jerusalem in Lamentations or those of a transgender Nigerian inhabited by gods and the humans in the opening chapters of Genesis who negotiate their identity in relationship with their divine creator.

The benefits accrued by pursuing the particular strategy of reading after that I have here are not limited to scholars like me from dominant social demographic contexts, because all of us can broaden our liberative imaginations in the hopes of creating interpretations that different minoritized groups involved in movements of resistance might find to be of use. Other interpreters, of course, might choose different strategies of reading after than the one I model in this monograph or, in pursuing the same one I have here, might notice different connections with different pieces of biblical literature after reading the same works by minoritized authors. Precisely how a given story might cause a specific reader to interpret a biblical passage differently than they did previously will depend on the story, the reader's context, the beliefs they hold, and how tightly they hold some of them. In other words, reading the same piece of literature by an author from a vulnerable social location will affect different people and their interpretation of biblical literature differently.

Of course, different interpreters will also be aware of different pieces of minoritized literature, and choosing other novels, plays, short stories, or memoirs will lead one to draw connections with different biblical writings to be read in light of them. In this monograph I largely read after works by minoritized authors from the United States, not only because they are writings I already knew and admired and that reminded me of specific pieces of biblical literature, sparking something like the rhyme to which Sechrest refers, but also as a reminder that minoritized communities do not only exist in the Two-Thirds World. I could, however, have followed the same hermeneutical process with other works I have also found deeply moving by authors from other countries, including Chinua Achebe, Chimamanda Adichie, Isabel Allende, Djaïli Amadou Amal, Miguel Ángel Asturias, Tsitsi Dangarembga, Achmat Dangor, Edwidge Danticat, Avni Doshi, Mariana Enríquez, Bernardine Evaristo, Aminatta Forna, Patricia Grace, Shehan Karunatilaka, Fernanda Melchor, Jennifer Nansubuga Makumbi, Rigoberta Menchú, Arundhati Roy, Mohamed Mbougar Sarr, and Zadie Smith, among many, many others. This particular process of reading after the minoritized has virtually unlimited potential to pair different works of literature with different biblical writings and so to vastly expand our literary imaginations and create a greater range of biblical interpretation potentially of use for emancipatory movements.

There is no set way to determine how to pair writings in this reading strategy; one must simply begin with a work by a minoritized writer featuring minoritized characters and their concerns, and then ask what resonances it has with a given piece of biblical literature, and how this act of reading after an author in a different social location than one's own could create imagination, reflection, and vision that movements of resistance against structural forces could potentially find useful. When I read *The Sympathizer*, a story about an immigrant to an imperial center who must struggle to determine his identity and sympathies in relation to the competing powers who claim his loyalty, I was struck by comparisons with the biblical figure of Daniel. Other readers, however, might find it easier to make connections with the story of Ruth, for example, noting that she shares the powerlessness and act of migration in common with the novel's narrator, and this act of reading after a work of literature by an author from a disadvantaged social location might cause them to understand Ruth and her plight differently, perhaps more as some scholars in different minoritized contexts do. Just as the Vietnamese characters in *The Sympathizer* are rejected by American society, we could see Naomi's insistence in Ruth that she migrate from Moab to Israel alone, without Ruth and Orpah, her recently widowed Moabite daughters-in-law (1:8–15), as a reflection of her belief that they do not belong in Israel as she, a native Israelite, does (so Sharp 2017, 155–56). Orpah does not accompany Naomi on her journey to Israel and returns instead to her Moabite family, while Ruth's expressed desire to leave the only people, religion, and homeland she has ever known—"your people will be my people, and your God, my God" (1:16), she tells Naomi, as she clings to her (1:14)—can be understood as the desperate plea of someone who has nowhere else to go (so Norton 2015, 266). Perhaps her Moabite family of origin is dead or perhaps they have disowned her for marrying into a family of Israelite foreigners who settled in Moab,[1] but reading this story after *The Sympathizer* can push us to see her as like the novel's narrator: someone ranked among the meanest and accepted by no culture, perhaps even someone whose own family rejects them.

This particular pairing of literature, then, allows us to see Ruth's struggles as a powerless and excluded migrant as key to her story, since in important ways she is like the nameless narrator of *The Sympathizer*, minoritized by a dominant society and a character whom no group is willing to fully accept. Readers whose identities are privileged in a dominant culture, just as Israel is the cultural center of the book of Ruth, might be prone to think that immigrants like Ruth yearn to abandon their homelands and migrate to what we see as the center of things, and we might fail to understand her as among the powerless who have no choice but to flee the only life they have ever known. *The Sympathizer* warns us of the danger of representing the powerless so that they become whoever the powerful want them to be, and that warning can make it easier for us to see Ruth not as someone who realizes her heart's desire in leaving her homeland but as someone who has lost her husband and family and who has run out of options to secure her survival.[2] Upon arrival in Israel, she and Naomi have no way to support themselves, so Ruth must follow men reaping a grain field, nursing the meager hope they would leave enough over to feed the two of them,[3] which puts her in a situation in which the harvesters can assault and rape her. The story uses the verb נגע in 2:9, 22 to refer to what

---

1. While not making this point exactly, Wil Gafney (2009, 30–32) sees Ruth and Orpah as women abducted by Naomi's sons as if they were spoils of war, with the result that Ruth remains with Naomi because she knows she will be shunned by other Moabites.

2. For a discussion of the significance of Ruth's losses in this story, see Yee 2021, 111–22.

3. As Harold Bennett (2002, 123–24) points out, the law of Deut 24:19 mandates that some of the harvest at the edge of fields must be left over for the poor and dispossessed, but Bennett also notes that the poverty of ancient society would mean that there would be virtually nothing left to glean.

men might do to a single woman in this vulnerable situation, and in other passages it can be used to refer to sexual assault (e.g., Gen 20:6; Prov 6:29) or physical attacks in general (e.g., Gen 32:26 [ET 25]; Deut 17:8). Naomi then sees a chance to have Ruth marry Boaz, one of her kin, who would be able to provide for both of them, and she pushes Ruth to go to him at night (3:1–4), once again placing her in danger of sexual assault (so, e.g., Masenya 2004, 58; Sharp 2014, 244). Boaz does marry Ruth, but when she gives birth to a son it is Naomi who takes him, and the women of the town say, "a son has been born to Naomi" (4:16–17), leaving Ruth, the vulnerable and exploited migrant, bereft even of her own child (e.g., Norton 2015, 277; Yee 2021, 85–100).

The larger point is not that Ruth has to be read this way—and certainly there are many scholars from a variety of vulnerable social locations whose contexts and experiences lead them to find different emphases in the book (e.g., Nadar 2001; Kalmanofsky 2014, 157–74; Nelavala 2015)—but that when read after *The Sympathizer*, interpreters from communities without recent experience of traumatizing migration could find that the novel opens new liberative hermeneutical paths. We do not suddenly become filled with the life experiences of destitute and vulnerable migrants once we have read *The Sympathizer*, but this particular act of reading after can make it a bit easier for Ruth's powerlessness to become visible to us and can make us ask who, if anyone, in her story decides to sympathize with her, a character who belongs to the undesirables among the undesirables, the group who, *The Sympathizer*'s narrator decides, truly deserves sympathy and loyalty.

We could also read different biblical texts after the novel and notice characters in different subjugated contexts, as one conceivably could after encountering any piece of minoritized literature. What matters in the process of reading after the minoritized in the specific way I have done in this book is to use that literature by authors from disadvantaged contexts other than one's own to notice and pay close attention to the characters we find in those narratives, thereby exposing us to different experiences of subjugation and resistance. The rhyme we see, to borrow Sechrest's term yet again, could not exist without paying close attention first to subaltern characters created by a minoritized author. This then allows us to ask how the characters and their concerns, contexts of oppression, and liberative struggles can help us better see and listen to and sympathize with subaltern figures we find in biblical literature or at least to focus on their absence as a problem if none are present and to ask how the story would be different if that were not the case.

6. CONCLUSION   229

Scholars from disadvantaged contexts might immediately be able to see how a particular interpretive act of reading after could spark imaginative vision and have liberative value at their own social locations, but the majority of biblical scholars do not belong to subjugated communities. If we want to urge those in the discipline's mainstream to privilege emancipatory goals by adopting hermeneutical practices of reading after the minoritized in their research and teaching in order to help create a better and more ethical field, however, we should also ask how scholars like me from the demographic mainstream could know if the work we produce could ever lead to useful imagination, vision, and reflection at any site of liberative struggle. Given the restrictions of epistemic humility, after all, we cannot be prescriptive as to the use and acceptance of such interpretative work in contexts outside of our own. However, as I point out in chapter 1, the kind of interpretive strategy I pursue in this book complements the act of reading after the scholarly work that our minoritized colleagues in the field produce as they read for liberation. It follows, then, that if biblical interpretation influenced by our reading of contemporary literature from minoritized contexts allows scholars from the demographic mainstream to produce work that resembles that of our peers in other contexts, we can have some confidence that it potentially has liberative value.

To apply this standard to my interpretive work in the previous chapters, I can see that approaching Gen 1–11 after *Freshwater* in chapter 5, for example, helps me notice some of the same things that queer interpreters of biblical texts do when they point out how ambiguous and unstable categories of gender and sexuality appear to be in some stories. Insofar as biblical scholars who use queer theory or gender studies as hermeneutical guides will show how such categories are things that social groups construct (e.g., Macwilliam 2011, 9–26; Tamber-Rosenau 2018, 15–20; Punt 2020)—which is precisely why they are sometimes contested and thus ambiguous and unstable—I read Gen 1–11 as, in important part, a story that specifically reflects on the change and construction of such categories in stories of humanity's beginnings. Or in chapter 3, where I feel compelled to imagine speech of powerless characters not reported by Ezra-Nehemiah, I find myself doing the same sort of thing that Funlọla Ọlọjẹde (2021) does when she retells the story of the daughters of Zelophehad in Num 27 and 36 from the perspective and in the voice of one of the daughters or that Gafney (2017b, 38–45) does when she retells the story of Hagar, Sarah's slave who is forced to have sex with Abraham, from Hagar's perspective, imagining how she might have experienced her slavery, rape, and interaction with God.

In chapter 4 I found it more appropriate not to speak for the subaltern characters in Lamentations, since that is a different situation than Ezra-Nehemiah where such figures have no speech at all. Because the subalterns do speak in Lamentations, we have a sense as to the different ways in which they view their context of being treated as subhumans, and so we have some sense as to possibilities for the ways in which their speech might continue. This is not entirely unlike the way Linzie Treadway (2022, 127–31) reflects on the story of Hagar and Ishmael from a Native American standpoint, as she notes that, while the biblical story may privilege the descendants of Sarah and Abraham's son, Ishmael receives a divine blessing of many descendants that sounds much like the one manifested through the birth of Isaac (Gen 17:16–20; 21:18). Hagar and Ishmael may have been dispossessed by the dominant characters in the narrative, writes Treadway, an experience reflected in Native American history, but the divine promise to Ishmael means that the dispossessed can imagine the story he and his descendants build outside of the ones related in biblical narratives. She does not go so far as to construct that story, but Native American experience has provided a context for her to imagine its basic contours, the role *Beloved* plays for my reading in chapter 4 as I imagine directions for subaltern speech in the context of Lamentations. And in both chapters 3 and 4, my basic strategy of imagining liberative subaltern speech shares some similarities with what Dube (2008, 108–11) describes as an important aspect of an African women's hermeneutic, their reimagining and retelling of biblical stories to make them more relevant to their specific liberative struggles.

When reading Daniel after *The Sympathizer* in chapter 2, I did not imagine what the powerless characters ignored by the book might say, but the very ability to notice and point to their absence and any concern for them in Daniel's discourse on empire reflects the suspicious readings seen frequently in the work of minoritized scholars writing for liberation. We could define suspicious readings as ones in which someone arrives at an interpretation of a text that can be used for oppressive purposes and then emphasizes the danger such a passage poses to those guided by an emancipatory hermeneutic. We can see readings like this when, for example, George Soares-Prabhu (1995) warns of the way that the mockery of divine images in Isa 44 devalues meaningful religious practice in India that has allowed readers of the chapter to destroy cultures and support colonialism.

We see a suspicious reading as well in the discussion by Clarice Martin (1991) of the household codes of the New Testament, in places such as Eph 5:22–6:9 and Col 3:18–4:1, which set out hierarchies and duties within the Christian household, subordinating wives to husbands and slaves to masters. Passages like these, Martin points out, were used to legitimate slavery in America and are still used to subjugate women. Or, to take just one more example of a suspicious reading from a minoritized context, we could point to Darden's (2015b, 195–200) interpretation of the story of Jesus meeting the Samaritan woman at the well in John 4. At first it seems as if exclusive gender and ethnic social boundaries will be broken, writes Darden, and that the woman will become one of Jesus's disciples, but in the end she is discarded, rendered an unnecessary figure in a story that concludes with her own community determining that they no longer need her testimony to Jesus's identity, as the social order that subordinates women to men is reinscribed.

We make decisions as to whether an interpretation is good on the basis of criteria relevant to our hermeneutical goals, and if we have decided to be guided by ethical ones that prioritize our obligations to those from disadvantaged contexts resisting subjugating forces, then we need to privilege interpretive strategies that could conceivably help us do that. Looking to the work of biblical scholars who are from vulnerable socioeconomic contexts and who write with emancipatory goals in mind is obviously one way to proceed, but the more we can broaden our literary and interpretive imaginations by learning about the many different sorts of experiences of those whose needs and liberative concerns must set the agenda for our work, the better off we will be. Reading after the minoritized in the way I have in the preceding chapters is certainly not the only way to do this, although it has allowed me, a reader at dominant intersections of social identity, to interpret texts in somewhat similar ways as some of my colleagues from disadvantaged contexts, which gives me some confidence that these readings might spark vision and imagination that could be of use in different sites of emancipatory resistance. The more that others in a white field, one with a mainstream that privileges and rewards scholarly work that benefits those in dominant social locations, can adopt this and other strategies oriented to privilege voices from minoritized contexts, the more ethically relevant the field of biblical studies will become.

BIBLIOGRAPHY

Adam, Klaus-Peter. 2020. "The Earth and the Earthling: Thoughts on Gen 2–3." *CTM* 47:35–37.

Ahmed, Sara. 2007. "A Phenomenology of Whiteness." *Feminist Theory* 8:149–68.

Ahn, John. 2023. "Made in Babylon: Daniel 1." Pages 317–28 in *T&T Clark Handbook of Asian American Biblical Hermeneutics*. Edited by Uriah Y. Kim and Seung Ai Yang. T&T Clark.

Albertz, Rainer. 1988. *Der Gott des Daniel: Untersuchungen zu Daniel 4–6 in der Septuagintafassung sowie zu Komposition und Theologie des aramäischen Danielbuches*. SBS 131. Katolisches Bibelwerk.

———. 2011. "From Aliens to Proselytes: Non-Priestly and Priestly Legislation Concerning Strangers." Pages 53–69 in *The Foreigner and the Law: Perspectives from the Hebrew Bible and the Ancient Near East*. Edited by Reinhard Achenbach, Rainer Albertz, and Jakob Wöhrle. BZABR 16. Harrassowitz.

Alderman, Isaac M. 2020. *The Animal at Unease with Itself: Death Anxiety and the Animal-Human Boundary in Genesis 2–3*. Lexington Books/Fortress Academic.

Allen, John. 2021. "On White Theology … and Other Lies: Redemptive Communal Narrative in Toni Morrison's *Beloved*." *Literature and Theology* 35:285–308.

Amzallag, Nissim. 2018. "The Authorship of Ezra and Nehemiah in Light of Differences in Their Ideological Background." *JBL* 137:271–97.

Anderson, Cheryl B. 2009. "Reflections in an Interethnic/Racial Era on Interethnic/Racial Marriage in Ezra." Pages 47–64 in *They Were All Together in One Place? Toward Minority Biblical Criticism*. Edited by Randall C. Bailey, Tat-siong Benny Liew, and Fernando F. Segovia. SemeiaSt 57. Society of Biblical Literature.

———. 2022. "The Struggles: A Personal Reflection." Pages 9–12 in *Black Scholars Matter: Visions, Struggles, and Hopes in Africana Biblical Studies*. Edited by Gay L. Byron and Hugh R. Page Jr. RBS 100. SBL Press.

Anderson, Melanie. 2013. *Spectrality in the Novels of Toni Morrison*. University of Tennessee Press.

Andrade Vinueza, María. 2017. "'We Don't Want Them Here': From the Politics of Rejection to Sustainable Relationships with Immigrants." *Journal of Latin American Theology* 12:79–99.

Anum, Eric. 2001. "Effective Scholarly Readings of the Bible in Africa." Pages 104–22 in *Interpreting the New Testament in Africa*. Edited by Mary N. Getui, Tinyiko Malukleke, and Justin Ukpong. ACS. Acton.

Anzaldúa, Gloria. 1987. *Borderlands/La Frontera: The New Mestiza*. Aunt Lute Books.

Assis, Elie. 2009. "The Unity of the Book of Lamentations." *CBQ* 71:306–29.

Bailey, Jonquil. 2017. "Breaking the Back of Words: Sound and Subversion in Toni Morrison's *Beloved*." *Palimpsest* 6:28–43.

Bailey, Randall C. 2010. "My Journey into Afrocentric Biblical Interpretation." Page 20 in *The Africana Bible: Reading Israel's Scriptures from Africa and the African Diaspora*. Edited by Randall C. Bailey. Fortress.

Bal, Mieke. 1987. *Lethal Love: Feminist Literary Readings of Biblical Love Stories*. ISBL. Indiana University Press.

Barnett, Claudia. 2014. "'More Life': Ethel Rosenberg's Ghost and *Angels in America*." *Women's Studies* 43:131–54.

Barnett, Pamela E. 1997. "Figurations of Rape and the Supernatural in *Beloved*." *PMLA* 112:418–27.

Barr, James. 2000. *History and Ideology in the Old Testament: Biblical Studies at the End of a Millennium*. Oxford University Press.

Barton, John. 2007. *The Nature of Biblical Criticism*. Westminster John Knox.

Batt, J. Daniel. 2021. "Do This in Remembrance of Me: Bits and Pieces in Re-membering the Body." *Renascence* 73:161–70.

Batto, Bernard F. 2013. *In the Beginning: Essays on Creation Motifs in the Ancient Near East and the Bible*. Siphrut 9. Eisenbrauns.

Bauks, Michaela. 2019. "Intertextual Exegesis in the Primeval History—the Literary Function of the Genealogies in View of the Formation of Gen 1–11." *ZAW* 131:177–93.

Bechtel, Lyn M. 1993. "Rethinking the Interpretation of Genesis 2.4b–3.24." Pages 77–117 in *A Feminist Companion to Genesis*. Edited by Athalya Brenner. FCB 2. Sheffield Academic.

Becking, Bob. 2011. *Ezra, Nehemiah, and the Construction of Early Jewish Identity*. FAT 80. Mohr Siebeck.
Bennett, Harold V. 2002. *Injustice Made Legal: Deuteronomic Law and the Plight of Widows, Strangers, and Orphans in Ancient Israel*. BibWor. Eerdmans.
Berges, Ulrich. 2002. *Klagelieder*. HThKAT. Herder.
Bergler, Siegfried. 1977. "Threni V: Nur ein alphabetisierendes Lied? Versuch einer Deutung." *VT* 27:304–20.
Berlinerblau, Jacques. 2002. "'Poor Bird, Not Knowing Which Way to Fly': Biblical Scholarship's Marginality, Secular Humanism, and the Laudable Occident." *BibInt* 10:267–304.
Beyerle, Stefan. 2006. "'If You Preserve Carefully Faith ...'—Hellenistic Attitudes towards Religion in Pre-Maccabean Times." *ZAW* 118:250–63.
Bier, Miriam J. 2013. "Theological Interpretation and the Book of Lamentations: A Polyphonic Reconsideration." Pages 204–22 in *Ears That Hear: Explorations in Theological Interpretation of the Bible*. Edited by Joel B. Green and Tim Meadowcroft. Sheffield Phoenix.
———. 2014. "'We Have Sinned and Rebelled; You Have Not Forgiven': The Dialogic Interaction between Authoritative and Internally Persuasive Discourse in Lamentations 3." *BibInt* 22:146–67.
———. 2015. *"Perhaps There Is Hope": Reading Lamentations as a Polyphony of Pain, Penitence, and Protest*. LHBOTS 603. Bloomsbury.
Bird, Michael F. 2012. *1 Esdras: Introduction and Commentary on the Greek Text in Codex Vaticanus*. Septuagint Commentary Series. Brill.
Bird, Phyllis A. 2015. *Faith, Feminism, and the Forum of Scripture*. Cascade.
Blenkinsopp, Joseph. 2009. *Judaism: The First Phase; The Place of Ezra and Nehemiah in the Origins of Judaism*. Eerdmans.
Blomberg, Craig L., and Jennifer Foutz Markley. 2010. *A Handbook of New Testament Exegesis*. Baker Academic.
Blount, Brian K. 1995. *Cultural Interpretation: Reorienting New Testament Criticism*. Fortress.
———. 2019. "The Souls of Black Folk and the Potential for Meaning." *JBL* 138:6–21.
Boase, Elizabeth. 2006. *The Fulfillment of Doom? The Dialogic Interaction between the Book of Lamentations and the Pre-exilic/Early Exilic Prophetic Literature*. LHBOTS 437. Continuum.
———. 2008a. "The Characterisation of God in Lamentations." *ABR* 56:32–44.

———. 2008b. "Constructing Meaning in the Face of Suffering: Theodicy in Lamentations." *VT* 58:449–68.

———. 2016. "Fragmented Voices: Collective Identity and Traumatization in Lamentations." Pages 49–66 in *Bible through the Lens of Trauma*. Edited by Elizabeth Boase and Christopher Frechette. SemeiaSt 86. SBL Press.

Boccaccini, Gabriele. 2002. *Roots of Rabbinic Judaism: An Intellectual History, from Ezekiel to Daniel*. Eerdmans.

Bortz, Anna Maria. 2018. *Identität und Kontinuität: Form und Funktion der Rückkehrerliste Esr 2*. BZAW 512. de Gruyter.

Bosman, Sean James. 2019. "Nguyen's Ghosts in *The Sympathizer*: Collapsing Binaries and Signalling Just Memory." *Scrutiny2* 24:3–12.

Bouson, J. Brooks. 2000. *Quiet as It's Kept: Shame, Trauma, and Race in the Novels of Toni Morrison*. SSPC. State University of New York Press.

Brandt, Stefan L. 2017. "History, Time, and Lived Experience in Toni Morrison's *Beloved* (1987), *Jazz* (1992), and *Paradise* (1997)." *Zeitschrift für Anglistik und Americanistik* 65:395–411.

Brayford, Susan. 2007. *Genesis*. Septuagint Commentary Series. Brill.

Brett, Mark G. 2000a. "Earthing the Human in Genesis 1–3." Pages 73–86 in *The Earth Story in Genesis*. Edited by Norman C. Habel and Shirley Wurst. Earth Bible 2. Sheffield Academic.

———. 2000b. *Genesis: Procreation and the Politics of Identity*. OTR. Routledge.

Burt, Sean. 2014. *The Courtier and the Governor: Transformations of Genre in the Nehemiah Memoir*. JAJSup 17. Vandenhoeck & Ruprecht.

Byron, John. 2008. "Cain's Rejected Offering: Interpretive Approaches to a Theological Problem." *JSP* 18:3–22.

Byttebier, Stephanie. 2011. "'It Doesn't Count if It's Easy': Facing Pain, Mediating Identity in Tony Kushner's *Angels in America*." *Modern Drama* 54:287–309.

Caesar, Terry Paul. 1994. "Slavery and Motherhood in Toni Morrison's *Beloved*." *Revista de Letras* 34:111–20.

Carden, Mary Paniccia. 1999. "Models of Memory and Romance: The Dual Endings of Toni Morrison's *Beloved*." *Twentieth Century Literature* 45:401–27.

Cardoso Pereira, Nancy. 2016. "We Sow Hope: For an Apocalyptic and Anticapitalist Solidarity with Palestine." *CrossCurrents* 66:185–92.

Carey, Greg. 2017. "Daniel as an Americanized Apocalypse." *Int* 71:190–203.

Carr, David M. 2020. *The Formation of Genesis 1-11: Biblical and Other Precursors*. Oxford University Press.
———. 2021. *Genesis 1-11*. IECOT. Kohlhammer.
Cataldo, Jeremiah W. 2020. "Lamenting Loss: A New Understanding of Trauma in Lam 1." *SJOT* 34:51-73.
Chia, Philip. 2006. "On Naming the Subject: Postcolonial Reading of Daniel 1." Pages 171-85 in *The Postcolonial Biblical Reader*. Edited by R. S. Sugirtharajah. Blackwell.
Chong, Sylvia Shin Huey. 2018. "Vietnam, the Movie: Part Deux." *PMLA* 133:371-77.
Claassens, L. Juliana M. 2013. "A True Disgrace? The Representation of Violence against Women in the Book of Lamentations and in J. M. Coetzee's Novel *Disgrace*." Pages 73-100 in *Fragile Dignity: Intercontextual Conversations on Scriptures, Family, and Violence*. Edited by L. Juliana Claassens and Klaas Spronk. SemeiaSt 72. Society of Biblical Literature.
———. 2018. "Cultivating Compassion? Abigail's Story (1 Samuel 25) as Space for Teaching Concern for Others." Pages 157-69 in *Considering Compassion: Global Ethics, Human Dignity, and the Compassionate God*. Edited by Frits de Laange and L. Juliana M. Claassens. Wipf & Stock.
———. 2020. *Reading and Writing to Survive: Biblical and Contemporary Trauma Narratives in Conversation*. BMW 74. Sheffield Phoenix.
Clarke, Sathianathan, and Sharon H. Ringe. 2009. "Inter-location as Textual Trans-version: A Study in John 4.1-42." Pages 58-70 in *Postcolonial Interventions: Essays in Honor of R. S. Sugirtharajah*. Edited by Tat-siong Benny Liew. BMW 23. Sheffield Academic.
Clauss, Jan. 2011. "Understanding the Mixed Marriages of Ezra-Nehemiah in the Light of Temple-Building and the Book's Concept of Jerusalem." Pages 109-31 in *Mixed Marriages: Intermarriage and Group Identity in the Second Temple Period*. Edited by Christian Frevel. LHBOTS 547. Bloomsbury T&T Clark.
Clines, David J. A. 1998. *On the Way to the Postmodern: Old Testament Essays 1967-1998*. 2 volumes. JSOTSup 292-293. Sheffield Academic.
Clune, Lori. 2016. *Executing the Rosenbergs: Death and Diplomacy in a Cold War World*. Oxford University Press.
Cobo-Piñero, Rocío. 2023. "Queering the Black Atlantic: Transgender Spaces in Akwaeke Emezi's Writing and Visual Art." *Cultural Studies* 37:280-97.

Collins, John J. 1993. *Daniel: A Commentary on the Book of Daniel.* Hermeneia. Augsburg Fortress.

Collins, Patricia Hill. 2019. *Intersectionality as Critical Social Theory.* Duke University Press.

Colón, Cristóbal. 1892. *Relaciones y Cartas de Cristóbal Colón.* Librería de la Viuda de Hernando y C.ª.

Conway, Mary L. 2012. "Daughter Zion: Metaphor and Dialogue in the Book of Lamentations." Pages 101–26 in *Daughter Zion: Her Portrait, Her Response.* Edited by Mark J. Boda, Carol J. Dempsey, and LeAnn Snow Flesher. AIL 13. Society of Biblical Literature.

Cook Steike, Elisabeth. 2010. *La Mujer como Extranjera en Israel: Estudio Exegético de Esdras 9–10.* Sebila.

Cooper, Jerrold S. 1983. *The Curse of Agade.* JHNES. Johns Hopkins University Press.

Corby, James. 2010. "The Audacity of Hope: Locating Kushner's Political Vision in *Angels in America*." *Forum for Modern Language Studies* 47:16–35.

Coxon, Peter. 1995. "Nebuchadnezzar's Hermeneutical Dilemma." *JSOT* 66:87–97.

Crawford, Cory. 2018. "Light and Space in Genesis 1." *VT* 68:556–80.

Cristofáni, José Roberto. 2005. "Resistência e Identidade em Daniel 1." *Teología y Cultura* 3:1–9.

Crouch, C. L. 2014. *Israel and the Assyrians: Deuteronomy, the Succession Treaty of Esarhaddon, and the Nature of Subversion.* ANEM 8. SBL Press.

———. 2016. "Made in the Image of God: The Creation of אדם, the Commissioning of the King and the *Chaoskampf* of Yhwh." *JANER* 16:1–21.

———. 2020. "Playing Favourites: Israel and Judah in the Marriage Metaphor of Jeremiah 3." *JSOT* 44:594–609.

Crowder, Stephanie Buckhanon. 2016. *When Momma Speaks: The Bible and Motherhood from a Womanist Perspective.* Westminster John Knox.

Cuéllar, Gregory Lee. 2008. *Voices of Marginality: Exile and Return in Second Isaiah 40–55 and the Mexican Immigrant Experience.* AUS 7/271. Lang.

Culbertson, Philip. 2009. "Bobbittizing God: On the Importance of the Divine Genitals Remaining Unmanageable." *TBC* 5.1:article 5.

Daniels, Steven V. 2002. "Putting 'His Story Next to Hers': Choice, Agency, and the Structure of *Beloved*." *Texas Studies in Literature and Language* 44:349–67.

Darden, Lynne St. Clair. 2015a. *Scripturalizing Revelation: An African American Postcolonial Reading of Empire*. SemeiaSt 80. SBL Press.

———. 2015b. "A Womanist-Postcolonial Reading of the Samaritan Woman at the Well and Mary Magdalene at the Tomb." Pages 183–202 in *I Found God in Me: A Womanist Biblical Hermeneutics Reader*. Edited by Mitzi J. Smith. Cascade Books.

Davies, Philip R. 1995. *Whose Bible Is It Anyway?* JSOTSup 204. Sheffield Academic.

Davis, Kimberly Chabot. 1998. "'Postmodern Blackness': Toni Morrison's *Beloved* and the End of History." *Twentieth Century Literature* 44:242–60.

Davis Bledsoe, Amanda M. 2014. "Attitudes toward Seleucid Imperial Hegemony in the Book of Daniel." Pages 23–40 in *Reactions to Empire: Sacred Texts in Their Socio-Political Contexts*. Edited by John Anthony Dunne and Dan Batovici. WUNT 2/372. Mohr Siebeck.

Day, John. 2012. "The Sons of God and Daughters of Men and the Giants: Disputed Points in the Interpretation of Genesis 6:1–4." *HeBAI* 1:427–47.

Delcor, M. 1993. "L'historique selon le livre de Daniel, notamment au chapitre 11." Pages 365–86 in *The Book of Daniel in Light of New Findings*. Edited by A. S. van der Woude. BETL 106. Leuven University Press.

Deutschmann, Barbara. 2017. "Partners in Crime? The Partnership of the Woman and Man in the Garden of Eden Narrative." *Pacifica* 30:255–67.

Dewey, John. 1998. "The Need for a Recovery of Philosophy." Pages 46–70 in vol. 1 of *The Essential Dewey*. 2 volumes. Edited by Larry A. Hickman and Thomas M. Alexander. Indiana University Press.

DiTomasso, Lorenzo. 2005. *The Book of Daniel and the Apocryphal Daniel Literature*. SVTP 20. Brill.

Dobbs-Allsopp, F. W. 1995. "The Syntagma of *bat* Followed by a Geographical Name in the Hebrew Bible: A Reconsideration of Its Meaning and Grammar." *CBQ* 57:451–70.

———. 1997. "Tragedy, Tradition, and Theology in the Book of Lamentations." *JSOT* 74:29–60.

———. 1998. "Linguistic Evidence for the Dating of Lamentations." *JANES* 26:1–36.

———. 1999. "Rethinking Historical Criticism." *BibInt* 7:235–71.

———. 2004. "R(az/ais)ing Zion in Lamentations 2." Pages 21–68 in *David and Zion: Biblical Studies in Honor of J. J. M. Roberts*. Edited by Bernard F. Batto and Kathryn L. Roberts. Eisenbrauns.

Dobbs-Allsopp, F. W., and Tod Linafelt. 2001. "The Rape of Zion in Thr 1,10." ZAW 113:77–81.

Dresner, Samuel H. 1990. "Homosexuality and the Order of Creation." *Judaism* 40:309–21.

Dube, Musa Wenkosi. 2008. *The HIV & AIDS Bible: Selected Essays*. Scranton University Press.

———. 2010. "Toward a Post-Colonial Feminist Interpretation of the Bible." Pages 89–102 in *Hope Abundant: Third World and Indigenous Women's Theology*. Edited by Kwok Pui-lan. Orbis Books.

———. 2015. "'And God Saw That It Was Very Good': An Earth-Friendly Theatrical Reading of Genesis 1." *Black Theology* 13:230–46.

———. 2018. "Border Crossing in Diasporic Academic Space." Pages 7–14 in *The Bible, Centres and Margins: Dialogues between Postcolonial African and British Biblical Scholars*. Edited by Musa Dube and Johanna Stiebert. T&T Clark.

Durkin, Anita. 2007. "Object Written, Written Object: Slavery, Scarring, and Complications of Authorship in *Beloved*." *African American Review* 41:541–56.

Dyck, Jonathan. 2000. "Ezra 2 in Ideological Critical Perspective." Pages 129–45 in *Rethinking Contexts, Rereading Texts: Contributions from the Social Sciences to Biblical Interpretation*. Edited by M. Daniel Carroll R. JSOTSup 299. Sheffield Academic.

Eidevall, Göran. 2005. "Spatial Metaphors in Lamentations 3,1–9." Pages 133–37 in *Metaphor in the Hebrew Bible*. Edited by P. Van Hecke. BETL 187. Leuven University Press.

Emezi, Akwaeke. 2018. *Freshwater*. Grove Atlantic.

———. 2021. *Dear Senthuran: A Black Spirit Memoir*. Riverhead Books.

Esler, Philip F. 2003. "Ezra-Nehemiah as a Narrative of (Re-Invented) Identity." *BibInt* 11:413–26.

Fanon, Frantz. 1963. *The Wretched of the Earth*. Translated by Constance Farrington. Grove Books.

Farisani, Elelwani. 2002. "The Ideologically Biased Use of Ezra-Nehemiah in a Quest for an African Theology of Reconstruction." *OTE* 15:628–46.

Federal Bureau of Investigation. 2023. "Hate Crime in the United States Incident Analysis." https://tinyurl.com/SBL6109m.

Fee, Gordon D. 2002. *New Testament Exegesis: A Handbook for Students and Pastors*. 3rd edition. Westminster John Knox.

Fewell, Danna Nolan. 1988. *Circle of Sovereignty: A Story of Stories in Daniel 1–6*. JSOTSup 72. BLS 20. Almond Press.

Finney, Brian. 1990. "Temporal Defamiliarization in Toni Morrison's *Beloved*." *Obsidian II* 5:20–36.

Finsterbusch, Karin, and Antonella Bellantuono. 2021. "Analyse der Struktur des masoretischen und nicht-masoretischen Danielbuches (MT-Dan und LXX967-Dan) unter besonderer Berücksichtigung der Zeitangaben." *BZ* 65:28–45.

Fish, Stanley. 1980. *Is There a Text in This Class? The Authority of Interpretive Communities*. Harvard University Press.

———. 1989. *Doing What Comes Naturally: Change, Rhetoric, and the Practice of Theory in Literary and Legal Studies*. PCI. Duke University Press.

Flores, Andrew R., Rebecca L. Stotzer, Ilan H. Meyer, and Lynn L. Langton. 2022. "Hate Crimes against LGBT People: National Crime Victimization Survey, 2017–2019." *PLoS ONE* 17:article 12.

Floyd, Michael H. 2012. "The Daughter of Zion Goes Fishing in Heaven." Pages 177–200 in *Daughter Zion: Her Portrait, Her Response*. Edited by Mark J. Boda, Carol J. Dempsey, and LeAnn Snow Flesher. AIL 13. Society of Biblical Literature.

Foertsch, Jacqueline. 1999. "Angels in an Epidemic: Women as 'Negatives' in Recent AIDS Literature." *South Central Review* 16:57–72.

Forti, Tova L. 2008. *Animal Imagery in the Book of Proverbs*. VTSup 118. Brill.

Fox, Michael V. 2009. *Proverbs 10–31: A New Translation with Introduction and Commentary*. AB 18B. Yale University Press.

———. 2010. "Scholarship and Faith in Bible Study." Pages 15–19 in *Secularism and Biblical Studies*. Edited by Roland Boer. BibleWorld. Equinox.

Francis, Donald. 2012. "Deadly AIDS Policy Failure at the Highest Levels of the US Government: A Personal Look back 30 Years Later for Lessons to Respond Better to Future Epidemics." *Journal of Public Health Policy* 33:290–300.

Frantzen, Allen. 1997. "Prior to the Normans: The Anglo-Saxons in *Angels in America*." Pages 134–50 in *Approaching the Millennium: Essays on Angels in America*. Edited by Deborah R. Geis and Steven F. Kruger. University of Michigan Press.

Frisch, Alexandra. 2016. *The Danielic Discourse on Empire in Second Temple Literature*. JSJSup 176. Brill.
Fröhlich, Ida. 2015. "Stars and Spirits: Heavenly Bodies in Ancient Jewish Aramaic Tradition." *AS* 13:111–27.
Frymer-Kensky, Tikva. 2006. *Studies in Bible and Feminist Criticism*. Jewish Publication Society of America.
Fuchs, Esther. 2003. "Men in Biblical Feminist Scholarship." *JFSR* 19:93–114.
Fulton, Deirdre N. 2015. *Reconsidering Nehemiah's Judah: The Case of MT and LXX Nehemiah 11–12*. FAT 2/80. Mohr Siebeck.
Fulton, Lorie Watkins. 2005. "Hiding Fire and Brimstone in Lacy Groves: The Twined Trees of *Beloved*." *African American Review* 39:189–99.
Gafney, Wilda C. 2009. "Mother Knows Best: Messianic Surrogacy and Sexploitation in Ruth." Pages 23–36 in *Mother Goose, Mother Jones, Mommie Dearest: Biblical Mothers and Their Children*. Edited by Cheryl A. Kirk-Duggan and Tina Pippin. SemeiaSt 61. Society of Biblical Literature.
———. 2011. "A Prophet-Terrorist(a) and an Imperial Sympathizer: An Empire-Critical, Postcolonial Reading of the No'adyah/Nechemyah Conflict." *Black Theology* 9:161–76.
———. 2017a. "A Reflection on the Black Lives Matter Movement and Its Impact on My Scholarship." *JBL* 136:204–7.
———. 2017b. *Womanist Midrash: A Reintroduction to the Women of the Torah and the Throne*. Westminster John Knox.
———. 2022. "Reflections on Teaching Biblical Interpretation through a Black Lives Matter Hermeneutic." Pages 139–56 in *Bitter the Chastening Rod: African Biblical Interpretation after* Stony the Road We Trod *in the Age of BLM, SayHerName, and MeToo*. Edited by Mitzi J. Smith, Angela N. Parker, and Ericka S. Dunbar Hill. Lexington Books.
Gandhi, Evyn Lê Espiritu. 2020. "Historicizing the Transpacific Settler Colonial Condition: Asian-Indigenous Relations in Shawn Wong's *Homebase* and Viet Thanh Nguyen's *The Sympathizer*." *MELUS* 45.4:49–71.
García Márquez, Gabriel. 2018. *Cien Años de Soledad*. 24th edition. Cátedra.
Garric, Nathaniel. 2008. "L'homme ou la représentation divine: Le terme 'çelem' en Genèse 1,26." *RB* 115:440–47.
Gatti, Nicoletta. 2017. "Toward a Dialogic Hermeneutics: Reading Gen. 4:1–16 with Akan Eyes." *HBT* 39:46–67.

Gericke, Jaco. 2012. "Spectres of Yhwh: Some Hauntological Remarks on Lamentations 3." *Scriptura* 110:166–75.
Gilan, Amir. 2013. "Hittites in Canaan? The Archaeological Evidence." *BN* 156:39–52.
Gladson, Jerry A. 2010. "Postmodernism and the *Deus absconditus* in Lamentations 3." *Bib* 91:321–34.
Gnuse, Robert K. 2021. "The 'Living Soul' in People and Animals: Environmental Themes from Genesis 2." *BTB* 51:168–74.
González, Justo. 1996. *Santa Biblia: The Bible through Hispanic Eyes*. Abingdon.
Gordon, Lewis R., and Jane Anna Gordon. 2006. "Introduction: Not Only the Master's Tools." Pages ix–xi in *Not Only the Master's Tools: African-American Studies in Theory and Practice*. Edited by Lewis R. Gordon and Jane Anna Gordon. Routledge.
Gossai, Hemchand. 2019. "The Exile of Cain and the Destiny of Humankind: Punishment and Protection." Pages 211–19 in *T&T Clark Handbook of Asian American Biblical Hermeneutics*. Edited by Uriah Y. Kim and Seung Ai Yeung. T&T Clark.
Grabbe, Lester L. 2016. "The Seleucid and Hasmonean Periods and the Apocalyptic Worldview—An Introduction." Pages 11–31 in *The Seleucid and Hasmonean Periods and the Apocalyptic Worldview*. Edited by Lester L. Grabbe and Gabriele Boccaccini. LSTS 88. T&T Clark.
Gradisek, Amanda. 2020. "Refocusing on Women and the Obscene in Viet Nguyen's *The Sympathizer*." *War, Literature, and the Arts* 32:1–27.
Graybill, Rhiannon. 2021. *Texts after Terror: Rape, Sexual Violence, and the Hebrew Bible*. Oxford University Press.
Grayson, Albert Kirk. 1975. *Assyrian and Babylonian Chronicles*. TCS 5. J. J. Augustin.
Greenstein, Edward L. 2002. "God's Golem: The Creation of the Human in Genesis 2." Pages 219–39 in *Creation in Jewish and Christian Tradition*. Edited by Henning Graf Reventlow and Yair Hoffman. JSOTSup 319. Sheffield Academic.
Grosfoguel, Ramón. 2007. "The Epistemic Colonial Turn: Beyond Political-Economy Paradigms." *Cultural Studies* 21:211–23.
———. 2012. "Decolonizing Western Uni-versalisms: Decolonial Pluri-versalism from Aimé Césaire to the Zapatistas." *Transmodernity* 1.3:88–104.
Guardiola-Sáenz, Leticia. 1997. "Borderless Women and Borderless Texts: A Cultural Reading of Matthew 15:21–28." Pages 69–81 in *Reading*

the Bible as Women: Perspectives from Africa, Asia, and Latin America. Edited by Katherine Doob Sakenfeld and Sharon H. Ringe. Semeia 78. Society of Biblical Literature.

Gudbergsen, Thomas. 2012. "God Consists of Both the Male and the Female Genders: A Short Note on Gen 1:27." *VT* 62:450–53.

Guest, Deryn. 1999 "Hiding behind the Naked Women in Lamentations: A Recriminative Response." *BibInt* 7:413–48.

———. 2006. "Lamentations." Pages 394–411 in *The Queer Bible Commentary*. Edited by Deryn Guest, Robert E. Goss, Mona West, and Thomas Bohache. SCM.

Guillaume, Philippe. 2009. "Lamentations 5: The Seventh Acrostic." *JHS* 9:article 16.

Habel, Norman C. 2007. "The Beginning of Violence: An Ecological Reading of Genesis 4." Pages 79–85 in *Ecumenics from the Rim: Explorations in Honour of John D'Arcy May*. Edited by John O'Grady and Peter Scherle. LIT Verlag.

———. 2013. "Reading as an Earth Being: Rereading Genesis 2–3—Again." Pages 95–104 in *Interested Readers: Essays on the Hebrew Bible in Honor of David J. A. Clines*. Edited James A. Aitken, Jeremy M. S. Clines, and Christl M. Maier. Society of Biblical Literature.

Hamilton, Cynthia S. 1996. "Revisions, Rememories and Exorcisms: Toni Morrison and the Slave Narrative." *Journal of American Studies* 30:429–45.

Hamori, Esther J. 2008. *When Gods Were Men: The Embodied God in Biblical and Near Eastern Literature*. BZAW 384. de Gruyter.

Harlin, Kate. 2023. "'One Foot on the Other Side': Towards a Periodization of West African Spiritual Surrealism." *College Literature* 50:295–322.

Harrington, Hannah K. 2012. "The Use of Leviticus in Ezra-Nehemiah." *JHS* 13:article 3.

Harris, Cheryl I. 1993. "Whiteness as Property." *Harvard Law Review* 106:1707–91.

Harrisville, Roy A. 2014. *Pandora's Box Opened: An Examination and Defense of Historical-Critical Method and Its Master Practitioners*. Eerdmans.

Harvey, Van Austin. 1996. *The Historian and the Believer: The Morality of Historical Knowledge and Belief*. University of Illinois Press.

Haydon, Ron. 2014. "'The Law and the Prophets' in MT Daniel 9:3–19." *BBR* 24:15–26.

Hayes, Christine E. 2002. *Gentile Impurities and Jewish Identities: Intermarriage and Conversion from the Bible to the Talmud*. Oxford University Press.
Hayes, John H., and Carl R. Holladay. 2007. *Biblical Exegesis: A Beginner's Handbook*. 3rd edition. Westminster John Knox.
Haynes, Matthew, and P. Paul Krüger. 2017. "Creation Rest: Genesis 2:1–3 and the First Creation Accounts." *OTE* 30:663–83.
Hecke, Pierre J. P. van. 2002. "Lamentations 3, 1–6: An Anti-Psalm 23." *SJOT* 16:264–82.
Heckl, Raik. 2016. *Neuanfang und Kontinuität in Jerusalem: Studien zu den hermeneutischen Strategien im Esra-Nehemia-Buch*. FAT 104. Mohr Siebeck.
Heider, George. 2012. "Cleaving and Cloven: Genesis and Gender." *BibRes* 57:39–50.
Heim, Knut M. 1999. "The Personification of Jerusalem and the Drama of Her Bereavement in Lamentations." Pages 129–69 in *Zion, City of Our God*. Edited by Richard S. Hess and Gordon J. Wenham. Eerdmans.
Hens-Piazza, Gina. 2021. "Silence Breakers: Woman Zion and the #Metoo Movement: Lamentation 2:20–22's Path to Transformation." Pages 20–35 in *Transgression and Transformation: Feminist, Postcolonial and Queer Biblical Interpretation*. Edited by L. Juliana Claassens, Christl M. Maier, and Fulọla O. Ọlọjẹde. LHBOTS 707. Bloomsbury.
Henze, Matthias. 1999. *The Madness of King Nebuchadnezzar: The Ancient Near Eastern Origins and Early History of Interpretation of Daniel 4*. JSJSup 61. Brill.
———. 2001. "The Narrative Frame of Daniel: A Literary Assessment." *JSJ* 32:5–24.
Herring, Stephen L. 2008. "A 'Transubstantial' Humanity: The Relationship between the Divine Image and the Presence of God in Genesis i 26f." *VT* 58:480–94.
Hickey, Walt. 2014. "The Dollar-and-Cents Case against Hollywood's Exclusion of Women." https://tinyurl.com/SBL61091.
Hickey, Walt, Ella Koeze, Rachael Dottle, and Gus Wezerek. 2017. "The Next Bechdel Test." https://tinyurl.com/SBLPress06109a1.
Hidalgo, Jacqueline M. 2018. *Latina/o/x Studies and Biblical Studies*. BRPBI 3.4. Brill.
———. 2021. "Defying the Meaning Line: Reading Brian Blount's Presidential Address alongside Lxs Atravesadxs." *BCT* 17.1:36–45.

———. 2023. "Reading between the Words: Learning to Interpret Worlds alongside Runagate Scriptural Studies." Pages 51–63 in *Remapping Biblical Studies: CUREMP at Thirty*. Edited by Stephanie Buckhanon Crowder and Mary F. Foskett. BSNA 31. SBL Press.

Hiebert, Theodore. 2019. "Retranslating Genesis 1–2: Reconnecting Biblical Thought and Contemporary Experience." *BT* 70:261–72.

———. 2022. "Genesis." Pages 81–94 in *The Oxford Handbook of the Bible and Ecology*. Edited by Hilary Marlow and Mark Harris. Oxford University Press.

Hillers, Delbert R. 1992. *Lamentations: A New Translation with Introduction and Commentary*. Revised edition. AB 7A. Doubleday.

Hinson, D. Scot. 2001. "Narrative and Community Crisis in *Beloved*." *MELUS* 26.4:147–67.

Hobbs, Heschel H. 1986. "Was Cain's Offering Rejected Because It Was Not a Blood Sacrifice? Yes." Pages 130–47 in *The Genesis Debate: Persistent Questions about Creation and the Flood*. Edited by Ronald Youngblood. Thomas Nelson.

Hoke, Jimmy. 2021. *Feminism, Queerness, Affect, and Romans: Under God?* ECL 30. SBL Press.

Holden-Kirwan, Jennifer L. 1998. "Looking into the Self That Is No Self: An Examination of Subjectivity in *Beloved*." *African American Review* 32:415–26.

Holm, Tawny L. 2013. *Of Courtiers and Kings: The Biblical Daniel Narratives and Ancient Story-Collections*. EANEC 1. Eisenbrauns.

Hoopen, Robin B. ten. 2017. "Genesis 5 and the Formation of the Primeval History: A Redaction Case Study." *ZAW* 129:177–93.

———. 2018. "Where Are You, Enoch? Why Can't I Find You? Genesis 5:21–24 Reconsidered." *JHS* 18:article 4.

Howard, Cameron B. R. 2008. "Animal Speech as Revelation in Genesis 3 and Numbers 22." Pages 21–29 in *Exploring Ecological Hermeneutics*. Edited by Norman C. Habel and Peter L. Trudinger. SBLSymS 46. Society of Biblical Literature.

Howard, Thomas A. 2006. *Protestant Theology and the Making of the Modern German University*. Oxford University Press.

Hsu, Ruth Y. 2023. "Trans-Species and Post-Human Oceanic Futures in Witi Ihimaera's *The Whale Rider* and James Nestor's *Deep*." *Atlantic Studies* 20:331–47.

Humphreys, W. Lee. 1973. "A Life-Style for Diaspora: A Study of the Tales of Esther and Daniel." *JBL* 92:211–23.

———. 2001. *The Character of God in the Book of Genesis: A Narrative Appraisal*. Westminster John Knox.
Intergovernmental Panel on Climate Change. 2022. *Global Warming of 1.5ºC*. Cambridge University Press.
Isasi-Díaz, Ada María. 1996. *Mujerista Theology: A Theology for the Twenty-First Century*. Orbis Books.
Iser, Wolfgang. 1978. *The Act of Reading: A Theory of Aesthetic Response*. Routledge & Kegan Paul.
Janz, Timothy. 2008. "Le deuxième livre d'Esdras: Clef de l'histoire textuelle de la Septante?" *Annali di Scienze Religiose* 1:101–17.
Janzen, David. 2017a. *Chronicles and the Politics of Davidic Restoration: A Quiet Revolution*. LHBOTS 655. Bloomsbury T&T Clark.
———. 2017b. "Yahwistic Appropriation of Achaemenid Ideology and the Function of Nehemiah 9 in Ezra-Nehemiah." *JBL* 136:839–56.
———. 2019. *Trauma and the Failure of History: Kings, Lamentations, and the Destruction of Jerusalem*. SemeiaSt 94. SBL Press.
———. 2021a. *The End of History and the Last King: Achaemenid Ideology and Community Identity in Ezra-Nehemiah*. LHBOTS 713. T&T Clark.
———. 2021b. *The Liberation of Method: The Ethics of Emancipatory Biblical Interpretation*. Fortress.
Japhet, Sara. 2006. *From the Rivers of Babylon to the Highlands of Judah: Collected Studies on the Restoration Period*. Eisenbrauns.
Jesser, Nancy. 1999. "Violence, Home, and Community in Toni Morrison's *Beloved*." *African American Review* 33:325–45.
Jobling, David. 1986. *The Sense of Biblical Narrative: Structural Analyses in the Hebrew Bible, II*. JSOTSup 39. JSOT Press.
Johnson, Bo. 1985. "Form and Message in Lamentations." *ZAW* 97:58–73.
Johnson, Willa M. 2011. *The Holy Seed Has Been Defiled: The Interethnic Marriage Dilemma in Ezra 9–10*. HBM 33. Sheffield Phoenix.
Jørstad, Mari. 2016. "The Ground That Opened Its Mouth: The Ground's Response to Human Violence in Genesis 4." *JBL* 135:705–15.
Joseph, Simon J. 2013. "Was Daniel 7.13's 'Son of Man' Modeled after the 'New Adam' of the *Animal Apocalypse* (*1 Enoch 90*)? A Comparative Study." *JSP* 22:269–94.
Joüon, Paul, and T. Muraoka. 2006. *A Grammar of Biblical Hebrew*. Editrice Pontificio Istituto Biblico.
Joyce, Paul. 1994. "First among Equals? The Historical-Critical Approach in the Marketplace of Methods." Pages 17–27 in *Crossing the Boundaries: Essays in Biblical Interpretation in Honour of Michael D. Goulder*.

Edited by Stanley E. Porter, Paul Joyce, and David E. Orton. BIS 8. Brill.

Junior, Nyasha. 2015. *An Introduction to Womanist Biblical Interpretation*. Westminster John Knox.

Kalmanofsky, Amy. 2007. "Their Heart Cried out to God: Gender and Prayer in the Book of Lamentations." Pages 53–65 in *A Question of Sex? Gender and Difference in the Hebrew Bible and Beyond*. Edited by Deborah W. Rooke. HBM 14. Sheffield Phoenix.

———. 2014. *Dangerous Sisters of the Hebrew Bible*. Fortress.

———. 2017. *Gender-Play in the Hebrew Bible: The Ways the Bible Challenges Gender Norms*. RIPBC. Routledge.

Kaminsky, Joel. 2009. "A Light to the Nations: Was There Mission and/or Conversion in the Hebrew Bible?" *JSQ* 16:6–22.

Karrer-Grube, Christiane. 2008. "Scrutinizing the Conceptual Unity of Ezra and Nehemiah." Pages 136–59 in *Unity and Disunity in Ezra-Nehemiah: Redaction, Rhetoric, and Reader*. Edited by Mark J. Boda and Paul L. Redditt. HBM 17. Sheffield Phoenix.

Kawashima, Robert S. 2004. "*Homo Faber* in J's Primeval History." *ZAW* 116:483–501.

———. 2006. "A Revisionist Reading Revisited: On the Creation of Adam and then Eve." *VT* 66:46–57.

———. 2015. "Violence and the City: On the Yahwist's Leviathan." *NEA* 78:264–72.

Kebaneilwe, Mmapula Diana. 2015. "The Good Creation: An Ecowomanist Reading of Genesis 1–2." *OTE* 28:694–703.

Kelly, Joseph R. 2013. "The Ethics of Inclusion: The גר and the אזרח in the Passover to Yhwh." *BBR* 23:155–66.

Kessler, John. 2010. "Images of Exile: Representations of the 'Exile' and 'Empty Land' in the Sixth to Fourth Century BCE Yehudite Literature." Pages 309–51 in *The Concept of Exile in Ancient Israel and its Historical Contexts*. Edited by Ehud Ben Zvi and Christoph Levin. BZAW 404. de Gruyter.

Kilner-Johnson, Allan. 2019. "'[God] is a Flaming Hebrew Letter': Esoteric Camp in *Angels in America*." *Literature and Theology* 33:206–22.

King, Emily. 2008. "The Overlooked Jewish Identity of Roy Cohn in Kushner's *Angels in America*: American Schmucko." *Studies in American Jewish Literature* 27:87–100.

King, Lovalerie. 2014. "Property and Identity in Toni Morrison's *Beloved*." Pages 159–71 in *Toni Morrison: Memory and Meaning*. Edited by Adrienne Lanier Seward and Justine Tally. University of Mississippi Press.

King, Shinman, and Pieter M. Venter. 2009. "A Canonical-Literary Reading of Lamentations 5." *HTS* 65:257–63.

Kirkpatrick, Shane. 2005. *Competing for Honor: A Social-Scientific Reading of Daniel 1–6*. BIS 74. Brill.

Kirova, Milena. 2020. *Performing Masculinity in the Hebrew Bible*. HBM 91. Sheffield Phoenix.

Klawans, Jonathan. 2000. *Impurity and Sin in Ancient Judaism*. Oxford University Press.

Koch, Klaus. 2007. "Der 'Menschensohn' in Daniel." *ZAW* 119:369–87.

Kolk, Bessel A. van der. 2014. *The Body Keeps the Score: Brain, Mind, and Body in the Healing of Trauma*. Viking.

Kornhaber, David. 2014. "Kushner at Colonus: Tragedy, Politics, and Citizenship." *PMLA* 129:727–41.

Korte, Anne-Marie. 2011. "Paradise Lost, Growth Gained: Eve's Story Revisited—Genesis 2–4 in Feminist Theological Perspective." Pages 140–56 in *Out of Paradise: Eve and Adam and Their Interpreters*. Edited by Bob Becking and Susanne Hennecke. HBM 30. Sheffield Phoenix.

Korzec, Cezary. 2021. "The Voice of Geber (Lam 3) in the Panorama of Speaking Voices in the Book of Lamentations." *The Biblical Annals* 11 (2021):637–57.

Kratz, Reinhard Gregor. 1991. *Translatio imperii: Untersuchungen zu den aramäischen Danielerzählungen und ihrem theologiegeschichtlichen Umfeld*. WMANT 63. Neukirchener Verlag.

———. 2005. *The Composition of the Narrative Books of the Old Testament*. Translated by John Bowden. T&T Clark International.

Krumholz, Linda. 1992. "The Ghosts of Slavery: Historical Recovery in Toni Morrison's *Beloved*." *African American Review* 26:395–408.

Kumamoto Stanley, Sandra. 2020. "Citizens of the Imagination: Refugee Memory in Viet Thanh Nguyen's *The Sympathizer* and *Nothing Ever Dies: Vietnam and the Memory of War*." *Modern Fiction Studies* 66:281–300.

Kushner, Tony. 2013. *Angels in America: A Gay Fantasia on National Themes*. Revised edition. Theatre Communications Group.

Kvanvig, Helen S. 2005. "Throne Visions and Monsters: The Encounter between Danielic and Enochic Traditions." *ZAW* 117:249–72.

Kwok Pui-lan. 1995. *Discovering the Bible in the Non-Biblical World*. Orbis Books.

Laird, Donna. 2016. *Negotiating Power in Ezra-Nehemiah*. AIL 26. SBL Press.

Lau, Peter H. W. 2009. "Gentile Incorporation into Israel in Ezra-Nehemiah?" *Bib* 90:356–73.

Law, David R. 2012. *The Historical-Critical Method: A Guide for the Perplexed*. T&T Clark.

Lee, Nancy C. 2002. *The Singers of Lamentations: Cities under Siege, from Ur to Jerusalem to Sarajevo, from Ur to Jerusalem to Sarajevo*. BIS 60. Brill.

Lee, Rachel. 1994. "Missing Peace in Toni Morrison's *Sula* and *Beloved*." *African American Review* 28:571–83.

Lee & Low Books. 2024. "Where Is the Diversity in Publishing? The 2023 Diversity Baseline Survey Results." https://tinyurl.com/SBL6109j.

Legaspi, Michael C. 2010. *The Death of Scripture and the Rise of Biblical Studies*. OSHT. Oxford University Press.

Lemaire, André. 2014. "Fifth- and Fourth-Century Issues: Governorship and Priesthood in Jerusalem." Pages 406–25 in *Ancient Israel's History: An Introduction to Issues and Sources*. Edited by Bill T. Arnold and Richard S. Hess. Baker Academic.

Levin, Saul. 1979. "The More Savory Offering: A Key to the Problem of Gen 4:3–5." *JBL* 98:85.

Liew, Tat-siong Benny. 1999. "Tyranny, Boundary and Might: Colonial Mimicry in Mark's Gospel." *JSNT* 73:7–31.

Liew, Tat-siong Benny, and Fernando F. Segovia. 2022. "Minority/Minoritized: A Note." Pages xiii–xiv in *Reading Biblical Texts Together: Pursuing Minoritized Biblical Criticism*. Edited by Tat-siong Benny Liew and Fernando F. Segovia. SemeiaSt 98. SBL Press.

Lim, Chin Ming Stephen. 2017. "The Impe(/a)rative of Dialogue in Asian Hermeneutics within the Modern/Colonial World System: Renegotiating Biblical Pasts for Planetary Futures." *BibInt* 25:663–78.

———. 2019. *Contextual Biblical Hermeneutics as Multicentric Dialogue: Towards a Singaporean Reading of Daniel*. BIS 175. Brill.

———. 2020. "Ruth as Esperanza? A Trans-textual Reading of Ruth with Foreign Domestic Workers in Singapore." Pages 122–39 in *Faith, Class, and Labor: Intersectional Approaches in a Global Context*. Edited by Jin Young Choi and Joerg Rieger. ITS. Pickwick.

Linafelt, Tod. 2000. *Surviving Lamentations: Catastrophe, Lament, and Protest in the Afterlife of a Biblical Book*. University of Chicago Press.
———. 2001. "The Refusal of a Conclusion in the Book of Lamentations." *JBL* 120:340–43.
Linehan, Thomas P. 1997. "Narrating the Self: Aspects of Moral Psychology in Toni Morrison's *Beloved*." *The Centennial Review* 41:301–30.
Lipschitz, Yair. 2012. "The Jacob Cycle in *Angels in America*: Re-performing Scripture Queerly." *Proof* 32:203–38.
Lohr, Joel N. 2009a. "Righteous Abel, Wicked Cain: Genesis 4:1–16 in the Masoretic Text, the Septuagint, and the New Testament." *CBQ* 71:485–96.
———. 2009b. "'So YHWH Established a Sign for Cain': Rethinking Genesis 4,15." *ZAW* 121:101–3.
López, Marta Sofía. 2022. "Border Gnoseology: Akwaeke Emezi and the Decolonial Other-than-Human." *Ecozon@* 13.2:77–91.
Lozada, Francisco, Jr. 2017. *Toward a Latino/a Biblical Interpretation*. RBS 91. SBL Press.
Macaskill, Grant. 2021. "Autism and Biblical Studies: Establishing and Extending the Field Beyond Preliminary Reflection." *Journal of Disability and Religion* 24:388–411.
Machinist, Peter. 1976. "Literature as Politics: The Tukulti-Ninurta Epic and the Bible." *CBQ* 38:455–82.
Macumber, Heather. 2015. "A Monster without a Name: Creating the Beast Known as Antiochus IV in Daniel 7." *JHS* 15:article 9.
Macwilliam, Stuart. 2011. *Queer Theory and the Prophetic Marriage Metaphor in the Hebrew Bible*. BW. Equinox.
Magaqa, Tina and Rodwell Makombe. 2021. "Decolonising Queer Sexualities: A Critical Reading of the *Ogbanje* Concept in Akwaeke Emezi's *Freshwater* (2018)." *African Studies Quarterly* 20.3:24–39.
Maher, John. 2019. "2018 VIDA Count Finds Mild Improvement in Lit Mag Gender Parity." *Publishers Weekly*. https://tinyurl.com/SBL6109h.
Ma'ilo, Mosese. 2018. "Island Prodigals: Encircling the Void in Luke 15:11–32 with Albert Wendt." Pages 23–36 in *Sea of Readings: The Bible in the South Pacific*. Edited by Jione Havea. SemeiaSt 90. SBL Press.
Maldonado-Torres, Nelson. 2007. "On the Coloniality of Being: Contributions to the Development of a Concept." *Cultural Studies* 21:240–70.
Mandolfo, Carleen R. 2007. *Daughter Zion Talks Back to the Prophets: A Dialogic Theology of the Book of Lamentations*. SemeiaSt 58. Society of Biblical Literature.

Marchal, Joseph A. 2019. "On the Verge of an Introduction." Pages 1–61 in *Bodies on the Verge: Queering Pauline Epistles*. Edited by Joseph A. Marchal. SemeiaSt 93. SBL Press.

Marks, Kathleen. 2002. *Toni Morrison's* Beloved *and the Apotropaic Imagination*. University of Missouri Press.

Martin, Clarice J. 1991. "The *Haustafeln* (Household Codes) in African American Biblical Interpretation: 'Free Slaves' and 'Subordinate Women.'" Pages 206–31 in *Stony the Road We Trod: African American Biblical Interpretation*. Edited by Cain Hope Felder. Fortress.

Martin, Dale B. 2008. *Pedagogy of the Bible: An Analysis and Proposal*. Westminster John Knox.

Masenya, Madipoane (ngwan'a Mphahlele). 2004. "Struggling with Poverty/Emptiness: Rereading the Naomi-Ruth Story in African-South Africa." *JTSA* 120:46–59.

Matskevitch, Karalina. 2019. *The Construction of Gender and Identity in Genesis: The Subject and the Other*. LHBOTS 647. T&T Clark.

May, Vivian M. 2015. *Pursuing Intersectionality, Unsettling Dominant Imaginaries*. CSP. Routledge.

Mbuwayesango, Dora Rudo. 2014. "Feminist Biblical Studies in Africa." Pages 71–85 in *Feminist Biblical Studies in the Twentieth Century: Scholarship and Movement*. Edited by Elisabeth Schüssler Fiorenza. BW 9.1. Society of Biblical Literature.

McLay, R. Timothy. 2005. "The Old Greek Translation of Daniel iv–vi and the Formation of the Book of Daniel." *VT* 55:304–23.

McNulty, Charles. 1996. "*Angels in America*: Tony Kushner's Theses on the Philosophy of History." *Modern Drama* 39:84–96.

Meadowcroft, Tim J. 1995. *Aramaic Daniel and Greek Daniel: A Literary Comparison*. JSOTSup 198. Sheffield Academic.

———. 2020. *Like the Stars Forever: Narrative and Theology in the Book of Daniel*. HBM 90. Sheffield Phoenix.

Melanchthon, Monica Jyotsna. 2013–2015. "Engaging Women's Experience in the Struggle for Justice, Dignity, and Humanity: Hebrew Bible Readings by South Asian Women." Pages 51–69 in vol. 2 of *Feminist Interpretation of the Bible in Retrospect*. 3 volumes. Edited by Susanne Scholz. RRBS 5, 8, 9. Sheffield Phoenix.

Mendieta, Eduardo. 2012. "The Ethics of (Not) Knowing: Take Care of Ethics and Knowledge Will Come of Its Own Accord." Pages 247–64 in *Decolonizing Epistemologies: Latina/o Theology and Philosophy*.

Edited Ada María Isasi-Díaz and Eduardo Mendieta. TTC. Fordham University Press.

Merrill Willis, Amy C. 2010. *Dissonance and the Drama of Divine Sovereignty in the Book of Daniel*. LHBOTS 520. T&T Clark.

Mettinger, Tryggve N. D. 2007. *The Eden Narrative: A Literary and Religio-historical Study of Genesis 2–3*. Eisenbrauns.

Meyers, Carol. 2014. "Was Ancient Israel a Patriarchal Society?" *JBL* 133:8–27.

Middlemas, Jill. 2005. *The Troubles of Templeless Judah*. OTRM. Oxford University Press.

———. 2012. "Speaking of Speaking: The Form of Zion's Suffering in Lamentations." Pages 39–54 in *Daughter Zion: Her Portrait, Her Response*. Edited by Mark J. Boda, Carol J. Dempsey, and LeAnn Snow Flesher. AIL 13. Society of Biblical Literature.

Middleton, J. Richard. 2022. "The Image of God in Ecological Perspective." Pages 284–98 in *The Oxford Handbook of the Bible and Ecology*. Edited by Hilary Marlow and Mark Harris. Oxford University Press.

Mignolo, Walter D. 2005. "On Subalterns and Other Agencies." *Postcolonial Studies* 8:381–407.

———. 2009. "Epistemic Disobedience, Independent Thought and Decolonial Freedom." *Theory, Culture & Society* 26.7–8:159–81.

Mignolo, Walter D., and Catherine E. Walsh. 2018. "Introduction." Pages 1–12 in On Decoloniality: Concepts, Analytics, Praxis. Edited by Walter D. Mignolo and Catherine E. Walsh. Duke University Press.

Miller, Althea Spencer. 2005. "Lucy Bailey Meets the Feminists." Pages 209–38 in *Feminist New Testament Studies: Global and Future Perspectives*. Edited by Kathleen O'Brien Wicker, Althea Spencer Miller, and Musa W. Dube. RCC. Palgrave Macmillan.

———. 2015. "Creolizing Hermeneutics: A Caribbean Invitation." Pages 77–95 in *Islands, Islanders, and the Bible: Ruminations*. Edited by Jione Havea, Margaret Aymer, and Steed Vernyl Davidson. SemeiaSt 77. SBL Press.

Minwalla, Framji. 1997. "When Girls Collide: Considering Race in *Angels in America*." Pages 103–17 in *Approaching the Millennium: Essays on Angels in America*. Edited by Deborah R. Geis and Steven F. Kruger. University of Michigan Press.

Moglen, Helene. 1993. "Redeeming History: Toni Morrison's *Beloved*." *Cultural Critique* 24:17–40.

Möller, Karl. 2011. "Images of God and Creation in Genesis 1–2." Pages 3–29 in *A God of Faithfulness: Essays in Honour of J. Gordon McConville*. Edited by Jamie A. Grant, Alison Lo, and Gordon J. Wenham. LHBOTS 538. T&T Clark.

Moore, Stephen D. 1996. "Gigantic God: Yahweh's Body." *JSOT* 70:87–115.

Morrison, Toni. *Beloved*. 2004. Vintage International.

Munnich, Oliver. 2015. "The Masoretic Rewriting of Daniel 4–6: The Septuagint Version as Witness." Pages 149–72 in *From Author to Copyist: Essays on the Composition, Redaction, and Transmission of the Hebrew Bible in Honor of Zipi Talshir*. Edited by Cana Werman. Eisenbrauns.

Murphy, Brian. 2017. "Is Same-Sex Marriage a Sin?" *MSJ* 28.2:135–44.

Nadar, Sarojini. 2001. "A South African Indian Womanist Reading of the Character of Ruth." Pages 159–75 in *Other Ways of Reading: African Women and the Bible*. Edited by Musa W. Dube. GPBS 2. Society of Biblical Literature.

———. 2012. "'Hermeneutics of Transformation'? A Critical Exploration of the Model of Social Engagement between Biblical Scholars and Faith Communities." Pages 389–405 in *Postcolonial Perspectives in African Biblical Interpretations*. Edited by Musa W. Dube, Andrew M. Mbuvi, and Dora Mbuwayesango. GPBS 13. Society of Biblical Literature.

———. 2023. "Epilogue: The Embodied Cost of Knowledge Activism." Pages 183–90 in *Activist Hermeneutics of Liberation and the Bible: A Global Intersectional Perspective*. Edited by Jin Young Choi and Gregory L. Cuéllar. RNCTRTBS. Routledge.

Nadella, Raj. 2023. "Remapping Biblical Studies: Shifts, Challenges and Opportunities." Pages 187–96 in *Remapping Biblical Studies: CUREMP at Thirty*. Edited by Stephanie Buckhanon Crowder and Mary F. Foskett. BSNA 31. SBL Press.

Nam, Roger. 2019. "Half Speak Ashdodite and None Can Speak Judean: Code-Switching in Ezra-Nehemiah as an Identity Marker for Repatriate Judeans and Koreans." Pages 119–31 in *Landscapes of Korean and Korean American Biblical Interpretation*. Edited by John Ahn. IVBS 10. SBL Press.

National Center for Transgender Equality. 2015a. "LGBTQ People behind Bars: A Guide to Understanding the Issues Facing Transgender Prisoners and their Legal Rights." https://tinyurl.com/SBL6109g.

———. 2015b. "The Report of the 2015 U.S. Transgender Survey: Executive Summary." https://tinyurl.com/SBL6109f.

Nelavala, Surekha. 2015. "Patriarchy, a Threat to Human Bonding: Reading the Story of Ruth in Light of Marriage and Family Structures in India." Pages 89–97 in *Reading Ruth in Asia*. Edited by Jione Havea and Peter H. W. Lau. IVBS 7. SBL Press.

Newsom, Carol. 2012. "Political Theology in the Book of Daniel: An Internal Debate." *RevExp* 109:557–68.

———. 2017. "'Resistance is Futile!': The Ironies of Danielic Resistance to Empire." *Int* 71:167–77.

Ng, Andrew Hock Soon. 2011. "Toni Morrison's *Beloved*: Space, Architecture, Trauma." *symplokē* 19:231–45.

Nguyen, Viet Thanh. 2015. *The Sympathizer*. Corsair.

———. 2018. "Dislocation is My Location." *PMLA* 133:428–36.

Nihan, Christophe. 2011. "Resident Aliens and Natives in the Holiness Legislation." Pages 111–34 in *The Foreigner and the Law: Perspectives from the Hebrew Bible and the Ancient Near East*. Edited by Reinhard Achenbach, Rainer Albertz, and Jakob Wöhrle. BZABR 16. Harrassowitz.

Niskanen, Paul. 2004. *The Human and Divine in History: Herodotus and the Book of Daniel*. JSOTSup 396. T&T Clark International.

Norton, Yolanda. 2015. "Silenced Struggles for Survival: Finding Life in Death in the Book of Ruth." Pages 265–79 in *I Found God in Me: A Womanist Biblical Hermeneutics Reader*. Edited by Mitzi J. Smith. Cascade Books.

Nussbaum, Martha C. 1995. *Poetic Justice: The Literary Imagination and Public Life*. Beacon.

———. 1997. *Cultivating Humanity: A Classical Defense of Reform in Liberal Education*. Harvard University Press.

Nzimande, Makhosazana K. 2008. "Being 'Apart' and 'Together' at the Same Time? A Response to Hans de Wit." Pages 31–35 in *African and European Readers of the Bible in Dialogue: In Quest of Shared Meaning*. Edited by Hans de Wit and Gerald O. West. SRA 32. Brill.

———. 2011. "*Imbokodo* Explorations of the Prevalence of Historical Memory and Identity Contestations in the Expulsion of the *Nāšîm Nokriyyōt* in Ezra 9–10." Pages 269–94 in *Texts, Contexts and Readings in Postexilic Literature: Explorations into Historiography and Identity in Hebrew Bible and Related Texts*. Edited by Louis Jonker. FAT 2/53. Mohr Siebeck.

O'Connor, Kathleen M. 2002. *Lamentations and the Tears of the World*. Orbis Books.

Oeming, Manfred. 2006. "'See, We Are Serving Today' (Nehemiah 9:36): Nehemiah 9 as a Theological Interpretation of the Persian Period." Pages 571–88 in *Judah and the Judeans in the Persian Period*. Edited by Oded Lipschits and Manfred Oeming. Eisenbrauns.

Ok, Janette H. 2023. "Minor Feelings and Embodied Strategies in Doctoral Biblical Education." Pages 251–56 in *Remapping Biblical Studies: CUREMP at Thirty*. Edited by Stephanie Buckhanon Crowder and Mary F. Foskett. BSNA 31. SBL Press.

Okonkwo, Christopher N. 2008. *A Spirit of Dialogue: Incarnations of Ọgbañje, the Born-to-Die, in African American Literature*. University of Tennessee Press.

Ọlọjẹde, Funlọla O. 2021. "Numbered with the Transgressors: The Story of the Daughters of Zelophehad as Retold by Noah." Pages 11–19 in *Transgression and Transformation: Feminist, Postcolonial and Queer Biblical Interpretation as Creative Interventions*. Edited by L. Juliana Claassens, Christl M. Maier, and Funlọla O. Ọlọjẹde. LHBOTS 707. Bloomsbury.

Olyan, Saul M. 1996. "Honor, Shame, and Covenant Relations in Ancient Israel and Its Environment." *JBL* 115:201–18.

———. 2004. "Purity Ideology in Ezra-Nehemiah as a Tool to Reconstitute the Community." *JSJ* 35:1–16.

Omer-Sherman, Ranen. 2007a. "The Fate of the Other in Tony Kushner's *Angels in America*." *MELUS* 32.2:7–30.

———. 2007b. "Jewish/Queer: Thresholds of Vulnerable Identities in Tony Kushner's *Angels in America*." *Shofar* 25.4:78–98.

O'Reilly, Andrea. 2004. *Toni Morrison and Motherhood: A Politics of the Heart*. State University of New York Press.

Otto, Eckart. 1996. "Die Paradieserzählung Genesis 2–3: Eine nachpriesterschriftliche Lehrerzählung in ihrem religionshistorischen Kontext." Pages 167–92 in *"Jedes Ding hat seine Zeit …": Studien zur israelitischen und altorientalischen Weisheit*. Edited by Anja A. Diesel, Eckart Otto, and Reinhard G. Lehmann. BZAW 241. de Gruyter.

Owens, Pamela Jean. 1990. "Personification and Suffering in Lamentations 3." *Austin Seminary Bulletin* 105:75–90.

Page, Philip. 1992. "Circularity in Toni Morrison's *Beloved*." *African American Review* 26:31–39.

Park, Suzie. 2019. "Saul's Question and the Question of Saul: A Deconstructive Reading of the Story of Endor in 1 Sam. 28:3–35." Pages

241–51 in *T&T Clark Handbook of Asian American Biblical Hermeneutics*. Edited by Uriah Y. Kim and Seung Ai Yang. T&T Clark.
Park, Wongi. 2021. "Multiracial Biblical Studies." *JBL* 140:435–59.
Parry, Robin. 2007. "The Ethics of Lament: Lamentations 1 as a Case Study." Pages 138–55 in *Reading the Law: Studies in Honour of Gordon J. Wenham*. Edited by J. G. McConville and Karl Möller. LHBOTS 461. T&T Clark.
Patte, Daniel. 1995. "Acknowledging the Contextual Character of Male European-American Cultural Critical Exegesis: An Androcentrical Perspective." Pages 33–55 in vol. 1 of *Reading from This Place*. 2 volumes. Edited by Fernando F. Segovia and Mary Ann Tolbert. Fortress.
Patterson, Brian Neil. 2019. "Postmodernism's Deconstruction of the Creation Mandates." *JETS* 62:125–40.
Perdue, Leo G. 2005. *Reconstructing Old Testament Theology: After the Collapse of History*. OBT. Fortress.
Perez, Richard. 2014. "The Debt of Memory: Reparations, Imagination, and History in Toni Morrison's *Beloved*." *Women's Studies Quarterly* 42:190–98.
Perrin, Andrew B. 2021. "Redrafting the Architecture of Daniel Traditions in the Hebrew Scriptures and the Dead Sea Scrolls." *JTS* 72:44–71.
Pfemmer De Long, Kindalee. 2012. "Daniel and the Narrative Integrity of His Prayer in Chapter 9." Pages 219–49 in *A Teacher for All Generations: Essays in Honor of James C. VanderKam*. Edited by Eric F. Mason, Samuel I. Thomas, Alison Schofield, and Eugene Ulrich. JSJSup 153. Brill.
Piggford, George. 2000. "'In Time of Plague': AIDS and its Significations in Hervé Guibert, Tony Kushner, and Thom Gunn." *Cultural Critique* 44:169–96.
Polaski, Donald C. 2004. "*Mene, Mene, Tekel, Parsin*: Writing and Resistance in Daniel 5 and 6." *JBL* 123:649–69.
Portier-Young, Anathea E. 2010. "Languages of Identity and Obligation: Daniel as a Bilingual Book." *VT* 60:98–115.
Prabhu, Anjali. 2018. "*The Sympathizer*: A Dialectical Reading." *PMLA* 133:388–95.
Punt, Jeremy. 2020. "Queer Bible Readings in Global Hermeneutical Perspective." Pages 65–79 in *The Oxford Handbook of Feminist Approaches to the Hebrew Bible*. Edited by Susanne Scholz. Oxford University Press.

Putnam, Amanda. 2011. "Mothering Violence: Ferocious Female Persistence in Toni Morrison's *The Bluest Eye, Sula, Beloved,* and *A Mercy*." *Black Women, Gender + Families* 5:25–43.

Pyper, Hugh S. 2001. "Reading Lamentations." *JSOT* 95:55–69.

Quijano, Aníbal. 2024. *Aníbal Quijano: Foundational Essays on the Coloniality of Power.* Edited by Walter D. Mignolo, Rita Segato, and Catherine E. Walsh. Duke University Press.

Quine, Cat. 2015. "Deutero-Isaiah, J and P: Who is the Image and Likeness of God? Implications for אדם and Theologies of Creation." *SJOT* 29:296–306.

Rad, Gerhard von. 1972. *Genesis: A Commentary.* Translated by John H. Marks. OTL. SCM.

Ramírez Kidd, José. 2015–2016. "Caín (Génesis 4,1–16): Su Presencia en la Literatura." *EstBib* 77–78:29–52.

Reay, Lewis. 2009. "Towards a Transgender Theology: Que(e)rying the Eunuchs." Pages 148–67 in *Trans/formations.* Edited by Lisa Isherwood and Marcella Althaus-Reid. CCTS. SCM.

Redding, Jonathan David. 2021. *Biography of a Dream: A Reception-Historical Study of the Fourth Beast in Daniel 7.* PHSC 34. Gorgias.

Redditt, Paul L. 1998. "Daniel 11 and the Sociohistorical Setting of the Book of Daniel." *CBQ* 60:463–74.

Remington Rillera, Andrew. 2019. "A Call to Resistance: The Exhortative Function of Daniel 7." *JBL* 138:757–76.

Rice, Alan. 1998. "'Who's Eating Whom': The Discourse of Cannibalism in the Literature of the Black Atlantic from Equiano's *Travels* to Toni Morrison's *Beloved*." *Research in African Literatures* 29.4:106–21.

Richard, Pablo. 2000. "El Pueblo de Dios contra el Imperio: Daniel 7 en Su Contexto Literario e Histórico." *RIBLA* 7:22–40.

Roberts, J. J. M. 1995. "Historical-Critical Method, Theology, and Contemporary Exegesis." Pages 131–41 in *Biblical Theology: Problems and Perspectives in Honor of J. Christiaan Becker.* Edited by Steven J. Kraftchick, Charles D. Myers Jr., and Ben C. Ollenberger. Abingdon.

Rody, Caroline. 1995. "Toni Morrison's *Beloved*: History, 'Rememory,' and a 'Clamor for a Kiss.'" *American Literary History* 7:92–119.

———. 2018. "Between 'I' and 'We': Viet Thanh Nguyen's Interethnic Multitudes." *PMLA* 133:396–405.

Rong, Lina. 2013. *Forgotten and Forsaken by God (Lam 5:19–20): The Community in Pain in Lamentations and Related Old Testament Texts.* Pickwick.

Rooke, Deborah W. 2007. "Feminist Criticism of the Old Testament: Why Bother?" *Feminist Theology* 15:160–74.
Rorty, Richard. 1998. *Truth and Progress: Philosophical Papers*. Vol. 3. Cambridge University Press.
Rosen-Berry, Judith. 2008. "Revealing Hidden Aspects of Divinity in the 'Queer' Face: Towards a Jewish 'Queer' (Liberation) Theology." *European Judaism* 41:138–54.
Rothenbusch, Ralf. 2012. *"... Abgesondert zur Tora Gottes hin": Ethnisch-religiöse Identitäten im Esra/Nehemiabuch*. HBS 70. Koch Neff & Volkmar.
Routledge, Robin. 2015. "The Nephilim: A Tall Story? Who Were the Nephilim and How Did They Survive the Flood?" *TynB* 66:19–40.
Ruiz, Jean-Pierre. 2011. *Readings from the Edges: The Bible and People on the Move*. SLC. Orbis Books.
Russaw, Kimberly. 2015. "Wisdom in the Garden: The Woman of Genesis 3 and Alice Walker's *Sophia*." Pages 222–34 in *I Found God in Me: A Womanist Biblical Hermeneutics Reader*. Edited by Mitzi J. Smith. Cascade Books.
Salters, Robert B. 2000. "Structure and Implication in Lamentations 1?" *SJOT* 14:293–301.
———. 2010. *Lamentations: A Critical and Exegetical Commentary*. ICC. T&T Clark International.
Sangtinuk. 2010. "Daniel: A Counter Paradigm to the Hellenistic Imperialism vis-à-vis Burmanization in Chin State." *AsJT* 24:32–51.
Savran, David. 1995. "Ambivalence, Utopia, and a Queer Sort of Materialism: How *Angels in America* Reconstructs the Nation." *Theatre Journal* 47:207–27.
Scapp, Ron. 1997. "The Vehicle of Democracy: Fantasies toward a (Queer) Nation." Pages 90–100 in *Approaching the Millennium: Essays on Angels in America*. Edited by Deborah R. Geis and Steven F. Kruger. University of Michigan Press.
Schindler, Melissa E. 2023. "From the Margin to the Fold: The Imprint of Toni Morrison on the Writing of Akwaeke Emezi." *Women's Studies* 52:227–45.
Schlimm, Matthew R. 2012. "At Sin's Entryway (Gen 4,7): A Reply to C.L. Crouch." *ZAW* 124:409–15.
Schmudde, Carol. 1993. "Knowing When to Stop: A Reading of Toni Morrison's *Beloved*." *CLA Journal* 37:121–35.

Schneider, Tammi J. 2019. "Scholarship of Promise." Pages 129–34 in *Women and the Society of Biblical Literature*. Edited by Nicole L. Tilford. BSNA 29. SBL Press.

Schniedewind, William M. 2006. "Aramaic, the Death of Written Hebrew, and the Language Shift in the Persian Period." Pages 137–47 in *Margins of Writing, Origins of Cultures*. Edited by Seth L. Sanders. OIS 2. The Oriental Institute of the University of Chicago.

Scholz, Susanne. 2017. *The Bible as Political Artifact: On the Feminist Study of the Hebrew Bible*. Fortress.

Schüle, Andreas. 2005. "Made in the 'Image of God': The Concepts of Divine Images in Gen 1–3." *ZAW* 117:1–20.

———. 2011. "Uniquely Human: The Ethics of the *Imago Dei* in Genesis 1–11." *TJT* 27:5–16.

Schüssler Fiorenza, Elisabeth. 1999. *Rhetoric and Ethic: The Politics of Biblical Studies*. Fortress.

———. 2000. *Jesus and the Politics of Interpretation*. Continuum.

Schwartz, Seth. 2005. "Hebrew and Imperialism in Jewish Palestine." Pages 53–84 in *Ancient Judaism in Its Hellenistic Context*. Edited by Carol Bakhos. JSJSup 95. Brill.

Scolnic, Benjamin. 2014. "Is Daniel 11:1–19 Based on a Ptolemaic Narrative?" *JSJ* 45:157–84.

———. 2022. "Her Story, History, and the Ancient Versions of Daniel 11.6." *BT* 73:227–39.

Sears, Brad, Neko Castleberry, Andy Lin, and Christy Mallory. 2021. "LGBT People's Experience of Workplace Discrimination and Harassment." https://tinyurl.com/SBL6109e.

Sechrest, Love Lazarus. 2022. *Race and Rhyme: Rereading the New Testament*. Eerdmans.

Segal, Michael. 2011. "The Chronological Conception of the Persian Period in Daniel 9." *JAJ* 2:283–303.

———. 2014. "Who is the 'Son of God' in 4Q246? An Overlooked Example of Early Biblical Interpretation." *DSD* 21:289–312.

———. 2016a. *Dreams, Riddles, and Visions: Textual, Contextual, and Intertextual Approaches to the Book of Daniel*. BZAW 455. de Gruyter.

———. 2016b. "The Old Greek and Masoretic Text of Daniel 6." Pages 404–28 in *Die Septuaginta—Orte und Intentionen*. Edited by Siegfried Kreuzer, Martin Meiser, and Marcus Sigisimund. WUNT 361. Mohr Siebeck.

———. 2017. "Daniel 5 in Aramaic and Greek and the Textual History of Daniel 4–6." Pages 251–84 in *Congress Volume Stellenbosch 2016*. Edited by Louis C. Jonker, Gideon R. Kotzé, and Christl M. Maier. VTSup 77. Brill.

———. 2018. "Harmonization and Rewriting of Daniel 6 from the Bible to Qumran." Pages 265–79 in *Hā-'îsh Mōshe: Studies in Scriptural Interpretation in the Dead Sea Scrolls and Related Literature in Honor of Moshe J. Bernstein*. Edited by Benjamin Y. Goldstein, Michael Segal, and George J. Brooke. STDJ 122. Brill.

Sellars, Wilfrid. 1997. *Empiricism and the Philosophy of Mind*. Harvard University Press.

Seow, C. L. 1985. "A Textual Note on Lamentations 1:20." *CBQ* 47:416–19.

———. 2004. "The Rule of God in the Book of Daniel." Pages 219–46 in *David and Zion: Biblical Studies in Honor of J. J. M. Roberts*. Edited by Bernard F. Batto and Kathryn L. Roberts. Eisenbrauns.

Settembrini, Marco. 2018. "Loyal to the Text and to the King? A Commentary on Dan 11,6–9." *Bib* 99:60–74.

Seufert, Michael. 2019. "Refusing the King's Portion: A Reexamination of Daniel's Dietary Reaction in Daniel 1." *JSOT* 43:644–60.

Sharp, Carolyn J. 2014. "Feminist Queries for Ruth and Joshua: Complex Characterization, Gapping, and the Possibility of Dissent." *SJOT* 28:229–52.

———. 2017. "Is This Naomi? A Feminist Reading of the Ambiguity of Naomi in the Book of Ruth." Pages 149–61 in *Feminist Frameworks and the Bible: Power, Ambiguity, and Intersectionality*. Edited by L. Juliana Claassens and Carolyn J. Sharp. LHBOTS 630. Bloomsbury.

Sheehan, Jonathan. 2005. *The Enlightenment Bible: Translation, Scholarship, Culture*. Princeton University Press.

Shostak, Debra. 2020. "Paternity, History, and Misrepresentation in Viet Thanh Nguyen's *The Sympathizer*." Pages 171–89 in *Twenty-First Century US Historical Fiction: Contemporary Responses to the Past*. Edited by Ruth Maxey. Palgrave Macmillan.

Sillin, Sarah. 2019. "American Sympathizers: Confessing Illicit Feeling from the Civil War to the Vietnam War." *Journal of American Studies* 53:613–35.

Ska, Jean-Louis. 2009. *The Exegesis of the Pentateuch: Exegetical Studies and Basic Questions*. FAT 66. Mohr Siebeck.

Smalley, Matthew. 2018. "The Unchurched Preacher and the Circulated Sermon: Literary Preaching in Toni Morrison's *Beloved*." *MELUS* 43.1:29–42.

Smith, Abraham. 2022. "Staying Awake: Constructing Critical Race Literacy and Reorienting Biblical Studies." Pages 111–32 in *Race and Biblical Studies: Antiracism Pedagogy for the Classroom*. Edited by Tat-siong Benny Liew and Shelly Matthews. RBS 101. SBL Press.

———. 2023. "Decolonizing Acts: Violence and the Politics of Knowledge in the Discipline of Biblical Studies." Pages 129–44 in *Remapping Biblical Studies: CUREMP at Thirty*. Edited by Stephanie Buckhanon Crowder and Mary F. Foskett. BSNA 31. SBL Press.

Smith, Mitzi J. 2017. *Insights from African American Interpretation*. Fortress.

Smith, Shively T. J. 2022. "Preliminary Thoughts: The Hermeneutical Dilemmas of the Allies, Colleagues, and Guild of African American Biblical Scholar-Teachers." Pages 39–45 in *Black Scholars Matter: Visions, Struggles, and Hopes in Africana Biblical Studies*. Edited by Gay L. Byron and Hugh R. Page Jr. RBS 100. SBL Press.

So, Richard Jean and Gus Wezerek. 2020. "Just How White Is the Book Industry?" *The New York Times*. https://tinyurl.com/SBL6109d.

Soares-Prabhu, George M. 1995. "Laughing at Idols: The Dark Side of Biblical Monotheism (an Indian Reading of Isaiah 44:9–20)." Pages 109–31 in vol. 2 of *Reading from This Place*. Edited by Fernando F. Segovia and Mary Ann Tolbert. Fortress.

Society of Biblical Literature. 2019. "2019 SBL Membership Data." https://tinyurl.com/SBL6109b.

Soesilo, Daud. 1994. "Why Did Daniel Reject the King's Delicacies (Daniel 1.8)?" *BT* 45:441–44.

Solomon, Alisa. 1997. "Wrestling with Angels: A Jewish Fantasia." Pages 118–33 in *Approaching the Millennium: Essays on Angels in America*. Edited by Deborah R. Geis and Steven F. Kruger. University of Michigan Press.

Song, Angeline M. G. 2022. "Why Did Naboth Say 'No!' to a King? Some Considerations *before* Attempting a Reading of 1 Kings 21." Pages 199–219 in *Reading Biblical Texts Together: Pursuing Minoritized Biblical Criticism*. Edited by Tat-siong Benny Liew and Fernando F. Segovia. SemeiaSt 98. SBL Press.

Southwood, Katherine E. 2012. *Ethnicity and the Mixed Marriage Crisis in Ezra 9–10: An Anthropological Approach.* OTRM. Oxford University Press.

Spargo, R. Clifton. 2002. "Trauma and the Specters of Enslavement in Morrison's *Beloved.*" *Mosaic* 35:113–31.

Spivak, Gayatri Chakravorty. 2010a. "'Can the Subaltern Speak?' revised edition, from the 'History' chapter of *Critique of Postcolonial Reason.*" Pages 21–78 in *Can the Subaltern Speak? Reflections on the History of an Idea.* Edited by Rosalind C. Morris. Columbia University Press.

———. 2010b. "In Response: Looking Back, Looking Forward." Pages 227–36 in *Can the Subaltern Speak? Reflections on the History of an Idea.* Edited by Rosalind C. Morris. Columbia University Press.

Stendahl, Krister. 1984. "Biblical Theology: A Program." Pages 11–44 in *Meaning: The Bible as Document and as Guide.* Fortress.

Stiebert, Johanna. 2013. *Fathers and Daughters in the Hebrew Bible.* Oxford University Press.

Stokes, Ryan E. 2008. "The Throne Visions of Daniel 7, *1 Enoch* 14, and the Qumran *Book of Giants* (4Q530): An Analysis of Their Literary Relationship." *DSD* 15:340–58.

Stone, Ken. 2006. "The Garden of Eden and the Heterosexual Contract." Pages 48–70 in *Bodily Citations: Religion and Judith Butler.* Edited by Ellen T. Armour and Susan M. St. Ville. GTR. Columbia University Press.

———. 2018. *Reading the Bible with Animal Studies.* Stanford University Press.

Stone, Mark Preston. 2021. "(More) on the Precative Qatal in Lamentations 3.56–61: Updating the Argument." *JSOT* 45:493–515.

Stout, Jeffrey. 1982. "What Is the Meaning of a Text?" *New Literary History* 14:1–12.

———. 1986. "The Relativity of Interpretation." *The Monist* 69:103–18.

Stuckenbruck, Loren T. 2006. "The Formation and Re-Formation of Daniel in the Dead Sea Scrolls." Pages 101–30 in vol. 1 of *The Bible and the Dead Sea Scrolls.* 3 volumes. Edited by James H. Charlesworth. Baylor University Press.

Sugirtharajah, R. S. 2003. "The End of Biblical Studies?" Pages 133–40 in *Toward a New Heaven and a New Earth: Essays in Honor of Elisabeth Schüssler Fiorenza.* Edited by Fernando F. Segovia. Orbis Books.

Sweeney, Marvin A. 2001. "The End of Eschatology in Daniel: Theological and Socio-Political Ramifications of the Changing Context of Interpretation." *BibInt* 9:123–40.

Talabi, Oluwadunni O. 2023. "Writing the Polyphonic African Queer Future: Reflections on Akwaeke Emezi's *Freshwater*." *Journal of the African Literary Association* 17:329–44.

Tamber-Rosenau, Caryn. 2018. *Women in Drag: Gender and Performance in the Hebrew Bible and Early Jewish Literature*. BI 16. Gorgias.

Taylor, Marion Ann. 2019. "Celebrating 125 Years of Women in the Society of Biblical Literature (1894–2019)." Pages 1–44 in *Women and the Society of Biblical Literature*. Edited by Nicole L. Tilford. BSNA 29. SBL Press.

Tevis, Britt P. 2021. "Trends in the Study of Antisemitism in United States History." *American Jewish History* 105:255–84.

Thiessen, Matthew. 2009. "The Function of a Conjunction: Inclusivist or Exclusivist Strategies in Ezra 6.21 and Nehemiah 10.29–30?" *JSOT* 34:63–79.

Thomas, Heath. 2011. "'I Will Hope in Him': Theology and Hope in Lamentations." Pages 203–21 in *A God of Faithfulness: Essays in Honour of J. Gordon McConville*. Edited by Jamie A. Grant, Alison Lo, and Gordon J. Wenham. LHBOTS 538. T&T Clark International.

Tiemeyer, Lena-Sofia. 2011. *For the Comfort of Zion: The Geographical and Theological Location of Isaiah 40–55*. VTSup 139. Brill.

———. 2017. *Ezra-Nehemiah: Israel's Quest for Identity*. TTCSGOT. Bloomsbury T&T Clark.

Toepel, Alexander. 2005. "Planetary Demons in Early Jewish Literature." *JSP* 14:231–38.

Tolbert, Mary Ann. 1983. "Defining the Problem: The Bible and Feminist Hermeneutics." Pages 113–26 in *The Bible and Feminist Hermeneutics*. Edited by Mary Ann Tolbert. SemeiaSt 28. Scholars Press.

Travis, Molly Abel. 2010. "Beyond Empathy: Narrative Distancing and Ethics in Toni Morrison's *Beloved* and J. M. Coetzee's *Disgrace*." *Journal of Narrative Theory* 40:231–50.

Treadway, Linzie M. 2022. "Freedom in the Wilderness between Two Worlds: A Native American Approach to Genesis 21:1–21." Pages 119–33 in *Reading Biblical Texts Together: Pursuing Minoritized Biblical Criticism*. Edited by Tat-siong Benny Liew and Fernando F. Segovia. SemeiaSt 98. SBL Press.

Trible, Phyllis. 1978. *God and the Rhetoric of Sexuality*. OBT. Fortress.

Trimm, Charlie. 2017. *Fighting for the King and the Gods: A Survey of Warfare in the Ancient Near East*. RBS 88. SBL Press.

Tsumura, David Toshio. 2005. *Creation and Destruction: A Reappraisal of Chaoskampf Theory in the Old Testament*. Eisenbrauns.

Turner-Smith, Sarah G. 2015. "Naked but Not Ashamed: A Reading of Genesis 2:25 in Textual and Cultural Context." *JTS* 69:425–46.

Twersky, Geula. 2017. "Lamech's Song and Cain's Genealogy: An Examination of Gen 4,23–24 within Its Narrative Context." *SJOT* 31:275–93.

Ukpong, Justin A. 1999. "Can African Old Testament Scholarship Escape the Historical Critical Approach?" *Newsletter on African Old Testament Scholarship* 7:2–5.

———. 2001. "New Testament Hermeneutics in Africa: Challenges and Possibilities." *Neot* 35:147–67.

———. 2002. "Intercultural Hermeneutics: An African Approach to Biblical Interpretation." Pages 17–32 in *The Bible in a World Context: An Experiment in Contextual Hermeneutics*. Edited by Walter Dietrich and Ulrich Luz. Eerdmans.

Ukwueze, Ogochukwu. 2023. "Nomadic Consciousness and Border Crossing in Virginia Woolf's *Mrs Dalloway* and Akwaeke Emezi's *Freshwater*." *Comparative Literature: East & West* 7.1:65–78.

Ulrich, Eugene. 2012. "The Parallel Editions of the OG and MT of Daniel 5." Pages 201–17 in *A Teacher for All Generations: Essays in Honor of James C. VanderKam*. Edited by Eric F. Mason, Samuel I. Thomas, Alison Schofield, and Eugene Ulrich. JSJSup 153. Brill.

United States Department of Justice. 2023. "FBI Releases Supplement to the 2021 Hate Crime Statistics." https://tinyurl.com/SBL6109a.

Vaka'uta, Nāsili. 2011. *Reading Ezra 9–10 Tu'a-Wise: Rethinking Interpretation in Oceania*. IVBS 3. Society of Biblical Literature.

Valentine, Katy E. 2020. "Examining Scripture in Light of Trans Women's Voices." Pages 509–23 in *The Oxford Handbook of Feminist Approaches to the Hebrew Bible*. Edited by Susanne Scholz. Oxford University Press.

Valeta, David M. 2005. "Court or Jester Tales? Resistance and Social Reality in Daniel 1–6." *PRSt* 32:309–24.

———. 2007. "Polyglossia and Parody: Language in Daniel 1–6." Pages 91–108 in *Bakhtin and Genre Theory in Biblical Studies*. Edited by Roland Boer. SemeiaSt 63. Society of Biblical Literature.

———. 2008. *Lions and Ovens and Visions: A Satirical Reading of Daniel 1–6*. HBM 12. Sheffield Phoenix.

VanderKam, James. 1992. "Ezra-Nehemiah or Ezra and Nehemiah?" Pages 55–75 in *Priests, Prophets and Scribes: Essays on the Formation and Heritage of Second Temple Judaism in Honour of Joseph Blenkinsopp*. Edited by Eugene Ulrich, John W. Wright, Robert P. Carroll, and Philip R. Davies. JSOTSup 149. Sheffield Academic.

Ventura, Patricia. 2018. "Dystopian Eating, Queer Liberalism, and the Roots of Donald Trump in HBO's *Angels in America*." *The Journal of Popular Culture* 51:317–36.

Vermes, Geza. 1991. "Josephus' Treatment of the Book of Daniel." *JJS* 42:149–66.

Vervenne, Marc. 1995. "All They Need Is Love: Once More Genesis 6.1–4." Pages 19–40 in *Words Remembered, Texts Renewed: Essays in Honour of John F.A. Sawyer*. Edited by Jon Davies, Graham Harvey, and Wilfrid G. E. Watson. JSOTSup 195. Sheffield Academic.

Villiers, Pieter G. R. de. 2013. "Entering the Corridors of Power: State and Church in the Reception History of Revelation." *AcT* 33:37–56.

Viviés, Pierre de Martin de. 2005. "Les séjours de Daniel dans la fosse aux lions: Regard narratif synoptique." Pages 131–43 in *Analyse narrative et Bible: Deuxième colloque international du RRENAB*. Edited by Camille Focant and André Wénin. BETL 191. Leuven University Press.

Wahman, Jessica. 2017. "The Idea(s) of America." *The Journal of Speculative Philosophy* 31:16–39.

Walker-Jones, Arthur. 2008. "Eden for Cyborgs: Ecocriticism and Genesis 2–3." *BibInt* 16:263–93.

Waller, David James. 2020. "Sympathy for a Great King: Nebuchadnezzar, Exile, and Mortality in the Book of Daniel." *BibInt* 28:327–46.

Walsh, Matthew L. 2020. "Sectarian Identity and Angels Associated with Israel: A Comparison of Daniel 7–12 with 1QS, 11QMelchizedek, and 1QM." Pages 169–98 in *Dead Sea Scrolls, Revise and Repeat: New Methods and Perspectives*. Edited by Carmen Palmer et al. EJL 52. SBL Press.

Walton, John H. 2011. *Genesis 1 as Ancient Cosmology*. Eisenbrauns.

Warner, Megan. 2017. "'Therefore a Man Leaves His Father and Mother and Clings to His Wife': Marriage and Intermarriage in Genesis 2:24." *JBL* 136:269–88.

Washington, Teresa W. 2005. "The Mother-Daughter Àjé Relationship in Toni Morrison's *Beloved*." *African American Review* 39:171–88.

Wasserman, Emma. 2013. "Beyond Apocalyptic Dualism: Ranks of Divinities in 1 Enoch and Daniel." Pages 189–99 in *"The One Who Sows Bountifully": Essays in Honor of Stanley K. Stowers*. Edited by Caroline

Johnson Hodge, Saul M. Olyan, Daniel Ullucci, and Emma Wasserman. BJS 356. Brown University Press.

Weems, Renita J. 1995. *Battered Love: Marriage, Sex, and Violence in the Hebrew Prophets*. OBT. Fortress.

———. 2022. "On Leaving but Not Going Far." Pages 47–51 in *Black Scholars Matter: Visions, Struggles, and Hopes in Africana Biblical Studies*. Edited by Gay L. Byron and Hugh R. Page Jr. RBS 100. SBL Press.

Weinberg, Joel. 1992. *The Citizen-Temple Community*. Translated by D. L. Smith-Christopher. JSOTSup 151. JSOT Press.

Werline, Rodney A. 2007. "Prayer, Politics, and Social Vision in Daniel 9." Pages 17–32 in vol. 2 of *Seeking the Favor of God*. 3 volumes. Edited by Mark J. Boda, Daniel K. Falk, and Rodney A. Werline. EJL 22. Society of Biblical Literature.

West, Gerald O. 1995. *Biblical Hermeneutics of Liberation: Modes of Reading the Bible in the South African Context*. BibLib. 2nd edition. Orbis Books.

———. 2001. "Contextual Bible Study in South Africa: A Resource for Reclaiming and Regaining Land, Dignity and Identity." Pages 595–610 in *The Bible in Africa: Transactions, Trajectories, and Trends*. Edited by Gerald O. West and Musa W. Dube. Brill.

West, Gerald O. and Charlene van der Walt. 2019. "A Queer (Beginning to the) Bible." *Concilium* 5:109–18.

Westermann, Claus. 1994. *Lamentations: Issues and Interpretation*. Translated by Charles Muenchow. T&T Clark.

White, Lynn Jr. 1967. "The Historical Roots of Our Ecologic Crisis." *Science* 155:1203–7.

Whitney, Elspeth. 2015. "Lynn White Jr.'s 'The Historical Roots of Our Ecologic Crisis' after 50 Years." *History Compass* 13.8:396–410.

Willey, Patricia Tull. 1997. *Remember the Former Things: The Recollection of Previous Texts in Second Isaiah*. SBLDS 161. Scholars Press.

Williamson, H. G. M. 2003. "The Family in Persian Period Judah: Some Textual Reflections." Pages 469–85 in *Symbiosis, Symbolism, and the Power of the Past: Ancient Israel and Their Neighbors from the Late Bronze Age through Roman Palaestina*. Edited by William G. Dever and Seymour Gitin. Eisenbrauns.

Williamson, Robert Jr. 2015. "Taking Root in the Rubble: Trauma and Moral Subjectivity in the Book of Lamentations." *JSOT* 40:7–23.

Wills, Lawrence M. 1990. *The Jew in the Court of the Foreign King: Ancient Jewish Court Legends*. HDR 26. Fortress.

Wilson, Stephen. 2017. "Blood Vengeance and the *Imago Dei* in the Flood Narrative (Genesis 9:6)." *Int* 71:263–73.

Wimbush, Vincent L. 2017. *Scripturalectics: The Management of Meaning*. Oxford University Press.

Wit, Hans de. 2008. "Exegesis and Contextuality: Happy Marriage, Divorce or Living (Apart) Together?" Pages 3–30 in *African and European Readers of the Bible in Dialogue: In Quest of a Shared Meaning*. Edited by Hans de Wit and Gerald O. West. SRA 32. Brill.

Wolde, Ellen van. 1994. *Words Become Worlds: Semantic Studies of Genesis 1–11*. BIS 6. Brill.

Wolfson, Roberta. 2023. "'A Man of Two Faces and Two Minds': Just Memory and Metatextuality in *The Sympathizer*'s Rewriting of the Vietnam War." *College Literature* 50:57–86.

Wright, Jacob L. 2004. *Rebuilding Identity: The Nehemiah-Memoir and its Earliest Readers*. BZAW 348. de Gruyter.

Wyatt, Jean. 1993. "Giving Body to the Word: The Maternal Symbolic in Toni Morrison's *Beloved*." *PMLA* 108:474–88.

———. 2021. "Dislocating the Reader: Slave Motherhood and the Disrupted Temporality of Trauma in Toni Morrison's *Beloved*." Pages 90–106 in *The Cambridge Companion to Literature and Psychoanalysis*. Edited by Vera J. Camden. Cambridge University Press.

Wynter, Sylvia. 2003. "Unsettling the Coloniality of Being/Truth/Power/Freedom: Towards the Human, after Man, Its Overrepresentation—An Argument." *CR: The New Centennial Review* 3:257–337.

Yamada, Frank M. 2009. "What Does Manzanar Have to Do with Eden? A Japanese American Interpretation of Genesis 2–3." Pages 97–117 in *They Were All Together in One Place? Toward Minority Biblical Criticism*. Edited by Randall C. Bailey, Tat-siong Benny Liew, and Fernando F. Segovia. SemeiaSt 57. Society of Biblical Literature.

Yee, Gale A. 2003. *Poor Banished Children of Eve: Women as Evil in the Hebrew Bible*. Fortress.

———. 2021. *Towards an Asian American Biblical Hermeneutics: An Intersectional Anthology*. Cascade.

Yoo, Philip Y. 2017. *Ezra and the Second Wilderness*. OTRM. Oxford University Press.

Yoon, Sarah. 2023. "The Cyborg's Plant: Trans-corporeality in Kim Cho-yeop's *The Greenhouse at the End of the Earth*." *Studies in Contemporary Fiction* 64:390–402.

Young, Ian. 2016. "The Original Problem: The Old Greek Text and the Masoretic Text of Daniel 5." Pages 271–301 in *Empirical Models Challenging Biblical Criticism*. Edited by Raymond F. Person Jr. and Robert Rezetko. AIL 25. SBL Press.

———. 2020. "What is Old Greek Daniel Chapter 8 about?" *JSOT* 44:693–710.

Zehnder, Markus. 2005. *Umgang mit Fremder in Israel und Assyrien: Ein Beitrag zur Anthropologie des "Fremden" in Licht antiker Quellen*. BWANT 168. Kohlhammer.

Zucker, David J. 2020. "My Punishment Is Too Great to Bear: Raising Cain." *BTB* 50: 7–21.

ANCIENT SOURCES INDEX

Hebrew Bible/Old Testament

Genesis
1	191
1–2	176
1–11	18, 175–79, 188–90, 192, 208–11, 213–17, 222, 229
1:1–2:3	193
1:2	190
1:4	194
1:12	194
1:18	194
1:21	194
1:25	194
1:26	189, 191–92
1:26–27	177
1:27	191, 214
1:28	177, 192, 194, 205, 214, 216, 221
1:29–30	192, 205, 221
1:31	194
2	194, 198, 211, 213
2–3	30, 175, 196
2:4	192
2:5	192
2:7	193–94, 220
2:7–20	211
2:8–9	193
2:15	193
2:17	193, 195, 197, 200, 204
2:18	193–94
2:18–19	220
2:19	194, 220
2:19–20	193
2:21–22	193–94, 211
2:23	194
2:24	211
2:25	194
3	198, 218, 220
3:1	195–96, 218–19
3:1–5	194–95
3:3	195
3:4–5	195
3:5	177, 218
3:6	196
3:7	196
3:13	219
3:14–15	197
3:15	219
3:16–18	197, 204, 211–13, 215
3:17	199, 206
3:17–18	206
3:19	197–98
3:20	198
3:21	198
3:22	189, 196–97, 203
3:22–23	208
4	199
4:1	199
4:2	199
4:3–4	199
4:5	199
4:7	200
4:8	199
4:10–16	200
4:11–12	201
4:13–15	200
4:14	201
4:15	201
4:16	201
4:17	200, 204

Genesis (*continued*)

4:17–18	202	8:21	175, 206, 212
4:17–24	202	9:1	205, 214
4:18	201–2	9:1–6	205, 221
4:18–24	202	9:2–3	207, 221
4:20–22	201	9:4	221
4:23–24	201	9:5–6	205, 221
4:26	202	9:6	177, 214
5	203	9:7	205, 214
5:1–2	202	10	207, 213
5:1–5	202	10:1a	213
5:1–28	202, 214	10:2–7	213
5:3	191, 202	10:20	213
5:18–24	202	10:22–23	213
5:21–24	203	10:31–32	213
5:21–27	202	11	213
5:25–28	202	11:1–9	207–8
5:29	202	11:3	207
5:30–31	202	11:4	204, 208
5:30–32	202, 214	11:6	208
6:1–2	203	11:7	189, 208
6:3	203	11:8–9	208
6:4	204, 208	11:10–32	204, 214
6:5	175, 204, 206	11:29–31	214
6:5–8	205	12	213
6:5–17	205	17:16–20	230
6:5–9:17	205	20:6	228
6:9	203	21:18	230
6:11–13	205	32:26 [ET 32:25]	228
6:19	206	34	13
7:1	206		
7:1–5	205	Exodus	
7:2–3	205	12:19	123
7:4	205	12:48–49	123
7:10	205	12:49	124
7:12	205	21:37 [ET 22:1]	157
7:16b–17	205	22:20 [22:21]	123
7:17	205	34	122
7:22–23	205	34:11–16	113, 121
7:24	205		
8:2b	205	Leviticus	
8:3	205	11	59
8:6	205	15:19–33	113
8:6–12	205	18:24–30	113
8:20–22	205	19:18	123
		19:33	123

19:34	124	4:16–17	228
21:1–5	113		
22:2–3	113	1 Samuel	
22:18–20	123	25:11	157
24:22	124		
25:43	192	2 Samuel	
25:46	192	8:11	192
26:17	192	13	13
Numbers		1 Kings	
3:22	192	5:4 [ET 4:24]	192
3:29	192		
9:14	124	2 Kings	
15:15–16	124	21:1–16	150
15:29	123–24	21:15	150
24:19	192	23:26–27	150
27	229	24:2–4	150
36	229		
		1 Chronicles	
Deuteronomy		22:18	192
1:39	195		
7	113, 122	2 Chronicles	
7:1–4	113, 121	36:15–17	150
14	59		
14:3–21	59	Ezra	
16:11	123	1–6	89, 112–13, 119
16:14	123	1–10	89–90
17:8	228	1:1	119
23:4 [ET 23:3]	122	1:2	108
24:17	123	1:3	108, 112, 119
24:19	227	1:7–11	108
28	150	1:11	109
28:15–68	150	2	89, 109
28:31	157	2:1	109
		2:1–2	109
Joshua		2:2	110
18:1	192	2:3–63	109
		2:59	109–10
Ruth		2:59–63	109
1:8–15	226	2:62	109
1:14	227	2:64	109–10
1:16	227	2:70	109–10
2:9	227	3–4	111
2:22	227	3:1	110
3:1–4	228	3:2	110

Ancient Sources Index

Ezra (continued)
3:3	110
3:7	110
3:8	109
4:1	109–10
4:2	111, 121
4:3	110–11
4:4	110
4:4–5	111
4:8–23	89
5:11–12	114
5:12	150
6:8–10	112
6:16	109
6:19	109
6:20	109
6:21	109–11
7	89
7–10	89, 112
7:7	110
7:10	110
7:15–24	112–13
7:25	113
7:26	113
7:28	110
8:25	110
8:25–27	112
8:29	110
8:35	109–10
9	89
9–10	89, 117, 122, 127
9:1	122
9:2	113
9:4	109
9:6–15	113
9:7	109, 113, 150
9:8–9	114
9:10–12	113
9:10–15	118
9:11	113, 122
9:13–15	114
10	89
10:1–4	114
10:3	122
10:6	109
10:7	109
10:8	109–10
10:10–11	114
10:14	110, 114
10:15	120
10:16	109

Nehemiah
1–13	89–90
1:2	109
1:3	109
1:6	110
1:6–8	114
2:2	110
2:7–8	112
5:13	110
7:6	109
7:7	110
7:66	110
7:73	110
8	89, 112, 114
8–10	115
8:2	110
8:9	114
8:17	109–10
9	89, 118
9:2	114
9:4–5	114
9:6	114
9:6–37	114
9:16–25	115
9:26–30	115, 150
9:28	192
9:31	115
9:36–37	115
10	89, 122
10:29–30 [ET 10:28–29]	115
10:31 [10:30]	115
10:32 [10:31]	115
10:33–40 [10:32–39]	115
11:1–24	112, 115
13	89, 122
13:1	110
13:6	116
13:10–13	116

13:15–18	116–17	1:6	152–53
13:23–24	117	1:7	152–53, 155, 158–59
13:23–27	116, 122	1:8	147, 153, 156
13:28	116, 120	1:9	153–54, 158, 162, 166
		1:10	147, 156
Job		1:10–11b	154
5:12	195	1:11	154, 162
15:5	195	1:11–12	147
42:2	208	1:11–22	154
		1:12–15	154
Psalms		1:13	156, 159
37:35	123	1:13–16	161
		1:14	154
Proverbs		1:16	154, 156, 159, 166–67
6:8	220	1:17	152, 154, 166
6:29	228	1:18	154
12:16	195	1:19	147
12:23	195	1:20	147, 154, 156
13:16	195	1:20–22	154
14:8	195	1:21	154–55, 166
30:24	220	1:21–22	161–62
30:24–28	220	1:22	154
		2	152, 155–58, 160–61, 167–68, 170
Isaiah		2:1	156
14:2	192	2:1–8	155
34:6	157	2:1–19	155
44	230	2:1–20	155
		2:2	152, 156
Jeremiah		2:3	152, 161
3	151	2:4	156, 159
3:6–10	150	2:5	152, 156
11:19	157	2:6	152
29:1–23	77	2:8	152, 156
29:12–14	77	2:8–9	156
		2:9	161
Lamentations		2:11	152, 156, 161
1	14, 152, 155–56, 160–61, 166, 168	2:11–12	156, 161
1–2	147, 152, 159, 166	2:12	147
1–4	170	2:13	152, 156, 161, 167
1:1	147, 153, 155–56, 169	2:14	155, 161
1:1–9b	153	2:15	152
1:2	153–54, 156, 166, 170	2:15–17	159
1:3	152, 156, 158, 161	2:16	156
1:4	153, 161	2:17	156
1:5	153–54, 161	2:18–19	160

Lamentations (continued)

2:19	147, 156–57
2:19–20	161
2:20	147, 155, 157, 161
2:20–22	162
2:21	147, 157
3	152, 158–60, 166–67, 169–70
3:1	153, 158
3:1–3	170
3:1–20	158
3:1–39	152
3:4–6	170
3:5–9	159
3:8	160
3:11	159
3:12	158
3:14	159
3:18	159
3:19	159
3:21	159
3:21–41	159, 161, 166
3:22	159
3:23	159
3:24–26	159
3:31–33	159
3:40–41	159–60
3:40–47	152–53
3:40–51	167
3:42–44	160
3:42–51	162
3:48–51	160
3:48–66	152
3:52	160
3:52–62	160
3:52–66	161
3:56–61	160
3:57	157
3:63	162
3:63–66	160–62
3:64–66	170
4	147, 153, 161–62, 165–67, 169–70
4:2	148
4:3–4	161
4:4	161
4:5	161
4:6	147
4:9	162
4:9–10	147, 161
4:10	161
4:11	161
4:13–16	161
4:17–20	161–62
4:18	162
4:21–22	161
4:22	161
5	153, 162–63, 165, 167, 169–71
5:1	162–63
5:2	163
5:6	163
5:7	163
5:8	163
5:9–10	163
5:11	147, 163
5:12	147, 163
5:13	147, 163
5:16	163
5:20	163
5:21	163
5:22	163

Ezekiel

16:35–43	150
23:9–10	150
23:22–35	150
23:46–49	150

Daniel

1	60–61
1–2	60
1–4	42, 62
1–5	57
1–6	42, 58, 62, 64, 66, 68–69
1:1–2	62, 69
1:3	58
1:3–4	1
1:4	57–58
1:5	58
1:7	57
1:8	59
1:10–15	61

1:12	59	4:19 [ET 4:22]	65
1:17	60, 65	4:24 [ET 4:27]	75
1:18–19	72	4:31–32 [ET 4:34–35]	63, 69
1:18–20	60	4:31–33 [ET 4:34–36]	62
1:20	72	5	45–46, 64
1:21	72	5:1–4	64
2	60, 62, 67–69, 82	5:10	64
2–4	62	5:17–28	65
2–6	58	5:18–22	64
2:1	60	5:19	68, 76
2:1–17	60	5:20–21	69
2:4	64	5:23–28	64
2:4b–7:28	57	5:28	68
2:5	69	5:29	66
2:12–13	69	5:30–6:1 [ET 5:30–31]	64
2:24	82	6	41, 57, 61, 63–64, 71, 74, 78
2:36–45	65	6:3 [ET 6:2]	63
2:37–38	62, 67	6:4 [ET 6:3]	1, 63, 66, 74
2:37–41	67	6:5 [ET 6:4]	63
2:38	65	6:5–6 [ET 6:4–5]	64
2:40	68	6:7 [ET 6:6]	64
2:44	67–68	6:15 [ET 6:14]	63–64
2:46	63, 66	6:19 [ET 6:18]	64
2:47	63, 65	6:22 [ET 6:21]	2, 64, 71
2:48–49	60	6:23 [ET 6:22]	1, 64, 82
3	41, 45, 61, 64, 78	6:24 [ET 6:23]	64
3:4	68, 76	6:25 [ET 6:24]	71, 82
3:6	69	6:26 [ET 6:25]	68, 76
3:7	68, 76	6:27–28 [ET 6:26–27]	65
3:9	64	6:29 [ET 6:28]	66
3:11	69	7	42, 67–73, 79
3:17	61	7–8	45, 57
3:18	61	7–12	42, 45, 58, 66–67, 82
3:28	65	7:1	1, 69
3:29	63, 68–69, 76	7:2–8	1
3:31 [ET 4:1]	68, 76	7:5	68
3:31–33 [4:1–3]	63, 69	7:7	68
4	45, 62–64, 67	7:9	68
4–6	45–46	7:11	68
4:2 [ET 4:5]	63, 67	7:13–14	68
4:5 [ET 4:8]	63	7:14	76
4:6 [ET 4:9]	63	7:15	67, 69
4:15 [ET 4:18]	63	7:15–16	67
4:16 [ET 4:19]	63, 67	7:17	67, 69
4:16–24 [ET 4:19–27]	65	7:19	1, 67

ANCIENT SOURCES INDEX

Daniel (*continued*)

7:21	1, 68–70, 73	11:2–3	72
7:21–22	73	11:5	73
7:22	73	11:5–39	73
7:23	68	11:5–45	73
7:23–27	67	11:21	73
7:24	69	11:31	73
7:25	70, 73, 80	11:33–35	73
7:26	70, 73	11:35	80
7:26–27	68	11:36	73
7:27	1, 69, 73, 76	11:40	80
7:28	67, 69	11:45	73
8	45, 70–73	12:1	73, 80
8–12	42, 66	12:2	73
8:1	1, 70	12:3	73, 75
8:4	1, 70	12:4	67, 73, 80
8:6–11	1	12:7	72
8:10–12	70	12:8	72
8:13	73	12:9	80
8:15–16	67	12:13	74, 80, 82
8:17	80		
8:19	80	Zechariah	
8:19–26	70	9:15	192
8:24	1, 70, 73		
8:25	70	Ancient Near Eastern Texts	
8:26	67	*ABC*	
8:27	70–71	19	149
9	77–78		
9–12	57	RINAP	
9:1–3	77	4.104.i.8–13	149
9:4–19	77	4.104.i.34–ii.1	149
9:15–19	77	4.105.i.27–37	150
9:24–27	77	4.106.i.10–ii.3	149
9:26	80	4.108.i.1–16	149
10–12	71	4.108.ii.2–iii.14	149
10:1	72, 82	4.110.ii.13–23	150
10:4	72	4.111.i.3–9	150
10:5	72	4.113.11	150
10:13	72		
10:16	72	SAA	
10:18	72	2.6.418a–c	150
10:20	72	2.6.428–430	150
10:20–12:4	72	2.6.449–450	150
10:21	73	2.6.519–520	150
11	45, 73	2.6.530–532	150

ANCIENT SOURCES INDEX 279

2.6.547–550	150	Mark	
2.6.599–600	150	9:42–48	80
		10:14	145
Deuterocanonical Books		10:17–31	79
		10:42	79
Sirach		12:28–34	79
25:24	175	14:21	80
1 Esdras		Luke	
5:53	110	15	14
8:23	113	18:16	145
9:14	120		
		Romans	
Pseudepigrapha		5:12	175
1 Enoch		1 Corinthians	
1–36	68	15:21	175
14	68		
		Ephesians	
2 Baruch		5:22–6:9	231
48.42	175		
54.19	175	Colossians	
		3:18–4:1	231
4 Ezra			
3.21	175	Rabbinic Works	
4.30	175		
7.118	175	b. Ketubot	
		51b	175
Testament of Asher			
1.8	175	b. Yoma	
3.2	175	69b	175
Dead Sea Scrolls		Genesis Rabbah	
		9.7	175
4Q422			
I, 12	175	Sifre Deuteronomy	
		45	175
4Q436			
I, 10	175	Early Christian Writings	
New Testament		Jerome, *Commentary on Daniel*	
		prologue	42
Matthew			
19:14	145		

MODERN AUTHORS INDEX

Achebe, Chinua	226	Bier, Miriam J.	153, 156, 159, 168
Adam, Klaus-Peter	212	Bird, Michael F.	113
Adichie, Chimamanda	226	Bird, Phyllis A.	22
Ahmed, Sara	8	Blenkinsopp, Joseph	89
Ahn, John	60	Blomberg, Craig L.	21
Albertz, Rainer	46, 123	Blount, Brian K.	23
Alderman, Isaac M.	196	Boase, Elizabeth	129, 156, 159, 167
Allen, John	146	Boccaccini, Gabriele	41–42
Allende, Isabel	226	Bortz, Anna Maria	89
Amal, Djaïli Amadou	226	Bosman, Sean James	55
Amzallag, Nissim	89	Bouson, J. Brooks	140
Anderson, Cheryl B.	6, 87, 117	Brandt, Stefan L.	134
Anderson, Melanie	136, 140	Brayford, Susan	200
Andrade Vinueza, María	127	Brett, Mark G.	196, 202
Anum, Eric	37	Burt, Sean	89
Anzaldúa, Gloria	198, 218	Byron, John	200
Assis, Elie	129	Byttebier, Stephanie	95
Asturias, Miguel Ángel	226	Caesar, Terry Paul	142
Bailey, Jonquil	139	Calarco, Matthew	217
Bailey, Randall C.	11	Carden, Mary Paniccia	141, 144
Bal, Mieke	211	Cardoso Pereira, Nancy	76
Barnett, Pamela E.	103, 141	Carey, Greg	44
Barr, James	19	Carr, David M.	190, 213
Barton, John	20, 29	Cataldo, Jeremiah W.	167
Batt, J. Daniel	142	Chia, Philip	59, 62
Batto, Bernard F.	193, 197, 211	Chong, Sylvia Shin Huey	53–54
Bauks, Michaela	202	Claassens, L. Juliana M.	13–14, 147
Bechtel, Lyn M.	193	Clarke, Sathianathan	30
Becking, Bob	89, 113	Clauss, Jan	113
Bellantuono, Antonella	45	Clines, David J. A.	189, 204
Bennett, Harold V.	227	Clune, Lori	96
Berges, Ulrich	152	Cobo-Piñero, Rocío	184–85
Bergler, Siegfried	170	Coetzee, J. M.	14
Berlinerblau, Jacques	21	Collins, John J.	41, 46, 60, 66
Beyerle, Stefan	45	Collins, Patricia Hill	11

Columbus, Christopher	81	Floyd, Michael H.	152
Conway, Mary L.	156, 167	Foertsch, Jacqueline	93
Cook Steike, Elisabeth	117	Forna, Aminatta	226
Cooper, Jerrold S.	149	Forti, Tova L.	220
Coxon, Peter	62	Fox, Michael V.	21, 220
Crawford, Cory	191	Francis, Donald	93
Cristofáni, José Roberto	59	Frantzen, Allen	93
Crouch, C. L.	150–51, 192	Frisch, Alexandra	68
Crowder, Stephanie Buckhanon	10, 30	Fröhlich, Ida	68, 72
Cuéllar, Gregory Lee	23	Frymer-Kensky, Tikva	6
Culbertson, Philip	214	Fulton, Deirdre N.	89
Dangarembga, Tsitsi	226	Fulton, Lorie Watkins	144
Dangor, Achmat	226	Fuchs, Esther	34
Daniels, Steven V.	146	Gafney, Wil	33, 127, 148, 227, 229
Danticat, Edwidge	226	Gandhi, Evyn Lê Espiritu	50
Darden, Lynne St. Clair	30, 80, 231	García Márquez, Gabriel	24–25
Davies, Philip R.	21	Garric, Nathaniel	191
Davis, Kimberly Chabot	135, 147	Gatti, Nicoletta	200
Davis Bledsoe, Amanda M.	62	Gericke, Jaco	161
Day, John	203	Gilan, Amir	121
Delcor, M.	73	Gladson, Jerry A.	160
Deutschmann, Barbara	193	Gnuse, Robert K.	194
Dewey, John	32	González, Justo	23
DiTomasso, Lorenzo	41, 60, 72	Gordon, Jane Anna	36
Dobbs-Allsopp, F. W.	20, 130, 147, 152, 155–56, 158, 161	Gordon, Lewis	36
		Gossai, Hemchand	200
Doshi, Avni	226	Grabbe, Lester L.	42
Dresner, Samuel H.	176	Grace, Patricia	226
Dube, Musa	8, 30, 35, 192, 230	Gradisek, Amanda	54
Durkin, Anita	146	Graybill, Rhiannon	13, 147, 153, 156, 164
Dyck, Jonathan	109		
Eidevall, Göran	159	Grayson, Albert Kirk	149
Ellison, Ralph	46	Greenstein, Edward L.	193
Emezi, Akwaeke	18, 176, 180, 187	Grosfoguel, Ramón	11, 217
Enríquez, Mariana	226	Guardiola-Sáenz, Leticia	35
Esler, Philip E.	85	Gudbergsen, Thomas	192
Evaristo, Bernadine	226	Guest, Deryn	147–48
Fanon, Frantz	130	Guillaume, Philippe	170
Farisani, Elelwani	86	Habel, Norman C.	193, 200
Fee, Gordon D.	21	Hamilton, Cynthia S.	145
Fewell, Danna Nolan	63, 65, 75	Hamori, Esther J.	204
Finney, Brian	134	Harlin, Kate	185, 187
Finsterbusch, Karin	45	Harrington, Hannah K.	113
Fish, Stanley	27–28	Harris, Cheryl I.	9
Flores, Andrew R.	177	Harrisville, Roy A.	20

Harvey, Van Austin	20	Kebaneilwe, Mmapula Diana	216
Haydon, Ron	77	Kelly, Joseph R.	124
Hayes, Christine E.	113	Kessler, John	111
Hayes, John H.	21	Kilner-Johnson, Allan	94, 102
Haynes, Matthew	192	King, Emily	97
Hecke, Pierre J. P. van	158	King, Lovalerie	136
Heckl, Raik	85	King, Shinman	155
Heider, George	211	Kirkpatrick, Shane	63
Heim, Knut M.	152	Kirova, Milena	191
Hens-Piazza, Gina	157	Klawans, Jonathan	113
Henze, Matthias	42, 46, 64	Koch, Klaus	69
Herring, Stephen L.	192	Kolk, Bessel A. van der	137
Hickey, Walt	14–15	Kornhaber, David	106
Hidalgo, Jacqueline M.	8, 36	Korte, Anne-Marie	196
Hiebert, Theodore	192–93	Korzec, Cezary	159
Hillers, Delbert R.	170	Kratz, Reinhard Gregor	42, 190
Hinson, D. Scot	142	Krüger, P. Paul	192
Hobbs, Heschel H.	199	Krumholz, Linda	144
Hoke, Jimmy	11	Kumamoto Stanley, Sandra	46, 56
Holden-Kirwan, Jennifer L.	140	Kushner, Tony	16, 86, 88
Holladay, Carl R.	21	Kvanvig, Helen S.	68
Holm, Tawny L.	46	Kwok Pui-lan	9
Hoopen, Robin B. ten	202–3	Laird, Donna	85
Howard, Cameron B. R.	218–19	Lau, Peter H.	111
Howard, Thomas A.	2	Law, David R.	20
Hsu, Ruth Y.	178	Lee, Nancy C.	152, 155
Humphreys, W. Lee	64, 196, 199	Lee, Rachel	147
Isasi-Díaz, Ada María	34	Legaspi, Michael C.	2
Iser, Wolfgang	23	Lemaire, André	112
Janz, Timothy	89	Levin, Saul	199
Janzen, David	23, 109, 112, 116, 161, 163	Liew, Tat-siong Benny	2, 79–80
		Lim, Chin Ming Stephen	13, 37, 61
Jesser, Nancy	147	Linafelt, Tod	147, 159, 163
Jobling, David	211	Linehan, Thomas P.	145
Johnson, Bo	170	Lipschitz, Yair	100
Jørstad, Mari	199	Lohr, Joel N.	199, 201
Joseph, Simon J.	69, 73	López, Marta Sofía	217, 222
Joüon, Paul	189	Lorde, Audre	36
Joyce, Paul	22	Lozada, Francisco, Jr.	34
Junior, Nyasha	35	Macaskill, Grant	11
Kalmanofsky, Amy	159, 197, 228	Machinist, Peter	149
Kaminsky, Joel	124	Macumber, Heather	68
Karrer-Grube, Christiane	89	Macwilliam, Stuart	229
Karunatilaka, Shehan	226	Magaqa, Tina	181
Kawashima, Robert S.	195, 200, 204, 211	Maher, John	15

MODERN AUTHORS INDEX

Ma'ilo, Mosese	14	Nihan, Christophe	123
Makombe, Rodwell	181	Niskanen, Paul	41
Makumbi, Jennifer Nansubuga	226	Norton, Yolanda	227–28
Maldonado-Torres, Nelson	130	Nussbaum, Martha C.	13, 15
Mandolfo, Carleen	151, 153	Nzimande, Makhosazana K.	6, 117, 127
Marchal, Joseph A.	178	O'Connor, Kathleen M.	156, 161
Markley, Jennifer Foutz	21	Oeming, Manfred	115
Marks, Kathleen	140	Ok, Janette H.	8
Martin, Clarice J.	231	Okonkwo, Christopher N.	180, 187
Martin, Dale B.	21	Ọlọjẹde, Fúnlọ́lá O.	229
Marx, Karl	53	Olyan, Saul M.	113, 153
Masenya, Madipoane (ngawan'a Mphahlele)	228	Omer-Sherman, Ranen	104, 123
		O'Reilly, Andrea	140
Matskevich, Karalina	211	Otto, Eckart	190
May, Vivian M.	11	Owens, Pamela Jean	158, 170
Mbuwayesango, Dora Rudo	10, 33	Page, Philip	142, 146
McLay, R. Timothy	42, 46	Park, Suzie	8
McNulty, Charles	106	Park, Wongi	7
Meadowcroft, Tim J.	42, 62	Parry, Robin	154–55
Melanchthon, Monica Jyotsna	33	Patte, Daniel	22
Melchor, Fernanda	226	Patterson, Brian Neil	176
Menchú, Rigoberta	226	Perdue, Leo G.	20
Mendieta, Eduardo	9	Perez, Richard	136
Merrill Willis, Amy C.	68, 73	Perrin, Andrew B.	45
Mettinger, Tryggve N. D.	195	Pfemmer De Long, Kindalee	77
Meyers, Carol	30	Piggford, George	97
Middlemas, Jill	129, 153, 162	Polaski, Donald C.	45, 65, 73
Middleton, J. Richard	194	Portier-Young, Anathea E.	58, 70
Mignolo, Walter D.	11, 37, 130	Prabhu, Anjali	54
Miller, Althea Spencer	33, 35	Punt, Jeremy	229
Minwalla, Framji	91, 101, 104	Putnam, Amanda	136
Moglen, Helene	147	Pyper, Hugh S.	170
Möller, Karl	192	Quijano, Aníbal	8, 217
Moore, Stephen D.	191	Quine, Cat	192
Morrison, Toni	17, 131, 133	Rad, Gerhard von	196
Munnich, Oliver	46	Ramírez Kidd, José	200
Muraoka, T.	189	Reay, Lewis	176
Murphy, Brian	176	Redding, Jonathan David	79
Nadar, Sarojini	9, 37, 228	Redditt, Paul L.	42
Nadella, Raj	6	Remington Rillera, Andrew	73
Nam, Roger	127	Rice, Alan	137
Nelavala, Surekha	228	Richard, Pablo	81
Newsom, Carol	42, 66	Ringe, Sharon H.	30
Ng, Andrew Hock Soon	133	Roberts, J. J. M.	31
Nguyen, Viet Thanh	16, 43, 56	Rody, Caroline	46, 141

Rong, Lina	153, 168	Smith, Zadie	226
Rooke, Deborah W.	197, 199	So, Richard Jean	15
Rorty, Richard	3	Soares-Prabhu, George M.	230
Rosen-Berry, Judith	176	Soesilo, Daud	59
Rothenbusch, Ralf	85	Solomon, Alisa	97
Routledge, Robin	204	Song, Angeline M. G.	12
Roy, Arundhati	226	Southwood, Katherine E.	113
Ruiz, Jean-Pierre	117	Spargo, R. Clifton	143
Russaw, Kimberly	196	Spivak, Gayatri Chakravorty	53, 164
Sa'at, Alfian	61	Stendahl, Krister	21–22
Said, Edward	53	Stiebert, Johanna	22
Salters, Robert B.	154, 163	Stokes, Ryan E.	68
Sangtinuk	65	Stone, Ken	212, 216
Sarr, Mohamed Mbougar	226	Stone, Mark Preston	160
Savran, David	94, 101–2, 105	Stout, Jeffrey	24, 26, 29–30
Scapp, Ron	106	Stuckenbruck, Loren T.	73
Schindler, Melissa E.	180	Sugirtharajah, R. S.	35
Schlimm, Matthew R.	200	Sweeney, Marvin A.	59
Schmudde, Carol	142	Talabi, Oluwadunni O.	215
Schneider, Tammi J.	6	Tamber-Rosenau, Caryn	229
Schniedewind, William M.	58	Tay, Hong Seng	13
Scholz, Susanne	21, 30	Taylor, Marion Ann	30
Schüle, Andreas	192–93	Tevis, Britt P.	90
Schüssler-Fiorenza, Elisabeth	30	Thiessen, Matthew	111
Schwartz, Seth	58	Thomas, Heath	159
Scolnic, Benjamin	45, 73	Tiemeyer, Lena-Sofia	85, 129
Sears, Brad	177	Toepel, Alexander	72
Sechrest, Love Lazarus	35–36, 38–39, 43, 57, 87, 224–25	Tolbert, Mary Ann	6
		Travis, Molly Abel	141
Segal, Michael	45–46, 61, 63, 69, 73, 77	Treadway, Linzie M.	230
Segovia, Fernando F.	2	Trible, Phyllis	211
Sellars, Wilfred	30	Trimm, Charlie	149
Seow, C. L.	41, 73, 154	Tsumura, David Toshio	190
Settembrini, Marco	45	Turner-Smith, Sarah G.	196
Seufert, Michael	59	Twersky, Geula	200
Shakespeare, William	24, 27	Ukpong, Justin A.	23, 33
Sharp, Carolyn J.	226, 228	Ukwueze, Ogochukwu	185
Sheehan, Jonathan	2	Ulrich, Eugene	46
Shostak, Debora	56	Vaka'uta, Nāsili	33, 88, 127
Sillin, Sarah	54	Valentine, Katy E.	211, 214
Ska, Jean-Louis	205	Valeta, David M.	58, 62, 65
Smalley, Matthew	145	VanderKam, James	89
Smith, Abraham	8–9	Venter, Pieter M.	155
Smith, Mitzi J.	10, 34–35	Ventura, Patricia	96, 101, 105
Smith, Shively T. J.	35	Vermes, Geza	46

Vervenne, Marc	203
Villiers, Pieter G. R. de	81
Viviés, Pierre de Martin de	64
Wahman, Jessica	91
Walker-Jones, Arthur	195–96
Waller, David James	62
Walsh, Catherine E.	11
Walsh, Matthew L.	72
Walt, Charlene van der	176
Walton, John H.	190
Warner, Megan	212
Washington, Teresa W.	133
Wasserman, Emma	72
Weems, Renita J.	6, 150
Weinberg, Joel	109
Wendt, Albert	14
Werline, Rodney A.	77
West, Gerald O.	37, 176
Westermann, Claus	170
Wezerek, Gus	15
White, Lynn Jr.	215, 221
Whitney, Elspeth	216
Willey, Patricia Tull	129
Williamson, H. G. M.	109
Williamson, Robert Jr.	168
Wills, Lawrence M.	46, 65
Wilson, Stephen	205
Wimbush, Vincent L.	6
Wit, Hans de	22
Wolde, Ellen van	199
Wolfson, Roberta	53
Wong, Sook Yee	13
Wright, Jacob L.	89
Wyatt, Jean	134, 140
Wynter, Sylvia	8, 217
Yamada, Frank M.	197
Yee, Gale	8, 30, 227–28
Yoo, Philip Y.	89
Yoon, Sarah	178
Young, Ian	45–46
Zehnder, Markus	123
Zucker, David J.	199

www.ingramcontent.com/pod-product-compliance
Lightning Source LLC
Chambersburg PA
CBHW050859300426
44111CB00010B/1299